The Function of Cynicism
at the Present Time

The Function of Cynicism at the Present Time

HELEN SMALL

OXFORD
UNIVERSITY PRESS

OXFORD
UNIVERSITY PRESS

Great Clarendon Street, Oxford, OX2 6DP,
United Kingdom

Oxford University Press is a department of the University of Oxford.
It furthers the University's objective of excellence in research, scholarship,
and education by publishing worldwide. Oxford is a registered trade mark of
Oxford University Press in the UK and in certain other countries

The moral rights of the author have been asserted

First Edition published in 2020

Impression: 1

Published in the United States of America by Oxford University Press
198 Madison Avenue, New York, NY 10016, United States of America

British Library Cataloguing in Publication Data
Data available

Library of Congress Control Number: 2019957935

ISBN 978-0-19-886193-5

Printed and bound by
CPI Group (UK) Ltd, Croydon, CR0 4YY

Preface

It is not unusual for a book of cultural criticism to reflect its time of writing. Indeed, any historical or political approach to reading will assume that it does— the relevant questions being how consciously and with what advantages or limitations of perspective. This book began in 2011, with an essay on George Eliot's cynicism, but it has taken its final content and form over the past three years, 2016–19. The engagement with contemporary politics is (with the partial exception of Chapter 2) at a remove, but the subject matter, modern cynicism, and the dominant preoccupations of the study—abrasive styles of public argument, debasing challenges to conventional morality, free speech, moral controversialism, the authority of reason and the limits of that authority, nationalism and resistance to nationalism, freedom of expression within the university generally and the Humanities specifically—are evidently topical. When I began writing, the tenor of public discourse around the world was already changing rapidly; it has become distinctly more acrimonious in the three years since. Neither 'American friends', as Matthew Arnold liked to say, nor European ones need reminding of how difficult the challenges of representative democracy have become, nor of the ease with which supposedly liberal cultures of public argument coarsen or fail.

In taking as my subject the function of cynicism at the present time, I am looking to cast light on the question of how moral and cultural ideals keep (or indeed, find) their value for people as those ideals come under pressure from political, social, and sometimes personal circumstances unamenable to any version of idealism that pitches too high. Cynicism, in the modern period, may keep contact with the ancient form of lived philosophy from which it takes its name, but it is also a common aspect of human psychological functioning, open to a normative description. In the forms in which it interests me most, it entails a capacity for tuning up the aggression of one's intelligence that offers to give edge, darkness, but also pleasure to the act of challenging conventional agreements on moral life. I treat cynicism, accordingly, as both a philosophical and a psychological phenomenon, repeatedly leading one back to the question of the relationship between these two disciplines. Underpinning all, I have a literary critic's concern with the stylistic means by which cynicism achieves its ethical effects. The 'debasing' of normative judgements and conventional moral agreements is, and has always been, an effect of speech that oversteps the perceived bounds of licence. The characteristic features of that overstepping—verbal impudence, shamelessness, 'biting' wit, circulating anecdote, vulgarization in all its linguistic forms— enable cynicism's anti-institutional forms of charismatic authority. In looking to chart the operations of cynicism at the level of style as well as argument, I own to some susceptibility to cynic flair. The original cynics would not have survived were it not that charisma opens the door to tolerance.

Chapter 1 provides the book's most concentrated account of how attention to ancient Cynicism has served philosophical efforts to articulate the proper scope of scepticism towards conventional morality. Taking a cue from Bernard Williams's observation in 1990 that most modern moral philosophy is 'surprisingly lacking' in 'a genuinely disturbing scepticism', this chapter considers the work of Nietzsche as our primary 'psychological and historically situated' exemplar.[1] I look to provide a more thorough account than has yet been offered of how far, and to what ends, Nietzsche's sceptical 'realism' was fashioned with an eye on Cynic styles of argument. Starting with the reappearance of Diogenes of Sinope in *The Gay Science*, I explore the histrionic characterization of the *tolle Mensche* and his 'untimeliness' in ways that open up Nietzsche's sense of the typology and stylistic gambits of Cynicism as helpful but inadequate models for the lived practice of philosophy. I then focus on how Cynicism helps to drive Nietzsche's thinking in two main respects: (i) his efforts to articulate what may be required to break the hold of convention, to be 'free-spirited' in one's philosophizing and fashion a philosophical style in the assumption of that freedom; and (ii) the important role of Cynicism in the articulation of the genealogy of morality.

I put Nietzsche first, though he disrupts the chronology, because he is the great philosophical writer of strategic Cynicism. But he is also of help to me because he offers a famously unflattering sidelong view of British writing about morality in the generation or two before him. With his caustic assessments (of Carlyle, Mill, Eliot, among others) in view, I then look before and after him, in Chapters 2–5, to locate in the main less technically demanding forms of cynicism operating as a critical test (often a critical brake) on moral and political ideals. Chapter 2, 'Speech beyond Toleration: Moral Controversialism (Then and Now)' treats one of the great confrontations in the history of British public moralism between cynical provocation and a more 'responsible' approach to free speech: Thomas Carlyle's deliberate offences against progressive sentiment in his 'Occasional Discourse on the Negro Question' (1849) and John Stuart Mill's swift and uncharacteristically angry response. Nietzsche (in pursuit of higher values and still freer speech) thought that Carlyle did not go nearly deep enough in the challenges he posed to conventional political morality—but the 'Occasional Discourse' went far enough to make Carlyle's own name a byword, still, for moral and political provocateurship. I argue that his cynicisms and Mill's astringent reply provide a helpful historical basis from which to consider similar challenges today to normative views of public argument and styles of expression.

---

[1] Bernard Williams, 'The Need to Be Sceptical', *Essays and Reviews, 1959–2002* (Princeton, NJ: Princeton University Press, 2014), 312–18 (317).

The central chapter, Chapter 3, turns to the terrain of cultural criticism, with a more literary focus. It develops an account of the attraction of Arnoldian criticism (with its 'free play of ideas') to the strong ironies, comic flair, and 'sarcastic turns' of cynicism—modes of argument that challenge and assist Arnold's critical authority, and that become the subject of his most explicit critical reflection when he writes about a German literary cynic, of the generation before him, for whom he had a keen affection: Heinrich Heine. I trace the process by which the kinds of scoriating cynicism that Arnold admired and (finally) found wanting in Heine became components of the style and content of his own public moralism, increasingly targeted to the work of describing and attacking the opponents of 'culture'. The final section of the chapter considers a late reanimation of Arnold's cynicisms in the context of his encounters with American democratic culture.

Chapter 4 turns to one of the most flexible and complex political effects of cynicism: its taking of distance on the politics of the nation state. I start, *reculant pour mieux sauter*, by re-reading the old story of cosmopolitanism's point of origin in the claim of Diogenes of Sinope to be 'not a citizen' of Athens, or any other city state, but *kosmopolites*, a citizen of the world. I examine the difference between the classical historical literature, in the main wary of giving Diogenes credit for advocating universal humanitarianism *avant la lettre*, and the more-or-less critical uses made of classical history by twentieth- and twenty-first-century political theorists. I then trace the lines of a specifically 'cynic cosmopolitanism' as it finds expression within two literary writers looking to challenge the role, and the rights, of Englishness in an international frame. The frame is predominantly European. But, in testing the validity and the limitations of Englishness in that near geographic extension of imaginary citizenship, the writers I focus on are assessing the ground for any more ambitiously inclusive global *politeia*. Both George Eliot and Ford Madox Ford held to the idea and the ideals of cosmopolitanism but recognized insuperable problems in the way of its realization in their present day. For both (and this may be a more arresting claim about Eliot than it is about Ford), cosmopolitanism was less a moral matter than a matter of psychology, requiring an internal balance to be found, in one's own mind, between idealism and a bracingly cynical realism.

The final chapter, Chapter 5, turns its attention to the university, deepening the critical-historical focus on the institutional settings within which cynicism (for all its anti-institutionalism) resides as a modern critical practice. I have a special interest in the university as a forum in which debate about the importance of, and the constraints on, free speech has in recent years generated unhappy and (in the US) occasionally violent levels of conflict. Attending closely to advocacy for professional freedom of expression in the work of Bertrand Russell, John Dewey, and Laura Kipnis (the latter operating in the context of Title IX legal disputes and the #MeToo movement), I examine the ways in which each of them has deployed cynicism in the course of advocacy for an ideal of the university as a place of free expression, while also anticipating and controlling charges of 'mere' cynicism or its assumed political endpoint, nihilism. One of the functions of cynicism, here, has been to assist articulation of the special nature, and (historically, at least) the privileged conditions of humanistic scholarship as a form of work. I ask what the implications are of the special protections Dewey, Russell, and Kipnis deem necessary for the support of university teaching and research, and explore the difficulties placed in the way of effective advocacy for the humanities by (sometimes starkly) differential conditions between academic labour and labour beyond the university; also, increasingly, differential conditions *within* the university.

A brief Coda wrestles with the scope of the claims made for a strategic cynicism. It begins with the uncomfortable play between sceptical cynicism and much more impoverished cynicisms in Dinaw Mengestu's novel *How To Read the Air*. I then turn to Bernard Williams's *Truth and Truthfulness*, a book that sought to clarify the virtues of truthfulness as our main resource against cynicism. I take Williams's reworking of the Nietzschean genealogy as a prompt to think critically about the strengths and limitations of cynicism's corrective or re-calibrating role for today. Acknowledging the invitation to doubt the speaker's authority that accompanies all versions of cynicism, I close by directing the 'black look' of suspiciousness towards my own assumptions here about the 'reality' of human psychology—my own, it-may-be temperamental inclinations—but also the special attraction cynicism may hold out to the literary writer and literary-critical reader responsive to the depths its abrasive surfaces may conceal.

The joined-up argument of *The Function of Cynicism at the Present Time* is that, with the exception of its earliest classical exponents (and even they provide only partial exceptions), cynicism has not been as eccentric to mainstream moral thought as is commonly claimed. I see cynical thinking and cynical speech not as the isolated posturing of a radical or psychologically damaged few, nor as an aspirational standard for radical-utopian trouble-making, but as a widely employed internal and external credibility check on those promoting moral ideals. Cynicism, in this analysis, can be a rebarbative mode of engagement with common morality by which those wanting to uphold ideals have often tested their plausibility, and that of idealism generally, against an imagined challenge from one disinclined to accept the authority of conventional reasoning and the persuasions of rhetoric. It is in the nature of cynicism that it gives rise to uncertainties about just how far that engagement is under control: how deeply the person espousing cynicism is committed to the propositions he or she makes. A fully committed cynicism, now, would be either a very strained mannerism or something much more psychologically worrying, and a long way from happiness. In its healthier forms, its function both for the individual and for the society may be more constructive. To define our normative practices and values by it would be to misunderstand its purpose and its scope, which are limited and reactive against commonly agreed behaviours and standards. But as a component of a flexible intelligence, cynicism, I suggest, has historically performed, and continues to perform, an occasional service to public debate about the morals, politics, and aesthetic principles that we do, and don't, agree to hold in common.

Acknowledgements

My first and greatest debt is to the Leverhulme Trust. A Leverhulme Research Fellowship from October 2017 to December 2018, supplemented by two terms of sabbatical leave, made possible the writing of the book—and forced me into coherence at the planning stage. The Trust's readiness to support individual research projects, and its non-interventionist policy towards grant recipients, have been indispensable in permitting me to shift ground when second thoughts seemed better than first.

I am grateful to the following people for guidance in areas where my own knowledge was wanting: to Adam Phillips, for steering me towards British psychoanalytic writers with an interest in cynicism, and for comments on the relevant section of the Introduction in its first draft; to Ritchie Robertson for giving the Nietzsche chapter the benefit of his admirably close critical eye, and to Katharina Herold for indispensable help with German sources and German translation; to Bruce Robbins, for characteristically astute critical responses to Chapters 4 and 5 as they took early shape. I have benefitted greatly from the kindness, and the sharpness, of 'critical friends' who read the whole of the book in draft: John Kerrigan (who put most chapters through their paces more than once), Stefan Collini (who held me to account in my dealings with nineteenth-century liberalism), and Fred Rush (a discerning reader for the press, whose influence tells especially in the Introduction and Chapter 1). Warm thanks, also, to the literary-critical reader for the press who has remained anonymous but whose reflections were of considerable help in the final revision stages.

Patricia Williams generously allowed me to work with Bernard Williams's Library. Though there is less of Williams in *The Function of Cynicism* than was at one stage expected and planned, it will be clear that he has played a significant part in my thinking about the tactical role of cynicism in Nietzsche and the importance of distinguishing a targeted, self-consciously limited cynicism from the 'inert' kind.

Not least: I thank my editor, Jacqueline Norton, who nurtured this book from the start, and who has the perfect knack for knowing when to inquire about its progress, when to hold off, and when to push firmly for completion. Whatever timeliness *The Function of Cynicism* has in its publication, it, and I, owe to her good steering. Niall Summers checked references and quotations with great care. A huge debt to Nick de Somogyi who corrected first proofs and indexed *The Function of Cynicism* at a time of COVID-19 quarantine, doing so with unimpaired professionalism, accuracy and (for my benefit) wit. Any remaining errors lie at my door.

Draft versions of material benefitted from being tested on the following audiences:

— Introduction: CRASSH, University of Cambridge; University of Freiburg; University of Sydney; University of Kent; Universitetet i Agder (Kristiansand);
— Chapter 2: Victorian Graduate Seminar, Faculty of English, University of Oxford
— Chapter 3: British Association for Victorian Studies/University of Liverpool
— Chapter 4: University of Leicester
— Chapter 5: University of Uppsala; Faculté des Lettres, University of Geneva; University of Pittsburgh; Utrecht University; University of York; University of Oxford; University of Nottingham; 'English: Shared Futures' (2017), Newcastle.

I am gladly indebted to many friends and colleagues for invitations to speak, and for assisting the work as it developed through discussion: Isobel Armstrong; Patrick Baert; Dinah Birch; Susan Bruce; Wout Cornelissen; Jos de Mul; Robert Douglas-Fairhurst; Kate Flint; John Frow; Frédéric Goubier; Margareth Hagen; Helge Jordheim; Benjamin Kohlmann; Jakob Lotthe; Johannes Waage Løvhaug; Sara Lyons; Gail Marshall; Lloyd Pratt; Sophie Ratcliffe; David Russell; Joanne Shattock; Matthew Sussman; Roxana Vicovanu; Sunniva Whittaker; Claire E. Wood.

Some elements of Chapter 1 were included, at an early stage of development, in 'Nietzsche and the Cynics', *Aeon*, 28 February 2018, https://aeon.co/essays/what-nietzsche-learnt-from-diogenes-the-cynic. A shorter version of Chapter 3 appeared under the title 'Speech beyond Toleration: On Carlyle and Moral Controversialism Now', in *New Literary History* 48.3 (2017), 531–54. Most of the discussion of George Eliot in the second section of Chapter 4 was first published as 'George Eliot and the Cosmopolitan Cynic', *Victorian Studies* 55.1 (Autumn 2012), 85–105. That material has been revised for publication here. The principal changes and additions are to the reading of *Impressions of Theophrastus Such*. I am sincerely grateful to the commissioning editors (Nigel Warburton, Rita Felski, Andrew Miller) and to anonymous readers for timely and astute commentary.

Contents

'Vices have a place in the composition of virtues.'

(La Rochefoucauld, after Epicurus)

'One should not hesitate to pursue a vice if it is the means to a worthy end.'

(Nietzsche)

'The cynic is a creature of over-statements
But an overstatement is something to achieve.'

(Louis MacNeice)

Introduction

The Function of Cynicism

Modern cynicism is standardly seen as a casting of doubt on the motives that guide right conduct, challenging the preferred self-image of those it targets.[1] On a richer description, the stance of the cynic is one of conscious detachment, or (it may be) alienation, from the common goals, projects, aspirations, ideals of others; he or she pursues a temperamental, quasi-vocational calling to expose the illusions and self-delusions sustaining, or helping to sustain, those goals, projects, aspirations, ideals. Self-styling along cynicism's non-conformist lines assumes, and potentially generates, a libertarian ethos: fearless in self-expression, untroubled by the consequences that might flow from disdaining accepted norms of behaviour in the public domain. Cynic speech is typically acid, terse, wilfully affronting, judgemental. While purporting to be self-sufficient it is, in practice, reactive.

As the characterization implies, identification of cynicism works, in the main, from the outside in, as an external description of what is being said and how it is being said: he/she/you appear cynical to others, rather than self-identifying as a cynic. This is unsurprising, given that in most contexts the word carries the whiff of opprobrium. Exceptions are to be expected: it is of a piece with cynic individualism that it will sometimes thrive on reproach. How and why a particular individual achieves the description are a matter for dispute. Is cynicism an intellectual or a psychological condition, or some combination of the two? Is it (insofar as any disposition may be) natural, temperamental? Or a response to external conditions? Any critical discussion of cynicism, the present one included, will sooner or later have cause to ponder where philosophy meets psychology, and which, if either, field of expertise has explanatory priority.

When contemporary critics complain that cynicism is ubiquitous, they express a concern that established moral agreements and the general psychological health of the society may be under threat. Without looking to recommend cynicism, this book gives reasons to take a less alarmist view. It explores the stylistic appeal and ethical significance of cynicism, understood as a widely employed form of

---

[1] Robin Hard notes (drawing on a large historical literature) that this aspect of cynicism is an Early Modern reinterpretation of Ancient Cynicism. Though Diogenes can sometimes seem to enter that terrain, his aim was to 'replac[e] false values with those which would (according to his conception) enable human beings to fulfil their true nature'. Introduction, in Diogenes the Cynic, *Sayings and Anecdotes with Other Popular Moralists*, trans. Robin Hard (Oxford: Oxford University Press, 2012), ix.

The Function of Cynicism at the Present Time. Helen Small, Oxford University Press (2020). © Helen Small.
DOI: 10.1093/oso/9780198861935.001.0001

credibility check on moral ideals.[2] I examine the role cynicism has played in the past, and continues to play now, in contesting norms of morality and public self-expression. The focus is on literature, public moralism, and philosophy (principally critical philosophy). The principal aim is to understand better how and to what ends writers in these fields have engaged with cynic models in order to recalibrate certain dominant moral values, judgements of taste, and political agreements. Not least, I am concerned with that aspect of the function of cynicism that has to do with creating or protecting a space for more affronting styles of engagement in public debate than are, by tacit agreement, commonly approved of. *Unlike* some others, I do not see cynicism as the isolated practice of a few atypical and difficult individuals, but as part of the remit of many writers—indeed, many people—and of significance primarily for the testing edge of dissent it imports into other, non-cynical discussions of public morality and shared values.

So compacted a summary of the terrain risks making cynicism sound like just a more sharply pugilistic version of the standard liberal requirement, set out by John Stuart Mill, that participants in public debate open themselves up to the challenge of disagreement from others.[3] But cynicism would be without the electric charge it still possesses if it did not retain the capacity to be genuinely undermining of conventional securities. I am not the first to observe (though I am looking to give the observation new point here) that the intellectual history of cynicism has often looked like a long contest over what constitutes a genuinely disturbing dissent from conventional morality.[4] The criteria for cynical 'disturbance' in literature, public moralism, and philosophy are not entirely the same. For the writer and critic of literature and public moralism, modern cynicism's characteristic attribution of low motives to human action opens up possibilities for moral provocation that may be dramatic, prompting strong disagreements between cynicism and its targets or interlocutors, or confined to the individual speech performance which is, typically, contrarian, careless of any offence given, but capable of a wide range of valences. (It is possible to be a 'hardened cynic' or 'somewhat cynical'; a 'good-natured cynic' or an 'embittered' one; to practise an 'inveterate' or an 'ironical' cynicism.) The writer/critic's interest in the moral affront of cynicism is, then, a concern with the operations of language and the delineation of the cynic character

---

[2] For a gestural argument along this line from within sociology, see Donald L. Kanter and Philip H. Mirvis, *The Cynical Americans: Living and Working in an Age of Discontent and Disillusion* (San Francisco: Jossey-Bass, 1989). Though they and I are in broad agreement on what 'the function of cynicism' is, Kanter and Mirvis's position is not developed in depth, and rests on a limited data set: a national telephone survey of 649 adults, in 1983.

[3] John Stuart Mill, *Essays on Politics and Society, Part I (On Liberty)*, in *The Collected Works of John Stuart Mill*, gen. ed. John M. Robson, 33 vols. (Toronto: University of Toronto Press; London: Routledge and Kegan Paul, 1963–91) [hereafter *CW*], vol. XVIII.

[4] Louisa Shea charts a long historical contest over who has the right to speak in the name of Cynicism (Rousseau the primitivist, Wieland the cosmopolitan, Frederick of Prussia the Enlightened despot, etc.). *The Cynic Enlightenment: Diogenes in the Salon* (Baltimore, MD: Johns Hopkins University Press, 2010), 92.

through language; it is also a concern with tone and the social, moral, character-ological, and psychological implications of tone. Good philosophical writing will have these considerations within its sights too, but philosophy brings other requirements to the discussion, many of them technical.[5] My primary interest is in those strands of modern philosophy from Nietzsche onward that have looked to cynicism's debasement of accepted *mores* to assist philosophical objectivity about morality, and (more especially) to articulate a serious scepticism about the sources and authority of morality today.

This introductory chapter presents the core critical-theoretical arguments of the book. I start with a fuller characterization of modern cynicism and a necessary critical account of the main features of early philosophical Cynicism from which it derives and departs. Psychologically aberrant, socially reprehensible today's cynic may appear, but the first Cynics were anti-normative by intellectual orientation and chosen way of life, and their ancient example confers weight on any conscious affront to conventionalism still associated with the name. The chapter then moves to the period that is my focus, roughly 1850 to the present, and to the terms on which I am looking to describe a function for cynicism as a set of linguistic practices aimed at calibrating a plausible, sufficiently robust articulation of ideals. Although, at its best, I see that function as positive, assisting the work of ethical discourse, I also deal with cases in which the cynic oversteps the mark of even a very liberal tolerance. I am not advocating for cynicism; I am interested in a better description of what cynical challenges to the dominant morality can offer as part of a wider conception of public argument.

Modern cynicism may lay claim, via etymology and history of ideas, to the charismatic allure of an old and rich characterization. Though histories of cynicism differ in their accounts of its modern (in the Renaissance and later) trajectories, they invariably trace the core features of today's typology back to the sayings and doings of the original Cynics in Greek antiquity: Antisthenes, Diogenes of Sinope, Crates, Hipparchia, and their followers up into the Roman Empire of the later fourth century CE.[6] The most striking, and arguably the most

---

[5] For more extensive consideration of the differences between academic philosophy and the requirements of 'criticism', see Mary Mothersill, 'Book Reviews', reviewing three early works by Stanley Cavell, *The Journal of Philosophy* 72/2 (1975), 27–48.

[6] The modern secondary literature on ancient Cynicism can be sourced to Donald R. Dudley's *History of Cynicism*, 2nd edn, Foreword and Bibliography by Miriam Griffin (Bristol: Bristol Classical Press, [1937] 2003). The more recent flourishing of scholarship in the field begins in the early 1980s with Gabriele Giannantoni's collection and ordering of the surviving texts documenting the lives and teachings of the Cynics, and other followers and reinterpreters of Socrates: *Socratis et Socraticorum Reliquiae* (reprinted Naples: Bibliopolis, 1990). Thereafter, see esp. Heinrich Niehues-Pröbsting, *Der Kynismus des Diogenes und der Begriff des Zynismus* (Frankfurt: Suhrkamp, 1988); Marie-Odile Goulet-Cazé and Richard Goulet (eds.), *Le Cynisme ancien et ses prolongements: Actes du colloque international du CNRS (Paris, 22–25 juillet 1991)* (Paris: Presses Universitaires de France, 1993); Robert Bracht Branham and Marie-Odile Goulet-Cazé (eds.), *The Cynics: The Cynic Movement in Antiquity and Its Legacy* (Berkeley, CA: University of California Press, 1996); Marie-Odile Goulet-Cazé, *L'Ascèse cynique: Un commentaire de Diogène Laërce, VI. 70–71* (Paris: Vrin, 1986); Luis E. Navia, *Classical*

influential, branch of the Socratic tradition, Cynicism 'revolutionized moral discourse' by insisting upon the animal nature of the human being.[7] Shameless in their manner of living—pissing and satisfying their sexual needs in public, like the dogs (κύνες/kynes) from whom their name partly derived[8]—the early Cynics sought independence from conventional material desires and, with that independence, freedom from emotional disturbance (ἀπάθεια/apatheia). Striving to live 'in accordance with nature',[9] they honed the art of doing without. Diogenes, famously, was said to have made his home in a tub or shack. Seeing a youth scoop up water in the hollow of his hand, he threw away the wooden cup he had been using, pleased to recognize its superfluity.[10]

In its recommendation of hardihood in the face of adversity, and insistence on 'poverty as the principle that should govern your entire life',[11] Cynicism fed directly into Stoicism and then into early Christianity: 'Christ preaching to the rich young man uses almost the same accents as Crates', notes Donald R. Dudley in his popular and still influential *History of Cynicism* (1937), 'exhorting him to renounce worldly goods and cleave to Philosophy, the only mother of virtue'.[12] Though the first Cynics abjured political action and made no detailed political recommendations, Cynic thought is often seen as providing the basis for modern conceptions of cosmopolitan humanism. In this (contested) genealogy of political

Cynicism: A Critical Study (Westport, CT: Greenwood Press, 1996); and Luis E. Navia, *Diogenes of Sinope: The Man in the Tub* (Westport, CT: Greenwood Press, 1998); R. Bracht Branham, 'Cynics', in Edward Craig (gen. ed.), *Routledge Encyclopaedia of Philosophy*, 10 vols. (London: Routledge, 1998), 753–9. Online, accessed 12 June 2019; John L. Moles, 'The Cynics', in C. J. Rowe and Malcolm Schofield (eds.), *The Cambridge History of Greek and Roman Political Thought* (Cambridge: Cambridge University Press, 2000), 415–34; and W. D. Desmond, *The Greek Praise of Poverty: The Origins of Ancient Cynicism* (Notre Dame, IN: University of Notre Dame Press, 2006); and W. D. Desmond, *Cynics* (Stocksfield: Acumen, 2008). A fuller bibliography with primary texts and attention to the Stoic-Cynic relationship can be found in Diogenes Laertius, *Lives of the Eminent Philosophers*, ed. James Miller, trans. Pamela Mensch (Oxford: Oxford University Press, 2018) [henceforth cited as 'Oxford text'], 630. The Oxford text translates the now standard edition of the Greek text by Tiziano Dorandi, Diogenes Laertius, Lives of *the* Eminent Philosophers (Cambridge: Cambridge University Press, 2013).

   [7] See R. Bracht Branham's authoritative summary of the Cynic tradition: 'Cynics'.
   [8] Etymologists have suggested a second root for 'κυνικός' in 'Κυνόσαργες' (Kynosarges), the gymnasium, open to 'illegitimate' Athenians, where the first Cynic, Antisthenes (c.446–366 BCE), was said to have lectured. This claim was standard in the nineteenth century, but 'skepticism now prevails'. See Susan Hukill Prince, *Antisthenes of Athens: Texts, Translations and Commentary* (Ann Arbor, MI: University of Michigan Press, 2015), 78, notes (13) for this contested claim. Also Shea, *Cynic Enlightenment*, 7.
   [9] The phrase is attributed to Diogenes in the apocryphal letter to the philosopher Hippon. 'Diogenes 25, to Hippon', in Diogenes, *Sayings and Anecdotes*, 170.
   [10] See various sources translated in Diogenes, *Sayings and Anecdotes*, 10–11. For the Greek and Latin texts (Jerome, *Against Jovinian* 2.14; *Gnomologium Vaticanum* 185; Simplicius, *Commentary on the 'Encheiridion' of Epictetus* 32), see Giannantoni, *Socratis et Socraticorum Reliquiae*: Diogenes Sinopaeus 175, 158, 160 in Giannantoni's numbering system, vol. II, 309, 303, 303.
   [11] 'Diogenes 26, to Crates', in Diogenes, *Sayings and Anecdotes*, 161.
   [12] Dudley, *A History of Cynicism*, 207. For the development of this theme, see Hans Dieter Betz, 'Jesus and the Cynics: Survey and Analysis of a Hypothesis', *The Journal of Religion* 74/4 (October 1994), 453–75.

thought, the ur-statement of the cosmopolitan philanthropic identification with the human species the world over (and not just human, John Moles suggests—with all inhabitants of the cosmos)[13] is Diogenes of Sinope's famous response to the question of where he comes from: 'κοσμοπολίτης/*kosmopolites*, "I am a citizen of the world."'[14] Above (or perhaps below) all, in their manner of living and their manner of speaking, Diogenes and his kind were understood to 'debase the currency of conventional *mores*' (παραχαράτειν το νόμισμα/*paracharattein to nomisma*). The metaphor alludes to the story that Diogenes was the son of a Sinopean banker, responsible for issuing and overseeing the local currency; when the coinage was found to have been adulterated, his father was imprisoned and Diogenes fled into exile.[15] Just so, in the eyes of its critics, Cynic philosophy devalues the moral currency of its day, chipping away at, or adulterating, the metal base. By implication, were the damaged coinage to circulate widely, the moral economy of public life would be compromised.

Hipparchia, the most famous of the female Cynics, signals a potentially attractive aspect to this inclusive outlook on the 'human': a disregard for conventional gender hierarchies. '[S]tand firm and continue to share the Cynic life with us', reads an apocryphal letter from Crates to Hipparchia: '(for you are by no way inferior to us by nature, any more than female dogs are inferior to male ones').[16] This should not to be mistaken for feminism. Insofar as Crates promises equality, it is equality by way of a shared commitment to living in accordance with nature, on a notoriously restrictive understanding of nature. There is plenty of misogyny on offer in the sayings and anecdotes of the Cynics.[17] On race, Robin Hard observes, they are comparatively benign: 'There is no hostility or cruelty in the jokes that are recorded about black people, in contrast to some of the jokes about women',[18] but they are racial slurs nonetheless and a long way from inclusive

[13] John L. Moles, 'Cynic Cosmopolitanism', in Branham and Goulet-Cazé (eds.), 105–20.

[14] Diogenes Laertius, *Lives of the Eminent Philosophers*, trans. Robert Drew Hicks, rev. and reprinted edn, 2 vols. (London: William Heinemann Ltd, 1950), 6.63 (II, 64–5); also Lucian of Samosata, 'Sale of Creeds' and 'A Cynic', in *The Works of Lucian of Samosata*, trans. H. W. Fowler and F. G. Fowler, 4 vols. (Oxford: Clarendon Press, 1905), I, 190–206 and IV, 172–81.

[15] Diogenes Laertius, *Lives of the Eminent Philosophers*, 6.20 (Oxford text, 269). For a discussion of the tradition and the flaws in its credibility, see Hard, Introduction, in Diogenes, *Sayings and Anecdotes*, xiv. Also Prince, *Antisthenes*, 115.

[16] 'Crates 29, to Hipparchia', in Diogenes, *Sayings and Anecdotes*, 173–4. For a classic feminist reclamation of Hipparchia, see Michèle Le Dœuff, *Hipparchia's Choice: An Essay Concerning Women, Philosophy, etc.* (1991), 2nd edn, trans. Trista Selous (New York: Columbia University Press, 2007), 205–7. The 'choice' is suggested by Hipparchia's rebuff to 'an imbecile who was criticizing her' for neglecting the loom in favour of philosophy: ' "…Do you think I have done wrong to spend on the getting of knowledge all the time which, because of my sex, I was supposed to waste at the loom?"'; 'Methodologically speaking, her remark suggests that if one opens a debate taking existential differences…as a starting point, it is impossible to open a theoretical debate…But philosophy is not purely and simply a theoretical activity' (205–6).

[17] Hard devotes a section of Diogenes, *Sayings and Anecdotes* to 'Misogynistic and Racial Humour'. See 71–2.

[18] Diogenes, *Sayings and Anecdotes*, 216n, quoting Antonius 2.32.60 (G385) and the Papyrus Sorbonne 826 nos. 4 and 5 (G466).

φιλανθρωπία/*philanthropia*. The three examples given in Hard's collection of Diogenes' *Sayings and Anecdotes* come not from Diogenes Laertius (our principal biographical source on the early Cynics) but from less well-known sources. Targeted at Ethiopian blackness, they depict Cynic wit at its most banal.[19]

Whatever the target of its attention, Cynicism favoured terse forms of speech in keeping with its reduced requirements for physical comfort. The first Cynics left no written texts, and their sayings and doings survive in pithy anecdotes, γνώμη/ *gnómē* or apophthegms, known collectively as χρεῖαι/*chreiai*, recorded several centuries after their deaths. Diogenes, as represented in Diogenes Laertius's *Lives of the Eminent Philosophers* (third century CE) is a figure given to swift and cutting rebuttals, aphoristic compaction and biting wit, rather than careful persuasion. He has something of the prankster about him. Entering the market-place with a lantern lit, though it is mid-morning, he demands to know where he can find 'a man' (anyone really or truly living in accordance with human nature). His conversational ripostes demonstrate a blunt disregard for courtesy or ordinary caution. When Alexander the Great announces himself, 'I am Alexander the Great King', Diogenes replies, 'I am Diogenes, the Dog.'[20] Plutarch elaborates a context: Alexander, newly proclaimed leader of the Greeks, expects a congratulatory visit from the philosopher, and when none eventuates goes in search of Diogenes and finds him sunning himself in a grove near Corinth. 'Ask whatever you wish of me', Alexander offers. 'Get out of my light', Diogenes replies.[21]

Such free speech, or παρρησία/*parrhēsia*, posed an affront to political power, to accepted modes of philosophical education, and to norms of public conduct more generally. But the aim was therapeutic, not simply contrarian. Luis Navia notes that:

> the Cynics in general and Crates in particular viewed themselves as 'physicians' of humanity, each one with his own idiosyncratic style of philosophical therapy: Diogenes appealed to various forms of confrontational challenge and vituper-ation, and, on occasion, even to physical blows, while Crates opted for jovial counselling and affectionate guidance. In all cases, however, the goal was one and

---

[19] Ibid., 71–2.

[20] Diogenes Laertius, *Lives of the Eminent Philosophers*, 6.60 (Oxford text, 287). In quoting the sayings of Diogenes of Sinope I have on some occasions preferred for pithiness either Hard's translation or that of R. D. Hicks. Here, cf. Hard's more confrontational rendition: '"And I", he replied, "am Diogenes the Dog."' *Sayings and Anecdotes*, 54.

[21] Diogenes Laertius, *Lives of the Eminent Philosophers*, 6.38 (Hicks II, 41). For further sources in Plutarch and Cicero, see Diogenes, *Sayings and Anecdotes*, 53–4. Cf. the respectfully literal 'Stand out of my light' found in Hard's *Sayings and Anecdotes* and in Mensch's Oxford text. The more demotic translation is widely preferred. See, for example, Richard Sorabji, *Gandhi and the Stoics: Modern Experiments on Ancient Values* (Oxford: Oxford University Press, 2012), 59; Martha C. Nussbaum, *The Cosmopolitan Tradition: A Noble but Flawed Ideal* (Cambridge, MA: The Belknap Press of Harvard University, 2019), 2.

the same, namely, to cure people from their τῦφος [typhos, literally 'smoke' or 'vapour'—the arrogance of false judgements of value which cloud reason].[22]

The ultimate goal was ἀτυφία/atyphia: the purging of 'unnecessary and disturbing thoughts', 'inconsequential and poorly conceived ideas', all the mental 'clutter' that impedes intellectual and spiritual lucidity.[23] According to Diogenes Laertius, Diogenes of Sinope 'often remarked that to get through life we need either reason (logon) or a noose (brochon)' (6.24).[24]

Diogenes' terseness proved negotiable: the later literary Cynics of the Roman Empire were expansive, masters of diatribe and satire in support of truth and austerity[25]—but the challenge to the hearer's assumptions was a constant, and with it (as Michel Foucault points out)[26] the implicit call for magnanimity. Crucially, Ancient Cynicism was non-argumentative. The description of Diogenes as 'A Socrates gone mad', attributed to Plato,[27] rings true on a number of levels—the austerity and self-control (karteria) taken to extremes, the perception that true wealth is a state of the soul and has nothing to do with material riches, the emphasis on reason—but it also merits attention as a comment on the characteristic mode of address to others. Early Cynic dialogue, such as it is,[28]

---

[22] Navia, Classical Cynicism, 138–9.

[23] Ibid.,140, citing Fernanda Decleva Caizzi, 'τῦφος. Contributo alla storia di un concetto', Sandalion 3 (1980), 53–66. See also Navia, Diogenes of Sinope, Chapter 5.

[24] Hicks translates 'right reason or a halter', Lives of the Eminent Philosophers, 6.24 (II, 27).

[25] On the development of Menippean satire, particularly, see Joel C. Relihan, Ancient Menippean Satire (Baltimore, MD: Johns Hopkins University Press, 1993) and 'Late Arrivals: Julian and Boethius', in Kirk Freudenberg (ed.), The Cambridge Companion to Roman Satire (Cambridge: Cambridge University Press, 2005), 109–22. For a longer historical view, see Eric McLuhan, Cynic Satire (Newcastle upon Tyne: Cambridge Scholars Publishing, 2015). A hugely influential figure in the twentieth-century critical take-up of Menippus is Northrop Frye, who gives the mode a crucial place in his Anatomy of Criticism, where he opposes the satirist's interest in 'mental attitudes' to the moral and sociological outlook of the novelist: 'The novelist sees evil and folly as social diseases, but the Menippean satirist sees them as diseases of the intellect, as a kind of maddened pedantry which the philosophus gloriosus at once symbolizes and defines.' Northrop Frye, Anatomy of Criticism: Four Essays (Princeton, NJ: Princeton University Press, 1957), 309. For later developments, see Howard D. Weinbrot, Menippean Satire Reconsidered: From Antiquity to the Eighteenth Century (Baltimore, MD: Johns Hopkins University Press, 2005); Florentine Hoelker, 'Menippean Satire as a Genre: Tradition, Form, and Function in the 17th and 18th Centuries' (PhD thesis, Loyola University of Chicago, 2003). ProQuest dissertation no. 3114131. For an extensive list of primary sources, see E. P. Kirk, Menippean Satire: An Annotated Catalogue of Texts and Criticism (New York: Garland, 1980).

[26] Michel Foucault, The Courage of Truth, in (The Government of Self and Others II): Lectures at the Collège de France, 1983–1984, ed. Frédéric Gros, gen. eds. François Ewald and Alessandro Fontana, English ser. Ed. Arnold I. Davidson, trans. Graham Burchell (London: Palgrave Macmillan, 2011), 11–13, and (on Lucian's uncharacteristically positive reading of Demonax, by way of classical precedent), 199; for commentary see Shea, Cynic Enlightenment, 178.

[27] Diogenes Laertius, Lives of the Eminent Philosophers, 6.54 (Hicks II, 55).

[28] According to Diogenes Laertius (6.17–19), Antisthenes' literary production was extensive, and the dialogue seems to have been a preferred mode. Little (perhaps nothing) of this writing has survived. See Prince, Antisthenes, 1, 15–16. Prince gives concise critical treatment to the proposition (from Winckelmann) that Antisthenes 'was a thinker as interesting and productive as Plato, whose intellectual influence [as a pupil and interpreter of Socrates] was suppressed through the success of that

closes matters down rather than opening them up: the Cynic issues a blunt challenge to conventional morality in no expectation of counter-argument or rebuttal. Typically the object of address is someone in a position of social or political power (Alexander) or someone who has posed a question of the philosopher. Occupying the marketplace, Diogenes puts his wisdom at the disposal of any passer-by. All of humanity stands to learn from the Cynic's acerbic wit, so the claim to *philanthropia* goes, but there is, famously, no Cynic 'School', since the Cynic despises institutions and the element of conformity all institutions bring with them. The partial exception is Antisthenes, often treated as a forerunner of Cynicism, not strictly a Cynic, and linked with the *Kynosarges* or gymnasium near Athens (a contested association).[29]

Cynicism puts conventional ideas of education under strain. A short story by the American late modernist and translator Guy Davenport, 'Mesoroposthonippidon', imagines what happens when the young Diogenes goes to seek instruction from Antisthenes:[30] 'as luck is a slut, Antisthenes despised students who ask questions. He also disliked the passive, the obedient, the suckers up, the complacent listeners. He disliked students, truth be told, altogether.'[31]

A free-wheeling rhetorical extemporization follows, seizing on Diogenes Laertius's brief remarks about Antisthenes' 'bitter reproof of his students' and elaborating them by way of 'extant titles, some likely guesses, and delight in anachronism' (Kenneth Haynes notes):[32]

---

younger rival', consequently suggesting that certain of the Platonic dialogues 'should be revisited under a modern understanding of intertexuality' with Antisthenes (15).

[29] As discussed earlier, a second root for '*κυνικός*' in '*Κυνόσαργες*' (Kynosarges), the gymnasium, has been suggested.

[30] Also disputed. See Diogenes, *Sayings and Anecdotes*, xiii. Susan Prince notes that the evidence for Diogenes' learning from Antisthenes comes from Dio Chrysostom, *Oration 1: On Virtue*, 'the most colourful surviving story of the relationship' between the two men and 'plausibly the oldest'. According to Dio Chrysostom, Antisthenes 'put[s] up with' Diogenes simply because he is 'amazed at the nature of the man'. Diogenes criticizes Antisthenes, comparing him to 'a war trumpet, for he did not hear himself, since he spoke the loudest'. In return, Antisthenes likens Diogenes to 'the wasps:...a small sound, of the wings, but a very bitter sting'. For text and commentary, see Prince, *Antisthenes*, 95–7 (96). Also 98 for Eusebius's more explicit claim that Diogenes was Antisthenes' 'pupil'.

[31] Guy Davenport, *Eclogues: Eight Stories* (San Francisco, CA: North Point Press, 1981), 107–21 (118).

[32] Kenneth Haynes, 'Eccentric Classics: The Fiction of Guy Davenport', in Kenneth Haynes (ed.), *The Oxford History of Classical Reception*, vol. 5: *After 1880* (Oxford: Oxford University Press, 2019), 549–75 (567). Andre Furlani nicely describes a 'vibrant ascesis': 'the Cynic is an inverted sensualist who gleefully tells his hedonistic disciple..."you have not learned the pleasure of despising pleasure"'. See Andre Furlani, *Guy Davenport: Postmodernism and After* (Evanston, IL: Northwestern University Press, 2007), 19. And see George Steiner, 'Rare Bird', in Robert Boyers (ed.), *George Steiner at the New Yorker* (New York: New Directions, 2009), 148–56, esp. 156 on Davenport's preference for the domain of the aesthetic—including the 'riddles and metaphors of the pre-Socratics'—over that of the economic and political: he 'seems to shield both himself and his readers from the full, perhaps anarchic deployment of his own strengths'.

What is teaching, the old boy bellowed, but thunder after lightning? With sharper fire than a Scythian arrow, thought splits the dark, crossing a chasm it can never close. The rent it tears in the placidity of opinion, in the weft of custom, closes itself along a crack of vacuum from cloud to oak, with a report and rumble, until of the fierce white clarity only a rumor is left, only a memory of light, a red afterglow.   (118–19)

What possible response might a student make? Silent spectatorship seems the safest bet ('That was Antisthenes' specialty, making a sight of himself', the narrator observes with perhaps not enough cynicism of his own.)[33] This is late-, some would say post-, modernist comedy, Joycean in its taste for the orotund, but alert—as Joyce was—to where the orotund can tip over into the silly. Antisthenes is not entirely coherent, if one presses his point (what is a cleft doing closing itself along a crack of vacuum?), but the 'old boy' is hamming it up, and either losing his grip or positively exerting himself to deter a student likely to be more demanding than most.[34] If Davenport's version of Cynicism traduces the historical record of its terseness, it stays true to the wit and the drama of a dialogue thwarted. In lieu of disciplined reduction to bare nature, we get nature's extravagance—the verbal equivalent of thunder and lightning: rhetorical afflatus, excess of allusion and quotation, burlesque of epic proportions, and, debasing it all, scatological wit. Antisthenes' speech is one giant fart—a 'report and rumble' issuing from his 'crack'; an offence against 'placidity'—though it is to Davenport's credit that it vents something more than just hot air. The non-teacher is, after all, saying something worth considering about teaching: that its communications are more often than not delayed reports from an illumination that has already happened, a rumbling of talk after the Sythian flash of insight. Not that thunder makes no impression of its own, but it is an after-effect or memory of clarification, not the thing itself.

Davenport is working that seam of the Cynic tradition that emphasizes energy of intelligence over polish, grafting his own literariness on to its rude wit. But his alertness to how Cynicism unbalances the critical conversation has wider purchase. Cynicism typically greets intellectual ambition, like all forms of loftiness, by accusing it of superficiality, pointing, again, to low motive: the self-interest that lies in taking one's own intelligence too seriously. Productive interchange is

[33] The narrator, Nippaki, a follower of Diogenes, is portrayed as a cheerful hedonist, and an object of mirth to the much older philosopher.

[34] Davenport wrote his BLitt thesis on Joyce at the University of Oxford. See Christopher Lehmann-Haupt, 'Guy Davenport Dies at 77; Prolific Author and Illustrator', *New York Times*, 7 January 2005, <https://www.nytimes.com/2005/01/07/books/guy-davenport-dies-at-77-prolific-author-and-illustrator.html>. Accessed 18 September 2019. On his debt also to Pound, see Dustin Illingworth, 'An Intellectual Love Affair: Guy Davenport and Hugh Kenner', *The Paris Review*, 14 November 2018. <https://www.theparisreview.org/blog/2018/11/14/an-intellectual-love-affair-guy-davenport-and-hugh-kenner/>. Accessed 18 September 2019.

unlikely to be the result. Cynicism thus opens up important questions about 'recognition': about whether philosophy and, by association, criticism must address its objects as 'equals' with whom it is 'in conversation'. Given to sarcasm and biting put-downs, Cynicism says not. It may be leavened in the delivery by irony, but it is not to be mistaken for irony, which makes an appeal to the insider: the offer of a shared perspective of intelligence is a form of recognition. (One can, of course, be one's own insider, savouring an irony to oneself.) The truculence of the Cynic, by contrast, implies 'take it or leave it': if its auditor does not get the point, too bad (or too good . . .). His or her taciturnity approaches, indeed, the silence of the hermit who does not deign to speak at all, but is not, finally, so self-isolating. The Cynic aspects of Nietzsche's Zarathustra, repeatedly retreating from and then re-engaging with the rest of humanity (see Chapter 1) play along this line, and indeed thin the line—at times unresponsive to others, at times too responsive. At least he knows his wavering is a problem.

Even in the early nineteenth century, familiarity with the classical credentials of Cynicism did not necessarily go very deep on the part of writers drawn to its moral and stylistic terrain. The primary texts recording the sayings and doings of the early Cynics, Diogenes Laertius's enjoyably anecdotal *Lives of the Eminent Philosophers* and Lucian's satiric dialogue between Alexander the Great and Diogenes the Cynic,[35] were not much taught in eighteenth- or nineteenth-century classrooms, other than in short excerpts as part of a general classical and historical education.[36] Thomas Francklin's (1780) English translation helped to return the

[35] 'Diogenes, Alexander', from 'Dialogues of the Dead', in *The Works of Lucian*, I, 129–30.
[36] M. L. Clarke, *Greek Studies in England, 1700–1830* (Cambridge: Cambridge University Press, 1945), notes that Lucian was 'much read' (12), but Diogenes Laertius was 'out of fashion' (161) for most of the eighteenth century in schools and universities—noting the exceptionality of Thomas Gray in being well acquainted with him. For the wider European story of Diogenes Laertius's long period in low regard, from the later sixteenth century to the late nineteenth, see Anthony Grafton, 'Diogenes Laertius: From Inspiration to Annoyance (and Back)', in *Lives of the Eminent Philosophers*, ed. Miller, 546–54. There were partial exceptions, both in the field of scholarship (see Grafton, 551–3) and among those deciding school syllabi. See Clarke, *Greek Studies*, 17, on the Eton curriculum's inclusion of Lucian, and 42 on the inclusion of the dialogues in the Edinburgh University curriculum at mid-century. There was dissent, even on the merits of Lucian. In *Classical Education in Britain, 1500–1900* (Cambridge: Cambridge University Press, 1959), Clarke quotes the *Edinburgh Review* on the 'obliquity of judgment' which led Eton to prefer Lucian to Thucydides in the eighteenth century (57). The widely used *Scriptores Graeci* (multiple editions through the eighteenth and nineteenth centuries) included extracts from 'Menippus' and 'Vitarium Auctio', both of which touch on Cynicism—'Menippus. A Necromantic Experiment' extensively so (it is a comic portrait of the Cynic Menippus, recounting his visit to Hades where he has witnessed the punishment of those who have been rich and powerful in life, and the happiness of Diogenes alone, who has set up his pitch within earshot of Midas and other 'specimens of magnificence': the 'sound of their lamentations and better-day memories keeps him in laughter and spirits; he is generally stretched on his back roaring out a noisy song which drowns lamentation; it annoys them, and they are looking out for a new pitch where he may not molest them' (*Works of Lucian*, I, 165); 'Vitarium Auctio' ('Philosophies for Sale', or 'Sale of Creeds') includes the sale of Diogenes—foreclosed because no buyer will have him (193–5). On the late eighteenth-century renaissance of teaching Greek in English schools, see Matthew Adams, *Teaching Classics in English Schools, 1500–1840* (Newcastle upon Tyne: Cambridge Scholars Publishing, 2015), 116. Lucian, Adams notes, was a great favourite of Erasmus, and one of the key figures in the introduction of humanism into

works of Lucian to favour on university Greek syllabi; and Diogenes Laertius, available in English translations from the late seventeenth and early eighteenth centuries, was given a wider readership by C. D. Yonge's 'literal translation' of 1853; but a basic, and for most cultural purposes, sufficient knowledge of Cynicism might amount to no more than a familiarity with a few famous anecdotes (Diogenes in his tub; Diogenes in his rough smock, carrying a crude lantern—in search of a true man; Diogenes as dog; Diogenes telling Alexander where to go).[37]

Knowledge of Classical Cynicism was, in short, both ubiquitous and (frequently) slight—as it still is. Arnold, Nietzsche, and Davenport are exceptional in this book in having had close knowledge of the original Greek texts: Nietzsche cut his philological teeth on the textual descent of Diogenes Laertius; Arnold immersed himself in the Stoic inheritors of Cynic ideas; the translations of Diogenes' sayings in the *Eclogues* are Davenport's own.[38] Appeals to the type often floated free of clear reference to ancient models, so that there is a judgement call to be made on whether continuity with early Greek and Roman philosophy and its later interpretations is intended or relevant in any given instance. Dictionary definitions indicate as much when they differentiate between the 'sect of philosophers in ancient Greece' (*OED* n. 1) and 'A person disposed to rail or find fault; now usually: One who shows a disposition to disbelieve in the sincerity or goodness of human motives and actions, and is wont to express this by sneers and sarcasms; a sneering fault-finder' (*OED* n. 2). It is not automatic that noun 2, with its quick shift from intellectual disposition to unlovely tonality, retains any strong connection to noun 1. The room for ambiguity notwithstanding, to assert a relationship with cynicism is, in post-classical contexts, to associate oneself with a set of well-known traits. The style is individualistic, but the familiarity of the form limits the scope for authenticity. This is so not only because Cynicism is remotely historic, no longer a fully lived or liveable practice

---

English schools (33). W. Tooke's 1820 translation of the dialogues suggests a nineteenth-century readership beyond the Classics classroom, but I have found little discussion or evidence of Lucian's presence in English translation on school curricula of the eighteenth and nineteenth centuries.

[37] For very recent examples, see Peter Robinson, '(Further Work on) Pissarro's Dream... Or... When Camille Pissarro the Impressionist Painter and Anarchist Met Diogenes of Sinope the Performance Artist and Cynic Philosopher...', *Peter Robinson artist painter*, 31 March 2017, Wordpress. <https://peterrobinsonartist.com/2017/03/31/further-work-on-pissarros-dream-or-when-camille-pissarro-the-impressionist-painter-and-anarchist-met-diogenes-of-sinope-the-performance-artist-and-cynic-philosopher/>; Daniel Anthony Ignatius Swanger, *Diogenes Throwing Away His Bowl*, painting (2014). <https://www.saatchiart.com/art/Painting-Diogenes-Throwing-Away-His-Bowl/330609/2022719/view>. And on cynicism and contemporary cynicism towards the institutionalization of art, see Peter Osborne, 'Disguised as a Dog', in Peter Osborne, *The Postconceptual Condition: Critical Essays* (London: Verso, 2018), 73–89.

[38] See 'Guy Davenport: The Art of Fiction. No. 174', interviewed by John Jeremiah Sullivan, *Paris Review*, 163 (Fall 2002) for a list of his translations. <https://www.theparisreview.org/interviews/355/guy-davenport-the-art-of-fiction-no-174-guy-davenport>. Accessed 15 September 2019.

of philosophy, but because naming cynicism is, as it always was, an act of characterization or self-characterization. To remark upon or adopt it is to activate a type: selecting and repeating from a narrow repertoire of well-recognized features. It is, as etymology reminds us, akin to scripting ('character' deriving from *kharaktēr* an instrument for writing or engraving).[39]

Every writer on cynicism faces the problem that there is no entirely satisfactory or secure way of denominating the form of characterization involved when the word starts playing between philosophical specificity and looser psychological gesturalism. So, though in some cases, primarily the philosophical ones, the object of discussion is clearly Cynicism, as I move out of that terrain to consider literary writing and public moralism of the nineteenth century and after, I am often discussing expressions of cynicism that put in play elements of the stricter characterization that are unconcerned with, and possibly not much cognizant of, its original remit. These looser cynicisms evince a continuing commitment to certain forms of debunking argument in the field of morality, a fondness for the tactic of debasing the motives of others (an Early Modern development in the remit),[40] and an appetite for stylistic aggressions in speech. Cynicism, as Ford Madox Ford deploys and scrutinizes it, for example, is primarily of this kind. Rather than clutter this book's prose, and try the reader's patience, with a hedging 'Cynicism/cynicism' in such cases, I have followed the convention and opted for the lower case.

A gradual drift in primary meaning is, then, clear, but it is the task of intellectual history to try to explain how and why Western cultures moved from early philosophical Cynicism to today's more dilute cynical disposition. Much scholarly labour has been expended to that end, thickening etymological derivation into intellectual genealogy by charting the detailed evolution of ancient philosophical Cynicism into its modern casualized namesake, from its popularization as a literary movement in the late Roman period, to its influence on early Christian and later humanist thinking about virtue, through to its richly generative impact on Early Modern satire and the shaping and self-regulation of Enlightenment rationalism.[41] There are serious and thorough accounts

---

[39] *OED*, 'character, *n.*' Accessed 27 September 2019.

[40] See Robin Hard's comments earlier on the Early Modern reinterpretation of ancient Cynicism.

[41] For the long inheritances of Cynicism into the Renaissance period, see the primary source texts collected in Niklaus Largier, *Diogenes der Kyniker: Exempel, Erzählung, Geschichte in Mittelalter und früher Neuzeit; mit einem Essay zur der Figur des Diogenes zwischen Kynismus, Narrentum und postmoderner Kritik* (Tübingen: M. Niemeyer, 1997), 165–359; and, for criticism, essays by Derek Krueger, Sylvain Matton, Joel C. Relihan, and Daniel Kinney in Branham and Goulet-Cazé (eds.), *The Cynics*, 240–328. Key critical works on the Enlightenment revival of Cynicism include: Heinrich Niehues-Pröbsting, 'Diogenes at the Enlightenment: The Modern Reception of Cynicism', in Branham and Goulet-Cazé (eds.), *The Cynics*, 329–65 (for the earlier German version, see 'Der Kynismus-Rezeption der Moderne: Diogenes in der Aufklärung', *Deutsche Zeitschrift für Philosophie* 40/7 (1992), 709–34); and esp. Shea, *Cynic Enlightenment*. See also Sharon Stanley, 'Retreat from Politics: The Cynic in Modern Times', *Polity* 39/3 (2007), 384–407, and Sharon Stanley, *The French*

demonstrating the continuation of cynic thought beyond this vigorous and well-recognized revival in the sixteenth to eighteenth centuries, and challenging the old view that cynicism suffered 'a fall from grace and memory' in the nineteenth century.[42] There is also an extensive literature looking at its more modern cultural and political expressions in, for example, the post-1980s United States.[43] I draw on some of those accounts in the course of this book as they have a bearing on the theoretical handling of cynicism or on specific instances, but I am not trying to write a modern history of cynicism, and it will be clear from the highly selective cast of writers assembled here that comprehensiveness is very far from my ambitions. My reasons for reviving the subject are more immediately presentist. The selection of materials reflects the several aspects of cynicism that seem to me to have been (and still are) most pertinent to the work of admitting a broader, more flexible, account of public debate than much (supposedly norma-tive) critical writing admits.

Like others who have taken up the topic in recent years, I am drawn to the questions cynicism raises about the nature and limits of normative thinking about public morality, public values, social commitments, and shared tastes, and the extent of any individual's capacity to take up a position of distance on 'the common currency' of ideas and values in a society. The 'self-fashioning' aspect of Cynic deportment (of interest to Foucault and reflected, under his influence, in the French 'Nouvelle philosophie' movement of the 1970s and 1980s)[44] is one way of framing the achievement of such critical distance, and of direct relevance to this book's discussion of how the literary and philosophical writers treated have cultivated independence of view and charismatic distinction of style in their

Enlightenment and the Emergence of Modern Cynicism (New York: Cambridge University Press, 2012)—arguing against accounts (esp. that of Sloterdijk, discussed below) which see a sudden emer-gence of cynicism towards politics after the 1960s. Stanley identifies the impulse towards cynicism 'in the thought of enlightenment itself' ('Retreat', 384). The idea that our modern troubles start from the eighteenth century (over-investment in certain kinds of scepticism drawing intellectual and political cultures too *much* towards cynicism) is also pursued by David Mazella. David Mazella, *The Making of Modern Cynicism* (Charlottesville, VA: The University of Virginia Press, 2007), esp. 96–7.

[42] See esp. Niehues-Pröbsting, *Der Kynismus des Diogenes* (esp. 262–372); Mazzela, *The Making of Modern Cynicism*, Chapter 6; and Osborne, 'Disguised as a Dog'.

[43] On the contemporary American political aspect, see esp. Kanter and Mirvis, *The Cynical Americans*; William Chaloupka, *Everybody Knows: Cynicism in America* (Minneapolis, MN: University of Minnesota Press, 1999); with a longer trajectory, Mazella, *The Making of Modern Cynicism*; Timothy Bewes, *Cynicism and Postmodernity* (London: Verso, 1997)—concentrating on contemporary political and cultural manifestations of cynicism; and Benjamin Schreier, *The Power of Negative Thinking: Cynicism and the History of Modern American Literature* (Charlottesville, VA: University of Charlottesville Press, 2009).

[44] Michel Foucault, *The Courage of the Truth*; also *The Government of Self and Others: Lectures at the Collège de France, 1982–1983*, ed. Frédéric Gros, gen. eds. François Ewald and Alessandro Fontana, English ser. ed. Arnold I. Davidson, trans. Graham Burchell (London: Palgrave Macmillan, 2010), 286–7, 292, 344, 346–8, 380. For the *Nouvelle philosophie* influence, see esp. André Glucksmann, *Cynisme et Passion* (Paris: Grasset, 1981)/*Cynicism and Passion*, Stanford French & Italian Studies 76 (Saratoga, CA: Anma Libri, 1995).

writing. Almost all the writers considered acquire deeper or new significance in such a reading: not just the recognized or regularly 'accused' cynics, such as Friedrich Nietzsche, Thomas Carlyle, Richard Rorty (briefly), Laura Kipnis, or those known, or sometimes considered, to have dabbled (Bertrand Russell, Ford Madox Ford, Bernard Williams) but several writers who normally are considered advocates for high moral and political ideals, who might be expected vigorously to oppose cynicism and in most contexts do: Matthew Arnold, George Eliot, John Dewey. Cynic voices tend to be read as individualistic,[45] but I am curious, also, about how their transgressions of norms of public debate and norms of morality may assist collective reappraisal, potentially the adjustment, and, in rare cases, the abandonment, of current norms. There is, of course, a topicality to the subject. 'Norm breaching' (acting, speaking, or writing in contravention of accepted standards) has of late become widespread, with correspondingly strong reactions in the direction of shoring up or enforcing normative principles where there is institutional scope and collective will to do so. A word, then, on norms.

Norms, in the widely adopted anthropological sense, are 'accepted rules or principles valid for particular communities'.[46] Rules and principles of this kind 'help us to pursue projects and goals, individually and collectively' and 'enable us to constitute social meanings'.[47] They are the empirical *mores* present in a society, generally applicable, affecting, and intended to affect, the behaviour of any agent. In Durkheim's terminology, they are 'social facts'.[48] Given the complex nature of societies, they are irreducibly 'pluralist in character',[49] though talk of norms often assumes a rigidity that conceals this social reality. Not infrequently, the norms of a group or community come into conflict with one another, requiring, in the way of everyday life, prioritization, choices, more and less strategic juggling. Not least, normative claims have an important role to play in shoring up public values. Most widely espoused public goods are supported not by simple or dogmatic standards but by multiple and overlapping systems of valuation. We have, for example, a variety of normative grounds for investing resources in humanities higher education, or care of the aged (subjects that have occupied me in the past). Locating and articulating the basis for these valuations bring most, though by no means all, participants to the work of articulating normative arguments as the ground of

---

[45] This claim is ubiquitous in the critical literature, though the Cynic proper would claim to be like everyone else—the difference being that others have not yet realized what they are.

[46] Geoffrey Brennan, Lisa Eriksson, Robert E. Goodin, and Nicholas Southwood, *Explaining Norms* (Oxford: Oxford University Press, 2013), 3–5.

[47] Ibid., abstract. I am omitting here the authors' comparison with philosophers' more demanding use of the term to denote 'objectively valid rules or normative principles'. That is not always the case: philosophers do not always hold that norms are 'objective', and when they do, what 'objective' means is a point of disagreement (universality, generality, pragmatic unavoidability, etc.).

[48] Emile Durkheim, *Les Règles de la méthode sociologique* (1895), trans. W. D. Halls, *The Rules of Sociological Method*, ed. with an Introduction by Stephen Lukes (New York: Free Press, 1982), *passim*.

[49] Brennan et al., *Explaining Norms*, abstract.

agreement with others, including those in positions of political power or responsibility.

Normative claims are not the only ones worth hearing, however, and anyone with an interest in the history of philosophy or the history of politics will have had occasion before now to think about varieties of non-normative or anti-normative expression and persuasion. The kinds of norm-breaching involved in, and figured by, cynic speech are unlike the several other varieties of radical critique, programmatic iconoclasm, contrarianism, exhortation, or even mystical evocation that may get a hearing within academic and wider public debate. Cynicism, in its ancient forms, was not only unconventional but anti-conventional. It based that anti-conventionality on its idea of a 'norm': living 'in accordance with nature'. Put simply, convention is, for the Cynic, a non-natural category. Cynicism was—and in its modern forms remains—strongly anti-idealist (of which more shortly), in the sense that it has no time for abstract ideals and theories that cannot stand the test of subjection to the basic animal condition of being human and inhabiting the marketplace of human affairs. It is, truculently, realistic about that condition— which is not to say that its realism is necessarily right or immune to objections from those who take ideals to have animating importance for individual and social action.

Cynicism in its original forms confronted the entitlement of individual representatives of power but it was, properly, anti-political in its designs even when political in its effects. Diogenes claimed the freedom of the exile as a warrant to spurn all political systems and challenge all political authority (the Cynic's cosmopolitanism was the negative condition of the person who belongs nowhere—who was 'not a citizen of your Greek cities').[50] He, and other Cynics after him, did not offer an alternative set of social or political actions to those currently in place: they reacted against the common currency, stopping at the point where a provocation had been issued to the 'intellectual and moral consensus'.[51] This is not to deny that Cynicism has been adapted over the centuries to purposes that are patently political, or that have reform of current ideas in their sights, but the affront of cynicism, now as in the past, lies in the stubbornness with which it holds itself at bay from the work of constructing consent (which may or may not follow in public reaction), and preserves to itself the tough-skinned isolation of the unaccommodated critic. The complaint that, in offering no programme of its own, it is not just by default conservative but corrosive has often been part of its negative description. A character in Iris Murdoch's *A Fairly Honourable Defeat* (1970) deliberately assays a cynical approach to her estranged husband's overtures, and thinks of her experimental cynicism as 'the opposite extreme from love: the cynicism of a deliberate contemptuous diminution of

---

[50] Dudley, *History of Cynicism*, 35. See also Desmond, *Cynics*, 271.
[51] Foucault, Lecture of 14 March 1984: First hour, *Courage of the Truth*, 232.

another person'.[52] I take this perception of the hostility of the cynic towards institutions and societies, as much as towards other persons, to be a key element in its negative reception. I demur from the default assumption that it makes nothing desirable happen: the potential to corrode seems to me indissociable from the power of cynicism to do intellectual, cultural, and political work by way of casting doubt on established agreements about what we value and why.

Norms of public expression do not usually rupture all of a sudden or entirely. War and periods of major civil unrest are the obvious conditions of exception. This is one reason for the high level of current interest in and agitation about what seems to many an abrupt weakening of norms of political discussion in Britain and America. Geoffrey Brennan and his co-authors locate a rationale for that weakening when they observe, in general terms, that acting in opposition to a norm involves a judgement that cooperating with it is not, or is no longer, in your interests: '[a]ny desire you may have to act in accordance with a norm, either for its own sake or to avoid sanctions for its breach, must compete with the various other desires you have'—the desire, for example, to have your voice heard, when the effect of complying with the norm would be to repress either the content or the level of feeling you want to express.[53] Current widespread hostility to 'liberalism', for example (in the American progressive-egalitarian, broadly leftist sense increasingly widely adopted in the UK), stems in large part from a perception on the political hard-right that the general rules and principles by which twentieth- and early twenty-first-century institutions have sought to secure tolerance, diversity, equality, have been exclusive rather than enabling. In endorsing public protections, some of them enforceable by law, on what can be said and how it can be said, modern democratic societies have, on this view, fostered a conformist public sphere that has claimed to listen to all comers but not given them equality of standing. One effect of the weakening of liberal norms has been growing counter-resistance to that view—a resistance visible in concerted efforts to strengthen public protections now perceived to have existed in name but not sufficiently in reality (the #MeToo and Black Lives Matter movements are prominent examples). And on the far left there is now a hardening radicalism willing to break contact with the principle of tolerance in seeking to enforce reform agendas.

Tuning in to cynic *parrhēsia* is a way of giving a philosophical lineage, but also a contemporary critical and psychological frame, to the principle that society should accommodate the person whose willingness to offend against broadly accepted standards of morality and its expression puts the liberal commitment to tolerance to a hard test. Clearly, given the argumentative move here from norm-breaking as a feature of recent political debate to the testing of free speech limits, I am not

---

[52] (London: Vintage, 2001), 146. But for divergent views on the negativity, see discussion in Shea, *Cynic Enlightenment*, Chapter 4.

[53] Brennan et al., *Explaining Norms*, 237.

assuming that cynicism's taking of extreme liberties has relevance only to theorists and critics of liberal thought, though they may take a special interest. Nor am I looking to conflate cynicism with the principle of free speech, though much of my discussion of cynic linguistic styles will centre on the taking of licence in speech.[54] *The Function of Cynicism at the Present Time* shows that cynicism's provocative dissent from agreed morality, standard modes of public disputation, and established political and intellectual authorities has appealed to writers and philosophers across the ideological spectrum, and with a wide variety of social and moral outlooks. It has attracted Tory radicals and those on the radical left as well as liberals. Its adoption has been more complete in some cases than others (and the partial cases are of special interest to me). In all its guises, its effects have been determined as much or more by the ways in which others have responded to its provocations than by any declared intentions or prior affiliations claimed by those exhibiting it.

*

Cultural criticism's interest in cynicism over recent decades can largely be attributed to two works, written contemporaneously but almost entirely in ignorance of one another.[55] Michel Foucault's last course of lectures at the Collège de France, *Le courage de la vérité* (1983–84)[56] and Peter Sloterdijk's *Kritik der zynischen Vernunft* (1983)[57] differ markedly in style and substance but have in common a genealogical impulse to anchor modern conceptions of critical freedom and philosophical independence in a line of thinking that connects today's philosophy back to the 'courageous freedoms' of Diogenes and later cynics. Like other philosophical genealogies written in the long wake of Nietzsche's critique of morality (though neither Foucault nor Sloterdijk is attempting genealogical work on that scale), the intellectual lineages described are retrospective fictions, making articulate a set of affiliations that is in part historical, in part literary (a matter of formal and perhaps stylistic continuity), in part philosophical. That is,

---

[54] For the pre-history of modern conceptions of 'free speech', in classical and early modern rhetoric, see David Colclough, '*Parrhesia*: The Rhetoric of Free Speech in Early Modern England', *Rhetorica* 17/2 (1999), 177–212.

[55] Foucault's lecture of 29 February 1984 (Second hour) includes a dismissive reference to Sloterdijk's work, of which he has just been made aware: '…a book by someone called Sloterdijk, which someone pointed out to me recently, but which I have not read bears the solemn title *Kriitk der zynischen Vernunft*…No critique of reason will be spared us, not of pure, or of dialectical, or of political reason.' He takes the wider evidence of German philosophical interest in the subject to be a topic worth pursuing in its own right: 'why and in what terms has contemporary German philosophy posed this problem?' It is clear from the comments that follow that he had not registered the distinctiveness of Sloterdijk's contribution (179).

[56] Foucault, *Le courage de la vérité: Le gouvernement de soi et des autres II: Cours au Collège de France, 1983-1984*, ed. Frédéric Gros, gen. eds. François Ewald and Alessandro Fontana (Paris: Seuil/Gallimard, 2009).

[57] First published in English as Peter Sloterdijk, *The Critique of Cynical Reason*, trans. Michael Eldred (London: Verso, 1988).

they offer a sharpened perception of principles held to be important for critical philosophy: primarily, a commitment to truth-telling understood as a courageous form of self-fashioning; a recognition that reasoning truthfully requires confrontation with the ways in which rationality tends to cooperate with power; a vigilant awareness lest the pursuit of critical freedom impose its own new norms and constricting forms of subjectification. (The intellectual-as-Cynic does not lack self-regard.)

Above all, the resuscitation of Cynicism in the early 1980s puts contemporary philosophy back in touch with an Ancient (and even when Ancient, 'radical') understanding that philosophy should be a lived practice, not an abstracted or institutionally formalized thing. For Foucault, 'Cynicism makes life...a manifestation of truth' (172)—courageous, spare, stripped of 'all the pointless obligations which everyone usually acknowledges and accepts and which have no basis in nature and reason' (171). Its 'reductive practice' makes space within life 'for truth-telling' (172). It is a reading that endows the Cynic with intellectual self-consciousness and virtue, downplaying the degree to which he or she might be operating reflexively. For Sloterdijk, the Cynic Diogenes 'talks with [other philosophers] in a dialogue of flesh and blood' (104), which is why Plato and Socrates found him impossible to deal with. The modern philosopher, Sloterdijk concludes, can find in him a courage that may 'make itself felt' either as a 'euphoric clarity' or as a 'wonderfully tranquil' seriousness (547).

The ends of Cynicism are not the same in Foucault and Sloterdijk, as the mystical turn of the last quotation might indicate. The likenesses and differences are well elaborated in the final chapters of Louisa Shea's *The Cynic Enlightenment: Diogenes in the Salon* (2010)—the richest and subtlest recent consideration of cynicism's long trajectories from antiquity, through the French Enlightenment, into modern critical theory. For that reason, I summarize relatively briefly here. Both take Cynicism as a model for a lived practice of philosophy that moves its practitioner beyond abstract reasoning and past the limitations of modes of critique deemed no match for a world in which 'the truth of rulers and that of servants are different', as Sloterdijk puts it (with Marx and the disappointments of Marxism in his sights) (218); or as Foucault sees the problem, a world in which 'the production of truth [*alētheia*], the exercise of power [*politeia*] and moral formation [*ēthos*]' do not coincide (68). Both men see in ancient Cynicism a model of vigilant self-fashioning that might be reworked to contest existing relations of power—and both can readily be interpreted within the context of a post-1960s attempt to keep 'radical critique' alive, albeit a description better fitted to Sloterdijk, whose work emerged directly out of his reading of Frankfurt School Marxism, in heterogenous mix with Nietzscheanism, Buddhism, Bakhtinianism, and early media studies (hinting at the techno-futurism that comes centre-stage in his later work), than to Foucault, who claimed to have come to Adorno and

Horkheimer belatedly and insisted on the plurality of 'rationalities'.[58] Both evince a strong hostility to organization of the work of dissent, and neither is free from what (with the clarity of hindsight) look like strongly Romantic elements of anti-institutionalism.

Foucault is much the more astringent. Shea rightly notes that what begins as a marginal interest in Cynicism gradually emerges as central to Foucault's efforts at reorienting his own critical attention from 'the historical analysis of the limits that are imposed upon us' to experimentation with 'the possibility of going beyond them' (172). An acute reader of the classical literature, Foucault picks up on the early Cynic's role as a kind of moral 'scout', revived in the lectures' description of a form of philosophical avant-gardism—though one notes also the replacement of the non-combatant scout with the combatant 'gardiste'. After years spent analysing the discursive structures of power, Foucault was grappling with how individuals 'position themselves with regard to the laws, codes, and attitudes available to them' in historical context (Shea, 173). To that end, he looked to connect critical-philosophical speech with a life lived according to demanding principles for free truth-telling. There are, perhaps inevitably, points at which 'principle' starts to sound like a source of tension in the entire enterprise. At one point he allows himself to admire the Cynics' enactment of 'well-defined rules [règles], conditions, or modes',[59] but in the main, he is more careful. Cynicism is a practice of intellectual virtue; it is a form of work directed at establishing an ethos or lived experience of philosophy. The alighting of that last quoted sentence on 'modes' relaxes the hint of regulation: there are no rules beyond the demand for courageous honesty at the risk of prompting one's interlocutor to anger or even violence. The means are individualistic, but Le courage de la vérité puts some distance between itself and the conventional association of Cynicism with individualism, insisting on the social ends of philosophy. Foucault has an opportune phrase for the modern intellectual qua Cynic: an 'aggressive benefactor', acting with a kind of missionary dedication, or as a doctor bearing unpleasant but necessary medication, to remedy the world by remedying, first, the self.[60]

The phrase 'strategic cynicism' can be found in Sloterdijk (525), but where I treat it normatively and allow for a range of valuations (how far its impact is positive or negative depends on numerous factors, including the fitness or otherwise of the cynicism to its object in the context), the Critique treats strategic cynicism

---

[58] This by contrast with the Marxist and subsequent Frankfurt critique of 'a rationality'. See Michel Foucault, Remarks on Marx: Conversations with Duccio Trombadori, trans. R. James Goldstein and James Cascaito (New York: Semiotext(e), 1991), 59–62, 115–29, 152. Foucault stresses the importance of Nietzsche's influence for him here. On his coming late to the Frankfurt School, see 116–17.

[59] Lecture of 29 February: First hour, 165. French text at Le courage de la verité, 252.

[60] Lecture of 21 March 1984: First hour, Courage of the Truth, 278–9 (279). And see Shea, Cynic Enlightenment, 183, for a discussion of the trope of benefaction.

as a spent force.[61] The phrase arises in the course of describing a *historic* crisis of the German Left confronted with the rise of Nazism. To cynically predict, as the 'supertactician' of Communism, Karl Radek, did, that 'Hitler will come to power and everything will go under' was 'to bet on a catastrophe', Sloterdijk observes: disastrous though it will be to have Hitler in power, there is 'something good' here for the Communist cause, in that he will 'help to bring about the total bankruptcy of the system' (525). It says something about Sloterdijk's argumentative priorities that he has no interest in thickening the historical picture of Radek's choice: the early *versus* later outlines of Nazism; the brutality of Stalinism. Objections on the particular case aside, plainly I am interested in quieter, less toxic forms of cynicism than this (a 'masochistic form of thinking', Sloterdijk calls it, 'that has transformed itself into a strategic consciousness') (526). The figures I have selected are not party-political tacticians plotting the expansion of their own power but writers, philosophical and literary, grappling with questions about how to make aspirations for personal and social improvement viable in a world where a Hitler or a Radek is from time to time a reality. They are, all of them, stylists, and none of them would be adequately accounted for by a critical approach that detached the content of their thinking about morality from the manner, style, tone, or affective charge of their cynicism. Even a cynicism that is 'strategic' in the sense that it serves an end will be subject to pressures of need, desire, fear, or ambivalence that may profoundly influence its operation.

Perhaps the most salient point of distinction between Sloterdijk and Foucault arises as they look to harness the radical potential of ancient Cynicism in the political sphere. Some much-quoted darkly poetic meditations on modernity's subjective incorporation of the nuclear 'bomb' notwithstanding (the bomb is the 'unfolding' of Western reason, 'a material representation of our essence'; it is 'not one bit more evil than reality and not one bit more destructive than we are' [Sloterdijk, 131]), *The Critique of Cynical Reason* looks less problematically keen than Foucault is, at key points, to ally itself with violence. Sloterdijk looks to dissolve the violence of reason and the limits of subjectivism in satiric laughter—freed from the chains of reason, the Kynical body, as he describes it,[62] experiences the freedom that comes with 'the liquefaction of the ego'. Foucault, by contrast, allows

---

[61] My use of the term does not presuppose allegiance to Michel de Certeau's distinction between the tactical and the strategic (sometimes invoked in writing about cynicism). The emphasis on the non-argumentative nature of cynicism, even or especially when it operates within wider frames of argument, allows for both terms to come in to play, depending on the circumstances. See Michel de Certeau, *The Practice of Everyday Life*, trans. Steven Rendall (Berkeley, CA: University of California Press, 1984), xix.

[62] The *Critique* has been criticized, understandably, for the unreconstructed crudity of the bodily provocations it entertains: farting, shitting, masturbating, pissing. 'Sloterdijk takes the modality of shock...with a naïve trust that only a child of the 1960s...could muster', Babette Babich comments sardonically. She does, however, give serious consideration to his proposal that 'artful...stupidification [*Verdummung*] is a kynik tactic', manifesting 'in a whole range of modern naturalisms: racism, sexism, fascism, vulgar biologism and egoism' (59). See 'Sloterdijk's Cynicisms: Diogenes in the Marketplace', in Stuart Elden (ed.), *Sloterdijk Now* (Oxford: Polity, 2011), 17–36 (22–3, 31).

himself some glamorizing reflections on nineteenth-century French terrorist revolutionaries as the heirs of Cynicism that 'no amount of theorizing will explain away' (Shea, 183). Militancy, Foucault observes, can be a 'style of existence' whereby 'one's life bears witness, breaks, and has to break with the conventions, habits, and values of society'; this aspect of bearing witness by one's own life was, and can still be, found 'especially in those movements which go from nihilism to anarchism or terrorism'.[63]

Both Foucault and Sloterdijk contrast their endorsement of a Cynic ethos of truth-telling with the limitations of Enlightenment and post-Enlightenment reasoning. Though Sloterdijk studiously avoids mention of 'scepticism', taking broad aim at the 'weapons of critique' that formed the 'arsenal' of Enlightenment, Foucault is, at least briefly, and late in the lecture series, interested in a historical proximity between 'Cynicism and Skepticism'. Cynicism, he observes in the manuscript version of the lecture for 29 February 1984, 'may be grouped with Skepticism', not just on the minimal basis of possessing a Greek pedigree, but on the grounds that 'the combination of Cynicism and Skepticism in the nineteenth century was a source of "nihilism"' [189n]). In pursuing a better description of what cynicism has offered and can still offer as part of a wider conception of public argument, my own approach may seem to bring the terms still closer. That is not the intention. In arguing that Cynicism has sometimes assisted the credibility and viability of ideals in the modern period by opening up areas of predictable and often valid doubt about the motives of the moralist and the tenability of high ideals, I keep in view a distinction between the confrontational affront of the Cynic and the frame in which that affront occurs. Though the deployment of cynicism may serve a purpose—recalibrating the level and credibility of moral claims—its debasements entail risk: not just the risk of alienating the reader or auditor who takes it seriously but (as Nietzsche saw) the risk of falling flat. It goes with the terrain of so established a type that it easily becomes tiresome, or must strain to recapture its one-time capacity to shock.

Given the difference between my approach and those of both Foucault and Sloterdijk, further clarification of the relation between cynicism and scepticism is germane. The aggression of modern cynical speech—its default explanatory recourse to low motives; its quick intolerance of convention in pursuit of truth and simplicity; its antipathy to the operation of power; its witty, quasi-intuitive sense of the drama of riposte; even its reductiveness—may superficially resemble

---

[63] See Foucault, Lecture of 29 February 1984: Second hour, *Courage of Truth*, 177–90 (183–6, quotations from 184, 185). And for commentary on Foucault's construction of Cynicism as a way of interrogating 'the status of his own speech, his own role as public intellectual, the stakes of his function . . . a little more than a professor and a little less than a militant, a little more than a scholar (*érudit*) and a little less than an ideologue', see Frédéric Gros, 'La *parrhesia* chez Foucault (1982–1984)', in Frédéric Gros (ed.), *Foucault: Le courage de la verité* (Paris: Presses Universitaires de France, 2002), 155–66 (155, my trans.).

the demeanour of the sceptic who requires that we scrutinize the basis of our claims to knowledge. Certainly, popular characterizations of the cynic and the sceptic have in common their willingness to cultivate the 'black look' of 'suspiciousness' (Bernard Williams).[64] For initial purposes, a standard, but not very satisfactory, description would be that scepticism belongs to epistemology, Cynicism to ethics. The former names a critical disposition towards knowledge or truth claims, the latter concerns itself with how one should live. Foucault indeed draws a version of this distinction when reflecting on the ancient relationship of Skepticism to Cynicism—before overriding it with his eye on present-day practices: 'Skepticism is an attitude of examination deployed systematically in the domain of knowledge, most of the time leaving the practical implications aside; whereas Cynicism is focused above all on the practical attitude and is structured around a lack of curiosity or a theoretical indifference and the acceptance of a few basic principles' (189).[65]

As he saw, this cannot be the last word on the subject.[66] To cultivate a sceptical disposition towards truth is to inhabit a disposition towards knowledge of the external world and our experience of it, including (it may be) our experience of other people: an 'examining' disposition, as Foucault puts it. By contrast with cynicism, scepticism is comparatively incremental and open to reformulation. The challenge it offers to 'true' conclusion leaves open a wide range of things that can be wrong with an argument: working on the inferences, it hopes to lodge doubt within a premise, but this in turn leaves open the work of adjusting premises, correcting for ambiguity or unwarranted assumption or exposed misstep. In other words, scepticism is highly rationalistic after its own fashion, a point both Kant and Nietzsche make over and over again: it is a form of dogmatism. Sooner or later, ethical considerations follow from the adoption of this testing perspective.

From the Cynic's side of the distinction, an ethical concern with living 'in accordance with nature' raises questions that have an epistemological cast to them, even if the Cynic himself or herself is decisive rather than questioning, and even if the questions provoked are not all of a form epistemologists would accept or want to clump together—questions about how (and in what sense) we know the truth of embodied experience; how we are to know what is and is not 'natural'; how we are to know the motives of others. Teasing out the implications

---

[64] Bernard Williams, 'The Need to Be Sceptical', in Bernard Williams, *Essays and Reviews, 1959–2002* (Princeton, NJ: Princeton University Press, 2014), 312–18 (318).

[65] Christian Thorne sharpens the contrast and adds a more contentious edge, when he makes Cynicism 'indicative of everything that is most distinctive about Hellenistic philosophy, understood as contemplative life-philosophy'—then opposes scepticism to philosophy on that basis: 'Philosophy is a cult, skepticism a deprogramming.' Christian Thorne, *The Dialectic of Counter-Enlightenment* (Cambridge, MA: Harvard University Press, 2009), 47, 49.

[66] Ian Cutler distinguishes between the two on the basis of their attitudes to truth, but in terms that would not satisfy most philosophers. Ian Cutler, *Cynicism from Diogenes to Dilbert* (Jefferson, NC: McFarland & Co., 2005), 17–18.

of his or her challenge to conventional thinking is not the way of the Cynic: s/he goes for the one-shot put-down, not argumentative engagement. In lieu of dogma, we get quick debunking.

Literary-critical readers will recognize the reflections on scepticism just made as being in line with the thinking of one of the most influential critics to have brought literary criticism and philosophy into conversation in recent decades: Stanley Cavell. Nothing said about scepticism here would falsify, or diminish the importance of, Stanley Cavell's distinction between scepticism as it assails the grounds of our knowledge about the external world and 'scepticism about other minds'. *The Claim of Reason* (1979) famously arrives at 'an intuition' (not a 'claim'; rather recognition of a nagging sense of how our reasons work upon us) that there may be an asymmetry in meaning and value between these two forms of scepticism: 'in the sense in which we can arrive at skepticism with respect to the external world, an initial sanity requires recognizing that I cannot live my skepticism, whereas with respect to others a final sanity requires recognizing that I can. I do'.[67] 'Cynicism' arises only once in the course of Cavell's deliberations. He is reflecting on how much of our reasoning about ethical behaviour takes the form of 'foregone' conclusions. When the naïve questioner in the room (the 'child', big or small) asks a question that rattles conventional ethical arrangements, s/he obliges us to confront the poverty of our reasoning about some very important matters: '"Why do we eat animals?" or "Why are some people poor and others rich?" or "What is God ... How did God get here?", I may find my answers thin, I may feel run out of reasons without being willing to say "This is what I do" (... what I sense, what I know) ... '

> Then I may feel that my foregone conclusions were never conclusions *I* had arrived at, but were merely imbibed by me, merely conventional. I may blunt that realization through hypocrisy or cynicism or bullying. But I may take the occasion to throw myself back upon my culture, and ask why we do what we do, judge as we judge, ...   (125)

The only point on which I need differ from Cavell here is that I accent the capacity of cynicism to assist the throwing of oneself back upon one's culture: its bluntness (not denied) may be, in some cases, a habitual reaction to the foregone conclusions of others (a characteristic of some of us more than others), but I allow also for cases where it rises to the level of *techne* and becomes a form of art. To regard it in that light at least blunts the charge of default bluntness. Taking cynicism as a perspective on other minds, it is surely a significant count against it that it does not trouble itself with such questions as whether it 'make[s] sense to say that there *is* a

---

[67] Stanley Cavell, *The Claim of Reason: Wittgenstein, Skepticism, Morality, and Tragedy*, new edn (New York: Oxford University Press, [1979] 1999), 451.

better position' for knowing other minds than the one I possess (353). Cynicism works on the assumption that 'I, the Cynic' *do* possess secure and pre-emptive knowledge of other minds, because I possess knowledge of *all* human nature, and I know self-interest to be a primary human motivation. It stands and falls on that assumption, not because the assumption is wrong but because it is incomplete, and in some cases culpably so.

Though the attention of this book is on modern philosophical and literary articulations of cynicism, my interest in the everyday, casualized *dispositional* cynicism that is, for most people, the primary connotation of the word requires more to be said about how philosophy relates to psychology. The explanatory priority commonly given to philosophy in cultural-critical discussion of cynicism is to some degree a reflection of a widespread disciplinary bias, only partly justified by the genealogical credentials of philosophical Cynicism. Why attention to modern cynicism's philosophical aspect should so often come at the *expense* of attention to psychology is therefore a question worth pausing over. Louisa Shea observes that '[t]he psychological interpretation of Cynicism is often brandished by those who wish to discredit Cynicism as a legitimate philosophical and social movement' (100). An odd circularity beckons here: designation of a piece of writing as 'cynical' is itself a potentially cynical reading of the motives for self-expression. Shea's passing comment helpfully identifies an element of distrust on the part of philosophical and literary criticism that repeatedly limits the permitted scope of psychological explanation for cynicism. She also encourages a rethink. As she points out, 'It is often the discomfort born from social marginalization or from the inability to understand the rules of right behavior that enables a person to perceive as contingent norms and laws [w]hat others accept as natural' (100). The modern cynic (whatever their field of work) may, on this reading, have had situational cause to think harder than those better situated in life about the norms of conduct that currently hold sway.

 This is helpful, but it does not eradicate the problem of what authority the cynic can point to for his or her own counter-normative stringencies. The focus on motive is critical here. Attribution of low motive is the characteristic venture of the cynic in response to other people's claims of attachment to higher ideals. You say you gave a sizeable donation to rebuilding Notre Dame because you care for its enduring religious, historical, and cultural significance in and beyond France; I, the cynic, say that you did so because it made you look good, distracted public attention from your unsavoury business practices, and helped your tax return. Debunking the preferred self-image is a confrontational gambit—one that, as we shall see, slides easily between the straight-speaking claim of the thoroughgoing rational sceptic and the more complex and difficult-to-assess motivations of the rhetorical provocateur.

In casual 'everyday' cynicism, the warrant for calling out the would-be idealist on his or her self-delusions is typically no more, and no less, than an assumption that human beings (individually and collectively) are naturally driven by self-interest, with all the negative associations of self-interest to the fore—egoism, a will to power, a desire to look better, stronger, or, in whatever relevant way, superior to how one really is. The ancient Cynics and their Stoic successors made the naturalist point but did not incline to judgementalism. A. A. Long, writing about Epictetus, captures an important element of neutrality in their view: 'everyone is naturally motivated by self-interest, which, when properly understood, is the precondition of a properly social identity'.[68] Epictetus himself is sinuously emphatic on the subject. In Robert Dobbin's pithy translation: 'It is a universal law—have no illusions—that every creature alive is attached to nothing so much as to its own self-interest' (2.22.15) (denominated in the Greek by the term *oikeiosis*: 'appropriation'; contextually, the balancing of self- and other-interests).[69] Acknowledgement of self-interest does *not* entail an assumption that competing interests may not displace the self as the centre of concern.[70] This, Long observes, is the 'starting point of early Stoic ethics': every normal person is deemed to be driven by basic 'instincts for self-preservation *and for sociability*' (182) [my italics].

Of course, a neutral 'just stating a fact' recognition of another person's self-interest may give offence in spite of the neutrality, especially if what is said contradicts a self-perception that is not just more flattering but genuinely held. How legitimate, after all, is the cynic's warrant for denying or downplaying a motivation to put 'other interest' or altruism above self-interest on certain occasions? This is, surely, a point of vulnerability in cynicism: it is as strong, but *only* as strong, as its assumption that the 'natural drive' to self-interest is at the fore in any given situation. Making that assumption protects the cynic from the errors of unworldliness and some of the sins of stupidity (naivety, in short); but it also makes the cynic's rationalization on some occasions too quick, too coarse, too complacent in its judgements, too slow to look at more generous alternatives.

In the absence of any historical account in English of cynicism's role in psychology comparable to the extensive accounts of Cynical philosophy,[71] I take

---

[68] A. A. Long, *Epictetus: A Stoic and Socratic Guide to Life* (Oxford: Clarendon Press, 2002), Oxford Scholarship Online version, at 180.

[69] Mark Holowchak, *The Stoics: A Guide for the Perplexed* (New York: Continuum, 2008), 77.

[70] Epictetus, *Discourses and Selected Writings*, ed. and trans. Robert Dobbin (London: Penguin, 2008), 137. And see 2.22.19: 'wherever "I" and "mine" are set, to that side the living creature must necessarily be inclined'. Epictetus, *The Discourses of Epictetus*, ed. Christopher Gill, trans. Robin Hard (London: Dent, 1995), 130.

[71] But see an important chapter in Niehues-Pröbsting's *Der Kynismus des Diogenes*, 298–373. Niehues-Pröbsting outlines changes in the meaning of the term *cynicism* over the past two centuries, starting from Friedrich Schlegel's intellectualized account of the superiority of moral cynicism to mere wit. A discussion of Nietzsche ('a neo-Cynic'?) concludes with the posthumously published fragments charging contemporary psychologists with fixation on the symptoms of Decadence and proffering the

some space here to elaborate on three psychological explanations of cynicism that are of particular interest to me and allow me to articulate the historically situated understandings of the mind with most relevance to this project as well as my own working assumptions. The first (readily recognizable) explanation employs cynicism as a diagnostic category within clinical psychology and psychoanalysis, where it contributes to description of an observable form, or a set of forms, of 'maladjustment' typically characterized as narcissistic self-defence. This modern application retains little connection to classical Cynicism. The second (much less discussed) line of response gives the original Cynics a historic, somewhat technical role to play in articulating and defending a notion of individual and embodied specificity as it comes into conflict with the typological work of psychological characterization. The third, almost entirely unremarked, introduces a critical (indeed, cynical) perspective on psychology as, itself, cynical in outlook—a discipline, or constellation of disciplines, founded on distrust of the motives human beings consciously avow.

Rarely identified as a condition in its own right, cynicism features within twentieth- and twenty-first-century clinical psychology as a contributing factor to the nosology of a variety of disorders. Indicatively, it makes its way into the American *Diagnostic and Statistical Manual of Mental Disorders*, 4th edition, as a symptomatic indicator for two types of adjustment disorder: Paranoid Personality Disorder (301.0) and Antisocial Personality Disorder (301.7).[72] In the Paranoid Personality type, 'a pattern of pervasive distrust and suspiciousness of others' develops, 'such that their motives are interpreted as malevolent' (p. 690); in the Antisocial Personality type, individuals tend to 'lack empathy and ... to be callous, cynical, and contemptuous of the feelings, rights, and sufferings of others' (p. 703).

Cynics (counted among the 'new barbarians' [*neue Barbaren*]) as an antidote (337). The third section (referenced as relevant below) concentrates on cynical jokes and humour in aesthetic and psychoanalytic theories. Niehues-Pröbsting then considers non-comic cynicisms, looking to Wilde as a prime example of a cynicism that aims to describe reality and not its distortion (the dandy's cynicism is a 'negative form of stoicism' [360]). Georg Simmel is credited with clarifying the 'somewhat perverse relationship' between modern 'negative' cynicism and the positive ethics of ancient Cynicism: ancient Cynicism assisted personal freedom whereas the modern cynic is trapped by a levelling [*Nivellierung*] of moral values, unable to distinguish between high and low. In modernity, money alone assigns value or meaning, the stock markets becoming 'hotbeds of modern cynicism' (363). The references are to Simmel's essay 'Bergson und der deutsche "Zynismus"' ['Bergson and German Cynicism'] (1914) and *Philosophie des Geldes* [*The Philosophy of Money*] (1900). The last section looks at then-recent theories of cynicism, including Fetscher's 'Thoughts on cynicism as an illness of our times' (1975), which takes illness to be a metaphor for contemporary forms of cynicism. See also Sloterdijk's analysis of the psychopolitical and sexual cynicisms of Weimar and the rise of Nazism: *Critique of Cynical Reason*, 521–8.

[72] American Psychiatric Association, *Diagnostic and Statistical Manual of Mental Disorders: DSM-IV-TR*, 4th edn, text revision (Washington, DC: American Psychiatric Association, 2000).

Both disorders present an inflated sense of self-worth coupled with hypervigilance towards perceived threats from others.[73]

The *DSM* is not an uncontroversial route into current clinical thinking. (It is often accused, especially in its most recent, 5th, edition, of pathologizing experiences of unhappiness and discontent that ought to be considered within the 'normal' range.) With respect to the place it affords cynicism, however, one can set that debate to one side, and recognize the *DSM*'s repetition of a pattern, common to the full range of approaches within clinical psychology, whereby cynicism does not in itself register as abnormal, but triggers the diagnostician's interest as part of a wider symptomatology of impaired or distressing behaviour, 'deviat[ing] markedly' from cultural norms. Behavioural medicine generally tends to consider cynicism one 'facet of hostility' among others, often grouped with anger, aggression, and depression.[74] (Only when attention shifts from diagnosis of individuals to ethical reflection on the professionals treating them does 'cynicism' appear as a problem in its own right—and part of a much wider clinical and sociological literature on cynicism in the workplace.)[75] Psychometric testing, primarily descriptive rather than diagnostic in its aims (and with all its now well-understood errors)[76] similarly treats cynicism as a commonplace behavioural tendency, problematic only as a matter of degree. Myers-Briggs tactfully list it under 'Potential Areas for Growth': both the ISTP and INTP types (Introverted Thinking with Extraverted Sensing, and Introverted Thinking with Extroverted

[73] A prospective study of 3,399 London civil servants, reporting in 2010, found a correlation between 'the personality trait of cynical hostility', which it took to be 'characterized by cynicism, distrust, resentment, and suspicion' and predilection towards depression. See Joan Arehart-Treichel, 'Cynical Hostility Personality Trait Strongly Predicts Depressed Mood', *Psychiatric News* 7 May 2010, <https://psychnews.psychiatryonline.org/doi/10.1176/pn.45.9.psychnews_45_9_028>. Accessed 3 June 2019; the research paper abstract is at <https://www.cambridge.org/core/journals/psychological-medicine/article/hostility-and-depressive-mood-results-from-the-whitehall-ii-prospective-cohort-study/76803E41FB196CED104304391C16FEEE>. Accessed 3 June 201]. Ray Corsini, *The Dictionary of Psychology* (London: Routledge, 2016) observes that cynicism may be one manifestation of 'character armour' as described in Wilhelm Reich's character-analytic approach to psychology: 'the assumption of an impenetrable front by a person to protect the self against intrusions by others'; like other hypothetical 'character patterns' (over-aggressiveness or ingratiation, for example), it may 'serve as [a] defenc[e] against anxiety, standing in the way of attempts to penetrate to the deeper, unconscious levels of the personality' (155).

[74] See, for example, Christian Hakulinen, Markus Jokela, Liisa Keltikangas-Järvinen, Päivi Merjonen, Olli T. Raitakari, and Mirka Hintsanen, 'Longitudinal Measurement Invariance, Stability and Change of Anger and Cynicism', *Journal of Behavioral Medicine* 37/3 (June 2014), 434–44; A. A. Nierenberg, S. N. Ghaemi, K. Clancy-Colecchi, J. F. Rosenbaum, and M. Fava, 'Cynicism, Hostility, and Suicidal Ideation in Depressed Outpatients', *The Journal of Nervous and Mental Disease* 184/10 (1996), 607–10.

[75] See, for example, Diane M. Plantz on the cynicism of health care professionals: 'Cynicism, with Consequences', *The Hastings Center Report* 41/2 (2011), 12–13; and, for a view of the growing cynicism said to be characteristic of the American workplace, Kanter and Mirvis, *The Cynical Americans*, including an elaborate detailing of the variety of cynical types ('obstinate', 'hard-bitten', 'squeezed', etc., 27ff.), and a proposal for 'managing cynicism' by ensuring 'honest dialogue' between workers and bosses (282 ff.).

[76] See Merve Emre, *What's Your Type?: The Strange History of Myers-Briggs and the Birth of Personality Testing* (London: William Collins, 2018).

Intuition) have a tendency, they observe, to become 'cynical and negative critics' if frustrated in their attempts to 'find a place where they can use their gifts and be appreciated for their contributions'.[77]

By contrast with clinical psychology and behavioural medicine, psychoanalysis has, from Freud onwards, retained a closer connection with ancient Cynicism's sceptical comportment towards *morality*. Freud himself seems to have had limited interest in cynical typing, with the exception of a short suggestive sketch on a 'special type' of male love, in which the 'cynical logic' of the boy is the psychological key to his adult desire for women who behave in the manner of prostitutes. 'The boy, having discovered his mother's sexual activity, tells himself that she is doing the same thing as a whore': he cynically 'takes the part for the whole', evidence of her desire being 'enough for her to be stamped as a prostitute'. The explanation rests on the boy's movement from a correct observation to a false generalization: having discovered the fact of the mother's sexual activity, he draws the unwarranted conclusion that all women who make love are prostitutes.[78] The most extensive (and they are not very extensive) of Freud's reflections on cynicism as a form of unconscious rationale arise in *Jokes and Their Relation to the Unconscious* (1905),[79] where he explores the cynical cast of certain kinds of jest. Differentiating between the '*innocuous* joke' and the '*tendentious* joke—the one with a 'tendency or intention'—Freud notes that this second kind of joke is the only one that 'runs the risk of coming up against persons who do not want to listen to it' (87). Tendentious jokes are themselves of two kinds: the *hostile* and the *obscene*, with 'cynical jokes' making up an important variety of the former type, whereby the joke-teller gives pleasurable vent to feelings of '[v]iolent hostility, forbidden by law', but permissible as 'verbal invective' (100). Intrigued as he is by anti-Semitic and misogynistic jokes, Freud latches on to their anti-institutional

---

[77] Isabel Briggs Myers, *Introduction to Type: A Guide to Understanding Your Results on the Myers-Briggs Type Indicator*, rev. Linda K. Kirby and Katharine D. Myers, 6th edn (Oxford: Oxford Psychologists Press Ltd, 2000), 22, 23. See also the Minnesota Multiphasic Personality Inventory (MMPI), which identifies a cynicism metric (measurement 8 (A-cyn) on the MMP1-S adolescent testing scale; RC3 (cyn) on the Restructured Clinical Scale and more refined Content Scale).

[78] See Sigmund Freud, 'A Special Type of Choice of Object Made by Men', in *Five Lectures on Psychoanalysis, Leonardo da Vinci, and Other Works* (1910), in *The Standard Edition of the Complete Works of Sigmund Freud*, gen. ed. and trans. James Strachey in collaboration with Anna Freud, assisted by Alix Strachey, Alan Tyson and Angela Richards, 24 vols. (London: Hogarth Press and the Institute of Psycho-Analysis, 1953–79), XI, 163–76 (171). For discussion see Alberto Eiguer, 'Cynicism: Its Function in the Perversions', trans. Philip Slotkin, *International Journal of Psychoanalysis* 80/4 (1999), 671–84 (671–2).

[79] Sigmund Freud, *Jokes and Their Relation to the Unconscious*, trans. Joyce Crick, Introduction by John Carey (London: Penguin Books, [1905] 2002). For commentary, see esp. Niehues-Pröbsting, *Der Kynismus des Diogenes*, 351–3. Niehues-Pröbsting also devotes some space (353–7) to developments of Freud's ideas by his pupil Theodor Reik, in *Psychoanalytical Notes on the Cynical Joke* (1913) and in the work of the Austrian-born American psychoanalyst Edmund Bergler, whose study 'On the Psychology of the Cynic' (published in German in *Psychoanalytische Bewertung* 5/1 and 2 [1933]) describes 64 sub-varieties of cynicism. A short English summary, 'On the Psychology of the Cynic', can be found in Bergler, *Selected Papers, 1933–1961* (New York: Grune & Stratton, 1969), 846–9.

thrust: the targeting of marriage as a constraint on individual sexual liberty, of Jewishness as it constrains the person to behave in accordance with cultural custom. The joke 'represents a rebellion against...authority' (102), disclosing the rebellious operation of the unconscious: it allows us to *get around restrictions and open up sources of pleasure that have become inaccessible* (100). By means of its linguistic aggression, we 'mak[e] our enemy small' (100).

One reason for pausing over Freud's account of cynical joking is that, unusually among psychologists, he emphasizes the capacity of cynicism to give pleasure to its auditors: the pleasure of inner superiority, of triumphalism. Even though, in theory, Freud thinks that innocuous jokes have more to tell us than tendentious jokes about the workings of the unconscious (we are less likely to be misled by an apparent rationality to the hostile or lustful content [91]), he has to concede that tendentious joking yields a more immediate and full-throated response from the listener: 'An un-tendentious joke scarcely ever achieves those sudden outbursts of laughter that make tendentious jokes so irresistible' (93–4). Consideration of cynical jokes also leads him to clarify the distinction between the object and the recipient of the joke. Three persons have a role to play in the cynical joke: the one telling the joke; the one taken as the object of the hostile or sexual aggression; and the one who takes pleasure in the joke (or, as he puts it, the one 'in whom the joke's intention of producing pleasure is fulfilled' [97]). This crucial distinction between the object of the joke's intention and its auditor is, one assumes (Freud does not exactly say so), a potential factor in the joke's concealment of its 'critical' work, 'well suited' as it is 'to attacking the great, the dignified and the mighty—powers protected from direct disparagement by internal inhibitions or external circumstances' (102). By implication, the recipient of the joke is not the person in power—but perhaps could (and sometimes should) be.

One can speculate that it is because Freud wants to accent the deep-cover strategic nature of cynical wit, and the pleasure it yields, that he has comparatively little to say about the dark colouring of these jokes—their capacity to register deep pessimism, plus the complacency and reassurance of a certain kind of despair. When the joke enters that territory, it becomes, for Freud, 'technically borderline', reliant on 'argot and skill in storytelling' lest it fail to raise a laugh (111). Later analysts have shown far greater interest in the darkness (arguably to the detriment of the analysis). In the main, I bypass the very technical literature, but one aspect of it is worth lingering over, and not evident from Freud's thinking about cynical jokes: the confrontational drama of the analyst's encounter with a cynic analys-and. The cynic is to be distinguished from the ironist, argues Alberto Eiguer,[80] by the causticity with which he denounces the hollowness of values, and by the degree to which he arrogates power to himself over his listener (in Eiguer's reading of the

[80] Eiguer, 'Cynicism', 671–2.

underpinning Freudian sexual theory, the cynic is assumed to be male). Where the ironist leaves to his interlocutor the work of intelligently decoding his hidden meaning, the cynic 'sets himself up as the founder of a different law, which is terrible and terrifying for his fellow human being, who is his victim and some-times his accomplice' (675). In this narrowly focused account of the cynic as pervert, illustrated by a case study of one of Eiguer's patients (a persistent *frotteur*), the pleasure that Freud associated with cynic logic has almost entirely disappeared. Whatever gratification the cynic promises to himself is fraudulent. Armed with a defensive theory that sensual pleasure is the aim of everyone, he goes about repeatedly 'proving' and proselytizing for that theory by his actions (touching up unknown women, in the case of the *frotteur*) and his speech (sneering caustically at all and sundry). He turns 'pleasure' into 'ideology', a mere mask for the assertion of his own power. He is, unsurprisingly, a challenge to the analyst (whose own bid for power then comes under aggravated self-scrutiny). During a 'particularly trying period' of analysis, the *frotteur* lashes out: 'Your house is a dark and dismal place, a constricted, suffocating and dead space, completely lifeless'; and the analyst duly worries over the force of the criticism: 'My waiting room does indeed give a dark and dismal impression. It is quite a while since I gave it a lick of paint. The plants have taken over ...' (680).[81] Dedicated to destabilizing the transference 'by attacks on thought', 'changing the analytic goals', turning pleasure to 'ideological struggle', the patient becomes (not without some cause?) an antagonist. The analyst, fretting over the force of the patient's criticism, in turn pays testimony to the contagion of cynicism—its invitation to be complicit rather than threaten the cynic's hard-won position.[82] The sessions, Eiguer confesses wryly, 'were certainly no picnic for me' (682).

The Kleinian tradition offers an ethically richer account of cynicism than the Freudian, in that it attends more closely to the social and political situations that may be conducive to cynicism in individual cases. In a brief but suggestive essay first published in 1944, Roger Money-Kyrle (one of the most influential of the mid-twentieth-century British Kleinians) identified cynicism as a condition of extreme disaffection, widespread (he observed) in inter-war society. Like Freud, but more explicitly, Money-Kyrle saw a clear component of rationality at cyni-cism's base, overlaid by a secondary emotional reaction.

> [Moral negativism is] the attitude of the disillusioned cynic, the man who feels that no end is worth striving for, fighting for, or still less dying for. It was rather common in [Britain] in the period between the two wars, and found its

---

[81] This scenario seems to appeal to Eiguer's sense of humour. See 'Docteur Alberto Eiguer', <http://alberto-eiguer-psy.fr>.

[82] Adam Phillips, who supplied the last nuance here, suggests also a connection with Winnicott's description of madness as the need to be believed: 'the cynic always needs to be believed, to find accomplices' (pers. comm.).

philosophical expression in ethical relativity—a system which quite rightly saw through the logical flaws in metaphysical ethics, and in view of the diversity of moral codes, concluded quite wrongly that no code was worth defending.[83]

By way of explanation for so radical a loss of attachment to moral ideals, Money-Kyrle drew on the Kleinian concept of unconscious fantasies: mental representations of libidinal and aggressive impulses and the defensive mechanisms an individual develops against them. When the 'bad or hostile figures' in the fantasy are perceived as 'so strong' that defence of the good ones is impossible, he observed, the despair that should follow is 'sometimes evaded by denying that the original good objects are good or worth defending'. In short: Negativism is 'a defence against depression' (183).

Money-Kyrle's clarifying contribution is to reconnect psychoanalysis with personal and social ethics by distinguishing between the cynic's initial scepticism towards metaphysics and the next step of a pervasive scepticism towards other people and their commitments. The cynic, in his guise as ethical relativist, correctly perceives the absence of a higher warrant for morality, incorrectly decides that this makes morality unworkable for ordinary purposes. The assumption (I take it) can hardly be that every cynic reaches his predicament by way of philosophical reflection on the metaphysics of morals; rather, ethical relativity, 'common...between the two wars', gives the condition of the cynic its clearest, most 'systematic' modern intellectual articulation.

It is germane to the description of cynicism here that it arises in the course of Money-Kyrle's attempt to formulate a secular account of psychological normality that might hold its own against a metaphysical or theologically based ethics (179), and on the basis of which it would be possible to say what ends a normal individual will feel they 'ought to seek'. Normality is very broadly defined by Money-Kyrle as 'an optimum freedom from neurosis', the character of which will be different for every individual, but with certain positive and negative characteristics forming a common pattern for all normal people, and 'something like a common pattern of ethical values' (179). Temperament is an acknowledged factor here, but within a wider picture that allows for significant circumstantial pressures on one's ethical formation. Of particular concern to him were the negative characteristics that come to the fore in wartime, and that would either be absent from the 'normal' pattern or only present in 'small degree' (179): 'Paranoia', 'Denial and Appeasement', 'Pacificism', 'Negativism'.

Initially discussed as just one element in this line-up of damaging characteristics encouraged by war, cynicism gains a more prominent place at the end of the

[83] Roger Money-Kyrle, 'Towards a Common Aim: A Psychoanalytic Contribution to Ethics' (1944), in *The Collected Papers of Roger Money-Kyrle*, ed. Donald Meltzer, assisted by Edna O'Shaughnessy (London: Karnac, 2015), 176–97 (182).

essay when Money-Kyrle considers the problem of how *much* divergence from 'primary morality' would occur in an optimally healthy society. The special threat cynicism poses to society resides, he argues, in its reduction of human activity to the individualistic pursuit of one's own interests and the exclusion of those of others. Cynical types, having 'no ideals themselves', are 'unable to believe that ideals can be more than a cover for self-interest in other people' (193). They are, in that sense, a manifestation of a wider problem with the modern interpretation of individualism. 'Part of the discredit into which individualism has fallen', Money-Kyrle continues, 'is the fault of its own theoretical apologists—the economists of the classical school—who imputed this motive only to their economic man' (193). In this socially corrosive scenario, the cynic imputes his or her own scepticism to others, crediting them (as it were) with the same intellectual apprehension that ideals have no metaphysical warrant. Once again, cynicism is exacting at the first stage of intellectual response, but generalizes incorrectly on that basis about the viability of everyday moral concern for the greater good. It is far from alone in doing so. The cynic's error repeats the error everywhere in evidence in the promotion of Adam Smith's 'self-interest' theory of economic motivation, without Smith's counterbalancing concern with the moral sentiments. Cynicism, on this reading, is individualism gone awry in ways that are symptomatic of a much larger social problem: the cynic individual is ethically impoverished for Money-Kyrle *just as* classical economic self-interest theory is seen to be ethically impoverished in its account of our motives to industry.[84]

Arguably Money-Kyrle moves too quickly here to exclude the cynic's possession of ideals. The cynic, Adam Phillips suggests, 'is his own ideal': knowing the truth about life and human nature, being unillusioned, he is in a position to claim that he is the most principled person of all. 'From a psychoanalytic point of view one could say that, developmentally, the cynic is living in the aftermath of a catastrophic disillusionment: the good things that had sustained him had let him down, betrayed him, tantalised him.' His cynicism is at once a refuge (from hope, and the dependence it brings on the object of hope) and a temptation (to omniscience, arrogance, megalomania, being 'the bearer of the real, terrible truth about life'). Cynicism, on this reading, is 'self-cure', a 'hospital' for those who, radically disappointed, fear being seduced back into life.[85] *Philosophically* this matters because it tells us that the idea of self-sufficiency so crucial to Cynical and cynic self-fashioning is less a goal than a fantasy: despite appearances, the cynic is always on the make for recognition by others.[86] The relation with narcissism looms larger, on Phillips's reading, than in Money-Kyrle's, but both

---

[84] A footnote from Money-Kyrle ventures that 'In reality, the average successful entrepreneur' spends much more time building the business than 'spending the profits' (193n).

[85] Phillips, pers. comm.

[86] Malcolm Bull makes a similar point about Nietzsche and his readers: to resist Nietzsche is not to escape him: only by failing to live up to his ideals can we move beyond him. See Malcolm Bull, *Anti-*

observe a crucial difference from narcissism in that the cynic has, at least in the past, recognized an object of desire outside the self: there is a capacity for holding ideals there that might potentially be retrieved.

In a Postscript to 'Towards a Common Aim', apparently from the 1970s, Money-Kyrle clarifies the principal suggestions he had made in 1944 for post-war ethical repair of a damaged society. In the course of a compressed six paragraphs he wrestles with the standard Freudian and Kleinian concentration on the primary emotion of guilt, understood as an outcome of tension between the ego and the super-ego when the latter imposes the primary taboos against incest and parricide. The *fears* aroused in response to the good and bad objects of fantasy are, for Money-Kyrle, as important as the guilt, because it is in the operation of fear (the persecution of the bad object) that we see the working of a kind of moral conscience. The cynic-depressive suffers to the extent that he or she confuses the good and the bad, but his or her abnormal level of vigilance against 'the enemy' offers a clue to a form of correct action 'in accordance with conscience' that, rightly interpreted, would enable psychoanalysis to replace ethical relativism with a 'universa[l] system of Ethics' (197). Money-Kyrle does not explicitly state that a measure of cynicism is no bad thing in a society where hostility is rife—a form of critical vigilance that might be harnessed to better ends—but I take that to be the implication.

A second point of interest in the history of psychological writing about cynicism raises a more fundamental question than those that belong to classification of individual cases: what validity can be claimed for psychological typing per se? Near the start of his classic exploration of the subject, *Psychological Types* (1921), Carl Jung turns his attention to the ancient Cynics. His initial consideration of the 'problem of types in the history of classical and medieval thought'[87] had addressed the earliest forms of personality 'typing' evidenced by Gnostic and early Christian considerations of the thinking/feeling distinction. He now introduces the 'incalculable consequences' of the conflict between nominalism and realism, as it comes under the spotlight of the Cynic challenge to Platonism. Nominalism, Jung glosses as, 'that school which asserted that the so-called universals ... generic or universal concepts such as beauty, goodness, animal, man, etc., are nothing but *nomina*, names, or words'; this by contrast with realism, which 'affirms the existence of universals ... hold[ing] that general concepts exist in themselves after the manner of Platonic universals' (23). Broadly speaking: 'nominalism is a sceptical tendency that denies the separate existence characteristic of abstractions.... Strict realism,

---

Nietzsche (London: Verso, 2011), Chapter 2. Fred Rush points out to me that Kierkegaard applies the same logic to Schlegel-style irony.

[87] C. G. Jung, *Psychological Types*, rev. R. F. C. Hull, trans. H. G. Baynes, with a new foreword by John Beebe (London: Routledge, 2017), 7.

on the contrary, transfers the accent on reality to the abstract, the idea, the universal, which it posits before the thing' (23). The relevance of Cynicism here is that it gave Jung the sharpest early articulation of the nominalist objection to abstractive realism in Western philosophy.[88] Antisthenes, Jung recalls, 'wrote a pamphlet against Plato, in which he scurrilously changed Plato's name to Σαθων/ sathōn', punning on boy/man and penis or cock, thus covertly implying 'what he is defending against Plato'—the 'delights of the senses', as against the thin abstraction of ideas (24).[89] The crude joke pits the individual material reality of the thing (Plato's cock) against Platonism's ideal and generic concepts.

This subject prompts Jung to an extended exploration of what 'kind of reality' is invoked when we produce generic concepts that purport to 'designat[e] the similarities or conformities of things' (29). Concepts of this kind are not 'merely' names, he argues (against the Cynic nominalists): they contain a great deal of reality, in his view—which is not to say that they are not vulnerable to the Cynic critique. That critique remains a problem for philosophy and for psychology that will not go away: we are left, he concludes, in a perpetual stand-off between the 'abstract standpoint' and the 'personal thinking and feeling' of the sentient and materially situated individual (32).

Can we take a step backwards, and speculate that the stand-off is itself a result of conflicting personality types?, Jung asks: Platonic introverts vs. Megarian Cynic extroverts? Well, no: this would be a false reduction of 'traditional universal values to personal undercurrents' (34). What kind of evidence, after all, would be sufficient to establish that Plato was of the introverted type, and Antisthenes an extrovert? The question is rather one of 'displacement of the accent of value'—of which mental processes 'for various reasons' come to the fore and which are subordinated. The extrovert may tend to place the accent of value on the external object, and not his relation to it, whereas the introvert does the opposite, but we all employ both types of thinking, on an everyday basis. Whether the idealist or the Cynic nominalist comes to the fore at any given moment is a matter of which way of thinking happens to be 'pushed into the foreground' (33). (One can see clearly here the line of thinking that flowed from Jung through into Myers-Briggs and other forms of personality type testing influential today.)

A final point of interest in the modern psychological response to cynicism requires another step back in order to entertain a quasi-structural view of the discipline's prevailing 'logic'. Freud might take some responsibility for a line of

---

[88] Jung correctly identifies Cynicism's significant place in the intellectual history of nominalist opposition to realism, with its insistence upon the concretion and particularity of things and refusal of the reality of abstractions and universals. For Antisthenes and his followers, Luis E. Navia summarizes, a 'thing can only be itself and nothing else, and as such cannot be subsumed under a general category or class'. See *Classical Cynicism*, 66.

[89] Jeffrey Henderson, *The Maculate Muse: Obscene Language in Attic Comedy*, 2nd edn (Oxford: Oxford University Press, 1991), 10, n. 13.

thought in which that logic looks tantalizingly close to cynicism, though it has not, to my knowledge, been laid at his door. In the *Introductory Lectures on Psycho-Analysis* (1915–16), Freud acknowledges a similarity between the psychologist, who endeavours to unmask certain 'banal' but frequently ignored or denied truths about the human condition and human relationships, and the role of the latter-day cynic philosopher. 'It is better', he quips (at least I take it there is humour here, though he makes a serious case) 'that the truth should be told by psychologists rather than that the task should be left to cynics.'[90] The psychologist, by implication, takes over the cynic's task of disclosing the impurity of human motives, and redirects cynicism to socially and personally productive ends. Freud summons (in jest?) a view of the psychologist as committed to something like a version of original sin, knowing in advance what human nature is and what its limitations are.

In *The Moral Animal* (1994), Robert Wright follows the same line of thought and presses harder, arguing provocatively that professional psychology is founded on a set of cynical conceptions about human beings and what motivates them. Concentrating on the imperfect alignment between Freudian and Darwinian approaches to explanation, Wright observes that they are nevertheless alike in their perspectives on the 'sly unconscious aims in our most innocent acts'.[91] Since their 'suspicion of a person's motives' is largely 'a suspicion of *unconscious* motives', the analytic and the evolutionary psychologist 'view the person—the conscious person at least—as a kind of unwitting accomplice' of those unaccessed motives: 'to the extent that pain is the price paid for the internal subterfuge, the person may [even] be worthy of compassion as well as suspicion. Everyone comes out looking like a victim' (314–15).

The cynically all-encompassing turn of the conclusion here mimics the disciplinary deformation towards cynicism that it identifies, and in ways that seem to reinforce rather than ironize it. Identifying an ongoing competition between Darwinian and Freudian psychology for the position of 'most influential behavioral paradigm' (314), Wright weighs in, in support of the Darwinians. The therapeutic model of mind offered by psychoanalysis implies (he thinks) a core 'honesty' struggling against self-deception. That assumption blinds the Freudian to something the (self-described) more radical Darwinian understands: that repression and the unconscious mind evolved 'long before civilization' in conditions that largely determined 'what kinds of self-deception are and aren't likely to be favored by evolution' (324). Darwinism, more accurate in its account of human development, will eclipse Freudianism before long, Wright predicts, unless

[90] Sigmund Freud, *Introductory Lectures on Psycho-Analysis (Parts I and II)*, in *The Standard Edition of the Complete Works of Sigmund Freud*, XV, 206.
[91] Robert Wright, *The Moral Animal: Evolutionary Psychology and Everyday Life* (London: Little Brown, 1994), 314.

present-day psychoanalysis starts discriminating between which of its theories of 'kin selection, parent-offspring conflict, parental investment, reciprocal altruism, and status hierarchy' are consistent with evolutionary theory and which are not (324). He is not optimistic, either about human beings (we really are fundamentally self-serving) or about the capacity of psychology to give us guidance (the utilitarian pursuit of the greatest happiness for the greatest number is 'just about all we have left', he concludes, with what looks like a late, and not entirely convincing, effort to soften his own cynicism).[92]

It is the concentration on motive that makes this analysis of psychology's cynical character something more than just another version of what commonly happens when a critic trained in a particular intellectual field (as Wright was in socio-biology) takes a position of distance on other fields and detects strong elements of self-promotion and self-defence against competition. In that broad sense, all critique of disciplinary formations is likely to contain (even bound to entertain) some portion of cynicism. But as Wright and, passingly, Freud frame matters, psychology is more-than-usually close to cynicism in that it has motive as one of its principal objects of study. What motive is, how it operates, what its relation is to other concepts including foresight, will, intention, reason, are all questions that fall within psychology's rubric. If the account of psychology in *The Moral Animal* exaggerates cynicism in order to make its point (Wright's 'highly partisan rendering of the subject has an admittedly cynical edge', observed Peter A. Corning, more tolerantly than not), this does not mean that the cynical imputation of cynicism is wholly misplaced. It may be true of some forms of psychology (the ones we would, in my view, do well to avoid). But it plainly does not give a full picture of a discipline that contains more expansive and complex accounts of self-interest and its socio-biological functions, as well as other more humanistic accounts that make space for singularity, eccentricity, and history.

I take several things from this short excursion into psychological writing about cynicism to have significance for writing about the subject outside the professional domains concerned.

First is the recognition, across widely variant forms of psychology and psychoanalysis, that cynicism is a capacity or tendency within the ordinary functioning of many, probably most, human beings: cynical personality disorder is a matter of excess or rigidity in that tendency. There are such things as temperaments, so that cynicism will be stronger or weaker in any given individual, but the cynic's disposition to distrust the good motives of others is psychological terrain we are

---

[92] For the problems with Wright's zero-sum view of human egoism, and its exclusion of a more systemic view of human societies as complex interdependencies, see Peter A. Corning, 'Evolution and Ethics ... An Idea Whose Time Has Come? Part Two: Review of Wright, The Moral Animal', *Journal of Social and Evolutionary Systems* 20/3 (1997), 323–31 (324–7).

familiar with and if it has its dangers (narcissism, hostility), it also has its uses and its pleasures. It can be right.

Second, there is a common understanding that the cynic's intelligence is astutely deployed as far as it goes (this is not in question in any of the models), and may even deserve approbation for the sharpness of its insight or the bravery of its willingness to confront unwelcome truths. It tends to err in judgement—either because the conclusions drawn are too absolute (the cynic goes low, not wanting to lose), or because the cynic confuses the impurity of moral motives, and the difficulty of accessing motives, with 'badness' of motive. Judgements are open to dispute, and judgement I take to be the point at which cynicism can and should most often be assailed.

Third, Cynicism, in its original intellectual formation, provides one of the earliest critical perspectives recorded on the limited validity of psychological typing. That there is some irony in this fact will be clear: the Cynic, as a type of (among other things) nominalist, gives his name to the nominalist hostility to typing.

Finally, psychology itself has a claim to disciplinary intimacy with cynicism, insofar as it inherits the cynic's quasi-vocational role of discovering the nature of human motivations—but not necessarily the Cynic's claim to always know better. Whether or not this intimacy amounts, as Freud hoped, to a making-good of cynicism, or, as Wright intimates, a reaffirmation of the cynic's supposed disaffection, very much depends on the variety of psychology and, perhaps, the disposition of the particular psychologist.

These four observations lead me to venture a normative view of psychology that situates cynicism's role within ethical discourse. The view I am proposing makes at least one unlovely but also unsurprising assumption about human motivation that can be inferred also from the literary and philosophical materials following, namely, that it is driven in part by self-interest or egotism. How *large* a part self-interest or egotism plays must remain a moot point, since this is the ground on which cynicism asserts itself, and on which its opponents fight back. I do not myself find Epictetus's view objectionable: 'everyone is naturally motivated by self-interest, which, when properly understood, is the precondition of a properly social identity'. Nietzsche, and, before Nietzsche, Carlyle, give that assumption a very strong interpretation; but it is possible to go some way with Nietzsche (as Bernard Williams does) or indeed without him, not making egoism the whole of our personal motivation for morality but acknowledging that it has a place and may assist as well as damage our collective moral life.

In asking my reader to consider that everyone, or very nearly everyone, has cynic capacity or moments, I may seem to create some possible tension with the more deliberate, debunking cynic perspective that provides the force of cynic intelligence. Here, too, a degree of 'mootness' is germane, and indeed unavoidable. Exactly how cynicism plays out in any given text, or any speech performance, will always be open to debate about how far characterization of cynicism, seen from the outside, emanates from the writer/speaker consciously putting into play debasing tactics that warrant description as a form of intelligence and/or a deliberate cultivation of style, and how far what is detected may be unconscious, or appears what it is by dint of the reader/auditor's unconscious imperatives. I allow that cultural and historical circumstance can make a difference (potentially a large difference) in how far cynicism thrives at some moments and some places more than in others, but at the core of my disagreement with Sloterdijk (especially), but also Foucault and many writers on postmodernism, is this claim that 'cynicism' names a set of traits with a strong enough hold in human psychology not to simply disappear or go weak or lose traction in conversation when they come up against other traits. These normative assumptions about human psychology will be an explicit subject of discussion again in relation to Nietzsche, Eliot, and Ford Madox Ford, and will come full circle in my Coda, but they have relevance to everything that follows.

1

On Nietzsche and Doing Less with Cynicism

> The Greeks were superficial—out of profundity.
>
> (Friedrich Nietzsche, Preface to Second Edition
> of *The Gay Science*)

> Any such attitude for us will be a different and more sophisticated
> thing, and it will represent an achievement.
>
> (Bernard Williams)[1]

Let us start with the obvious case: the implication of *The Gay Science* (1882) in the legacies of Cynicism. Diogenes of Sinope's appearance as *der tolle Mensch* ('the crazy man') who proclaims the death of God is a canonical scene of modern philosophy:

> Haven't you heard of that madman who in the bright morning lit a lantern and ran around the marketplace crying incessantly 'I'm looking for God! I'm looking for God!' Since many of those who didn't believe in God were standing around together just then, he caused great laughter. Has he been lost, then? asked one. Did he lose his way like a child? asked another. Or is he hiding? Is he afraid of us? Has he gone to sea? Emigrated?—Thus they shouted and laughed, one interrupting the other. The madman jumped into their midst and pierced them with his eyes. 'Where is God?' he cried; 'I'll tell you! *We have killed him*—you and I! We are all his murderers.'   (§125, 119–20)

The reported drama of the madman riffs elaborately upon the *Lives of the Eminent Philosophers*, vi. 41: 'He [Diogenes] lit a lamp in full daylight and walked around with it, saying, "I'm searching for a man."'[2] Tapping into the radicalism of the

---

[1] Friedrich Nietzsche, *The Gay Science: With a Prelude in German Rhymes and an Appendix of Songs*, ed. Bernard Williams, trans. Josefine Nauckhoff and Adrian del Caro (Cambridge: Cambridge University Press, 2001), 3–9 (9); and Introduction, vii–xxii (xxii).

[2] Diogenes the Cynic, *Sayings and Anecdotes with Other Popular Moralists*, trans. Robin Hard (Oxford: Oxford University Press, 2012), 19 (56a).

The Function of Cynicism at the Present Time. Helen Small, Oxford University Press (2020). © Helen Small.
DOI: 10.1093/oso/9780198861935.001.0001

ancient example, Nietzsche echoes its original cynicism[3]—the lamentable absence of anyone in Athens capable of understanding and living in the knowledge of what it means to be human—and gives it updated purchase. A new Diogenes declares the death of God, the collapse of the belief system that underpinned Judaeo-Christian morality and provided the culture's sources of valuation for hundreds of years. Or rather, he demands attention to what should have followed from that realization, since the collapse itself is hardly news. Nietzsche succinctly captures, later in *The Gay Science*, what is, relatively, novel here. By 'God is dead', he writes, we should understand that 'belief in the Christian God has become unbelievable' (§343, 199) (or, with the interpretative nudge of Thomas Common's older translation, has become 'unworthy of belief ').[4] The time has come for human beings to live truthfully, in accordance with as honest an apprehension of our situation as we are capable of.

Striking though the revival of the Cynic figure is here, what might be expected to impress a reader with equal force is how stylistically *unlike* the original Nietzsche's rendition is. Where Diogenes was concisely anecdotal, intellectually provocative but psychologically reticent, Nietzsche is expansive, even garrulous, and, if not psychologically intimate, certainly interested in staging a public psychological drama from his philosophical materials. The expansiveness is the more apparent in a work that elsewhere (albeit unevenly) looks to sharpen the aphoristic mode first fully essayed in *Human, All Too Human* (1878–79), confirming a dominant turn away from the 'effusive and often hyperbolic style' of the earlier writings.[5] Some broad characteristics of Diogenes Laertius's text remain. Though the concision of the original is foregone at §125, the *tolle Mensch* episode retains the anecdotal focus on a single event, and the narrative delivery suggestive of word-of-mouth transmission. It retains also the distinctive mixing of a whiff of philosophical scandal with an element of comedy that puts in question quite how much the sense of scandal is warranted, and what its presence might tell us about the conditions for, and effects of, the Cynic's challenge to accepted norms of morality. All this is consistent with Diogenes Laertius, yet much in §125 is (in Robert Pippin's phrasing) 'quite mysterious'[6] as the original story of the lamp lit in the morning light is not. To isolate, as so many readers have done, the declaration

---

[3] R. Bracht Branham rightly notes that the Cynicism/cynicism (in German, *Kynismus/Zynismus*) distinction between ancient philosophical Cynicism and modern, predominantly psychological, cynicism is not one Nietzsche himself makes. He uses only *Zynismus*. See 'Nietzsche's Cynicism: Upper or lowercase?', in Paul Bishop (ed.), *Nietzsche and Antiquity: His Reaction and Response to the Classical Tradition* (Rochester, NY: Camden House, 2004), 170–81 (171).

[4] Friedrich Nietzsche, *The Joyful Wisdom*, trans. Thomas Common, poetry rendered by Paul V. Cohn and Maud D. Petre, in *The Complete Works of Friedrich Nietzsche*, gen. ed. Oscar Levy, 18 vols. (London: T. N. Foulis 1910–13), X, 244.

[5] Brendan Donnellan, 'Nietzsche and La Rochefoucauld', *The German Quarterly* 52/3 (May 1979), 303–18 (311).

[6] Robert Pippin, *Nietzsche, Psychology, and First Philosophy* (Chicago: University of Chicago Press, 2010), 47.

of the 'death of God' as a summary statement of the modern human condition is to push to one side most of what §125 is about.

Much of the 'mysterious'-ness arises from the projection of the Cynic as an unstable psychology into a public encounter that is, on both sides, immersively interrogative. Nietzsche's *tolle Mensch* is a histrionic figure, his performance in the role of Diogenes significantly more complex than that of the original. Addressing an audience largely, but not entirely, committed to a view of itself as enlightened ('many of them' do not 'believe'), he appears initially absurd to them, coming late to recognition of what they consider an established understanding. The questions thrown out at the *tolle Mensch* as he makes his erratic progress—'Has he been lost?', 'Did he lose his way like a child?', 'Is he hiding?', 'Is he afraid of us? Has he gone to sea? Emigrated?'—are variants on a caustic theme: Where has he been? Enlightenment scepticism has been around a long time, Get up to speed! But comedy turns to embarrassment when the madman jumps into the midst of his audience, 'pierc[ing] them with his eyes' and charging them with murder. The neo-Cynic affront lies not in the debasement of conventional metaphysical certainties long gone, but in his embarrassing insistence that destruction of the old ideals has important consequences for how to live now: God's death, he urges, is a matter about which his listeners ought to care deeply and for which they should take responsibility; in failing to care enough, they stand freshly incriminated.

After the accusations, then, come the *tolle Mensch*'s own questions—a stream of them:

How did we do this? How were we able to drink up the sea? Who gave us the sponge to wipe away the entire horizon? What were we doing when we unchained the earth from its sun? Where is it moving to now? Where are we moving to? Away from all suns? Are we not continually falling? And backwards, sidewards, forwards, in all directions. Is there still an up and a down? Aren't we straying as though through an infinite nothing? Isn't empty space breathing at us? Hasn't it got colder? Isn't night and more night coming again and again? Don't lanterns have to be lit in the morning? Do we still hear nothing of the noise of the grave-diggers who are burying God? Do we still smell nothing of the divine decomposition?—Gods, too, decompose! God is dead! God remains dead! And we have killed him! How can we console ourselves, the murderers of all murderers! The holiest and the mightiest thing the world has ever possessed has bled to death under our knives: who will wipe this blood from us? With what water could we clean ourselves? What festivals of atonement, what holy games will we have to invent for ourselves? Is the magnitude of this deed not too great for us? Do we not ourselves have to become gods merely to appear worthy of it? There was never a greater deed—and whoever is born after us will on account of this deed belong to a higher history than all history up to now!

The length is part of the point. Focusing, hectoringly, not on the 'crime' but on its authorization and its consequences, the scene capitalizes far more intensively than Diogenes Laertius does on the symbolism of the Cynic lantern, lit after the night is over and 'bright morning', or Enlightenment, has come. Berating his listeners with the insouciance of their unbelief, the madman iterates painstakingly the problems a culturally acquired scepticism raises for life hereon in: what was the warrant for so profound a change in our philosophical outlook? *How* can we go on without metaphysical and ontological anchoring? Must we be entirely without external light to guide us? What now are the sources, and the guarantees, of value, the protections against suffering? And what are the routes to human ennoblement, or as Nietzsche would formulate it in *Thus Spoke Zarathustra* (1883–85), where are we to find the means of 'self-overcoming' and entering fully into the 'higher history' open to us?[7] Not least, how do we live with our guilt? There is, he tells an increasingly 'disconcerted' audience, a pressing requirement for new routes to valuation, new forms of philosophy fit for purpose in the wake of a murderous but heroic act of unprecedented cultural magnitude; but there is also (and it is arguably his most perplexing claim) a need for atonement, and, looking forward, for justification through new and better ways of living. (I take this to be a spiralling overshoot beyond what our response should be—equivalent to asking, 'How could we atone, and should we think it would help?') Part of what is wanted are new artistic forms that no longer monumentalize dead modes of thought but grasp the challenge of our freedom in music, architecture, literature, painting. The water-colourist, having wiped away the old painted 'horizon', can start to fashion new perspectives.[8]

The *tolle Mensch*'s mode of address is ill-suited to any request for exemplarity. Faced with incomprehension and resistance, he falls silent, then casts aside the Cynic prop. Smashing his lantern upon the ground (a tired gimmick), he continues without it, 'forcing his way' into churches and interrupting proceedings with a sacrilegious parody of the funeral service: *requiem aeternam deo*/eternal rest for God! Having declared himself resigned to going unheard, he nevertheless persists, an unstable figure, urgent in his address to present and future but himself of the past, as the gesturally deictic narrative mode (akin to parable) tells us: 'it is still recounted' how he acted '*that very day*' [*des selbigen Tages*] (the accents are those of the Lutheran Bible). With hindsight, the *tolle Mensch*'s most sonorous claims are not 'God is dead!', 'we have killed him', but 'I come too early', 'deeds

---

[7] Friedrich Nietzsche, *Thus Spoke Zarathustra*, eds. Adrian del Caro and Robert B. Pippin, trans. Adrian del Caro (Cambridge: Cambridge University Press, 2006), *passim*.

[8] It is a universal law Nietzsche argues, in 'On the Uses and Disadvantages of History for Life', that 'a living thing can be healthy, strong, and fruitful only when bounded by a horizon'. Friedrich Nietzsche, *Untimely Meditations*, ed. Daniel Brezeale, trans. R. J. Hollingdale (Cambridge: Cambridge University Press, 1997), 63. For commentary, see Keith Ansell-Pearson, *An Introduction to Nietzsche as Political Thinker: The Perfect Nihilist* (Cambridge: Cambridge University Press, 1994), 69.

need time'—self-reflexive declarations to the effect that the prophetic philosopher's time is out of joint. Too late in the eyes of others, he is too soon in his
own, though that claim is, of course, open to various suspicions, including the
suspicion of being histrionic (if we take the *tolle Mensch* to be one of Nietzsche's
many guises)[9] and the suspicion that the future does not lie securely ahead of us as
'coming too early' might imply.

What, and how much, does Nietzsche's philosophy have to do with the
untimeliness of Cynicism itself, at once antique and modern, immature
(Nietzsche often suggests) and sophisticated, 'superficial' and 'profound'? It is a
question that the later philosophical writings, especially, seem to want to provoke
as they look to the typology and the stylistic gambits of Cynicism as helpful, but
inadequate, models for the lived practice of philosophy. 'There is no doubt,'
remarked Elisabeth Förster-Nietzsche (an unreliable witness), that 'my brother
tried a little bit to imitate Diogenes in the tub: he wanted to find out how little a
philosopher could get by with.'[10] She was, perhaps, recalling a sentence in *Human,
All Too Human* where Nietzsche contemplates the conditions necessary for
spiritual strength: 'a *minimum* of living, an unchaining from all coarser desires,
an independence amid every sort of external misfortune, together with the pride in
being able to live under this misfortune: a bit of cynicism perhaps, a bit of "the
tub"'.[11] Three facets of classical Cynicism come briefly into view in this sentence: a
stripped-back life, requiring the barest material supports; an ascetic life of philosophy, without unwanted psychological entanglements; a life equipped with the
internal resources (the pride) to deflect 'misfortune'. But though he is identifying
with Diogenes, Nietzsche is in jesting mode and taking a peculiar slant on
Cynicism: a 'minimum of life', yes, but the early Cynics did not shun the 'coarser',
or 'baser', desires ['*gröberen Begehrlichkeiten*'][12] (on the contrary, they were
notoriously shameless in satisfying them); Diogenes and his followers claimed

---

[9] A perceptive account of Nietzsche's use of masking is given in Alexander Nehamas, *Nietzsche: Life
as Literature* (Cambridge, MA: Harvard University Press, 1985), Chapter 1—but see p. C1.P43 below
on the difficulties arising in relation to Cynicism, and what those difficulties indicate more broadly
about Nietzsche's recourse to masks.

[10] '*Es ist kein Zweifel, dass mein Bruder damals ein wenig Diogenes in der Tonne nachzuahmen
versuchte, er wollte einmal sehen mit wie wenig ein Philosoph auskommen kann*'. Elizabeth Förster-
Nietzsche, *Der einsame Nietzsche* (1914) (Bremen: Unikum, 2012), 80. Trans. Anthony K. Jensen, in
'Nietzsche's Unpublished Fragments on Ancient Cynicism: The First Night of Diogenes', in Bishop
(ed.), *Nietzsche and Antiquity*, 182–91 (185). I have slightly rephrased for idiomatic fluency.

[11] Preface to Vol. 2. On this occasion I have preferred the more exact rendition given by Gary
Handwerk in the Stanford edition, but have restored the italicization of *minimum* in the original
German ('ein *Minimum* von Leben'): Friedrich Nietzsche, *Human, All Too Human II and Unpublished
Fragments from the Period of* Human, All Too Human II *(Spring 1878–Fall 1879)*, trans. with afterword
by Gary Handwerk (2013), in *The Complete Works of Friedrich Nietzsche*, gen. eds. Alan D. Schrift,
Duncan Large, and Adrian del Caro (Stanford, CA: Stanford University Press, 1995–), Vol. IV, 8–9. Cf.
Friedrich Nietzsche, *Human, All Too Human: A Book for Free Spirits*, trans. R. J. Hollingdale, intro-
duction by Richard Schacht (Cambridge: Cambridge University Press, 1996), 212–13.

[12] 'Base' perhaps captures better the dual resonance here: 'coarse/indecent' but also 'basic/funda-
mental'—the '*grob*' actions required to stay alive (eating, sleeping, etc.).

'independence', yes—from conventional morality, from conventional material wants, from emotional disturbance—but 'external misfortune' (more literally, 'outer adversity' [*äussere Ungunst*]) seems the wrong idiom, too small, too fretful for their thick-skinned *apatheia*—hinting at Nietzsche's resistance to his critics;[13] 'pride' was a target of Cynic scorn, not a source of self-validation. In short: this is a rewriting of the philosophy of the tub, not a straightforward recapitulation.

The overall nature and extent of Nietzsche's debts to the Cynic legacy are already the subject of a large literature, with many critics drawn to the *odi et amo* quality of his relationship with Diogenes and later French *moralistes* who placed themselves in his tradition, pre-eminently La Rochefoucauld, Molière, La Bruyère, Vauvenargues, Chamfort.[14] I give a brief account of the intellectual-biographical terrain in the section that follows, emphasizing the function of Cynicism as an argumentative and stylistic toolkit for Nietzsche's writing, employed with an eye on its obvious limitations. My initial focus is on how tactical adoptions of Cynicism assisted the articulation of his thinking about two crucial dimensions of modern life: (i) what it would mean to break the hold of convention and be 'free-spirited' in one's philosophizing; and (ii) how best to fashion a philosophical style (and a philosophical outlook on life, though I will have little to say about biography) in the assumption of that freedom. I then turn to the principal application of Cynicism: its role in the articulation of the geneal-ogy of morality. That role is well enough recognized but has attracted little close commentary to date. I am primarily concerned with the limited but dramatic and psychologically pungent role Nietzsche accords to Cynicism as an astringent questioning of our motives for attachment to moral norms, in attempting to articulate nobler, future-oriented modes of living outside 'the cage' (as *The Gay Science* puts it [§125]). Just how Cynicism about morality, so handled, relates to scepticism about morality is a key consideration, not least in the light of Nietzsche's well-known antagonism to more standard, discursive forms of rational scepticism.

---

[13] The Cambridge translation 'nuisances' may be attempting to register the implication of philo-sophical rather than material enmities, but the word seems too weak.

[14] See esp. the pioneering work of Heinrich Niehues-Pröbsting, *Der Kynismus des Diogenes und der Begriff des Zynismus* (Frankfurt: Suhrkamp, 1988); Heinrich Niehues-Pröbsting, 'Die Kynismus-Rezeption der Moderne: Diogenes in der Aufklärung', *Deutsche Zeitschrift für Philosophie* 40/7 (1992), 709–34; English version, Heinrich Niehues-Pröbsting, 'Diogenes at the Enlightenment: The Modern Reception of Cynicism', in Robert Bracht Branham and Marie-Odile Goulet-Cazé (eds.), *The Cynics: The Cynic Movement in Antiquity and Its Legacy* (Berkeley, CA: University of California Press, 1996), 329–65. Also, Robert Bracht Branham, 'Nietzsche's Cynicism: Upper or Lowercase?', in Bishop (ed.), *Nietzsche and Antiquity*, 170–81; Jensen, 'Nietzsche's Unpublished Fragments'; Donnellan, 'Nietzsche and La Rochefoucauld'; Marion Faber, 'The Metamorphosis of the French Aphorism: La Rochefoucauld and Nietzsche', *Comparative Literature Studies* 23/3 (Fall 1986), 205–17; Ian Cutler, *Cynicism from Diogenes to Dilbert* (Jefferson, NC: McFarland & Co., 2005), 68–91. See also Thomas H. Brobjer, *Nietzsche's Philosophical Context: An Intellectual Biography* (Urbana, IL: University of Illinois Press, 2008), 20.

A Limited and Strategic Cynicism

Diogenes Laertius was the subject of Nietzsche's earliest scholarly work in the field of philology, and a point of repeated return for his later thinking about philosophy's mode of public address when it ventures to disturb conventional thinking about morality (the *tolle Mensch* is the most striking example, but far from the only one). He read the *Lives of Eminent Philosophers* for the first time probably in his late teens, borrowing the two-volume edition by Hübner while a student at Schulpforta.[15] The essay 'De Laerti Diogenes Fontibus' ('On the Sources of Diogenes Laertius') with which he won the Leipzig University Prize in philology a few years later was composed during the Christmas holidays 1866–67, and published in two parts over 1868–69.[16] Wider reading in the early records of philosophy and the theory of textual transmission followed, feeding into two essays, *Analecta Laertiana* and *Beiträge zur Quellenkunde und Kritik des Laertius Diogenes* (both 1870,[17] in effect appendices to the prize essay). Exploring the evidence for textual influence, with almost no room for reflection on the content of the *Lives*, the essays argue for Diogenes Laertius's dependence on two principal authorities: Diocles of Magnesia and Favorinus (Diogenes is 'often merely a slavish copyist' of both); also, more speculatively, a third author, Theodosius, to whom Nietzsche attributes Book IX's account of Pyrrhonian scepticism.[18]

The textual claims have not, in the main, stood up to later scrutiny. Jonathan Barnes identifies some cavalier rushing to conclusions, convenient exclusions of potential conflicting evidence, and a tendency to 'substitut[e] rhetoric for logic' in

---

[15] See Brobjer, 'Table 1: Chronological List of Nietzsche's Philosophical Reading', in *Nietzsche's Philosophical Context*, 185–236 (192). And for Nietzsche's personal library of Diogenes Laertius (he possessed at least eleven copies of the *Lives*, including two in German translation), see G. Campioni et al. (ed.), *Nietzsches Persönliche Bibliothek*, *Supplementa Nietzscheana*, vol. VI (Berlin: Walter de Gruyter, 2003), 191–5. Max Oehler (ed.), *Nietzsches Bibliothek* (Weimar: Nietzsche-Archivs, 1942) lists only two.

[16] See J. Mansfeld and D. T. Runia, *Aëtiana: The Method and Intellectual Context of a Doxographer*, vol. I: *The Sources* (Leiden: Brill, 1997), 93–4.

[17] Jonathan Barnes, 'Nietzsche and Diogenes Laertius', *Nietzsche-Studien* 15/1 (1986), 16–40. Barnes's account is extended by James I. Porter, *Nietzsche and the Philology of the Future* (Stanford, CA: Stanford University Press, 2002), who examines in detail the innovative nature of Nietzsche's philological work, drawing special attention to its 'theatrical' quality (116–21) and argues for the ongoing significance of his training in this field for his work as a philosopher. See Friedrich Nietzsche, *Kritische Gesamtausgabe* [*KGW*], gen. eds. Giorgio Colli and Mazzino Montinari (Berlin: Walter de Gruyter, 1967–), vol. II/I. Also Friedrich Nietzsche, *Historisch-kritische Gesamtausgabe*, ed. Hans Joachim Mette, 9 vols. (Munich: C.H. Beck, 1934–40) [*BAW*], vols. IV and V for the extensive *Nachlass* notes, essays and preliminary sketches on Diogenes Laertius. His recorded reading in this period includes F. Ueberweg's *Grundriss der Geschichte der Philosophie*, 3 vols. (1866–67), Mullach's *Fragmenta philosophorum graecorum*, and F. Schleiermacher, 'Über das Verzeichnis der Schriften des Demokritus bei Diogenes Laertius' (1835). See Brobjer, *Nietzsche's Philosophical Context*, 194–5. Also Curt Paul Janz, *Friedrich Nietzsche: Biographie*, 3 vols. (München: Hanzer, 1978–79), esp. vol. I, 190 and 591.

[18] Barnes, 'Nietzsche and Diogenes Laertius', 22.

pursuit of a theory—not surprising in a 22-year-old focusing on the subject for just a few months.[19] But Barnes also affirms what is remarkable about Nietzsche's essays: the clarity and panache with which they engage a set of scholarly problems that still resist definitive solutions;[20] and the zeroing in on the poetic attractions of a text that, for all its borrowed knowledge, its stupidity and its laziness ('wretched little Laertius'),[21] preserves 'the spirit of the old philosophers'[22] as more substantial early accounts do not.

From very early in Nietzsche's writing life, the *Lives of Eminent Philosophers* functioned as a touchstone when articulating principles for his own philosophical style. 'Diogenes Laertiades' was the signature he placed on a letter to Erwin Rohde of 26 August 1872 ('son of Laertius', or literally 'sprung from Laertius').[23] Jokey letters between members of his friendship group suggest that his liking for Diogenes of Sinope was well known to them.[24] Direct evidence appears in notebook fragments only recently translated into English—occasional memoranda, a comic couplet 'Aus der Tonne des Diogenes' ('From the Tub of Diogenes'), a notebook entry from 1874 praising Diogenes' radical life-philosophy ('As long as philosophers do not muster the courage to seek an entirely different lifestyle and demonstrate it by their own example,' the entry concludes, 'they will come to nothing').[25]

The philosophical views given public airing in Nietzsche's early teaching practice support the Nachlass evidence of his interest in Cynicism. But, from the start, the Cynics were an aid to his thinking about other topics rather than a primary focus. His University of Basel lectures on Philosophical Literature (*'Die philosophische Litteratur'*), of 1874–75, gave some consideration to the Cynics' influence on the development of satire and philosophical genre of 'conversations with the dead'.[26] His lecture course on the Pre-Platonic philosophers (first given in the winter of 1869–70; reworked in the summer of 1872, 1873, and 1876)[27] turned again to Diogenes Laertius as the main ancient source of information about earlier Greek philosophy. Drawing his historical line at Plato, Nietzsche has no cause to look ahead at the Cynics but the characteristics applauded in the earlier writers

---

[19] Barnes summarizes the, at that stage, largely dismissive literature on Nietzsche's philological achievements (ibid., 36–8).

[20] See Tiziano Dorandi, '"A la Recherche du Text Perdu": The Manuscript Tradition of Diogenes Laertius' *Lives of the Eminent Philosophers*', in Diogenes Laertius, *Lives of the Eminent Philosophers*, ed. with introduction by Tiziano Dorandi (Cambridge: Cambridge University Press, 2013), 577–81, and, by way of summary, James Miller's Introduction to *Lives of the Eminent Philosophers*, ed. James Miller, trans. Pamela Mensch (Oxford: Oxford University Press, 2018), vii–xviii.

[21] *De fontibus* 131.2, quoted in Barnes, 'Nietzsche and Diogenes Laertius', 20.

[22] 'Schopenhauer als Erzieher', the third of the *Unzeitgemässe Betrachtungen* (1874), *KGW* 33 III/l, 413—as translated and quoted in Barnes, 'Nietzsche and Diogenes Laertius', 21.

[23] Quoted in Introduction to Friedrich Nietzsche, *The Pre-Platonic Philosophers*, ed. and trans. Greg Whitlock (Urbana. IL: University of Illinois Press, 2006), xliv.

[24] Jensen, 'Nietzsche's Unpublished Fragments', 180.

[25] *KSA* 7, 31 (11), 752; trans. Jensen, 'Nietzsche's Unpublished Fragments', 183.

[26] See ibid., 191, 4n.   [27] Whitlock, Introduction to *The Pre-Platonic Philosophers*, xxii–xxvi.

show him aiming, like Diogenes Laertius, to capture the 'spirit of the old philosophers' with a premium on traits that the Cynics made their own: stylistic
individuality; 'free-spiritedness'; a philosophical approach that, even on so
abstract a subject as philosophy of numbers, can register a transformative individual intelligence at work. The lectures make a case for a radical strain within
Pre-Platonic Greek philosophy, presenting the 'philosophy of numbers' as a 'new
path' on which the Pythagoreans were 'emboldened' by the failure of earlier
theories when applied to problems.[28] Individual genius is to the fore. Nietzsche's
belief in 'nobility' of mind becomes more pronounced, understood both 'literally'
(he lingers over the distinguished family trees of Heraclitus and Empedocles) and
'expressively' (foregrounding the stylistic individuality of Homer, Hesiod,
Anaxagoras). Heraclitus finds special favour: 'intuitive, oracular, internalized,
deeply reflective, self-searching, self-critical, and self-challenging'.[29] Not least,
the lectures show Nietzsche probing the logic and narrative power of intellectual
genealogy, rejecting established sources such as Theophrastus and Demetrius in
order to establish 'a chain of student-teacher relations down through time'.[30]

In Diogenes Laertius, Nietzsche found encouragement for his increasingly
wayward relationship to accepted modes of academic philosophy. The
lectures—a mélange of 'philosophical myths, proverbs, poems, fragments, mis-
cellania, and anecdotes'[31]—show him imitating Diogenes' attention to the person
and cultural influence of the philosopher, and preferring the unconcealed personal
element in doxography to the dusty analysis of ancient systems of thought. A letter
to Lou Salomé on 16 September 1882 makes the aim explicit, in retrospect:

My beloved Lou, your idea of reducing philosophical systems to the status of
personal records of their authors is a veritable 'twin brain' idea. In Basel I was
teaching the history of the ancient philosophy in just this sense, and liked to tell

---

[28] Letter to Erwin Rohde, 11 June 1872, quoted by Whitlock, Introduction to *The Pre-Platonic
Philosophers*, xxxix–xl (xl). Hugo Drochon notes a further key attraction of the Pre-Platonics for
Nietzsche: in his eyes, they 'were "pure" in the sense that their philosophy sprung naturally from their
personality'. After Plato, all philosophy becomes 'hybrid' (a mix, in Plato's own case, of Socrates,
Heraclitus, and other influences) and, politically, it aims no longer at the 'salvation of the whole' (as
Socrates is understood to have done, in his care for the *polis*) but at 'the salvation of [the philosopher's]
own small sect'. Hugo Drochon, *Nietzsche's Great Politics* (Princeton, NJ: Princeton University Press,
2016), 7.

[29] Whitlock, 'Translator's Commentary', in *The Pre-Platonic Philosophers*, 153–264 (210). Whitlock
helpfully draws out Nietzsche's concentration on the early Greek philosophical struggle against the
'dogmatisms' of science, myth, and religion: he approaches the history of science, Whitlock observes,
with a conviction that '[a]ll natural science is but an attempt to understand that which is anthropological, humanity' (166–7).

[30] Ibid., xlv. It is evidently a theme close to Whitlock's heart: his 'Translator's Preface' to the lectures
opens with an emotive testimony to the influence upon him of Walter Kaufmann, and a tutor directly
taught by Kaufmann (see xiii).

[31] Whitlock, Introduction to *The Pre-Platonic Philosophers*, xxii.

my students: 'This system has been disproved and it is dead; but you cannot disprove the person behind it—the person cannot be killed.'[32]

Nietzsche's first philosophical (as distinct from philological) publications touch only occasionally on Cynicism. *The Birth of Tragedy* (1872) anticipates the lectures of 1874–75 with approving references in passing: Cynicism (like tragedy) 'absorbed into itself all the earlier varieties of art'; the 'most promiscuous style' of the Cynics was a literary protest against the efforts of Socrates and Plato to banish the Dionysian elements of life in the name of reason.[33] By the time he writes *Human, All Too Human* (1878–79), Nietzsche is adopting a more ambivalent stance: at I, 8 §457, he approves of the Cynic's ability to see through the over-valuation of status that allows people to tolerate conditions of work worse than slavery ('The Cynic thinks differently because he despises honour:—and thus Diogenes was for a time a slave and private tutor');[34] but when he observes, at II, Pt II, §18, that the search for man requires a lantern and asks 'Will it have to be the lantern of the cynic?', there can be little doubt that the implied answer is in the negative. *Untimely Meditations* (1880) is specific about the shortcomings of Cynic teaching, detecting a flaw in all philosophies which make 'happiness' the desired end of individual and collective life. Nietzsche scoffs at the 'fatal' reduction of outlook: happiness is the limiting preoccupation of the Cynic 'animal', content to forget history, ignore futurity, and 'sink down on the threshold of the moment' (62).[35] *Daybreak* (1881) expands upon the objection:

> in Greece in the third century,...there were not a few philosophers who...believed that their happiness was the best refutation of other ways of life, and in pursuit of that all they had to do was to seem happy; but by doing that they were bound in the long run to *become* happy! This, for example, was the fate of the Cynics. (§367, 168)

The formal risks and benefits of any recourse to Cynicism for present-day purposes are brought sharply into focus in *Daybreak*. §266 identifies a kind of theatrical mannerism about Cynic philosophizing that has grown more rigid over the years.

---

[32] Quoted in Brobjer, *Nietzsche's Philosophical Context*, 28.

[33] Friedrich Nietzsche, *The Birth of Tragedy*, ed. and trans. W. M. A. Haussmann (Edinburgh: Foulis, [1872] 1910), 109.

[34] There is, surely, humour in the conjunction.

[35] Also *Beyond Good and Evil*, §26: for the most part, those who deal in Cynicism are not the real thing: they are 'so-called cynics', Nietzsche asserts here. They 'easily recognize the animal, the commonplace, the "norm" within themselves'—but among them will be a few who 'still have a degree of spiritedness and an urge to talk about themselves and their peers *in front of witnesses*', and show a 'subtle and exceptional understanding'. Friedrich Nietzsche, *Beyond Good and Evil: Prelude to a Philosophy of the Future*, eds. Rolf-Peter Horstmann and Judith Norman, trans. Judith Norman (Cambridge: Cambridge University Press, [1886] 2002), 27.

[The actor is] WITHOUT CHARM.—He lacks charm and knows it. Ah, how skilful he is in masking this defect! He does it by a strict virtue, gloomy looks, and acquired distrust of all men, and of existence itself; by coarse jests, by contempt for a more refined manner of living, by pathos and pretensions, and by a cynical philosophy—yea, he has even developed into a character through the continual knowledge of his deficiency.   (§266)

Laboured virtue-signalling marks the limit of the modern Cynic's 'knowledge'. He has not moved with history, but rather ossified into a set of traits that make up a 'character', pre-scripted—as character always is—by etymology and enduring usage. What potential prestige Cynicism might hope to accrue here by way of a recognizable and concentrated performance in the interpretation of 'strict virtue' it loses by dint of inflexibility and irremediable 'coarseness'.

There is a context for the increasingly hostile case of Nietzsche's comments here in his general movement away from pessimism (and especially from the influence of Schopenhauer). But the tactical deployment of the Cynic after this point, especially with the prominence it achieves in §125 of *The Gay Science*, is in line with the continuing interest in Cynicism as a kind of magnifying glass held over the operation of philosophical style and form. The foregrounding of the Cynic as a 'character' in trouble (a character in distress, as he will become in *The Gay Science*) befits a growing concern with strategies of address to a readership presumed not just ill-equipped to comprehend what the philosopher is saying but resistant to becoming better equipped. This is a posture, or rather, one side of a double posture, most intensively worked in *Zarathustra* and *Ecce Homo*: the philosopher at once in despair of finding readers capable of hearing him, and defiantly aloof, willing his own self-sufficiency.[36] Contemplation of the Cynic 'as character' serves both attitudes, and offers to loosen the hold of 'posturing' itself, making clearer what the posture is and what it may hope to achieve.

For the Nietzsche of the 1880s, critical 'types' (not just the Cynic, but the Fool, the Scholar, the Sceptic, the Fanatic) are not true: they are valuable to the extent that they unsettle modern complacency, useful irritants almost every use of which is qualified lest it harden back into something that looks like authenticity. Silted over as the Cynic is with conventional interpretation, the primary facet of his ancient characterization still has validity for Nietzsche, as it will do subsequently for Jung (steeped as he was in Nietzsche):[37] his resistance to typing. (Theophrastus

[36] See Henry Staten, *Nietzsche's Voice* (Ithaca, NY: Cornell University Press, 1990), Chapter 1, for this rich line of inquiry.

[37] Deirdre Bair, *Jung: A Biography* (London: Little Brown, 2004), 285–7, for the Nietzschean influence on his thinking about psychological types (but with no mention of the Cynic specifically); more generally 35, 51, 284, 395, and 662 75n. See also C. G. Jung, *Jung's Seminar on Nietzsche's Zarathustra*, ed. James L Jarrett, abridged edn (Princeton, NJ: Princeton University Press, 2004) (the Introduction provides an overview of Jung's engagement with Nietzsche, culminating in the seminar of 1934–39). For Jung's interest in Diogenes with his lantern, as a figure for primitive man's need of

picks up on that resistance when he excludes the Cynic from his *Characters*—as George Eliot had also done much more recently. See pp. 161–64.) When Nietzsche writes that the Cynic 'has even developed into a character through the continual knowledge of his deficiency', he is, in part, telling us that deficiency is of the essence of the Cynic type, who indeed exhorts us by example to strip ourselves back (our desires and needs) to essentials; but he is also picking up what is implied through him about the act of characterization in general: reduced to type, stripped of what does not fit, the Cynic character makes available certain associated ideas (including critical antagonism, reductiveness, self-sufficiency, free speaking) that can then be put into circulation as if *with all due warning* of their limitations.

An indirect element of that warning relates to what Nietzsche terms the 'democracy of concepts'. 'The Wanderer and His Shadow' clinches the point:

> *Tyrants of the Spirit.*—In our age anyone who was so completely the expression of a single moral trait as are the characters of Theophrastus or Molière would be regarded as sick and one would in his case speak of an '*idée fixe*'. The Athens of the third century would, if we could pay it a visit, seem to us populated by fools. Nowadays a democracy of concepts rules in every head—*many together* are master: a single concept that *wanted* to be master would now, as aforesaid, be called an '*idée fixe*'. This is *our* way of disposing of tyrants—we direct them to the madhouse.   (*Human, All Too Human*, II, I, 230)

The democracy of concepts has it that each person gains a paltry conception of themselves as an individual, given their idiosyncratic mix of common traits. I am me, and different from you on account of the particular way in which I am common. Individuality rests on that basis. Ancient character types (as we read them off from Aristotle and Theophrastus) were not such hybrids. The pedant was essentially a pedant, the miser nothing but. In the modern period of hybrids, character so expressed can only be caricature and indeed deviant: 'mad', or a 'fool', and 'tyrannical' in its concentration of a '*fixed idea*'.

But just because such characters are radically out of place in modern life, Nietzsche prizes them as disconcerting probes. Where self-satisfaction and homo-geneity of belief reign, they have disruptive potential. The difficulty is that, given how readily moderns ignore distilled characters like the Cynic (they have long gone stale on us), being cynical must amplify or distort itself to have any effect at all. It must needs be hypertrophic. This is part of why Nietzsche holds that the ancient Cynic is either 'out of time' or trapped in it: Cynic compression of speech

consciousness, given his 'pretty blurred and obscured' knowledge of the world, see lecture VI, 27 February 1935, 124–35 (125–6). Paul Bishop's discussion of typology, in Paul Bishop, *The Dionysian Self: C. G. Jung's Reception of Friedrich Nietzsche* (Berlin: Walter de Gruyter, 1995), is germane but makes no reference to the Cynic or Cynicism.

could function critically in a rhetorical culture so long as the authority of that compression, and of the rhetorical scheme it affronts, held; but the modern world is a world of endless gab, for Nietzsche; so, the Cynic is driven to rant. Hence the flood of speech from Zarathustra, when the fool raises his ire in the marketplace ('At this point...Zarathustra interrupted the foaming fool and clapped his hand over the fool's mouth' [142]).

I noted above that Nietzsche's handling of the aphorism gradually gained in formal and expressive flexibility over the course of the early works.[38] From *The Gay Science* onwards Cynicism assists a sharpening of the aphorism's contrarian edge, though not its succinctness. More than in the preceding works, the manner of address in certain sections pulls toward insult, invective, mockery in the name of urgency. It is a stylistic development that would be taken to extravagant excesses in the 'skirmishing' passages (*Streifzüge*) of *The Twilight of the Idols* (1889), with their notorious and exhilarating attacks on, among others, George Sand ('smug...fertile little writing cow'); John Stuart Mill ('insulting clarity'); Thomas Carlyle ('an English atheist who stakes his honour on not being one'); and, not least, the reader ('Don't try to be clever').[39] Clearly, Nietzsche did not regret the toughening up of his style after the 'squandering of goodness' in *Zarathustra*, as *Ecce Homo* denotes it retrospectively.[40] But he was already alert, in *The Gay Science*, to the questions raised by such aggressive freedoms and to the placing of Cynicism within a wider gamut of aggressive philosophical play.

When Nietzsche writes, in *The Gay Science* §379, that 'we are artists of contempt' (p. 243), he has in view internal differences in the kind and quality of antagonistic free speech available to the writer. Although he does not on this occasion explicitly confine contempt to the perspective of the Cynic, the section implicitly deploys that association (already made in *Daybreak* §266) as it circles around the challenge of identifying parameters of 'virtue' for 'the writer of this book'. 'Contempt' finds an alternative here not in 'respect' but in 'hatred', which Nietzsche takes to be an older and narrower art than the one he aspires to. 'Hatred' is based on a presumption of equality with other people—an unwanted equality; hence hatred is 'misanthrop[ic]' (243). Its practice was raised to its artistic height, he tells us, in Shakespeare's *Timon of Athens*: in Shakespeare's wake, one could aim at 'hat[ing] *the* human being, Timonically, wholly, without exception, with

---

[38] Most relevantly, *Untimely Meditations, Human, All Too Human, The Wanderer and His Shadow* (1880), and *Daybreak: Thoughts on the Prejudices of Morality* (1881).

[39] 'Skirmishes of an Untimely Man', 6, 1, 12, 9, in Friedrich Nietzsche, *The Anti-Christ, Ecce Homo, Twilight of the Idols, and Other Writings*, eds. Aaron Ridley and Judith Norman, trans. Judith Norman (Cambridge: Cambridge University Press, 2005), 194, 192, 198, 196.

[40] See esp. Nietzsche's justification in *Ecce Homo* of the change in psychological outlook between *Zarathustra* and *Beyond Good and Evil*: the latter marks a '*deliberate* turning away from those instincts that make a *Zarathustra* possible—...psychology is applied with avowed hardness and cruelty,—there is not a single good-natured word in the book'; what is looked for now is a reactivation of the will to liberation in those higher beings who are 'master[s] by nature' (*Ecce Homo, Beyond Good and Evil*, §2, 135).

one's whole heart, with the whole *love* of hatred'. But now 'refined contempt is our taste and privilege, our art, our virtue perhaps'. It offers to be the higher art, operating (as hatred does not) in the assurance of its own superiority.

If this looks like arrogance (as it well might), Nietzsche's recourse to a higher form of Cynic aggression is nevertheless tormented by recognition that the present-day philosopher operates under a severe external restraint, in the form of a widespread cultural commitment to tolerance that makes philosophical free-speaking peculiarly difficult to invest with force. Whatever freedoms s/he broaches, the philosopher-artist need have no serious fear of reprisals.

> We will hardly be decapitated, or imprisoned or exiled; not even our books will be banned or burned. The age loves the spirit [i.e. the spirit of 'the fearless ones']; it loves and needs us, even if we should have to make clear to it that we are artists of contempt; that every association with human beings makes us shudder slightly...   (§379, 244)

In such a context, whatever liberation the philosopher's 'contempt' may demonstrate lies in contempt's resistance to the even-handed, levelling 'spirit of the age': contempt will not of itself provide sufficient scope for growth.[41] The squeamish shudder that characterizes the affirmation of higher consciousness looks all too likely to congeal into another affectation ('we cannot persuade our noses to give up their prejudices').

One can deduce from what is said here of hatred that *parrhēsia* on the model of the (bad) Cynic Apemantus, who goads Shakespeare's Timon on his way to misanthropy instead of the philanthropy of Diogenes of Sinope, is not going to take philosophy very far towards the higher freedoms Nietzsche seeks. Not least, free speech along old Cynic lines rests on a notion of direct intelligible address that levels an audience (as §381 will go on to protest), instead of appealing to its higher elements. 'Fool's mockery', or, less freely, 'the Fool's interlude' [*Zwischenrede des Narren*] (the title given to 379),[42] is perhaps looking to fend off that threat when it supplies two final specifications to the rubric for its own free speech that offer to temper contempt's pomposity and prevent it hardening into the characteristic of a Cynic: 'we love nature the less humanly it behaves' (alluding to and rewriting the Cynic *philanthropia*); we love 'art...if it is the artist's mockery of himself' (p. 244). This is Cynicism as a puncturing, not an assertion, of the authority of

---

[41] For Nietzsche's articulation of what he means by 'growth', see esp. *The Gay Science*, 230.

[42] Thomas Common's (otherwise questionable) translation of *The Joyful Wisdom* goes with a simpler option, 'The Fool's Interruption' (346). There is, perhaps, a Goethean note to the original, recalling both the poem 'The Fool's Epilogue' and the '*Lustige Person*' (Merry-Andrew) in *Faust* I ('*Vorspiel auf dem Theater*'), in which the fool interjects and interrupts the manager and poet. For the wider resonances from the German literary tradition, see Joel B. Lande, *Persistence of Folly: On the Origins of German Dramatic Literature* (Ithaca, NY: Cornell University Press, 2018), 243.

free speech; Cynicism as (at best) one among several points from which the ideal of a more genuinely free speech might come into view.

To claim, then, that *The Gay Science* locally recasts the act of public philosophizing about morality as a *neo*-Cynic performance of free speech is correct as far as it goes—but that means not very far. The significance of the *tolle Mensch*'s strained (and aphoristically contained) performance is finally that it articulates a version of Cynicism which is, as it can *only* now be, locally tactical—opening up questions of public address, of the effectiveness or otherwise of criticism, and the authority or lack of authority possessed by the 'philosopher of the future', while itself claiming no exemplary force or authority. What authority it *can* claim is that of the *Ur*-type: so singular that it inspires others *not* to copy but to understand what individuality might amount to. The best relationship the 'higher man' can have with Cynicism, Nietzsche implies, will be at once instrumental and wary: there are 'real short-cuts and aids' here 'to make his work easier', he indicates in *Beyond Good and Evil* §26, but the philosopher must remain on the look-out for the inevitable betrayal of Cynicism's limitations: 'the higher man needs to open his ears to all cynicism, crude or refined, and congratulate himself every time the buffoon speaks up without shame, or the scientific satyr is heard right in front of him'.

Both the buffoon and the scientist are Cynics in the sense that they debase, or limit, the possibility of human freedom by conceiving of no greater goal for life than happiness and health. The higher man nevertheless has cause to give them a hearing, 'open[ing] his ears' not to the *content* of what they have to say but to the shamelessness of their complacency—recognition of which may be the philosopher's best recourse against such complacency in himself.

The same section revives Nietzsche's long-standing objection to the low horizons of Cynic philosophy. Some of those who deal in it (the 'so-called cynics', who do not follow their insight all the way towards the ascetic life of Diogenes and his kind) will be of service to us, §26 asserts, because their critique of the current human condition is right, as far as it goes, and because its limitations are also helpfully apparent: they 'easily recognize the animal, the commonplace, the "norm" within themselves'. To their credit, they 'still have a degree of spiritedness and an urge to talk about themselves and their peers *in front of witnesses*: sometimes they even wallow in books as if in their own filth'. Cynicism, Nietzsche affirms (and it is the strongest endorsement he ever gives to it), 'is the only form' in which such 'common souls come close to honesty' (*Redlichkeit*)— the chief virtue he attaches to truthfulness. So, even in his modern, reduced, 'so-called' form, entranced with his own intellectual credentials, the Cynic has value for us, Nietzsche claims, if he can be made to serve a higher philosophy. There is a capacity for self-examination here, however under-developed, and a degree of 'spirit', however constrained, that may aid the higher man towards self-overcoming.

The Gay Science sets the underlying terms for all Nietzsche's dealings with Cynicism thereafter. Like the first Diogenes, the philosopher of *The Gay Science* is at once self-negating and theatrically self-affirming. *Unlike* the Cynic of settled 'character', he is driven by the idea of artistic growth, actively willing a higher future for the individual. He is not, himself, a figure of achieved liberation. The closing sections of the book weigh the question of how far it will ever really be possible to free oneself from conventional ideas, especially in the sphere of morality. Any attempt to stand outside morality and see the moral system of Europe from a distance means endeavouring to command, or rid oneself of, 'value judgements that have become part of our flesh and blood', §380 reflects. The philosopher (now designated 'The wanderer') seems here to be looking to export Cynicism from its ancient role as a form of critique internal to the society, performing its work in the central marketplace, to make it serve the purposes of a more radical detachment. The philosophic wanderer must 'leav[e] the town' to see it in its true proportions (to gauge 'the height of its towers', as Nietzsche puts it [§380]). Like the original Cynics, he must be divested of 'many things that oppress, inhibit, hold down, and make heavy'. The hardest thing of all to shed may be the posture, the instinct perhaps, of antagonism itself: one's 'aversion and opposition *against*' one's own time; one's 'suffering from this time', one's 'untime-liness' and '*romanticism*'. One must, in short, free oneself from oneself, where once Cynicism looked to take oneself back to oneself, to one's 'nature'.

Nietzsche's modern, strategically invoked, Cynic thus remains true to the element in ancient Cynicism that would a few decades later appeal most strongly to Jung: the ability of its radical individualism to import resistance to what 'individualism' normally implies in the way of a charismatic forging of one's own values. To the limited extent that the figures or masks of the philosopher in late Nietzsche remain in touch with Cynicism, they signal through it a hostility to the idea of the exemplary individual, historical or literary, as much as they signal the allure of free-speaking antipathy to convention. The exemplary type can only be anathema to a body of writing directed towards the goal of living a life that will be, as far as possible, not just self-asserting but heroically self-transforming.

If it remains tempting, as it may well do, to look beyond the *tolle Mensch* to Zarathustra as Nietzsche's subsequent effort to figure forth such a philosophical life, even keeping in view his own caveats against providing models for emulation, there are warnings aplenty to step very cautiously. Residual elements of Diogenes are not hard to find in Zarathustra—living a radically simpler life than the majority of his kind; consorting with animals; drawn especially to dogs and they to him; charismatic yet uninterested in commanding or even teaching others, repeatedly leaving his hermetic retreat to re-engage with the world only to retreat again. Like the ancient Cynics, he is a figure drawn to the goal of a radical self-reliance. More to the point, however, are the ways in which this dramatization of the philosopher as poetic prophet departs from the Cynic's investment in the idea of living in accordance with his 'truth'. There is no authenticity to be found in human 'nature', as Zarathustra sees it. He strenuously resists the 'bovine contentment', the lack of a will for self-transformation, that (in keeping with *The Birth of Tragedy*) he associates with the pursuit of happiness. And he understands early on that what he offers in its stead will find little traction with the philosophy-reading public.

The role of Cynicism in helping to draw the limit of the philosopher's public authority, and secure his avoidance of exemplarity, crystallizes briefly, in a famous scene where Zarathustra addresses a crowd gathered in the marketplace. His audience is distracted by a tightrope walker who falls suddenly, scattering the watchers. Kneeling beside the dying man, Zarathustra sees in the man's actions a more compelling demonstration of the 'sense of [our] existence' than any lesson the philosopher might endeavour to convey in words. To the tightrope walker, he gives a reassurance that he, Zarathustra, is no devil luring him to hell: nothing awaits beyond the point of death. The tightrope walker fears that he has received a last-minute Cynic lesson in the untranscendable materiality of human existence: 'If you speak the truth . . . I am not much more than an animal that has been taught to dance by blows and little treats.' Not so, Zarathustra reassures him: 'you have made your vocation out of danger, and there is nothing contemptible about that' (First Part, §6). Zarathustra is, at this moment, a more compassionate figure than the *tolle Mensch*, but the tie to Cynicism is still visible. Both figures are constructed out of a lingering, pointedly ambivalent debt to the Diogenes type. Historically defunct, ignobly reductionist in his conception of the 'human', the Cynic plays a part, but only a minor part, in articulating the modern philosopher's commitment to a higher future for humanity.

'Oh, sky above me', Zarathustra sighs, enraptured, at a later point in his wanderings, as he turns his back on mere 'happiness': 'Gazing at you I shudder with godlike desires!' He then reflects on the antagonisms that have goaded him onward in the past: 'Whom did I hate more,' he asks, 'than drifting clouds and everything that stains you? . . . I would much rather sit in the barrel [*der Tonne*] under a closed sky, would rather sit in the abyss without sky, than see you, sky of light, stained by drifting clouds' (Third Part, §XLIII).[43]

Like so much of the symbolic writing in late Nietzsche, it is an image of philosophy endorsing the highest possible aspirations for humanity (an 'awesome and infinite saying of Yes and Amen' [§XLIII]), but compelled, for their

---

[43] I have used the Cambridge translation (131) as the base, here, but have restored the 'much' before 'rather'—'*Lieber will ich noch unter verschlossnem Himmel in der Tonne sitzen*'—and preferred the literal 'the barrel' to 'a barrel', with its clearer pointer to Diogenes. Also the more correct and idiomatic 'the abyss' for 'an abyss'. Thomas Common's 1909 translation is syntactically closer to the German: 'Rather will I sit in a tub under a closed heaven, rather will I sit in the abyss without heaven, than see thee, thou luminous heaven, tainted with passing clouds!' Friedrich Nietzsche, *Thus Spake Zarathustra: A Book for All and None*, ed. and trans. Thomas Common (Edinburgh: T. N. Foulis, 1909), 200.

articulation, to go back to the unsatisfactory 'rag-and-bone shop' of the human condition, as Yeats would have it. For a short space of time, Zarathustra chooses the Cynic tub, confining himself within its limits, as within the limits of the old language of religion, in preference to any evident reduction of the light aspired to—but all the while willing, and waiting on, a better philosophical mode.

The Genealogical Debasement of Morality

What, then, of Cynicism's role in the genealogy of morality? Here its presence goes beyond facilitating philosophical 'free-spiritedness' to touch on the definition of morality itself: what it is, where it comes from, how far we can, and should want, to be free of it. Though the reductive 'character' of the Cynic plays in here, too, the role of Cynicism in the genealogy has more to do with Cynic *tactics* and their evident limitations than with the deployment of the Cynic as mouthpiece in some kind of relation, however strongly ironized, to the philosopher himself.

That we have 'moral prejudices'[44] is, famously, of less interest to Nietzsche than where those prejudices come from. By 'moral prejudices', we should understand not *unwarranted biases within our systems of morality, viewed from a correct moral perspective* but *prejudices in favour of thinking as we now do morally*. The fundamental focus on how we came to be moral in the way we did puts the Nietzschean genealogy of morality in a distinctive relation to Cynicism: at once closely indebted to its characteristic modes of 'debasing the moral currency' and importantly askew from them.

The genealogist of the descent of morality makes his first appearance in *Human, All Too Human*, with a recurrent denial of the conventionally assumed motives for morality that is, so far as the manner of reasoning goes, thoroughly Cynical: 'He who has the power to requite, good with good, evil with evil... is called good; he who is powerless and cannot requite counts as bad' (I, 45).[45]

And again: 'Justice goes back naturally to the viewpoint of an enlightened self-preservation, thus to the egoism of the reflection: "to what end should I injure myself uselessly and perhaps even then not achieve my goal"' (I, 92). That is: 'good' and 'bad' are the names originally given to the power (or the absence of the power) to repay another person's actions; justice (more sophisticated) arises when the power balance between me and the other person is roughly equal and I deem it in my interests to satisfy their demands of me. What drives morality, here, is not virtue, or a desire to see good people or good acts prevail and bad people or bad

---

[44] Friedrich Nietzsche, *On the Genealogy of Morality and Other Writings*, ed. Keith Ansell-Pearson, trans. Carol Diethe (Cambridge: Cambridge University Press, 2017), 4.

[45] Friedrich Nietzsche, *Human, All Too Human*, trans. R. J. Hollingdale, intro. by Erich Heller (Cambridge: Cambridge University Press, 1986), 36–7.

acts frustrated, but self-interest latching on to a disparity in power and weighing the advantages and disadvantages of reaction. 'Our present morality', as Nietzsche represents it in *Human, All Too Human*, is the collective psychological and behavioural playing out, from pre-history, of self-interest—self-preservation and competitive self-advancement—within the framework of social hierarchies.

The 'Cynicism' rhetorically at work here lies in identifying hidden motives that are not just *other* but (from the perspective of our current morality) *lower* (in the eyes of the conventional) than those we standardly attach to moral behaviour, thereby looking to destabilize the currency of our attachments. As the genealogy becomes further elaborated over the course of Nietzsche's writings leading up to *On the Genealogy of Morality* (1887) and the revised text of *The Gay Science* in the same year, the logic of debasement becomes locally more intensive, rhetorically sharper.

Here, for example, is *Human, All Too Human*, on the moral relation with one's neighbour: '—If there were no curiosity, little would be done to further the wellbeing of one's neighbour. But curiosity creeps into the house of the unfortunate or needy under the name of duty or pity' (§363).

Here is *Daybreak: Thoughts on the Prejudices of Morality*: 'The compassionate Christian:—The reverse side of Christian compassion for the suffering of one's neighbour is a profound suspicion of all the joy of one's neighbour, of his joy in all that he wants to do and can' (1. 80).

And here is *Beyond Good and Evil* (1886), on the impossibility of any morality of 'love thy neighbour': 'In the final analysis, "love of one's neighbour" is always something secondary, partly conventional and arbitrarily illusory in relation to *fear of the neighbour*' (§201).[46]

In each case, and with increasing pungency, a quality to which modern cultures have agreed to give the name and value of a virtue—concern for a neighbour's well-being—is reread as something other than virtue and, from today's dominant moral perspectives, less admirable. The rhetorical effect, at full force, is one of unmasking. By such routes, 'duty' can be decoded as 'restoration of wounded self-regard' (*Daybreak*, II. 112), 'striving for distinction' as 'assault on another' (II, 113); fear can be said to be 'the mother of morals' (*BGE*, 201). We think we are doing *this* but more truthfully we are doing *that*; we think we want *this*, but we 'rather' want (or don't want) *that*; quality (a) is in reality derived from, 'secondary, partly conventional and arbitrary' by comparison with quality (b).

Some of the genealogy's work of explanation has a claim to be 'history', Bernard Williams observes; much of it is a 'helpful fiction'.[47] It is especially germane to the

---

[46] I have preferred Carol Diethe's translation, which is closer to the German than Judith Norman's (and others') on this occasion; see 'Supplementary Material' to *On the Genealogy of Morality*, 152.

[47] Bernard Williams, *Truth and Truthfulness: An Essay in Genealogy* (Princeton, NJ: Princeton University Press, 2002), 19.

focus on Cynicism that Nietzschean genealogy so often mimics, in its story-telling, the aims and methods of evolutionary anthropology. When *Human, All Too Human* asks us to think of justice 'go[ing] back naturally to enlightened self-preservation' (I.92) or *Beyond Good and Evil* tells us that 'it is utterly impossible that a person might *fail* to have the qualities and propensities of his elders and ancestors in his body' (§264), these early writings on morality are, like evolutionary anthropology, running with the trope of genealogy as a form of temporally articulated inquiry into the prompts of human behaviour. For Nietzsche, the exercise is critical not descriptive: a crucial function of the genealogy is to forge a connection between the quasi-historical work of thinking backwards through 'earlier' conceptual stages of our psychological outlook (philological work, of a kind, applied to the explanation of morals rather than to texts) and the philosopher's present-day work of freeing the individual from the grip of 'dead' ways of thinking to enable a freer, 'higher' future. (Morality, in a much quoted phrase, has 'grown up in the soil of the *ruling* tribes and castes' where 'the individual' can never flourish [I, 45; see also *Human, All Too Human* II.45].) In both the backward-looking explanatory and present-day liberatory endeavours, 'Cynic' styles of argument and Cynic modelling of defiant, free-speaking individualism provide a set of philosophic tools. The fitness-for-purpose of those tools is greater on the first count than on the second; in neither case are they presented as satisfactory.

Certain sections of the genealogical writings take pronounced relish in Cynic manoeuvring: the core gambit of debasing the moral currency by calling out the supposedly ubiquitous operation of self-interest; the charismatic stylistic sharpness—'biting' wit, epigrammatic sayings, strong ironies, sarcastic turns. 'What really are our reactions to the behaviour of someone in our presence?', asks *Daybreak* at the start of a much-quoted rhetorical flourish often made to stand as a kind of epigraph for the entire genealogical project:

> —First of all, we see what there is in it *for us*—we regard it only from this point of view. We take *this* effect as the *intention* behind the behaviour—and finally we ascribe the harbouring of such intentions as a *permanent quality* of the person whose behaviour we are observing and thenceforth call him, for instance, 'a harmful person'. Threefold error! Threefold primeval blunder! Perhaps inherited from the animals and their power of judgement! Is the *origin of all morality* not to be sought in the detestable petty conclusions: 'what harms *me* is something *evil* (harmful in itself); what is useful *to me* is something *good* (beneficent and advantageous in itself); what harms me *once or several times* is the inimical as such and in itself'.   (*Daybreak* I, §102)

'*O pudenda origo*', §102 pronounces: 'oh shameful origin' of morality. The moral texture of our psychological relations with others *goes back*, or *comes down*, in this locally elaborated Cynic interpretation, to the 'detestable' as-it-were-primal rationales of pursuing our own advantage and avoiding harm: we judge the other by whether s/he serves our self-interest or harms it; we ascribe to that other, falsely, an *intention* to serve or harm our self-interest; we make that attribution of intention the basis of a permanent characterization of the other as 'dangerous', 'evil', 'hostile', 'injurious'. By such mental operations, we over-interpret the 'merely accidental relations' others have with us, and make ourselves, with immodest folly, 'the standard of what is good' and evil.

The reduction of self-other relations to the projections of egoism is clear enough, but what is the appropriate *response* to the genealogist's disclosure? 'Moral indignation' is a sure sign that the philosopher has lost his 'sense of philosophical humour', *Beyond Good and Evil* warns (II.25), and there are goads aplenty here to prompt the reader's recognition that it would equally be a failing on the part of the reader—further evidence of morality's psychological and cultural grip. This is, after all, a passage whose provocations may be such that they take one's eye off the speculative cast of the claims ('perhaps...'; 'Is [this] not...'). Employing strategies of reduction to egoism, the genealogist is never-theless looking to incorporate recognition that 'this whole antithesis between "egoistic" and "unegoistic"' is itself a sign that morality has taken hold (*On the Genealogy of Morals*, I.2). Irony and other strategies of stylistic estrangement thus have an open door. With respect to §102, as with so much of Nietzsche, one ignores the presence of literary burlesque at one's peril. Aping the voice of outraged conventionality, the prose looks for an injection of scepticism towards its own authority at just the point where a reader may be predisposed, if not to resist the psychologist's disclosures about morality, then to have recourse to morality in appraising them.[48] Like the ventriloquization of the 'primeval blunder itself' ('whatever harms *me* is something *evil*', etc.), the ventriloquization of modern 'shame' holds the moralizing response at bay. It asks us to entertain that response at a remove—as irony or comedy or both. Pippin is right that the '*O pudenda origo*' gesture of unmasking is continuous with the tradition of La Rochefoucauld and others in that long Enlightenment inheritance of Cynicism, and as such it registers a familiar sceptic demand for 'clarity about human frailty and failings'.[49] But the prose is also, and it may be disconcertingly, stylistically agile and mimetically '*de trop*' in ways that even La Rochefoucauld is not. Its

---

[48] An alternative way of phrasing the more general point here is that, whatever Nietzsche's scepticism amounts to, it has to be compatible with his constant claim that the philosophers of the future will 'wear masks'. The masks (as Fred Rush puts it) are 'not for hiding: they are to make patent that, given any purported appearance of something beneath, there is always something presupposed (for every *Begründung* an *Abgrund*) (*Beyond Good and Evil*, §§289, 295)'.

[49] Robert Pippin, 'How to Overcome Oneself: Nietzsche on Freedom', in Ken Gemes and Simon May (eds.) *Nietzsche on Freedom and Autonomy* (Oxford: Oxford University Press, 2009), 69–87 (74). And on La Rochefoucauld, see Faber, 'Metamorphosis of the French Aphorism'.

Cynicisms come laced with a relish for mimicry that goes beyond the intellectual requirements for clarity.

The implication is that *reasoning about morality*, as much as *morality* itself, has become imprisoning, bound by 'cords that seem almost unbreakable' (*Human, All Too Human*, Preface, 3). The genealogical texts accordingly work hard to prevent morality simply ceding the floor to intellectual judgement. Nietzsche gives frequent vent to castigatory statements (like that in *Daybreak*) that treat our conventional belief in morality as a kind of 'primitive' incompetence in psychological reasoning. The *excess* of the denunciation wards off the more general error: the tendency of philosophers to 'make the whole cosmos out of th[e] intellectual faculty' (*Human, All Too Human*, I, 2). 'Primeval blunder', 'not much better than the judgements of animals!', 'detestable petty conclusions!' We don't strictly need the emotional excess of any of this—of 'blunder' or 'detestable' or 'petty', or for that matter 'primeval' and 'animal-worthy'—but such hyperbolic notes create a stylistic intimacy between the ravelling work of morality and the unravellings of philosophy that should put us on our guard against both. They warn us against the tenacity of morality as we have inherited it *and* against any claim the philosopher might want to make to avoid error and afford a value perspective that we could call 'true'.

I follow in the wake, here, of Alexander Nehamas, Sarah Kofman, Robert Pippin, Henry Staten, and others who have drawn attention to the implications of Nietzsche's hyper-literariness: that extravagant 'stylistic pluralism' by which (in Nehamas's phrase) his writing 'denies the possibility of . . . eliminat[ing] illusion and falsification', while recognizing (and, perhaps, meeting halfway) our persistent attraction to illusions.[50] It is in this light that we can best interpret the metaphorical flexibility with which Nietzsche depicts the work of 'debasing' conventional morality. The Cynic association with coinage is occasionally in play. The *Genealogy*, for example, sources the original investment of value in the idea of the 'good' to those powerful ones who 'first took for themselves the right to create values, to coin names for values' (*Namen der Werthe auszuprägen*) (I.2);[51] *Beyond Good and Evil* is pithier: 'in the world of historical values, counterfeit rules'; or, in Helen Zimmern's 1907 translation, 'spurious coinage PREVAILS'[52] (§269). Translators have sometimes taken it upon themselves to introduce the association, going beyond the German original, as when John

---

[50] Nehamas, *Nietzsche: Life as Literature*, 18, 61. See also Pippin, *Nietzsche, Psychology, & First Philosophy*; 'Figurative Philosophy in Nietzsche's *Beyond Good and Evil*' (13 May 2017), <https://www.youtube.com/watch?v=j_1OSwcS37M>. Accessed 28 February 2019; Christopher Janaway, *Beyond Selflessness: Reading Nietzsche's* Genealogy (Oxford: Clarendon Press, 2007); and Lawrence Hatab, *Nietzsche's* On the Genealogy of Morality: *An Introduction* (Cambridge: Cambridge University Press, 2008).

[51] Del Caro's translation is closest to the original German here: Nietzsche, *Beyond Good and Evil/On the Genealogy of Morality*, trans. Adrian del Caro (Stanford, CA: Stanford University Press, 2014), 219.

[52] *Beyond Good and Evil* (1907), 245.

McFarland Kennedy renders *Daybreak*'s sigh of regret, prompted by overvalu-ation of 'altruism'—'*wie immer die ganze Niedertracht unserer lieben Thierwelt heisst, in der wir leben*'—as the 'odious expressions which the beautiful animal world in which we live chooses to coin' (§147) (this takes a very liberal way with the verb *heissen*, to name).

But Nietzsche is at least as interested in alternative applications of 'base'. *Human, All Too Human* (I, 1) asks us to consider the idea in its chemical-structural sense:

> Alles, was wir brauchen...ist eine **Chemie** der moralischen, religiösen, ästhetischen Vorstellungen und Empfindungen,...wie, wenn diese Chemie mit dem Ergebniss abschlösse, dass auch auf diesem Gebiete die herrlichsten Farben aus **niedrigen**, ja verachteten Stoffen gewonnen sind?
>
> All we require...is a *chemistry* of the moral, religious and aesthetic conceptions and sensations...what if this chemistry would end up by revealing that in this domain too the most glorious colours are derived from base, indeed from despised materials?[53]

The English translation allows for easy slippage between the language of chemistry and the language of morality, from chemical 'base' to what is judged 'base...and indeed...despised'. There is no such ready connection in German between '*niedrigen*' and '*verachteten*', rather an experimental metaphoric reconfiguration of the problem of approaching an explanation for the psychological hold of morality. Associated with chemistry, the 'base' might seem to describe psycho-logical structures without particular consideration for their temporal develop-ment,[54] but here too Nietzsche is interested in 'descent': how 'glorious colours' may have derived 'from base, indeed from despised materials'. To be a chemist of morality would be, by analogy, to have technical expertise in the reverse-engineering of solutions or compounds, recovering a 'basic element' that appeared 'almost to have dispersed' (*verflüchtigt*) (I.1).[55]

More often than not the metaphors evoke the hypothetico-deductive reasoning of evolutionary psychology and linguistics.[56] Imagining the earliest interactions of

---

[53] *Human, All Too Human* (1996), 12.

[54] Cf. Todd Gooch, 'Atheism', in Michael N. Forster and Kristin Giesdal (eds.), *The Oxford Handbook of German Philosophy* (Oxford: Oxford University Press, 2015), 829–51 (846). Gooch points out the multiple scientific influences making conceivable Nietzsche's call for 'a *chemistry* of the moral [and other] conceptions', but does not distinguish between the temporally and non-temporally articulated.

[55] The Stanford edition has 'in which the fundamental element appears to have almost evaporated' (15).

[56] On Nietzsche's interaction with contemporary work in the life sciences, see Thomas H. Brobjer, *Nietzsche and Science* (London: Routledge, 2017); Gregory Moore and Thomas H. Brobjer, *Nietzsche and Science* (Aldershot: Ashgate, 2004); Christian J. Emden, *Nietzsche's Naturalism: Philosophy and the Life Sciences in the Nineteenth Century* (Cambridge: Cambridge University Press, 2014).

human beings within social formations ('simplified' for the genealogy's purpose),[57] Nietzsche plays with the model of a progressive sophistication in 'primitive' or 'prehistoric' names and concepts—from those belonging to the 'wild beast' phase to more finely tuned perceptions of agency (*Beyond Good and Evil*, 229). 'A *high* degree of humanization had first to be achieved', the *Genealogy* tells us, so that 'the animal "man"' could begin to differentiate' between 'much more primitive nuances' of causality than are apparent in 'guilt' and 'retribution' alone (2.4). A long list of 'primitive nuances' is then specified—more finely graded assessments of responsibility, investing value in new concepts or 'names': '"intentional", "negligent", "accidental", "of sound mind" and their opposites'). Once again, the performativity of the metaphoric handling (with another rash of distantiating quotation marks) holds any truth claim at bay.

Notwithstanding the insistent undermining of 'truth', something important is being said about what it means to argue on the grounds of what is or is not natural to human beings ('the terrible basic text of *homo natura* must again be recognized', *Beyond Good and Evil*, §230 intones). The natural condition to which the genealogy takes us back is not a given. Sarah Kofman puts the point eloquently (her Derridean affiliations very much in evidence):

> When Nietzsche writes that one must reconstitute behind every text the original text *homo natura*, that does not mean finding a text cut off from all interpretation, a 'being in itself', an ontological truth. On the contrary, it means he is going against a metaphysical reading which conceals the text as interpretation behind the rags it has woven. Unmasking the metaphysical illusion does not mean removing from the text a cloak veiling the truth;... it means showing the clothing which an apparent 'nakedness' conceals... seeing [the spirit of the text, its 'body'] as a falsified and distorted inscription of the instinctive writing of the will to power.[58]

The tension thus generated in the term 'instinct', as it comes loose from its temporary moorings in the biological sciences, to point the reader towards the act of interpretation and evaluation 'which aims at power', shows clearly in Nietzsche's argumentative handling of *ressentiment* as instinct gone wrong. Part 1 of the *Genealogy* observes that the 'herd instinct' which drove adoption of morality as a common currency of Christian societies was not always in the ascendancy: it took 'long enough' for it to become 'sufficiently dominant' for the 'valuation of moral values' to stick (1.2). Morality's hard-won dominance came at the price of 'old instincts', 'healthier' instincts than the herd instinct—those of 'the

[57] Williams, *Truth and Truthfulness*, 21.
[58] Sarah Kofman, *Nietzsche and Metaphor*, trans. with an Introduction, Additional Notes, and a Bibliography by Duncan Large (London: Athlone Press, 1993), 92.

wild, free, roving man', which (Part 2 tells us) were gradually forced under (2.16). Denied an outlet for their expression, over time, those instincts 'turn[ed] creative' (1.10) and began to work inwardly *against man himself* in the form of 'bad conscience' (2.16)—a 'forcible breach' of man 'with his animal past' (2.16).

For Nietzsche, instinct itself 'evolves'. The point is made right at the start of the genealogical project in *Human, All Too Human*, though it is not until the *Genealogy* that it finds a full temporal articulation: 'the philosopher ascribes "instinct" to contemporary man and assumes that this is one of the unalterable facts regarding man himself, ... Yet everything evolved: there are no eternal facts as there are no absolute truths' (*Human, All Too Human*, II, 2). The same must then be true of the concept of 'evolution'. There are specific dangers attached to this metaphorical terrain. If instinct is going to mislead us, Richard Schacht suggests, it is not only because we may overvalue the interpretations offered by the natural sciences, but because, in that context, it may suggest a power untouched by what is 'higher'. Clearly, it is defined in opposition to 'the labored, uncertain and fumbling "consciousness" operative in non-instinctive action', but that opposition is as far as the metaphor safely takes us. When Nietzsche sets his sights on a 'higher freedom' for humanity, 'instinct' is, indeed, the internal driver he envisages taking us there. What is sought is an intelligent movement forward, an *advance beyond* non-instinctive action so that the 'hesitancy and clumsiness' of non-instinctive action are overcome, 'but *not* the intentionality and awareness'.[59]

In one perspective, 'instinct' is subject to historical change, capable of developments and refinements, most of which are deemed to have been, hitherto, 'unhealthy' (as Schacht observes, Nietzsche associates development, in this view, with an increase in complexity that has produced a decline in fitness of civilized humanity: the '"highest types" ... by virtue of their very complexity and accumulated energy may be the most fragile and unstable and therefore the least durable' (256). Later nineteenth-century theories of degeneration are evidently in play here.)[60] In the other perspective, however, there remain 'primal' instincts: *un*changing and indispensable to 'the total health of the people', the instincts for 'health, future, growth, power, life' (*The Gay Science*, Preface §2).

These (as it were) continuous instincts play a larger but also an increasingly freer part in the later works as Nietzsche starts to invest less in debasing arguments and more in the positive effort at a revaluation of our values needed for man to reach 'his *highest potential power and splendour*' (Preface, 6). For that, he tells us, we need to tap back into, or as he puts it much more expressively, encourage the

[59] Richard Schacht, *Nietzsche* (London: Routledge, 1983), 280 (my emphasis).
[60] See Steven E. Aschheim, 'Max Nordau, Friedrich Nietzsche and *Degeneration*', *Journal of Contemporary History* 28/4 (1993), 643–57; and Steven E. Aschheim, *The Nietzsche Legacy in Germany 1890–1990* (Berkeley, CA: University of California Press, 1992).

'external discharge' of healthy instincts. (This is surely part-parody and not simple endorsement of contemporary medicine.)[61] 'Every naturalism in morality', *Twilight of the Idols* asserts, '—which is to say: every *healthy* morality—is governed by an instinct of life.'[62] There are two main spheres in which Nietzsche invites us to imagine the desired liberation: art and politics. Both put further pressure on the neo-Cynic attachment to what is 'natural' and, indeed, what is 'healthy'. In the case of art, liberated instinct, 'higher naturalness',[63] will see a flourishing of 'joyful' creativity, realizing 'larger and higher (interpretive, creative, competitive, etc.) intentions and values'.[64] Nietzsche's 'favourite model', Nehamas rightly notes, is 'that of the artist who finds the greatest freedom and the most natural state to be the result of strict and subtle obedience to a "thousandfold" laws that are internalized and finally become instinctive' (47; quoting *Beyond Good and Evil*, 188). In the case of politics, it is less easy to say what 'higher naturalness' would amount to, but the key role of instinct in determining 'health' is consistent. In the *Genealogy*, Nietzsche's theory of the forces that led to the creation of the political state is presented as a kind of analogy 'on a grand scale' with the forces that produced morality (2.18). The 'artists of violence and organisers' who brought the political state into being were, the *Genealogy of Morality* tells us, operating instinctively to 'create and imprint forms' (2.18). 'Ignorant of the meaning of guilt, responsibility, consideration', they were 'master[s] by nature', bringing 'live' schemes of sovereignty straight into existence. The 'formative and rapacious' forces of 'secret self-violation' that generate *ressentiment* are 'at bottom' the same, only inward- rather than outward-working in their direction: 'an identical *instinct of freedom*', 'constructive' and 'tyrannous', is 'let loose' in the 'labyrinth of the breast' (2.18).[65] *How* a 'Revaluation of All Values' in the political sphere will make the move from liberating instinct to constructing healthy social and political forms is never fully articulated, though various attempts have been made to flesh out the bones of Nietzsche's thinking.[66] 'To establish an

---

[61] For sources, in medicine and psychology, and (behind them) physics (esp. Mayer, Helmholtz, Joule, and special attention to the influence on Freud's circle, see Ronald Lehrer, 'Freud and Nietzsche, 1892–1895', in Jacob Golomb, Weaver Santaniello, and Ronald L. Lehrer (eds.), *Nietzsche and Depth Psychology* (Albany, NY: State University of New York Press, 1999), 181–204 (185–9).

[62] Friedrich Nietzsche, 'Morality as Anti-Nature', §4, in *The Anti-Christ, Ecce Homo, Twilight of the Idols, and Other Writings*.

[63] Schacht, *Nietzsche*, 280—channelling Nietzsche.   [64] Ibid., 281.

[65] This notoriously abusable, and historically abused, theory of state formation is an inevitable focus of attention for any attempt to rescue a positive account of Nietzsche's 'great politics'. See esp. R. Hinton Thomas, *Nietzsche in German Politics and Society, 1890–1918* (Manchester: Manchester University Press, 1983); Mark Warren, *Nietzsche and Political Thought* (Cambridge, MA: MIT Press, 1988); and Drochon, *Nietzsche's Great Politics*, on the implications of the claim that the state begins with an act of primal violence—cf. the Hobbesian social contract, 'thought up precisely to get away from this primal hostility' (59); also 98–9; and, on the continuing influence of Nietzsche's early thinking about Socrates as the corruptor of an archaic healthy instinctiveness, 31–2.

[66] In addition to Warren and Drochon, see esp. Staten, *Nietzsche's Voice*, Chapter 4; and cf. Tamsin Shaw, *Nietzsche's Political Skepticism* (Princeton NJ, Princeton University Press, 2007) on (as she sees it) Nietzsche's profound scepticism towards modern political legitimacy and political authority.

infrastructure...', reads a somewhat aspirational Notebook entry for 1887, 'on which becomes at last possible a *stronger* species...State and society as infrastructure: global economic viewpoint, education as breeding.'[67]

In the artistic and the political contexts alike, the Cynic move to 'debase the moral currency' comes under greater strain as Nietzsche looks more urgently to articulate a vision of the future. Where debasement, historically and logically, has carried economic connotations of a *loss* of value (a coinage that has been adulterated or chipped-away-at is worth less than its face value), Nietzsche puts that thought to work only as the first step towards the more important task of positive revaluation, creating new and higher values hereafter. The critical 'debasement' of conventional morality thus performs a strictly limited function. It exposes and undermines the 'arbitrary' valuations of a moral system that has thwarted older, healthier as-it-were original instincts; it may help to model an idea of free-speaking truthfulness (not of truth) and some other, closely related 'formal excellences' historically associated with it (freedom of self-rule, the will—and perhaps the capacity—to give form to one's own life);[68] its stylistic charisma may also be of some assistance, enhancing the appeal of the critique, and (perhaps) of the philosopher who delivers it. But the philosophical and psychological errors Cynicism entails are rarely out of sight with Nietzsche. Only with such curtailing of its authority is the field open for more creative and sophisticated instincts to flourish.

The pressure brought to bear on the idea of debasing morality towards an honest account of human 'nature' in the genealogical writings is not, of course, felt only through Nietzsche's increasingly strenuous efforts to recalibrate the meaning of 'instinct'. Other terms similarly offer at once to engage and to dislodge the standard implications of arguing by reference to what is natural: 'animal man', 'the animal past', 'primitive', 'prehistorical', 'primal or first'. In all such cases, we are cautioned against giving credence to received interpretations that would import biological determinism, let alone biological reductionism. It is in the seduction of the word 'instinct' towards simple hierarchical valuations (lower and higher, more and less primitive, healthier and less healthy) that the pressure to revalue, not dispense with, 'nature' (so important to the Cynics) shows most clearly. Nietzsche wants a perspective on morality that recognizes the fundamental role of physiological forces, states, functions, as conditioning but not determining human behaviour and understanding. The risk is that exploitation of the metaphorical terrain of instinct brings him close to making the 'natural' synonymous with the

---

Drochon draws also on an unpublished manuscript by Bernard Williams, 'Can There Be a Nietzschean Politics?' (see Drochon, Introduction, for a summary).

[67] Quoted in Drochon, *Nietzsche's Great Politics*, 35.
[68] See Edward Harcourt, 'Nietzsche and the Virtues', in Lorraine Besser-Jones and Michael A. Slote (eds.), *The Routledge Companion to Virtue Ethics* (New York: Routledge, 2015), 165–79 (175–6).

'socially conditioned'—only to have to call on something fundamental, 'universal and unconditional' (*Beyond Good and Evil*, 22) but not in any conventional sense 'natural', in human behaviour, that (in those strong enough, noble enough, possessed of sufficient will) presses for liberation.

How far, then, does the idea of 'human nature' have a usefulness for Nietzsche that provides a new licence for Cynicism (or even a licence for neo-Cynicism)? One way of reading Nietzsche sees naturalism as having residual authority in spite of so much that works to dislodge it. A problem arises, as Brian Leiter, for example, sees the question, from the *Genealogy*'s appeals to nature in the service of delivering a more accurate account of 'reality'. Nietzsche's genealogist 'appears to be very much interested in "the nature of things" as they *really* are, not simply as some arbitrary interpretation would have them be'. While it is correct, then, to say that the aim is 'critical not positive',[69] the distinction does not settle the kind and degree of naturalism in play and the extent of Nietzsche's reliance on it.[70] An element of positivity remains. Among the several sources of difficulty identified by Leiter, three are worth bringing forward in this context: (i) Nietzsche does not establish that hatred, *ressentiment* and the other emotions that are held to have driven morality in the past still possess (deep down) the causal role, or motivating power, ascribed to them in the genealogy; (ii), relatedly, it is not at all clear from his description how much continuity the genealogical method requires between motives that had sway in the past and those that drive moral behaviour now; and, (iii) one looks in vain to Nietzsche for evidence, or a more complete argument, to establish that we *suffer* from our enrolment in morality as he plainly takes it we do.[71]

The last of these problems might be answered by a quick look around at Nietzsche's society. The first two rather go with the terrain of a mode of argument that wants to tell more than one kind of story about humanity and apply that story to a corrective purpose. Sublimating 'primal' drives into 'sophisticated' morals, the genealogy tells an anthropological-evolutionary story about how human behaviour came to be as it is. To that story it appends an optimistic, but necessarily more gestural account of what humanity might be, if freed from the errors that have become habitual to it. As Leiter cuts through the difficulties: the repeated invoking of 'shameful origins' may best be understood with the aid of a phrase from that problematic (because not reliably Nietzschean) text *The Will to Power*: 'by revealing the "shameful origin"' of [morality],[72] the *Genealogy*...brings a *feeling of*

[69] Brian Leiter, *The Routledge Philosophy Guidebook to Nietzsche on Morality* (London: Routledge, 2002), 167.
[70] On this much-debated topic, see esp. Williams, *Truth and Truthfulness*, 22–7.
[71] On (i) and (ii), see Leiter, *Routledge Philosophy Guidebook to Nietzsche on Morality*, 174; on (iii) 177–9.
[72] Leiter has 'MPS' at this point, or '"morality" in his pejorative sense'—his standard way of identifying morality as the object of Nietzsche's critique as distinct from its more general understanding.

diminution in value of the thing that originated thus and *prepares the way* to a critical mood and attitude toward it'.[73]

This invests quite a lot, still, in the technical and, in effect, logical capacity of the idea of debunking. We might remain closer to the spirit of Nietzsche's text if we borrow a metaphor from Amia Srinivasan, who writes of the 'vertigo' effect of the well-turned debunking argument, encouraging a change of ground.[74] With respect to psychology, the effect is 'realistic' rather than 'naturalistic'. There is pleasure, wit, appetite for the incongruity or excess of one's own rhetorical move here that seems truer to the positive imperatives of desire and aspiration in Nietzsche's late writing. One aim of the *Genealogy of Morality*, he writes, famously, at 2.1, is to teach us how 'nature' came to 'breed an animal with the prerogative to *promise*' (68), meaning a creature capable of orienting itself towards a future over which it can, in some degree, assert control: 'what a lot of preconditions there are for this! In order to have that degree of control over the future, one must first have learnt to distinguish between what happens by accident and what by design, to think causally, to view the future as the present and anticipate it...' (37).

The task of the philosopher, having grasped the present condition of morality through reconstruction of those preconditions, is to assist the future conditions for 'willing'—'suspend[ing] forgetfulness' (the 'inertia of habit' [First Essay, I]), opening the 'doors and windows of consciousness for a while', and running the risk that we will not be able to 'cope' (the cautionary quotation marks are there in the German) (36).[75] The later Nietzsche is constantly shifting expressive and psychological ground in the endeavour to realize such an opening out in his own philosophical practice. To exhibit a freeing of the will, 'giving earth its purpose and humans their hope again' (2.24), requires a philosophical voice capable of so radical a self-overcoming that what is said will be, the *Genealogy* tells us, metaphorically intimate with death—'a rebellion against the most fundamental prerequisites of life' (3.28).[76] At this point Nietzsche's late works have, clearly, left Cynicism behind, both in its attachment to a reductive account of Nature (and the ascetic practices the Cynic deemed appropriate to Nature) and in its sturdy animal contentment. Not 'coping', making a parade of one's dyspepsia and unhappiness and fraughtness, as the late works do, even as they put 'health'

[73] Leiter, *Routledge Philosophy Guidebook to Nietzsche on Morality*, 179; quoting *Will to Power* §254, second emphasis Leiter's. On the rhetorical purpose trumping critical clarity here, see 176–9.

[74] Amia Srinivasan, 'The Archimedean Urge', *Philosophical Perspectives* 29/1 (December 2015), 325–62 (341).

[75] A more literal translation of '*er wird mit Nichts "fertig"*' would be 'is not able to finish anything', the German '*mit etwas (nicht) fertig werden*' having a double meaning of 'to cope' but also 'to bring to an end, conclude, accomplish'. The Stanford edition has 'he cannot "finish" anything' (247).

[76] Simon May, 'Why Nietzsche Is Still in the Morality Game', in Simon May (ed.), *Nietzsche's* On the Genealogy of Morality: *A Critical Guide* (Cambridge: Cambridge University Press, 2011), 78–100 (78–9).

before us as a modern virtue,[77] is a way of making that departure rhetorically clear.

Bernard Williams identifies the crucial remaining question for the reader interested in the scope and quality of the genealogy's recourses to Cynicism: if these are the benefits of Cynicism (a recognized tool-kit for prizing open conventional thinking about morality; a long association with philosophical free-speaking; *épatant* reaches of philosophical style; a vocabulary for returning us— though we must be more critical here—to the idea of our 'nature'), what are the risks? And how seriously should we take them? What—and it need not be a *merely* Cynic question—is the cost-benefit ratio of Nietzschean Cynicism? In the Introduction to *The Gay Science* (2001), Williams reflects on the errors attaching to 'the reductive spirit':

> he is very clear that mere reductionism, the readily cynical explanation of all such attitudes in terms of self-interest, is a mistake. Partly this is because he does not think that self-interest is an individual's basic motive anyway,... But, more broadly, Nietzsche thinks that the reductive spirit itself can be in error, a form of vulgarity (3), and that the 'realists' who congratulate themselves on having the measure of human unreason and self-deception are usually themselves in the grip of some ancient fantasy.[78]

It is worth taking separately the brakes on Cynicism identified here, before asking in what spirit, given such reservations, Nietzsche has recourse nevertheless to Cynic strategies. The first rebuff to tactical reductionism of this kind, taking us back *as if to the natural state*, is that Cynicism—'the readily cynical explanation of [moral sentiments] in terms of self-interest'—has a very limited warrant for its conclusions. (This was and is, as we saw in the Introduction, the abiding problem with Cynicism—and, indeed, with its namesake in moral psychology, small-c cynicism.) As far as moral psychology goes, the effect is rather 'realistic' than 'naturalistic'.[79] The identification of 'self-interest' as 'an individual's basic motive' is too quick and too sweeping: a basic egoism can account for some of our motives, but not all. To this objection is added another: that the 'reductive spirit' is an error not just in reasoning but in intellectual taste, that comes of participation in the realist 'fantasy' that it is possible to get a grip on the 'unreason and self-deception'

---

[77] See Harcourt, 'Nietzsche and the "Aesthetics of Character", in May (ed.), *Nietzsche's On the Genealogy of Morality*, 265–84 (279–81), and Harcourt, 'Nietzsche and the Virtues', 176–7.

[78] Introduction to *The Gay Science*, ix.

[79] On this distinction, see Williams, 'Nietzsche's Minimalist Moral Psychology': 'Nietzsche's approach is to identify an excess of moral content in psychology by appealing first to what an experienced, honest, subtle, and unoptimistic interpreter might make of human behaviour elsewhere. Such an interpreter might be said to be—using an unashamedly evaluative expression—"realistic", and we might say that what this approach leads us towards is a realistic, rather than a naturalistic, moral psychology. What is at issue is ... an informed interpretation of some human experiences and activities in relation to others.' In Bernard Williams, *The Sense of the Past: Essays in the History of Philosophy*, ed. with an introduction by Myles Burnyeat (Princeton, NJ: Princeton University Press, 2006), 302.

that are reliable, generalizable traits of human beings (the realist supposing himself or herself to be the exception). I take it that, for Nietzsche, the second objection has more weight than the first, since the limitations of Cynic reasoning are (or ought to be) recognized and built into any use of the model today. The internal dialogue of the philosopher as tactician then goes something like this: *I, the modern philosopher of morality, know that Cynic debasement of values is an error; it is 'useful to me' even so in trying to move humanity forward; but how far, how long, do I want to go on associating with it, and do I not run the risk of falling victim to the fantasy of its supposed 'realism'?*

2

Speech Beyond Toleration

Moral Controversialism (Then and Now)

Caveat lector.

> It was International Women's Day on Wednesday of last week. The *Guardian* had enjoined its readers to send in reports of what they had done to advance the struggle, or how they had been in some way oppressed by men—perhaps raped, or talked to as if they were stupid, or looked at a little coldly when they squirted breast milk over fellow diners at The Ivy. I tried to think of something I had done for the cause but came up short, sad to say.
>
> So instead I tried to show solidarity by spending a substantial amount of International Women's Day looking at a photograph of Emma Watson's tits. The actress is a radical feminist campaigner and has even been given some kind of role at the United Nations to advance the cause of female liberation across the globe. Presumably as part of this drive to stop men regarding women as sex objects, Emma got her tits out for *Vanity Fair*.
>
> I have to say, I heartily approve. They seemed to me attractive and exquisitely English breasts [*&c.*] (Rod Liddle, 'What I did on International Women's Day', *The Spectator*, 11 March 2017)[1]

A significant aspect to present-day confrontations between those looking to shore up norms of acceptable public speech and their opponents is disagreement over how far transgressions should be tolerated by a healthily 'liberal' culture. Moral controversy makes a space for itself, as do some kinds of satire, in the gap between the tolerant and the intolerant. The defence, in theory (typically, both the controversialist and the satirist scorn to make it explicit), is that crossing the line of broadly agreed acceptability functions as a diagnostic test: those who move to sanction or censor the provocation, put their liberalism in doubt; those who react with laughter, or limit their protest to the restrained raising of an eyebrow, confirm their open-mindedness. It is to the point that disputants on either side of the divide will often object to appeals to 'tolerance' as the relevant principle. The

---

[1] <https://www.spectator.co.uk/2017/03/what-i-did-on-international-womens-day/>. Accessed 22 March 2017.

The Function of Cynicism at the Present Time. Helen Small, Oxford University Press (2020). © Helen Small.
DOI: 10.1093/oso/9780198861935.001.0001

person moved to protest against excessive licence may ask, for example, why tolerance should trump 'respect' or 'decency' or 'taste'. The person not so inclined may protest that laughter is, as Thomas Carlyle put it, the 'cipher-key':[2] where it operates, generosity takes precedence, moral judgementalism retreats.

Liddle's response to International Women's Day says less about the condition of feminism today (beyond a strong implication that 'the cause' may not be well served by a celebrity-struck media) than about the condition of a modern 'liberal culture', where the calculated offence provoked by his lingering over the sight of Emma Watson's 'tits' is guaranteed to hit a higher point on the public outrage barometer, beyond the readership of *The Spectator*, than her baring of them. This is rhetorically high-risk humour: a casual grammatical running together of 'the struggle' (the dated locution makes mockery of 'solidarity' on his part) with an undiscriminated list of offences against women (a naughty conflation of rape, casual disrespect, and the up-market diners' moue against implausibly misfired breast milk), hinting cynically that demonstrated commitment to 'the cause' on 8 March 2017 is no more than self-promotional display.

'What I Did on International Women's Day' is designed to bait left-leaning 'progressives' in a magazine that is a historic vehicle for such gestures, not always as closely allied to political conservatism as it has been in recent years. Liddle has a critical point—not confined to outlooks on the political right. Viewed from one direction, modern Western societies are freer than they were forty years ago (taking your top off no longer looks like much of a political act, especially when the image is curated by *Vanity Fair*); but, viewed from another, public toleration of moral controversialism, and of satire in some of its riskier forms, is not what it was. Christopher Hitchens, who may stand as the presiding spirit of intrepid liberty as it crosses the bounds of left-liberal consensus, narrows the grounds of Carlyle's observation when he asks us to think of 'wit' as 'the unfailing symptom of intelligence'.[3] That is almost certainly too self-serving, but it will appeal to anyone who sees danger in constraining the style and tenor as well as the content of 'opinion'. The joke, for those who find Liddle funny, is still on the putative feminist without a sense of humour; but it is also on *Vanity Fair*, on International Women's Day, on the UN, for having—apparently—not enough to evidence in the way of progress. (It would not be hard to do better, but the dig at the 'liberal media' rather depends on not trying. The intelligent reader who spends time on this material is, in effect, slumming it, laughing not so much at the 'wit' as at the thought of *Guardian* red lines being crossed and predictable sensitivities being predictably offended.)

[2] Thomas Carlyle, *Sartor Resartus: The Life and Opinions of Herr Teufelsdröckh*, in *The Works of Thomas Carlyle*, Centenary Edition (hereafter *CE*), 30 vols. (London: Chapman and Hall, 1896–99), I, 26.

[3] Christopher Hitchens, 'Why Women Aren't Funny', *Vanity Fair*, 1 January 2007, <http://www.vanityfair.com/culture/2007/01/hitchens200701>. Accessed 15 September 2019.

In the given case, an expansive tolerance can be assumed on the part of the primary audience: few readers will, one imagines, pick up *The Spectator* or click on its website without knowing its reputation. This is a long-established magazine (first issue, 6 July 1828) that has kept contact with the guiding ethos established by its Scottish founder-editor Robert S. Rintoul, who made it for a time 'one of the most politically influential weekly newspapers in Britain'.[4] At the time of his death, in 1858, *The Spectator* could fairly claim that it spoke to a 'class' of reader 'not affected by partisan spleen: its circulation being chiefly, as it must always aim to be, among the men of culture who like to listen to all sides of controversies'. There was a rider: 'provided the argument is conducted with fairness and moderation'.[5] On key political issues, Rintoul made his political position clear: immediate abolition of slavery was a cause dear to his heart, and he wrote repeatedly to that effect in 1831–32—yet he allowed his reviewers to back more gradualist reform.[6] Antedating the Liberalism of Gladstone, and indeed of the Liberal Party, this was a broad church radicalism that could admit advanced thinkers of the John Stuart Mill type alongside those who identified rather with the libertarian strand of Toryism. The latter strain is where (reputationally at least) the magazine now finds most of its following. With the exception of a significant period between 1858 and 1861 when it was hijacked by American interests to provide a platform against English abolitionism (seen as threatening the American Union),[7] it can claim to have been consistently hospitable, over its long history, to controversialism of the kind that resists pinning down to the libertarianism of the right.

But if the provocateurship of 'What I Did' makes sense within the traditions of its host magazine, it acquires an added edge of risk from Liddle's personal track record. Repeatedly the cause of legal and Press Complaints Commission proceedings against his employer, he has become a lightning conductor for arguments about whether and where the controversialist's goads distort 'radical liberalism' into bigotry.[8] I take him as a present-day point of entry to a problem of long standing that has, at present, more than usual urgency for our cultures of public argument: how to read and respond to the argumentative practices of the cynical rhetorician, operating as a moral and political provocateur in a context where it is vividly clear that the norms framing and regulating 'free speech' are disputed in principle, heavily context-dependent for their operation, and often violated in

---

[4] Richard Fulton, '*The Spectator* in Alien Hands', *Victorian Periodicals Review* 24/4 (Winter 1991), 187–96 (187).

[5] *The Spectator* 1 May 1858, 466. Quoted by Fulton, ibid., 187. The author was almost certainly Thornton Hunt (son of Leigh Hunt, and in effect Rintoul's sub-editor for many years).

[6] See Richard D. Fulton, 'Rintoul, Robert Stephen (1787–1858)', *Oxford Dictionary of National Biography* (2004). Accessed 26 September 2019.

[7] See Fulton, '*The Spectator* in Alien Hands'.

[8] For a more measured assessment than most, see Will Self, 'Why Is He So Angry?': Review of Rod Liddle, *Selfish, Whining Monkeys*, *The Guardian*, 22 May 2014, <https://www.theguardian.com/books/2014/may/22/selfish-whining-monkeys-rod-liddle-review>. Accessed 20 September 2019.

practice. Wider changes in the 'temperature' of the public sphere intensify the difficulties here. In a political climate of reaction against dampened or restricted self-expression, cynic provocations may appear more authentic for no better reason than that they violate soft norms (and sometimes hard laws)[9] about what ought to be said and how it may be said. They may also be, for many readers, simply more entertaining than sincerity—and the substitution of entertainment for truth-seeking allows cynicism of both the serious and the casual sort to flourish.

That there should be some expressive latitude available to 'liberty of opinion' was a principle endorsed by John Stuart Mill in his classic statement on the subject, *On Liberty* (1859). He was more demanding than is sometimes recalled in his insistence that 'free discussion' (233 and *passim*) means giving a hearing to opinions beyond the pale even of a capacious tolerance: 'The best government has no more title to [constrain freedom of opinion] than the worst ... If all mankind minus one, were of one opinion, and only one person were of the contrary opinion, mankind would be no more justified in silencing that one person, than he, if he had the power, would be justified in silencing mankind.'[10]

The lone dissenter will not always be persuasive but Mill gives him or her at least the prima facie right not to be shut down. What *On Liberty* requires of good government in the way of permissiveness, it requires all the more of the individual, who must listen keenly and constantly hold established authorities to the test of contrary views: 'In the case of any person whose judgment is really deserving of confidence, how has it become so? ... Because it has been his practice to listen to all that could be said against him' (41). The risk of constraining free speech is the falsification of the avowed commitment to liberty itself; the risk of failing to constrain it is that the liberal gate-keeper opens a door on views that may prove not only testing but toxic.

How to know the difference? In drawing attention to a particular kind of free speech 'offence'—moral controversialism that deploys cynic tactics to test the bounds and the seriousness of the society's liberalism—I am identifying an especially taxing category of discourse. Thanks to Amanda Anderson and others over recent years, the field of cultural criticism and theory now possesses sophisticated descriptions of the stylistic flexibility and complexity of modern liberalism's argumentative ethos as it developed over the course of the nineteenth and twentieth centuries (the doubts and negativities as well as optimism; the creative

[9] On this distinction, see Timothy Garton Ash, *Free Speech: Ten Principles for a Connected World* (London: Atlantic Books, 2016), 83–6.

[10] John Stuart Mill, *Essays on Politics and Society, Part I (On Liberty)*, in *The Collected Works of John Stuart Mill*, gen. ed. John M. Robson, 33 vols. (Toronto: University of Toronto Press; London: Routledge and Kegan Paul, 1963–91) [hereafter *CW*], XVIII, 229.

utopianism as well as prosaic rationalism).[11] The moral controversialist who uses cynicism to assert a more *radical* liberal outlook complicates matters: it is unclear how far so individualistic a gambit, protected though it is by its publishing context, generates something we are warranted in describing as an ethos—i.e. an effect owned by the social group and not just the particular speaker or writer who offers to overstep the bounds of licence even within his or her group. Liddle is a case in point: performances that go too far (I have chosen not to repeat the instances for which he and/or *The Spectator* have been fined and or for which apologies have been made) are liable to be portrayed as not of the ethos (narcissistic or temperamentally contrarian or just badly behaved, and in any event illegitimate).[12]

Cynic moral controversialism has a special claim to consideration within wider assessments of liberal free speech, on the grounds that it can appeal to a historic model and (I have been suggesting) a continuing psychological rationale for the disruption caused in the system: an apparently hostile challenge to conventionally held values and ideals serves the public (and, it may be, private) good (see Introduction, pp. 4, 6–8). Since not all freedoms of speech that violate agreed norms of expression are cynical, ascertaining the manner of address is crucial; reception of it even more so. The affront to the auditor—or to the auditor's views, if they are willing and able to see that distinction—is characteristic of the scene of cynic controversialism. It involves some cognizance of the other as an object of speech or discourse. Non-argumentative, uninterested in dialogue though the cynic is, s/he engages the addressee—in some cases, the self—who is at once the target of an affront and the recipient of a concealed offer of ethical assistance. There is, as Foucault puts it, a 'kind of pact' between the free-speaking cynic, or parrhesiast, and the person s/he addresses, 'which means that if the parrhesiast demonstrates his courage by telling the truth despite and regardless of everything, the person to whom this *parrhēsia* is addressed will have to

[11] See Amanda Anderson, *The Way We Argue Now: A Study in the Cultures of Theory* (Princeton, NJ: Princeton University Press, 2006) and Amanda Anderson, *Bleak Liberalism* (Chicago: University of Chicago Press, 2016). It is a measure of Anderson's influence especially, but also of the extent to which cultures of public argument in America and Britain have altered since the first of these books, that literary criticism and political thought today seem much less in need of persuasion that they *have* normative ethical dimensions than of clear differentiation between norms that are indispensable, and those that are contingent or relatively loose (perhaps flexible) agreements. For early criticism along these lines, see Stefan Collini, '"What, Ultimately, For?": The Elusive Goal of Cultural Criticism', *Raritan* 33/2 (2013), 4–26 (12). Also Bruce Robbins, 'On Amanda Anderson's *The Way We Argue Now*', *Criticism* 48/2 (2006), 265–71. For a more Victorian-focused treatment of these issues, see Elaine Hadley, *Living Liberalism: Practical Citizenship in Mid-Victorian Britain* (Chicago: University of Chicago Press, 2010).
[12] The distinction between 'ethos' and 'character' that has been the focus of much recent work within critical theory is one helpful way of articulating these interrelated components of argumentative practice: 'ethos', Amanda Anderson reminds us in *The Way We Argue Now*, is largely a matter of 'the ambient social conditions and norms that guide practice'; 'character' has more to do with 'the inculcation – and reflective cultivation – of values in the form of habits, dispositions, styles' (3n).

demonstrate his greatness of soul by accepting being told the truth'.[13] The terms of description generated around this effect are significantly not quite the same, though the basic insight is constant: Mill speaks of 'tolerance'; Carlyle of 'generosity'; Foucault avoids the judgementalism of the first term, and goes for a still larger poetic flourish than the second—'greatness of soul'.[14]

Distinctions must be made in how deep the cynicism goes. The modern cynic may be anti-normative in the sense that s/he is consciously rule-breaking but not rule-denying: acknowledging that certain norms command wide adherence, but testing the strength and latitude of those norms. (This is how *The Spectator* construes its contribution to public debate.)[15] Or s/he may be anti-normative in a more radical sense, denying the value of norms others consider settled. The impulse in that case may be merely contrarian; it may (as with Nietzsche) reflect alternative values; in the most problematic cases it emanates from denial of the existence of norms. Mill rightly considered such cases very rare. *Whatever* the philosophical depth of the challenge to convention, violation of the conventional terms of engagement tends to gain what political traction it finds from the 'authenticity' associated with refusing to play by the rules. Authenticity (it follows) may be a more or less calculated effect.[16]

Proponents of a deliberate illiberalism in speech or writing, testing rather than denying norms, are more likely than the intuitive controversialists to have exemplary models in view. Rod Liddle engages in a helpful piece of literary self-credentialling here:

[13] Michel Foucault, *The Courage of Truth (The Government of Self and Others II): Lectures at the Collège de France 1983–1984*, ed. Frédéric Gros, gen. eds. François Ewald and Alessandro Fontana, English ser. ed. Arnold I. Davidson, trans. Graham Burchell (London: Palgrave Macmillan, 2011), 12–13.

[14] There is some irony in the flourish, given that Foucault explicitly states that the 'rhetor' cannot be a parrhesiast, and is for that reason (as so often) in the inferior role: 'rhetoric does not entail any bond, a bond of power between what is said and the person to whom it is said. Rhetoric is the exact opposite of *parrhēsia*, [which entails a] strong, manifest, evident foundation between the person speaking and what he says...' Foucault is, by his own account, working 'very schematically' here, with the definitions and practices of 'Antiquity'. Ibid., 13. The schematism is, as I see it, rather less valid when applied to practices in the modern period, where Cynic free speech has become one among other styles available to the rhetorical writer.

[15] See the magazine's formal statement of purpose: 'Our writers'...only allegiance is to clarity of thought, elegance of style, and independence of opinion'; also a comment, drawn from an interview with its current editor Fraser Nelson (like many of his predecessors, of Scottish origin), 'If *The Spectator* can be said to have a radical cause—in the present [Brexit-dominated] context—it is freedom of speech.' 'We're the magazine for the queen and the scaffolder', interviewed by Emily Hill, *Spiked*, 13 September 2019, <https://www.spiked-online.com/2019/09/13/were-the-magazine-for-the-queen-and-the-scaffolder/>—referring the reader to David Butterfield, *The Spectator: A Historical Sketch* (forthcoming 2020).

[16] For discussion by someone at the editorial front line, see Mark Thompson, 'Trump, Brexit, and the Broken Language of Politics', lecture delivered at Hertford College, University of Oxford, 17 March 2017, <https://www.hertford.ox.ac.uk/alumni/hertford-today/john-donne-lectures/mark-thompson>. Accessed 23 March 2017.

Now that post-Marxian vacuous liberalism is over, it is surely about time that we revived the vigorous writings of Thomas Carlyle and made him fashionable once again. He is too little read and admired these days, perhaps partly on account of his arguably controversial treatise 'Occasional Discourse on the Negro Question' (1849)—which, while well intentioned, may nonetheless these days ruffle one or two feathers on our university campuses, or within the BBC. But there was of course a lot more to Thomas Carlyle than simply a benign, if misguided, wish to abolish slavery while keeping a few blacks on as indentured house servants. He was very astringent on celebrity culture, economics, the French revolution and, perhaps most importantly, prisons.[17]

If one is looking to model moral and political rhetoric that, as a matter of principle, oversteps the conventional boundaries on free expression of opinion, Carlyle has as good a claim as anyone to exemplarity. But his is a curious case. Where Mill has remained philosophically influential—still the most articulately exacting and urgent exponent of the ground rules for free public discussion in a democracy—Carlyle's tenure in the culture has proven less secure. That he is an *imaginative* rather than strictly philosophical writer on morality makes a large difference. Once a fixture on undergraduate literature and history syllabuses (it makes sense that Liddle and other 'undoubtedly pretentious and very left-wing working-class kids' were reading him as teenagers in the 1970s),[18] he has been much less in favour since, roughly, the 1980s. In part, as Nietzsche observed, a casualty of his own excesses (see p. 51), he looks stylistically more alien at this historic distance than Mill, whose clean rationality (or 'insulting clarity'[19]) has survived better.

That Carlyle is enjoying a minor revival at present[20] has much to do with recognition (variously motivated) of how far the arch-antagonist of normative

---

[17] Rod Liddle, '*The Spectator* Has Gone Soft – Prisons Should Be Much Nastier Places', *The Spectator*, 26 November 2016, <https://www.spectator.co.uk/2016/11/the-spectator-has-gone-soft-prisons-should-be-much-nastier-places/>. Accessed 24 March 2017.

[18] Rod Liddle, 'Don't Judge a Play by its Audience', *The Spectator*, 13 October 2018 [online via Nexis]. He explains: 'The 1970s were a more enlightened time – that meant stuff from the political right, as well as the despised soft centre and the bourgeois left. I could enjoy Céline while accepting that he was a thoroughly horrible anti-Semite. Ivan Turgenev's storytelling could enthrall despite the fact that he was a vacillating liberal, wary of revolution. We devoured conservatives such as Evelyn Waugh and Thomas Carlyle and Edmund Burke, alongside the lefties…' See also 'Bercow the Brazen', *The Spectator*, 23 March 2019 [online via Nexis] (on the attractions of Carlyle's prose).

[19] Friedrich Nietzsche, *The Anti-Christ, Ecce Homo, Twilight of the Idols, and Other Writings*, eds. Aaron Ridley and Judith Norman, trans. Judith Norman (Cambridge: Cambridge University Press, 2005), 192. See p. 51.

[20] See esp. Eliza Tamarkin, 'Why Forgive Carlyle?', *Representations* 134 (Spring 2016), 64–92; Ranjan Ghosh, *Transcultural Poetics and the Concept of the Poet: From Philip Sidney to T. S. Eliot* (London: Routledge, 2016); Paul E. Kerry and Marylu Hill (eds.), *Thomas Carlyle Resartus: Reappraising Carlyle's Contribution to the Philosophy of History, Political Theory, and Cultural Criticism* (Madison, NJ: Farleigh Dickinson University Press, 2010); Porscha Fermanis and John Regan, *Rethinking British Romantic History, 1770–1845* (Oxford: Oxford University Press, 2014);

moral and political assumptions in the nineteenth century shared Mill's basic precepts, above all the understanding that 'Habit is the deepest law of human nature...our supreme strength; if also, in certain circumstances, our miserablest weakness.'[21] A core aim of Carlyle's 'modern Gnosticism',[22] as of Mill's liberalism, was to dislodge habit and make his reader aware of the ways in which narrow upbringing, limited experience, insufficient familiarity with differences of custom and language, blinker us to (for Mill) a wider range of perspectives, (for Carlyle) higher truths. But where Mill looks to persuade an intelligent reader, point by point, logically, through careful accumulation of evidence, Carlyle wants to take a 'besom of destruction' to logic. His ideal audience is not critical but 'ardent' and 'boundlessly tolerant'.[23] Even Nietzsche himself cannot represent as effectively the literary history of the rhetorical affront calculated to stretch settled habits of thought, since Nietzsche's Cynically-assisted challenge was to morality itself, and Carlyle remains, finally, a moralist of a very taxing sort. Nietzsche rightly recognized in him a significant but incomplete challenge both to substantive beliefs (equality, humanitarianism, and so on) and to norms of expression.

Taking the satirist at his provocative word, then, this chapter goes back to Carlyle to elaborate the ethical provocation of the cynic as moral controversialist: the rhetorical gambit of making a bad example of oneself and thereby calling out a blinkered illiberalism identified as residing within a culture ostensibly committed to 'free discussion'. I focus on the essay that led Mill himself to sever his long friendship with Carlyle and draw a line beyond which tolerance should not be asked to go—the essay so disgraceful that even Liddle does not risk endorsing it, though he flirts with its notoriety.[24]

'An Occasional Discourse on the Negro Question' (1849), first published in the 'liberal' but conservative-leaning magazine Fraser's, and retitled and revised to inflammatory effect as a separate pamphlet, 'The N—— Question' (1853),[25] goes

John Plotz, 'Crowd Power: Chartism, Carlyle, and the Victorian Public Sphere', *Representations* 70 (Spring 2000), 87–114; and Duke University's ongoing digitization project, *The Carlyle Letters Online: A Victorian Cultural Reference* (Durham, NC: Duke University Press, 2007), <http://carlyleletters. dukeupress.edu>. Kerry and Hill provide a helpful review of important work over the last thirty years. See *Thomas Carlyle Resartus*, 14–15.

[21] Carlyle, *Past and Present*, CE X, 126; and, for discussion, Ghosh, *Transcultural Poetics*, 2–3.
[22] G. B. Tennyson, *Sartor Called Resartus: The Genesis, Structure, and Style of Thomas Carlyle's First Major Work* (Princeton, NJ: Princeton University Press, 1965), 286.
[23] Letter to Ralph Waldo Emerson, 29 May 1839, XI, 119–21 (120).
[24] Once a staple text of Victorian period teaching, this essay is (on an informal survey) strikingly absent from most current teaching curricula. Indicatively, it is excluded from the *Norton Anthology of English Literature* and from Norton Topics Online; also from James Eli Adams, *A History of Victorian Literature* (Chichester: Wiley-Blackwell, 2012). Victoria Shea and William Whitla (eds.), *Victorian Literature: An Anthology*, (Chichester: Wiley-Blackwell, 2015) includes only a short extract (148–9), and it receives the briefest of mentions in Kate Flint (ed.), *The Cambridge History of Victorian Literature* (Cambridge: Cambridge University Press, 2012), 101.
[25] [Thomas Carlyle], 'Occasional Discourse on the Negro Question', *Fraser's Magazine for Town and Country* XL (December 1849), 670–9; rev. and reprinted as 'The N—— Question' (1853), CE

out of its way to offend. Like Liddle's more recent homages to Carlylean 'astringency' in public discussion, the essay occupies a platform with a defined readership, self-selectingly (given *Fraser's* articulated purposes and reputation), but still selectively, 'open-minded' on the matter of free expression of opinion.[26] In the 'Occasional Discourse', Carlyle looks both to gratify that self-image and to test it. Abrasively goading, he calls implicitly for readers tolerant or intelligent enough not to rush to hostile judgement (deep-cover flattery is crucial to the tone of address), but he fully expects to fall foul of readers whose commitment to open-mindedness does not go so far. Rejecting the assumption that the public moralist must model right thinking, Carlyle breaks the common framework, 'absconding' from normal reporting (as he has it in the framing conceit of the essay) to undertake a more 'speculative' line of inquiry (348).

To that end, Carlyle conceals himself (as so often) behind a series of frame narrators who offer the flimsiest of disguises to his own authority—a putative editor, who has 'accepted the article, at a cheap market rate' from its putative author Dr Phelin McQuirk (felon/feline? quirky/of the kirk?)...or rather from McQuirk's landlady. Left in the red when her tenant absconds, she wants what profit she can extract from the typescript on his desk. The editor agrees to 'give it publicity', 'without, in the least, committing ourselves': its views, he suspects, are pretty much in a 'minority of one' (348). The person (or persona) exposing others to the controversialist's view thus warns away those likely to take offence (*caveat lector*), not merely declining responsibility but pointing helpfully to discreditable elements of self-interest in the system: the editor who fills his pages at a discount (not the real editor, John William Parker, Jr, who is by implication on side with the joke, certainly is permitting it), and the fictional landlady who wants her rent (she, at least, can plead entitlement). McQuirk himself sounds a more belligerent note: 'you shall hear what I have to say on the matter', and 'probably you will not in the least like it' (349).

One of Mill's lesser objections to Carlyle was that the charade of concealment is very thin. (It is, of course, meant to be.) Mill was perhaps alert to the somewhat risqué nature of such jesting over one's sources, given that just over a year before Carlyle had persuaded *Fraser's* to publish fraudulent letters purporting to be

XXIX, *Critical and Miscellaneous Essays* IV, 348–83. References are to the Centenary Edition unless otherwise stated.

[26] A contributor to *The Spectator* (see 'Ireland and Sir Robert Peel', *The Spectator* 14 April 1849, 343), Carlyle had a closer relationship with *Fraser's*, publishing extensively in its pages. His subjects for the magazine included Goethe, Schiller, Boswell's *Life of Johnson*, 'Biography', 'Thoughts on History,' 'The Diamond Necklace', 'Count Cagliostro' and, most famously, *Sartor Resartus* (discussed on pp. C2. P40-C2.P42). A letter from Mill to Carlyle suggests that Carlyle found it, at least initially, a less than 'congenial' location for his work (22 December 1833, *Letters* I, 200–3 [202])—but, considering the latitude editors afforded him, that feeling may reflect his fierce desire for independence as much or more than any ideological friction. See also John Morrow, 'Thomas Carlyle, "Young Ireland" and "The Condition of Ireland Question"', *The Historical Journal* 51/3 (2008), 643–67.

written by a soldier in the retinue of Oliver Cromwell. That Carlyle had himself been hoaxed had only recently become clear to him, and the experience perhaps lent vim to his artful distancing of his own authority (better to promote the freedom of fiction than accept diminishment of one's reputation as a historian?).[27] Even without that context in view, the elaborate editorial framing of the 'Occasional Discourse' is not hard to recognize for what it is: a somewhat hackneyed literary gambit, warding off naïve, crude, or potentially litigious objectors. Later readers have sometimes argued for a deeper rationale. Geoffrey Hartman, for example, sees amplification of the business of mediation as preventing a 'regress into solipsism'.[28] Certainly Carlyle was alert to the risk, and prone to connect it with the Diogenes strain in his make-up (too much writing, and low mood, were—he worried to Mill—drawing him 'into total abstraction from mankind, into some Diogenes' Herring-barrel, with not even the sun to shine on me'[29]); but there may be a temptation to over-rationalize. It is at least easy to agree that the ground of reasoning in the 'Occasional Discourse' is made highly unstable from the start.

In addressing 'the Rights of Negroes' (349), Carlyle selects a subject that can be, he suggests, a gauge of progressive morality more generally: on it can be hung 'innumerable other rights, duties, expectations, wrongs and disappointments, much argued of, by logic and by grape-shot, in these emancipated epochs of the human mind!' (348). The indisputable racism of much of the rhetoric ('a few black persons rendered extreme "free" indeed. Sitting yonder with their beautiful muzzles up to the ears in pumpkins' [350], calling 'Higher wages, massa; higher' [352] &c.) is of a piece with much of Carlyle's private writing about race. It sounds casual, but in this context it is instrumental: a linguistic weapon against the self-congratulatory posturing of a generation of philanthropists and politicians still living off the moral derivatives of the Slavery Abolition Act (1833). The rhetorical

---

[27] Mill, in effect, outs Carlyle as the writer of the essay when he observes that 'This pet theory of your contributor about work, we all know well enough, though some persons might not be prepared for so bold an application of it.' [J. S. Mill], 'The Negro Question', *Fraser's Magazine for Town and Country* XLI (January 1850), 25–31; reprinted in *CW* XXI, 85–95 (90). On the Cromwell hoax, see Clyde de L. Ryals, 'Thomas Carlyle and the Squire Forgeries', *Victorian Studies* 30/4 (Summer 1987), 495–518. Carlyle had at last met his hoaxer, William Squire, in January 1849, finding him oddly appealing: 'Untruth I nowhere detected or suspected in him; but everywhere exasperation [because of "his social, economical, intellectual condition"], and reason even keen reason became "semi-delirious".' Quoted in ibid., 509. The full extent of Squire's duplicity became known to Carlyle only in the same month that the 'Occasional Discourse' was published, December 1849 (ibid., 512–13).

[28] Geoffrey Hartman, *Criticism in the Wilderness: The Study of Literature Today*, 2nd edn (New Haven, CT: Yale University Press, 2007), 48.

[29] Letter to J. S. Mill, 12 July 1836, *The Collected Letters of Thomas and Jane Welsh Carlyle* [hereafter *CL*], eds. Ian Campbell, Aileen Christianson, and David R. Sorensen, 47 vols. (Durham, NC: Duke University Press, 1970–), IX, 6–7 (6). <https://carlyleletters.dukeupress.edu/home>. Also the characterization of Diogenes Teufelsdröckh in *Sartor Resartus*, discussed on pp. C2.P40-C2.P42. For comparative discussion of Carlyle and other writers on this theme, see Reino Virtanen, 'The Spectre of Solipsism in Western Literature', *The Journal of the Midwest Modern Language Association* 19/1 (Spring 1986), 59–76.

gambit is clear enough, even if Carlyle would not put it so explicitly: if anti-racism has become a signature expression of progressive achievement and liberal toler-ance, racism, it might follow, can be made a signature goad of opposition to progressive complacency.

Both the first and second titles and the deployment of the rhetoric of blackness throughout decline to participate in the work of cultural specification that, on a standard affirmation of anti-racism, would require Carlyle to distinguish the many forms of blackness under his eye: the former slaves of British Jamaica, the indentured workers of Dutch Java, the African 'war-captives' (381) brought in as cheap labour to replace West Indian slaves, black Haitians currently embroiled in civil war, the free negro populations of most Northern and some Southern American states, the still-enslaved African-Americans of many remaining states in the South. The revised title of 1853 of course ups the ante. Modern lexicographers remark on the passage of the 'n——' word in recent decades from being a 'contemptuous term in dictionaries...treated similarly to ethnic and religious slurs' to 'taboo' status.[30] Historical change is evident, here, but it is not the case that the word was neutral in the mid-nineteenth-century: commentators were aware of its pejorative connotations and polite liberal discourse tended to shy away from it.[31] (Indicatively the word is more extensively employed in the private correspondence of Victorian men and women of letters than in their public writings—fictional representation being a case apart.)

Decoupled, insofar as it can be, from its racist delivery, the 'Occasional Discourse' advances a series of cynical 'astringencies' directed against three targets: (i) philanthropic sentimentalism; (ii) political economy, famously dispar-aged as 'the Dismal Science' (354); and, (iii) a broader target than either, the mismatch between the rhetoric of progress adopted by contemporary politicians and their present political failings. The essay has some substantive political points to make. First, that the end of slavery in Jamaica, expensive as it was to the British state (the compensation package to slave owners cost £20m), was not accompan-ied by the necessary investment in restructuring the local sugar industry that would have prevented the need for sugar duties at the expense of 'our own English labourers'.[32] Cheap political capital is still being extracted from the abolition of British slavery sixteen years on from the Slavery Abolition Act, Carlyle observes. Witness Prime Minister John Russell's recent reassurance to Parliament that the end of slavery has been a good thing for the former slave populations of Jamaica

---

[30] Sidney I. Landau, *Dictionaries: The Art and Craft of Lexicography*, 2nd edn (Cambridge: Cambridge University Press, 2001), 234–7.

[31] See Randall Kennedy, *N——: The Strange Career of a Troublesome Word* (New York: Vintage, 2002).

[32] '[W]hile the sugar-crops rot round [the Jamaicans] uncut, because labour cannot be hired, so cheap are the pumpkins;—and at home, we are but required to rasp from the breakfast-loaves of our own English labourers, some slight "differential sugar-duties," and lend a poor half-million or a few poor millions now and then, to keep that beautiful state of matters going on' (350).

(349): the historic achievement of abolition gives cover to a persistent failure to redress the grievances of those colonists now complaining of wage inflation and lack of cooperation from the local administration. Progressivist back-patting over abolition is also distracting attention from other pressing problems of the day: English poverty, Irish poverty, Chartism, Irish republicanism, parliamentary allocation of funds across the several colonial administrations.

On the subject of race, Carlyle's strongest anti-progressive thrust is that the Whig/Liberal government's current policies towards Jamaica rest on a sinister hypocrisy: the importation of African indentured labour (financed by loans) to make good a labour deficit in the wake of emancipation. His racism, however, grossly distorts his description of the characterological consequences said to have followed from emancipation and from attempts by the British and Foreign Anti-Slavery Society (BFASS) to block 'wage-slavery' by plantation owners extending exploitative apprenticeships beyond the 12-year period of permitted post-abolition dependency.[33] The political illiberalism stems largely from the view Carlyle takes of the value of work; the racism from his readiness to accept (and amplify) the stereotype of the work-averse negro. In all cases, he rates work much higher than liberty. His cynicism on this score is modified, however, by the spiritual convictions that frame it. No human being, in his view, is free in anything other than a trivial sense: I am free to read this book instead of that, to befriend this person and not that; I am *not* free, except at the margins, to be (for example) prosperous, or socially high or low placed, or loved, or even healthy, by my own efforts. The collapse of the ancient clarifying distinctions between the powerful and their dependants is a constant source of regret to him. 'The old Feudal circumstances never can return,' he laments to a friend in 1860, 'nor anything practically like them (however much wanted, and indeed at last indispensable) till people have quite laid aside immense quantities of stuff (especially [a]bout "liberty" &c &c) which they now babble of, with one accord.'[34] The Jamaican labour problem results from the former West Indian slave now finding it too easy to provide for himself and therefore falling into extreme indolence, while the white man who 'himself cannot work' must import African indentured labour to keep the estates going. This is, Mill will explain, a fantasy, based on an account of a strike that Carlyle has read in a parliamentary Blue Book,[35] and one of very

---

[33] Jenna M. Gibbs, *Performing the Temple of Liberty: Slavery, Theatre, and Popular Culture in London and Philadelphia, 1760–1850* (Baltimore, MD: Johns Hopkins University Press, 2014), 216. The BFASS was also instrumental in exposing local abuses of law, including the burning of black settlements. See cruel.org, 'The Carlyle-Mill "Negro Question" Debate', <http://cruel.org/econthought/texts/carlyle/negroquest.html>. Accessed 3 September 2019.

[34] Letter to C. A. Ward, 24 September 1860, in *Collected Letters* XXXVI, 262–4.

[35] For an enlightening account of how quickly and effectively opponents of the government moved to use the state's publications against it, making 'shrewd' critical use of information, the veracity of which the state had vouched for, see Oz Frankel, 'Blue Books and the Victorian Reader', *Victorian Studies* 46/2 (2004), 308–18.

inferior quality: he has taken as fact 'the wildest prophecies of the slavery party before emancipation' (89).

Carlyle does not always appeal to 'nature' as the source of his racial discriminations. Like Mill (up to a point), he holds that character can be assisted or corrupted by circumstance: the Jamaican former slave and the Irish pauper, persistently twinned in the 'Occasional Discourse', are said to be idle and immoral not because it is in their nature to be idle and immoral but because (unlike the 'heroic' European colonists to whom Carlyle gives the sole credit of making Jamaica fertile) they have been prevented from doing what it is every man's divinely ordained purpose to do: work to the best of his ability. (Women's labour does not interest him.) The problem with importing African labour to the Caribbean is that it lowers the local price of labour, further disincentivizing the West Indian worker who sees others working at lower wages than it is worth his while selling his own labour for. This is, in essence, an early Victorian articulation of present-day hostility to the effects of a globalized labour market—though Carlyle is not suggesting protectionism as a solution and he is scathing about attempts to 'blockade the continent of Africa itself, and to watch slave-ships along the extremely extensive and unwholesome coast? . . . The slave-traders will only re-route through Brazil and Cuba anyway . . . ' (382). His answer comes in the form of a plea to Heaven, rather than any economic recommendations:

> The idle Black man in the West Indies . . . will again . . . , if it please Heaven, have the right (actually the first 'right of man' for an indolent person) to be *compelled* to work as he was fit, and to *do* the Maker's will who had constructed him with such and such capabilities and prefigurements of capability. And I incessantly pray Heaven, all men, the whitest alike and the blackest, the richest and the poorest, in other regions of the world, had attained precisely the same right, the divine right of being compelled (if 'permitted' will not answer) to do what work they are appointed for, and not to go idle another minute, in a life which is so short.   (357)

'Oh Lord, our Maker', in short, 'deliver us from the iniquity of idleness.' 'Why not at once say', Mill will retort, 'that, by "some wise means", every thing should be made right in the world?' (90).

The provocation of the 'Occasional Discourse' to contemporary Victorian public discourse lay less in its economic arguments, most of which were commonly made from both the Conservative and Whig benches of Parliament,[36] than in the aggravated racism with which it drew its cartoon Jamaican negro,

---

[36] For the internal liberal critique, see, for example, [Henry George Grey], 3rd Earl Grey, *The Colonial Policy of Lord John Russell's Administration*, 2 vols. (London: Richard Bentley, 1853), 166–95.

'Quashee',[37] now living in indolence. There is cynicism in the representation of liberal motives and liberal self-congratulation, but the real cynic disturbance comes with the affront to acceptable freedom of expression on the subject of race. 'Our beautiful Black darlings are at last happy', McQuirk rejoices sarcastic-ally, 'with little labour except to the teeth [i.e. feasting on the ready supply of pumpkins], *which*, surely, in those excellent horse-jaws of theirs, will not fail!' (350). The illustration goes well beyond the passing image that facilitates satire (breast-feeding at The Ivy, as it were), and is almost entirely supererogatory to the critique of political economics.

> Where a black man, by working half an hour a day (such is the [government] calculation), can supply himself, by aid of sun and soil, with as much pumpkin as will suffice, he is likely to be a little stiff to raise into hard work! Supply and demand, which, science says, should be brought to bear on him, have an up-hill task of it with such a man. Strong sun supplies itself gratis – rich soil, in those unpeopled or half-peopled regions, almost gratis: these are *his* supply; and half an hour a day, directed upon these, will produce pumpkin, which is his 'demand.' The fortunate black man! very swiftly does he settle his account with supply and demand; not so swiftly the less fortunate white man of these tropical localities. He, himself, cannot work; and his black neighbor, rich in pumpkin, is in no haste to help him. Sunk to the ears in pumpkin, imbibing saccharine juices, and much at his ease in the creation, he can listen to the less fortunate white man's 'demand,' and take his own time in supplying it. Higher wages, massa; higher, for your cane crop cannot wait; still higher – till no conceivable opulence of cane crop will cover such wages!

The anti-Philanthropic message rests on a perception that the Jamaican negro character has been corrupted by politics and by the misplaced moral sentimen-talism guiding the politics. Depicting the imaginary black man as the beneficiary of a climate that encourages laziness, Carlyle might be defended on the grounds that the same would apply to any human group so situated (his point would then have universal application)—but 'nature' determines otherwise. The impoverished English of the North Riding, whose plight is compared to that of 'our beautiful black darlings', cannot fall back on the generosity of nature. Moreover, while the 'fortunate' black man is readily satisfied by pumpkin, the same is not true of his white neighbour (former owner?) who 'cannot work'—one assumes because he is physically unfitted to the climate (Carlyle is not explicit on this point but it was a commonplace justification for black slavery)—and is culturally? physically?

---

[37] 'A British racial slur equivalent' to the 'n——' word. Susan Meyer, *Imperialism at Home: Race and Victorian Women's Fiction* (Ithaca, NY: Cornell University Press, 1996), 47.

unfitted for so poor a diet. Pumpkin is a food standardly given to cattle and, in America, to horses in the colder months.[38] 'Horse-jaws' are fit to take it.

Above all, the white man is culturally primed to know the dignity of work as the black man is not. This is a historical contingency, Carlyle recognizes, but a powerful one. Among his few relatively clear recommendations for practical action is:

> it ought to be rendered possible, ought it not, for white men to live beside black men, and in some just manner to command black men, and produce West Indian fruitfulness by means of them? West Indian fruitfulness will need to be produced. *If the English cannot find the method for that, they may rest assured there will another come (brother Jonathan or still another) who can.* (381)

The allusion here is, as so often, biblical (to the loved brother of King David, in the Old Testament) but it steers a threat, more than a promise, for the political power currently wielded by the white man: make the land fruitful and profitable or some other group will. 'He it is whom the gods will bid continue in the West Indies, bidding us ignominiously, Depart, ye quack-ridden incompetent!—' (381). What the black man possesses in lieu of a right apprehension of the value of work is an instinctive grasp of his current advantage: seeing the gap between his needs and those of his white neighbour, he forces up the price of his labour, recognizing no moral limit on his opportunism. There is a hint of mischief, surely, malice even, in his spelling out the advantage he enjoys: 'Higher wages, massa; higher, for your cane crop cannot wait . . .' With 'Massa', Carlyle is of course deep in the territory of racial stereotyping. As *OED* observes, 'Massa', first sourced to the late 1770s, in 'later use . . . typically highlight[s] offensive expectations or stereotypes of black servility, referring back to the era of slavery'.[39] The word is specific to that history, but the broader technique chimes with a persistent feature of Carlyle's writing, well described by John Plotz: its depletion of agency from the potential political subjects represented. Just as his Chartist crowds are, in his account of them, 'strip [ped] . . . of language', accorded only (in Carlyle's words) a 'deep, dumb inarticulate want', his negroes speak only to confirm that they have no independence.[40] They operate like 'jolly Sambo' mechanical money boxes popular a little later in the century (the outsized jaws opening to swallow a coin).

Carlyle's point is, precisely, that 16 years after the official end of slavery, British handling of the West Indian economy continues to create the conditions of psychological servility for Jamaicans of African descent. He is, to that extent,

---

[38] For mid-nineteenth-century (trans-Atlantic) practices, see John Stewart, *The Stable Book: Being a Treatise on the Management of Horses* (1855), American edn (New York: A. O. Moore, 1858), 192.

[39] 'massa, *n.*', *OED*. Accessed 21 September 2019.

[40] Plotz, 'Crowd Power', 97, 98—quoting Carlyle, 'Signs of the Times' (1829).

ironizing the stereotype; but there would be less cause for 'offence' were there not a clear implication that the imaginary black man is himself cynically working the stereotype for all it is worth. So persistent are the racist provocations to 'philan-thropic' sensibility that it is, indeed, difficult to know where interpretation should stop: by 'unpeopled or half-peopled regions' does Carlyle mean to imply that negroes do not count as people, or only that the density of population, especially in the interior of Jamaica was low (and, prior to the importation of slaves, 'naturally' so)?

'Mere racism does not yield so pungent a phantasmagoria', Harold Bloom suggests, as he contemplates the culmination of the pumpkin-eating trope in an image of Oliver Cromwell (one of Carlyle's great 'heroes') lying beneath the soil 'pushing up pumpkins so that unbreeched Blacks might exercise their potent teeth'.[41] We see here Carlyle's 'demi-Gnosticism at its worst', reimagining time's generative seed-bed as Shakespeare's 'devouring time, Kronos chewing us up as so many pumpkins' (Bloom, 93). This is right but it does not quite capture the complexity of a projection of fantasy that functions, disconcertingly, along more than one axis, and with so questionable a level of commitment, on the author's part, to any particular claim. Though the most striking aspects of the stereotype are animalistic (standard, if aggravated, racist caricature—lazy, greedy, horse-jawed Jamaicans), Carlyle has a different, in some sense 'larger', target in his sights when he taps into the data-driven geographic-comparativist languages of the emerging political sciences: 'our interesting Black population,—equalling almost in number of heads one of the Ridings of Yorkshire, and in *worth* (in quantity of intellect, faculty, docility, energy, and available human valour and value), perhaps one of the streets of Seven Dials [the impoverished Irish-immigrant quarter abutting Covent Garden]...' (350). If we are to take him at his word here, and in similar passages on statistical reports in the latest govern-ment 'Blue Books', the true object of his targeted cynicism is not the 'negro question' at all, but the state's reliance on quantifications of 'supply' and 'demand' that are, themselves, culpably cynical in that they fail to recognize human 'inter-ests' beyond food, cash, a diminished and diminishing conception of happiness.

In such high-risk satire, the reader, whatever the extent of his or her liberalism, is likely to see a tipping point from the cartoonist's artful elaboration of his picture to excessive investment in its derogatory wit and cynical bite. This was terrain Carlyle had been working up to (or perhaps down to) for several years. A keen reader both of the classical record of Cynicism and of English, French, and German Enlightenment developments in its reception (Byron, Rousseau,

---

[41] *Essayists and Prophets*, Bloom's Literary Criticism 20th Anniversary Collection (Philadelphia, PA: Chelsea House, 2005), 93. Bloom points us, suggestively, to the young Teufelsdröckh in *Sartor Resartus*, thwarted in his search for meaningful work: 'Me, however, as a Son of Time, unhappier than some others, was Time threatening to eat quite prematurely.' *Sartor Resartus*, *CE* II, 104.

Wieland, and Heine were all close objects of study), he gave early evidence of personal attraction to the figure of Diogenes.[42] 'Had I lived at Athens,' he wrote, aged 22, to Robert Mitchell, 'in the plastic days of that brilliant commonwealth, I might have purchased "a narrow paltry tub,"[43] and pleased myself with uttering gall among them of Cynosarges.' Contemporary times seemed to him less flexibly intelligent. 'Political institutions and increased civilization have fixed the texture of society': when 'the aberrations of philosophical enthusiasm are rewarded not by admiration but contempt—when Plato would be dissected in the Edin*r* review, and Diogenes laid hold of by a "society for the suppression of beggars"—in these times—it may not be.'[44] This sounds more like a man working himself up to 'aberrations' than ruling them out. Increasingly, over the following years, the association with Diogenes was one Carlyle positively courted—not least, Alexander Jordan observes, because he saw in the Cynic 'a model of the independent intellectual that he himself longed to become.'[45] Loathing the idea of reliance on a patron (Coleridge's acceptance of this constraint disgusted him[46]), Carlyle was equally reluctant to massage the reputations of others and advance his own by playing the reviewing and article-writing game in the manner that kept so many of his fellow-writers' literary careers burnished and contemporary periodicals stocked with material. Diogenes' free-speaking rebuff to Alexander strongly attracted him: 'the one the conqueror of all the world, in his pride and glory and splendour; the other a poor needy man, with nothing besides his skin save the soul that was in him'. To speak as Diogenes did 'was certainly a great thing', he wrote in *Lectures on the History of Literature* (1838), 'and altogether worthy to be recognized; it was much for a man'.[47]

There was persistent financial rationale for Carlyle to cultivate the asceticism of a Cynic identity. Writing to his brother, John, in 1831, he complained, only semi-comically, that no other route than the Cynic one might be feasible for him: 'I told [Jeffrey] I...did not see that Literature could support an *honest* man otherwise than *à la Diogenes*; in which fashion too I meant to experiment, if *nothing* else could be found,...'[48] But Alexander Jordan is surely right that the primary drivers behind Carlyle's constant pitting of the 'Natural' against the 'Artificial' and the 'Sham' were intellectual and ideological: a confluence of Scottish Presbyterianism, Swift, and the Menippean satire tradition, Wordsworthian and Byronic

---

[42] See Alexander Jordan, 'That Scotch Diogenes: Thomas Carlyle and Cynicism', *International Journal of the Classical Tradition* 26/3 (September 2019), 295–318 (esp. 300–5 for signs of early reading).
[43] The quotation is from Samuel Butler's *Hudibras* (1684), and befits the mock-heroic mode of the letter.
[44] 6 November 1818, *Collected Letters* I, 141–7 (142).   [45] 'That Scotch Diogenes', 307.
[46] Ibid., 306.   [47] Quoted in ibid, 307.
[48] Letter to John A. Carlyle, 12 July 1831, *Collected Letters* V, 301–4 (303).

Romanticisms, and a strong strain of later Stoicisms, mixing with the original example of Diogenes of Sinope.[49]

By the time Carlyle published *Sartor Resartus* in *Fraser's Magazine* (1833–34), the association was settled. *Sartor* brought it to the fore. Employing as his mouthpiece the fictious German philosopher Diogenes Teufelsdröckh,[50] Carlyle looked to shine a light on how the naked animal, man, has 'mask[ed] himself in Clothes' (2)—that is, in the changing material and symbolic draperies of historical and cultural circumstance. Like the original Cynic, the new Diogenes 'speaks out with a strange plainness', casting a debasing eye on society and its *mores*: a 'Drawing-room' is simply a portion of 'Space'; 'within the most starched cravat there passes a windpipe and weasand [oesophagus]' (21). Taking aim at all 'Cant' and seeking the undistorted truth of humanity, Teufelsdröckh is, in the Editor/ Carlyle's somewhat acidic description, a 'speculative radical' (47), for the most part abrasively terse in his public communications, just occasionally breaching the apoliticism expected of a Cynic and endorsing 'The Cause of the Poor' (11). Like the first Diogenes, he gives signs of deeply philanthropic aspiration, sometimes looking as if 'he could clasp the whole Universe into his bosom', and yet his dominant manner is offensively 'indifferent', showing a 'malign coolness towards all that men strive after' (25).

Unlike the first Cynics, Carlyle looks ultimately to raise rather than lower the bar of valuation in support of moral tenets that are capable of a very conservative interpretation: famously, Teufelsdröckh reaffirms the hard-won insight of Goethe's Wilhelm Meister, '*Do the Duty which lies nearest thee*' (156).[51] This is the aspect of Carlyle that gravely disappointed Nietzsche. Though the conclusion to Diogenes' developmental survey of human history resembles the Cynic's reductive attention to material realities ('man is a Tool-using Animal' [30]), that debasing insight serves a higher idealism: the truth about humanity is discovered not in the body but in the soul. Diogenes Teufelsdröckh is a Transcendentalist employing Cynicism to ends that Diogenes would not recognize (and Nietzsche would recognize but resist): men are 'God-created Souls' (21) who will find the true value in their lives through work—including the work of 'Imagination'. Carlyle's Diogenes no longer inhabits the marketplace in person; he lives at the top of a high tower above it, looking down upon it (14–15), speaking through the comically arduous efforts of his German followers and English editor who, like a

---

[49] Jordan accents the Cynicism somewhat at the expense of these other elements. But see 'That Scotch Diogenes', 308, n. 75.

[50] The influence of Jean Paul Richter (his '*Humoristen*' and his 'buckram'-casing of sarcasm) on the conception of Teufelsdröckh is also important. See J. W. Smeed, 'Thomas Carlyle and Jean Paul Richter', *Comparative Literature* 16/3 (1964), 226–53 (esp. 233); and Joanna Aleksandra Malecka, 'Between Herder and Luther: Carlyle's Literary Battles with the Devil in his Jean Paul Richter Essays (1827, 1827, 1830) and in *Sartor Resartus* (1833–34)' (MPhil(R) thesis, University of Glasgow, 2013). <http://theses.gla.ac.uk/4343/>.

[51] Carlyle translated the novel in 1824.

latter-day Diogenes Laertius, endeavours to make sense of scraps of written record. The biographical story those scraps at last yield is not the tissue of anecdotes or *chreiai* familiar from the *Lives of the Eminent Philosophers*, though it sometimes pretends to be. It is the story of a man taken very close to a destructive cynicism but rescued by something like Divine revelation.

Having developed a habit, as a young man, of ironies and sarcasms, taking down (and earning the hostility of) 'persons of weight and name', Teufelsdröckh comes philosophically unstuck after being bitterly disappointed in love. This is Goethe's *Sorrows of Young Werther* minus the tragic ending: Carlyle's philosopher-in-the-making wanders Europe with the *Enchiridion* of Epictetus for company (see p. C1.P44) (his English editor is scathing, rebuking Teufelsdröck's Stoic interests by an appeal to Aristotle—'*The End of Man is an Action, and not a Thought*'): but Teufelsdröckh himself finds his text increasingly wanting. From an abyss of cynicism, unbelief, and depression, he passes to an intermediate stage of 'Indifference' in which the stars seem to look down, mockingly, on 'this paltry little Dog-cage of an Earth' (138). He keeps faith, throughout, with the first Diogenes' holistic view of Nature (154) (Diogenes was 'the greatest man of Antiquity, only that he wanted Decency' [168]) and with the Cynic determination to 'stan[d] on the adamantine basis of his Manhood' (168), but a reawakened Teufelsdröckh recognizes the need of something more to 'rais[e] us up' (231). Work is his answer (again famously, reworking John 9:4): 'Work while it is called Today; for the Night cometh, wherein no man can work' (157).[52]

The critical success of *Sartor* helped guide contemporaries' recurrent depictions, thereafter, of Carlyle as Cynic: a 'Scotch Diogenes', 'modern Diogenes', 'Diogenes Carlyle', 'the grand sullen Diogenes'.[53] The association was thoroughly familiar to the public by the time *Vanity Fair* caricatured Carlyle as 'The Diogenes of the Modern Corinthians without his Tub', in late 1870: a thin, glowering figure whose straw hat makes fun of the original Cynic's desire for sunlight (Fig. 2.1). This Diogenes looks like a miserabilist. He is (says the accompanying text):

> the profoundest cynic, the most daring satirist of his age; but so far as cynicism, or satire, or daring conveys a mean idea, the expression is inappropriate. All his characteristics, good or bad, are on a grand scale, and if he be a devil he is the muckle deil himself....No such hatred of shams, no such contempt for the slavery of words, is to be found anywhere as in the works of Thomas Carlyle—

---

[52] 'I must work the works of him that sent me, while it is day: the night cometh, when no man can work' (King James Bible).

[53] Respectively, the Chicago*Chronicle* (1849), E. P. Hood, anonymously, in *The Eclectic Review* (1861), the *Methodist Review* (1870); quoted with many further examples by Jordan, 'That Scotch Diogenes', 314.

Fig. 2.1 Jehu Junior, 'Men of the Day. No. 12. Thomas Carlyle', *Vanity Fair*, 22 October 1870, in *The Vanity Fair Album: A Show of Sovereigns, Statesmen, Judges, and Men of the Day; with Biographical and Critical Notices by Jehu Junior*, 2 vols (London: "Vanity Fair" Office, 1870), no pag. (image No. 103). The Bodleian Libraries, The University of Oxford, 2106 b. 1, Vol. 2, 1870, 22 October 1870, No. 103.

> the realist, *par excellence*, of Moral Philosophy and History, the Diogenes of the Modern Corinthians without his tub . . . [54]

Visually, the subject was more elaborately worked out in Frederick Waddy's 1873 cartoon, depicting an outsized Carlyle leaning out of a barrel labelled 'Chelsea' (the edge of satire in Carlyle's other popular soubriquet, 'the sage of Chelsea', has rather worn off over time). Waddy depicts him with contemplative head on hand, suffering under the efforts of a small bugler atop the tub, busily offering to wake the world (Fig. 2.2).[55] The accompanying verbal 'sketch' contextualizes a little:

---

[54] [Jehu Junior], 'Men of the Day. No. 12. Thomas Carlyle', *Vanity Fair*, 22 October 1870, in *The Vanity Fair Album: A Show of Sovereigns, Statesmen, Judges, and Men of the Day; with Biographical and Critical Notices by Jehu Junior*, 2 vols. (London: "Vanity Fair" Office, 1870), no pag. (image No. 103).

[55] Frederick Waddy, *Cartoon Portraits and Biographical Sketches of Men of the Day* (London: Tinsley Brothers, 1873), opposite 114.

A LATTER-DAY PHILOSOPHER.

Fig. 2.2 Frederick Waddy, *Cartoon Portraits and Biographical Sketches of Men of the Day* (London: Tinsley Brothers, 1873). The Bodleian Libraries, The University of Oxford, (OC) 210 h. 210, facing p. 114.

when he took up public lecturing, 'our philosopher was remarkable for rough vigour, masterlike handling of his subject, and rude language to his audiences. The last, no doubt, did them good, and did not displease them. They paid to go and see a nineteenth-century Diogenes, and they got their money's worth, and something more' (115).

Anachronism is part of the comedy: this is a fully clothed Diogenes, the bohemian connotations of contemporary Chelsea not much in evidence. The weary frown on the sage's face suggests irritation with the marketplace rather than willing occupation of it, and—if we are to connect the frown with the bugler—no doubt pokes fun at Carlyle's long-standing vendetta against street musicians (the bugler being more of that ilk than of the army). The tub is hardly the sound-proof study Carlyle had tried, and failed, to achieve for himself in 1853.[56] On the other hand,

---

[56] 'The "sound-proof room" was a flattering delusion of an ingenious needy builder, for which we after-wards paid dear,' Carlyle later wrote. The room was 'by far the noisiest in the house,' 'a kind of infernal "miracle" to me then and ever since.' John M. Picker, 'The Soundproof Study: Victorian Professionals, Work Space, and Urban Noise', *Victorian Studies* 42/3 (April 1999), 427–53 (436).

there is no public audience in evidence—and no Cynic dog for companionship, only the inscrutable front-facing owl, its facial 'brow' feathers mirroring the philosopher's frown. He is, perhaps, the owl referred to in the 'Model Prisons' essay of *Latter-Day Pamphlets*, and there to represent the intellectual myopia of the age, as Carlyle saw it: '—not eagles soaring sunward, not brothers of the lightnings and the radiances we; a dim horn-eyed, owl-population, intent mainly on the catching of mice!'[57] Significant, then, that he has his back to both Diogenes and bugler. This is an owl unmoved by Carlylean 'noise'.

Emanating from this already well-established Cynic character, the cynicism of the 'Occasional Discourse'—in content, genre, and style—must be beyond question.[58] It lies in the assault on conventional morality: specifically, on the 'rosepink Sentimentalism' of 'Benevolence', 'Fraternity', the 'Emancipation-principle', 'Christian Philanthropy', even as Carlyle looks to raise, rather than lower, standards (he holds himself to be defending truer conceptions of, at least, Benevolence and Fraternity; on Emancipation and Christian Philanthropy, he has graver doubts—ironically, it is the purpose of this modern Cynic's free speaking to tell us that we are fundamentally unfree). Cynic models equally support the essay's offer to ground morality back in 'Fact' and 'Nature': we need, Carlyle urges, to discriminate between reality and the false facts given to us by the 'social sciences' (there is scorn in the title, as he uses it); in his own words, we must 'ascertain a little better what it is that Fact and Nature demand of us, and what only Exeter Hall [the centre of the Anti-Slavery movement] wedded to the Dismal Science, demands' (354). Unlike the original Diogenes, Carlyle does proffer a few practical suggestions—binding the Jamaican negroes into a limited 'serf[dom]' ('bound, by royal authority, to give so many days of work a year') as the Dutch are said to be doing in Java might be a 'first step' (381); less clearly, stop trying to station 'policeofficers' at 'every henroost' on the African coast and go after 'the fox' (the traders, or those who pay them). But beyond this, nothing that is not awash with ironies and sarcasms to a degree that renders all recommendations unstable. Most of all there is that matter of tone: nowhere was Carlyle more shocking than in this, his most notorious work, and if the *Latter-Day Pamphlets* come close, there is nevertheless the sense sometimes of straining to repeat the effect.[59] It was, surely, among the matters tugging at his conscience when he rebuked himself, late in life:

---

[57] Thomas Carlyle, 'Model Prisons', in *Latter-Day Pamphlets*, CE XX, 48–86 (84).

[58] Carlyle had, possibly, been rereading Lucian near to the time of writing. In an undated manuscript, thought to have been written 'between 1844 and 1851', he quotes Lucian's 'Apology for "The Dependent Scholar"', warming to the strictures of the Cynic-influenced satirist against writerly servility to patrons. See Lucian, *The Works of Lucian of Samosata*, trans. H W. Fowler and F. H. Fowler, 4 vols. (Oxford: Clarendon Press, 1905), II, 1–16. The case for Cynic influences on the 'Occasional Discourse' is secure without this additional context, though it may enhance it. For the reference to Lucian, and the dating, see Michael Timko, 'Carlyle, Sterling, and the Scavenger Age', *Studies in Scottish Literature* 20/1 (1985), 11–33 (31).

[59] 'Have you quite done your interesting Negroes in the Sugar Islands?', he has the Reformers of 'Modern Prisons' ask: 'Rush to the Jails, then.' *Latter-Day Pamphlets*, 48–86 (69). That essay

'I have given far too much in to [it]—*sniggering at things*.'[60] The problem for his contemporaries, in 1849, was how to react.

Mill's response, sent to *Fraser's* within days of Carlyle's essay appearing,[61] was characteristically lucid, uncharacteristically fierce. Coming from a man often now castigated for not going far enough in his criticisms of British imperialism,[62] it is a reminder of how pungently critical Mill was of the illiberal assumptions about race on which British foreign and domestic policy operated.[63] He is tolerant insofar as he acknowledges the 'Occasional Discourse' as a significant contribution to a public debate, angrily *in*tolerant of the gross abuses of fact, unwarranted interpretations of evidence, and baseless assertions he identifies in Carlyle's essay. Mill treats the racism as secondary but substantive and (given the scope for emboldening anti-abolitionists in the American South) dangerous. (Carlyle would, indeed, insert into the 1853 pamphlet edition an address to 'Senator Hickory Buckskin' in which he explicitly advocates the retention of slavery in the South, made 'fair' by a 'proper code of law' that, as a precaution against revolt, would set a price at which slaves might buy their freedom.)[64]

As Mill decodes Carlyle, he is a reactionary of a grossly misleading sort: the 'Occasional Discourse' peddles 'the old law of the strongest' rhetorically repackaged as a 'great ethical doctrine' (92). He is culpably uninterested in evidencing his claims (when he does look to sources he is conveniently without scepticism).[65] He deals, Mill points out, in stirring appeals to the duty of work, the beauty of European heroism, the wisdom of established power, all backed by 'divine' authority—a word Mill consistently loads with sarcasm ('If "the gods" will this, it is the first duty of human beings to resist such gods' [87]). On the duty of work Mill is especially caustic:

substantially repeats the main terms of the 'Occasional Discourse' in the context of its extended attack on 'philanthropic twaddle' (68). See 66–7.

[60] Quoted in Ian M. Campbell, 'David Masson and Thomas Carlyle', *Studies in Scottish Literature* 40/1 (2014), 134–45 (141).

[61] See Letter to John William Parker, 21 January 1850, returning a cheque sent in payment for the essay: 'I regarded your insertion of an attack on an article which had appeared in Fraser, as a favour done to me rather than the opposite, & think it quite unfair that I should be paid for it.' *Additional Letters of John Stuart Mill*, CW XXXII, 80.

[62] See esp. Uday Singh Mehta, *Liberalism and Empire: A Study in Nineteenth-Century British Liberal Thought* (Chicago: University of Chicago Press, 1999), and David Theo Goldberg, 'Liberalism's Limits: Carlyle and Mill on "The Negro Question"', *Nineteenth-Century Contexts* 22/2 (2002), 203–16.

[63] For a nuanced view, see Lauren M. E. Goodlad, *The Victorian Geopolitical Aesthetic: Realism, Sovereignty, and Transnational Experience* (Oxford: Oxford University Press, 2015), esp. Chapter 2.

[64] See F. S. J. Ledgister, 'Racist Rantings: Travelers' Tales, and a Creole Counterblast: Thomas Carlyle, John Stuart Mill, J. A. Froude, and J. J. Thomas on British Rule in the West Indies', in Kerry and Hill (eds), *Thomas Carlyle Resartus*, 106–32 (110).

[65] Mill: 'Because he reads in some blue-book of a strike for wages in Demerara, such as he may read of any day in Manchester, he draws a picture of negro inactivity, copied from the wildest prophecies of the slavery party before emancipation' ('Negro Question', 89).

this 'gospel of work'... to my mind, as justly deserves the name of a cant as any of those which he has opposed.... There is nothing laudable in work for work's sake. To work voluntarily for a worthy object is laudable; but what constitutes a worthy object? On this matter, the oracle of which your contributor is the prophet has never yet been prevailed on to declare itself. He revolves in an eternal circle round the idea of work, as if turning up the earth, or driving a shuttle or a quill, were ends in themselves, and the ends of human existence. (90)

This is a scathing attack not only on the 'Occasional Discourse' but on an extensive body of Carlylean writing, by 1849, in which the duty of work had been a constant theme. The contentlessness of that duty here stands exposed, the more starkly because Mill makes no special provision for the writer's labour (Carlyle's included) as having any greater (or less) merit or virtue than that of the farm labourer or road digger or factory hand. Whatever its sphere, work only acquires dignity from the value of its object, Mill counters. Implicitly, he discounts the value of Carlyle's work done *on this occasion*: he might have 'driven his quill' to much better ends. The point is substantive (bad work would be better not done), but Mill pitches the rebuke perhaps higher than need be: work can and does often have value beyond its 'objects' and 'ends' (the value, for example, of welcome distraction or the purely personal value of acquiring technical skill).

Mill's main point of attack on Carlyle's text (after he has dealt with its self-serving theology) concerns the misrepresentation of what liberalism has and has not achieved by 1849. The abolition of slavery was not the outcome of 'philanthropic sentiment':

It depended no more on humane feelings than any cause which so irresistibly appealed to them must necessarily do. Its first victories were gained while the lash yet ruled uncontested in the barrack-yard and the rod in schools, and while men were still hanged by dozens for stealing to the value of forty shillings. It triumphed because it was the cause of justice; and, in the estimation of the great majority of its supporters, of religion. Its originators and leaders were persons of a stern sense of moral obligation, who, in the spirit of the religion of their time, seldom spoke much of benevolence and philanthropy, but often of duty, crime, and sin. (88)

Nothing so flattering to the national self-image as humanitarian compassion gears this corrective account of recent history: it is a hard-headed view of a belated stirring by 'men' (Mill does not even call them 'good' persons) to rectify an 'iniquity' so extreme that the British treatment of the Irish makes for a bad comparison. The comparison was Carlyle's: his Paddy/Negro paralleling points to the hypocrisy of a 'philanthropy' that rejoices in the freedom of its 'black darlings' while ignoring the problems it has created across in Ireland and that are now spilling over to England:

> look at that group of *unsold*, unbought, unmarketable Irish 'free' citizens, dying there in the ditch, whither my Lord of Rackrent and the constitutional sheriffs have evicted them; or at those 'divine missionaries,' of the same free country, now traversing, with rags on back and child on each arm, the principal thoroughfares of London, to tell men what 'freedom' really is;—and admit that there may be doubts on that point!   (381–2)

And by reverse token, Britain need only look to its record on Ireland to see the dangers of failing to do better in its dependencies abroad: 'That will be a consummation. To have "emancipated" the West Indies into a *Black Ireland*; "free" indeed, but an Ireland, and Black!' (353). Mill is having none of it: 'It is a mockery to talk of comparing it with Ireland. [Slavery] went on, not, like Irish beggary, because England had not the skill to prevent it—not merely by the sufferance, but by the laws of the English nation' (88). In this fine-tuned analysis of historical circumstances, 'civilizational self-accusation', as Bruce Robbins has recently denominated it,[66] requires an understanding of comparative scales of injustice: unless we can discriminate between a colonial political and economic system, enforcing by law the extraction of wealth through enslavement of an entire racial group, and a union where 'beggary' is the result of successive failures of political 'skill' in dealing with the long legacies of colonization, we have (Mill suggests) no basis on which to say where there has been progress, nor how much injustice remains to be rectified in the world. 'Is our cholera comparable to the old pestilence—our hospitals to the old lazar-houses—our workhouses to the hanging of vagrants?', he asks (94). If there is a danger in seeming to underrate the importance of Britain's exploitation of the Irish, it is a danger he is prepared to run.[67]

Narratives of 'civilizational self-accusation', whereby individual writers name the disasters for which their own political cultures should take responsibility, can be, in tune with what Robbins suggests, a marker of the capacity for a critical articulation of unevenness in history.[68] The 'Occasional Discourse' is an extreme

---

[66] 'On the Non-Representation of Atrocity', *b2o* [*boundary2 online*], 7 October 2016, <http://www.boundary2.org/2016/10/bruce-robbins-on-the-non-representation-of-atrocity/>.   Accessed   24 March 2017.

[67] On a technical note: the critique of historical indiscriminateness is in tune with Mill's internal critique of utilitarianism's tendency to synchronic indiscriminateness. The point is developed by Frances Ferguson, who argues that 'the progressivist narrative' is 'not merely historically indefensible' (as Bernard Williams claims), it is as 'philosophically unproductive' as 'the most flat-footed utilitarian [ism...]. For the utilitarian assessment of more and less, it substitutes a before and after' without adequate attention to the complexity and diversity of experience. Frances Ferguson, 'What Should I Do and What Was I Thinking?: Philosophical Examples and the Uses of the Literary', *boundary 2: An International Journal of Literature and Culture* 40/2 (2013), 9–23 (14).

[68] 'On the Non-Representation of Atrocity'.

example of the genre—too extreme for Mill, who brings to his criticism an imperative sense of the need for discrimination and not just moral rectitude (of either the liberal-philanthropic or reactionary kind). When Geoffrey Hartman describes Carlyle's deployment of language as 'a form of terror-ism',[69] he captures the extremity of a rhetoric that is prepared to let fine discriminations go in order to jolt complacencies that are, he thinks, too easily fed by singular achievements. The liberal smugness Carlyle has in his sights is (unsurprisingly) not of the cultural-egalitarian globalist kind Robbins has in view—rather, an internal British smugness about the nation's supposed achievements in bringing its colonial system up to the moral mark. The political affront he offers is, on the surface, presentist in thrust: stop paying attention to the historic injustice of slavery in Jamaica; start looking at the consequences today of preferential treatment given to black labourers (or as he would have it, non-labourers) abroad over white labourers and non-labourers in Britain. Mill's response is far more historically robust: if self-accusation is to be morally persuasive, it had better be accurate in the story it tells about past and current actions and their motives, he observes. 'Every age has its faults,' he acknowledges,

> and is indebted to those who point them out.... [But w]e must beware...of mistaking its virtues for faults,... Your contributor thinks that the age has too much humanity, is too anxious to abolish pain. I affirm, on the contrary, that it has too little humanity...and I point to any day's police reports as the proof. I am not now accusing the brutal portion of the population, but the humane portion; if they were humane enough, they would have contrived long ago to prevent these daily atrocities.   (94)

The question, as ever when Mill is read in company with Carlyle, must be whether the liberal philosopher's point-by-point exacting rationality, impressive as he is in correcting his opponent's errors, and challenging his moral principles, and look-ing to dampen the emotional appeal of his rhetorical extremism, can be a sufficient rebuttal to the stylistic and emotional excitement Carlyle creates when he oversteps the normal bounds of political debate in the periodical press. The classic demurral is that, though Mill's criticisms are 'decisive in their own terms', they make little or no impact on a Carlylean perspective from which 'enthusiasm for human justice' is a 'weak-kneed, self-deluded evasion of the facts of a power-

---

[69] Hartman, *Criticism in the Wilderness*, 150. Cf. John P. Farrell, *Revolution as Tragedy: The Dilemma of the Moderate from Scott to Arnold* (Ithaca, NY: Cornell University Press, 1980), 187–245. Farrell reads Carlyle rather as a thwarted extremist, for whom heroic radicalism is the 'gravest' of his many masks (203). Only occasionally, he argues, does 'sheer exasperation excee[d] his capacity for the sense of tragedy'.

governed universe'.[70] It is a criticism that looks forward to Nietzsche as the fuller expression of a 'transvaluation of all values' that Carlyle's prose partly anticipates[71]—crediting the earlier writer with (no small thing) the power to place the argument elsewhere, to elude a framework of liberal debate that, though it would not close him down entirely, seeks to rein him back into the fold of progressivism.

Publishing Mill's response, the editor of *Fraser's* encouraged the magazine's readers to view the critique of the 'Occasional Discourse' in that light: 'If all the meetings at Exeter Hall be not presided over by strictly impartial chairmen, they ought to be. We shall set an example to our pious brethren in this respect, by giving publicity to the following letter. Our readers have now both sides of the question before them, and can form their own opinions upon it.'[72] This is all well and (placatingly) Millian, but Carlyle's goading sarcasms, vehement exhortations, stylistic excesses make for a kind of rhetoric that, as Hartman's metaphor implies, does not aim at participation in argument. Pointing beyond itself to a higher authority, it demands a hearing but does not look to persuade—indeed, expects *not* to persuade. Carlyle was content to create a strongly antipathetic reaction. At first self-protectively dismissive of the 'little dud of a thing' he had written, he was pleased when it provoked a response: 'The Saint-Howard people [Evangelical philanthropists of the John Howard type] are in a terrible tempest here about the N——s; chaunting mournful "*Ichabods!*" over me. Which is all right.'[73] The reaction against the 'Occasional Discourse' in fact went well beyond self-defensive anger from the philanthropic community: the essay gave 'universal offence', as Carlyle's friend and first biographer, J. A. Froude admitted. Admirers on all sides 'drew back', and 'walked no more with him'.[74] Carlyle, who had expected intelligent friends to be exceptions, professed bafflement when some (Mill chief among them) were not.[75] Even twenty years later, George Meredith could recall the 'Occasional Discourse' as a moment of singularly repugnant excess in Victorian public moralism: 'his method of applying his sermon to his "n——" is intolerable.—Spiritual light he has to illuminate a nation. Of practical little or none, and he beats his own brains out with emphasis.'[76]

---

[70] Stefan Collini, 'Introduction to Mill', *CW* XXI, xxi. And see Helen Small, 'The Liberal University and Its Enemies', John Stuart Mill Lecture, delivered at the University of St Andrews, 3 February 2017.

[71] Collini, 'Introduction', xxi.   [72] 'The Negro Question', *Fraser's Magazine*, 25.

[73] Letter to Margaret A. Carlyle, 1 Dec 1849 ('The *dud* of a thing is come out in *Fraser*') and Letter to John A. Carlyle, 14 Dec 1849; in *Collected Letters* XXVII, 299, 310–12 (311).

[74] II, 26. For a telling account of Froude's response to Jamaica when he visited in 1887, forearmed with Carlylean prejudices, see Ledgister, 'Racist Rantings', 113–18.

[75] See Tamarkin, 'Why Forgive Carlyle?', for an ethical reading of the reaction against Carlyle as (in some cases) the first prompt to an enlarged conception of forgiveness.

[76] George Meredith, Letter to Frederick A. Maxse, 2 Jan 1870, in *Letters of George Meredith*, ed. C. L. Cline, 3 vols. (Oxford: Clarendon Press, 1970), I, 442–3 (443). 'Philosophy, while rendering its dues to a man like Carlyle, and acknowledging itself inferior in activity, despises his hideous blustering impatience in the presence of progressive facts.'

Carlyle was prepared to make a bad example of himself to society in a way that involves a quite different form of exemplarity from the kind Thomas Keenan has in mind when he writes of important moral work done by monitory examples ('the bad example', as he puts it). Keenan's subject is the exemplarity of fable: the sheep deceived by the wolf in sheep's clothing; Peter, who cried wolf—didactic cases of immorality or imprudence or plain stupidity that get their due come-uppance. These are, Keenan suggests, the best kinds of moral example because, more than any good example that is set before us to encourage emulation, these tutelary cases call forth 'imitation, interiorization, and identification'.[77] The 'bad example', in other words, excites us, as good examples, with their implicit coercion to fall in line with conventional expectations, do not. Without that excitement, their medicinal function would have less effect. 'What would we humans do...without our regular inoculation?' Keenan asks. 'Responsibility', as Nietzsche saw, 'begins in' such bad examples. The classic Nietzschean object-lesson is, he reminds us, the fable of the lambs and the great birds of prey in the *Genealogy of Morals*.[78] As Nietzsche revises the original fabula, it ceases to be a didactic device modelling good/prudent/wise behaviour and becomes a means to decoding the operation of morality as it takes hold in the language.

> That lambs dislike great birds of prey does not seem strange: only it provides no ground for reproaching these birds of prey for bearing off little lambs. And if the lambs say among themselves: 'these birds of prey are evil; and whoever is as little as possible like a bird of prey, but rather its opposite, a lamb—would he not be good?' ... the birds of prey might view it a little ironically (*spöttisch*) and perhaps say: '*we* don't dislike them at all, these good little lambs; we even love them: nothing is more tasty than a tender lamb.'[79]

Nietzsche goes on: 'only thanks to the seduction of language,...which under-stands and misunderstands all effects as conditioned by something that causes effects, by a "subject"', do the birds appear to have made a moral decision about how to treat the lambs. 'Language', Keenan comments, 'makes action without a subject impossible, allowing what Nietzsche calls "popular morality" to separate strength from expressions of strength, as if there were a neutral substratum behind the strong man, which was *free* to express strength or not to do so' (135). In the Nietzschean account, there is no moral agency in the case: the greater strength of the one animal over the other is a fact, and it is the work of the Nietzschean

---

[77] 'Fables of Responsibility', in Alexander Gelley (ed.), *Unruly Examples: On the Rhetoric of Exemplarity* (Stanford, CA: Stanford University Press, 1995), 121–41 (121).

[78] Ibid., 135.

[79] Friedrich Nietzsche, *The Genealogy of Morals*, trans. Walter Kaufmann and R. J. Hollingdale (New York: Vintage Books, 1969), 44–5 (this is the translation cited by Keenan).

philosopher/critic to expose the error of morality and affirm the nobility of strength.

Nietzsche's insightfulness as a reader of Carlyle lies, as this celebrated passage helps us to see, in his resistance to those elements in Carlyle that, while offering to be bad, want, underneath, to be more than conventionally good. Carlyle gets the point about power (all too well, many would say), but he cannot do away with the false 'substratum' of moral freedom altogether. He wants ('needs', Nietzsche says) to retain an anchoring belief that morality has metaphysical security. His prose accordingly models a less than clear-cut form of misbehaviour—a violation of norms of free speech that anticipates Nietzsche in its affronting sarcasms and ironies at the expense of conventional morality and its flagrant breaches of discursive norms, but (unlike Nietzsche) appeals to a higher authority in matters of good and evil. In that light, the frame narrators perform a service beyond self-interested screening from blame: they model a deferral of authority that looks comic in the frame but operates quite seriously to moor the moral controversial-ism of the writing that follows. For all its hyper-literacy and its dazzling rhetorical energies, Carlyle's is a prose that, indeed, *must* deny or reject its own power and accept the consequences of its own abscension from some, not all, normal moral agreements.

Historically, the 'Occasional Discourse' stands alongside (and midway between) Swift's *Modest Proposal* and Nietzsche's *Ecce Homo*: a perplexing, if not quite paradoxical thing—'exemplary' cynicism, whose mode of relating rules to action is more 'internal' than external.[80] Nietzsche's own reaction to reading Carlyle via the laudatory account found in Froude's (1882) biography (it is unclear whether he had read Carlyle at first hand) singles out Carlyle's anti-scepticism as having particular diagnostic significance: 'The craving for a strong faith is no proof of a strong faith, but quite the contrary. If one has such a faith, then one can afford the beautiful luxury of skepticism.'[81] In other words, if Carlyle had felt able to risk some scepticism towards his own values and assertions, the metaphysical infrastructure of his rhetoric would have been less shaky—but the result a lot less interesting to Nietzsche himself. This is, of course, a criticism born of closely felt kinship (Nietzsche says as much).[82] The element of identification is no less

---

[80] Ridley, Introduction, in *Anti-Christ, Ecce Homo, Twilight of the Idols, and Other Writings*, xxiii: 'In the exemplary figure' the relation of rules to action is 'altogether internal: he does as he does because it is in his nature to do so'.

[81] *Twilight of the Idols*, trans. Kaufmann, 521.

[82] That Carlyle and Nietzsche stand in a near relation to one another is well known. See esp. Eric Bentley, *A Century of Hero-Worship: A Study of the Idea of Heroism in Carlyle and Nietzsche, with Notes on Wagner, Spengler, Stefan George, and D. H. Lawrence*, 2nd edn (Boston: Beacon Press, 1957); Albert J. LaValley, *Carlyle and the Idea of the Modern: Studies in Carlyle's Prophetic Literature and Its Relation to Blake, Nietzsche, Marx and Others* (New Haven, CT: Yale University Press, 1968); Jeremy Tambling, 'Carlyle through Nietzsche: Reading *Sartor Resartus*', *Modern Language Review* 102/2 (April 2007), 326–40; William Meakins, 'Nietzsche, Carlyle, and Perfectionism', *Journal of Nietzsche Studies* 45/3 (November 2014), 258–78.

significant, given that Nietzsche is so caustic about Carlyle in *Twilight of the Idols* (1888).[83] Carlyle emerges from the brief reflection on Froude's *Life* as barely worthy of applause (which is to say, much better than most in Nietzsche's judgement): a man not up to the task that Nietzsche sets for himself of asserting his own will towards a thoroughgoing atheistic scepticism. Restrained by a 'naïve' 'Romantic' yearning after a strong faith, restrained also by an outmoded code of 'honour', Carlyle is a shouty attitudinizer.[84]

There is, perhaps, no better example of the Nietzschean view that antagonism is the sincerest form of flattery than the younger man's insistence on Carlyle's systemic limitations: the 'dyspeptic philosopher' delivers 'pessimism as coughed-up lunch' (192). When Nietzsche writes of himself that he has cultivated a style 'with as much substance as possible at its base, a cold malice against "beautiful words" as well as "beautiful feelings"' (224), he might be describing a rhetoric that has learned from Carlyle's strengths while eradicating as far as possible his weakness. The Nietzschean 'great sceptic' needs no doctor: he thrives without 'regulative guidelines' and scorns the 'weak-willed person's failure to thrive'. Late Nietzschean style foregrounds 'concision and compression', as Julian Young notes: the outrageously stylish epigram is a form of compacted heterodoxy. 'You do not get hold of things that are open to question any more' (Nietzsche praises himself in *Ecce Homo*), 'you get hold of decisions'.[85]

It would be easy to mistake what Carlyle does in the 'Occasional Discourse'— and what some of the more strategic testers of free speech norms today are doing—as just a more demanding version of the kind of internal challenge to which Millian liberalism promised to expose itself (a line of response that would provide some reassurance to the liberal worried that the price of democracy may be that noise will sometimes trump reason). The challenge Carlyle poses is deeper, and politically salient again today. Looking to stir up conviction rather than to join in argument, he speaks over the heads of a limitedly tolerant 'liberal' readership to a 'boundlessly tolerant' audience that will forgive his peculiarities and respond to his ardour rather than his arguments (though he eschews the role of demagogue). In doing so he creates a discursive situation in which his audience is asked at once to discount much of what is said in favour of how authentically it is said; and yet also to understand that there is a deeper purpose to his speech (a confrontation

[83] The other direct references to Carlyle in the late works (*The Anti-Christ, Ecce Homo*) are gestural not palpable hits: 'that knowing and involuntary counterfeiter' (101), 'Carlylism...a need of the *weak*' for 'some unconditional yes or no' (54).

[84] One may intuit that part of the reason for Nietzsche's antagonism was that Froude had sought to establish Carlyle himself as an exemplary figure—'an example of integrity & simplicity to all English men of letters', as he put it in a private letter to Martin Tupper: 'We sorely need an example of this kind, for our profession tends to vanity and is not a wholesome one.' Froude to Martin Tupper, 3 December 1882, quoted by John Clubbe, Editor's Introduction to *Froude's Life of Carlyle* (Columbus, OH: Ohio State University Press, 1979), 31.

[85] Julian Young, *Friedrich Nietzsche: A Philosophical Biography* (Cambridge: Cambridge University Press, 2010), 498; quoting *Ecce Homo*, 137.

with the reality of power) that requires all of us to possess the strength of our own convictions.

Oddly, his ideal reader might, in theory, and had he chosen almost any other subject, have been the great African-American civil rights activist W. E. B. Du Bois, who felt, as many critics have noted, a 'great affinity' with Carlyle's prose.[86]

Reading Carlyle as a student at Fisk University (the Congregational school in Nashville, Tennessee, where he 'embraced' his 'Negro' identity for the first time), Du Bois warmed, his biographer observes, to the 'effulgent adjectives and magnificent invective' of 'authoritarian romanticism'. This was a prose capable of cutting through politeness, and steeling the reader to change the world. Discovering *Sartor* and *Heroes, Hero-Worship, and the Heroic in History* later, at Harvard, strengthened the attraction.[87] There was inspiration to be had in the idea of the strong leader; the injunctions to find purpose and value in work; the attacks on Mammon; the calls to find a better and higher happiness than a society greedy for money will tend to promote. 'What if to the Mammonism of America be added the rising Mammonism of the reborn South,' Du Bois asks in *The Souls of Black Folk* (1903), 'and the Mammonism of this South be reinforced by the budding Mammonism of its half-wakened black millions? Whither, then, is the new-world quest of Goodness and Beauty and Truth gone glimmering?'[88] 'Gone glimmering' puts a Byronic twist on the end, but Carlyle was fond of glimmer too, and Du Bois's moral rhetoric is drawn straight from Carlyle: 'I anticipate light in the Human Chaos, glimmering, shining more and more;... Our deity no longer being Mammon,—O Heavens, each man will then say to himself: "Why such deadly haste to make money?"'[89]

A prior basis for stylistic kinship may be found, Vanessa Dickerson observes, in the two writers' respective debts to the sermonic traditions of the Scottish Secession and the black-American Congregational church tradition in which they were raised—we should add, also in the degree to which they subsequently set themselves at a critical distance from these institutions.[90] But fellow-travelling to this degree seems explicable only on the assumption that Du Bois remained 'ignorant of Carlyle's infamous fulmination against blacks in "The N—— Question" as incapable of surviving outside slavery'.[91] He certainly came to

---

[86] Vanessa D. Dickerson, *Dark Victorians* (Urbana, IL: University of Illinois Press, 2008), 95.

[87] David Levering Lewis, *W. E. B. Du Bois: Biography of a Race, 1868–1919* (New York: Henry Holt and Company, 1993), 55, 72, 75.

[88] W. E. B. Du Bois, *The Souls of Black Folk*, with an Introduction and Chronology by Jonathan Scott Holloway (New Haven, CT: Yale University Press, [1903] 2015), 62.

[89] *Past and Present*, CE X, 270.

[90] On Carlyle, see Ian Campbell, 'Carlyle's Religion: The Scottish Background', in John Clubbe (ed.), *Carlyle and His Contemporaries: Essays in Honor of Charles Richard Sanders* (Durham, NC: Duke University Press, 1974) 3–20; on Du Bois, Barbara Diane Savage, 'W. E. B. Du Bois and "The Negro Church"', *The Annals of the American Academy of Political and Social Science* 568 (March 2000), 235–49.

[91] *Du Bois: Biography of a Race*, 75. Lewis thinks him 'undoubtedly' so.

understand that Carlyle could be dangerously irresponsible on the subject of race, and in *Black Reconstruction* (1935) picked out for special attention a notorious comment recorded by Grant Duff in the context of the American Civil War: 'Carlyle sneered at people "cutting each other's throats because one half of them prefer hiring their servants for life, and the other half by the hour"'.[92] Du Bois's debt to Carlyle was, Paul Gilroy suggests, a case where writerly influence is as significant for the limits drawn as for the inspiration taken. Carlyle's capacity to cut through politeness goes into the mix with, and is softened by, other influences (Emerson, Hazlitt, Lamb, all make their mark). We can, Gilroy concludes, see the various ways of addressing and 'interpellating' the reader 'as a deliberate experiment produced from the realization that none of these different registers of address could, by itself, convey the intensity of feeling that [he] believed the writing of black history and the exploration of racialized experience demanded'.[93]

In *Bleak Liberalism* (2016), Amanda Anderson, making a persuasive case for a return to 'character' as a term that can 'hel[p] us think through the ethical and existential dimensions of intellectual and political positions', observes that ascriptions of character 'often signal moments where the lived aspects of theory are making their force felt' (21). The controversialist possesses, almost by definition, a strong public character: confrontationally dissenting, putting 'reality' before 'ideals', careless of giving offence. The ethical corollary of that character in the shared work of debate is not always as apparent. In the Carlylean case, there are two primary aspects to it. The first can expect to find fairly wide agreement; the other has consistently failed to do so. The element of his performance as a modern controversialist that has to do with resetting the default modes of public argument has a valid point: it asks an ostensibly liberal public sphere to take seriously the high valuation it places on freedom of speech, and to extend that value to styles of expression—admitting power, passion, extravagance, disconcerting excess, as part of a broad palate of public discourse. The content he chooses to endow with these attributes is another matter: rightly reviled, as to its racial politics, and (as a consequence) largely unheard in the astute criticisms it has to make about the selectivity of his culture's view on its own progressivist credentials. A better reading than the standard account of Mill *vs.* Carlyle as a confrontation of liberal

[92] W. E. B. Du Bois, *Black Reconstruction in America, 1860–1880* (1935), with an Introduction by David Levering Lewis (New York: Free Press, [1935] 1998), 88. The Right Hon. Sir Mountstuart E. Grant Duff, *Notes from a Diary, 1851–1872* (London: John Murray, 1897), 204. And see David Levering Lewis, *W. E. B. Du Bois: The Fight for Equality and the American Century, 1919–1963* (New York: Henry Holt and Company, 2000), 310.

[93] Paul Gilroy, *The Black Atlantic: Modernity and Double Consciousness* (Cambridge, MA: Harvard University Press, 1993), 115. For further consideration of the limits of Carlyle's credibility as an influence, see Cornel West, 'Black Strivings in a Twilight Civilization', in Henry Louis Gates, Jr and Cornel West (eds.), *The Future of the Race* (New York: Alfred A. Knopf, 1993), 53–114 (65–71); and Orlando Patterson, *The Ordeal of Integration: Progress and Resentment in America's "Racial" Crisis* (Washington, DC: Civitas/Counterpoint, 1997), 104; and commentary by Dickerson, *Dark Victorians*, 105–6.

principle with reactionary offence, I have been suggesting, would allow for recognition on both sides that, at stake here, more than their friendship, was the dominant ethos of public debate, and the degree and kind of influence to be wielded in it by liberal political theory.

Right at the start of their friendship, Carlyle warned Mill that 'I set little store by this so celebrated virtue of Tolerance.'[94] It is worth recalling the context. Carlyle was writing in fulsome praise of a review Mill had just published of Alison's *Europe during the French Revolution*, welcoming what he saw as a new willingness in the democratic theorist and utilitarian to go beyond colourless reasoning and strike a more full-hearted and 'decided' tone:

> it is a really *decided* little utterance, with a quiet emphasis, a conscious incontrovertibility, which (heretic that I am) I rejoice to see growing in you. Such a feeling, such a mode of writing seems to me, in these days especially, the only fruitful one: emphasis in uttering, what is it but the natural result of entireness in believing; the *first* condition of all worth in words to be spoken, and quite especially precious in a despicable sceptical, 'supposing,' weathercock, foundationless era such as ours.

Being Carlyle, he did not stop there: 'Give me, above and before all things, a man that has legs to stand on: keep far from me, were it possible, the innumerable decrepit *culs-de-jutte* [cripples] that can stand, that can move nowhere, but only beg permission of all bystanders to move *whithersoever they are shoved!*' 'Tolerance', he writes, is a virtue he has scarcely ever seen in action—only, 'often enough, and with ever-increasing dislike, Indifferentism parading itself in the stolen garments' (445). It is a characteristic display of Carlylean 'bad exemplarity' in private rather than public mode—going a metaphor too far in search of the gut response he associates with integrity of belief.[95] Whether that gut response be laughter or revulsion does not, perhaps, matter to him, so long as there *is* a powerfully felt response.

The confrontation between Carlyle and Mill over 'The Negro Question' in 1849–50 was a sharper, and far more public challenge, sixteen years on, to Mill's manner of conducting public arguments—one that indeed compelled Mill to decide how tolerant or otherwise the character of his moralism should be. Nietzsche famously tells us that 'noble hospitality means keeping a room free

---

[94]   24 September 1833; *Collected Letters*, VI, 444–50 (445).

[95]   He was consistent on this point. 'Intolerance, with nothing to protect but empty pots and eggs that are fairly hatched addle, is doubly and trebly intolerable', he wrote in a private manuscript much nearer the time of composing the 'Occasional Discourse': '[Eheu, eheu!] [Alas, alas!]—There are a few men who have even at present a certain right, call it rather a certain terrible duty, to be intolerant, and I hope there will be ever more, and that their intolerance will grow ever nobler, diviner, more victorious; but how few are there in all the Earth!' See Murray Baumgarten, 'Carlyle and "Spiritual Optics"', *Victorian Studies* 11/4 (1968), 502-33 (512).

for the unwanted guest' (*Twilight of the Idols*, 25)—a radical challenge that has attracted many recent critics in the wake of re-readings of Nietzsche by Levinas and Derrida.[96] But Mill, while he requires us to listen and deliberate, does not ask us to be as generous as many of these advocates of critical hospitality (especially those in the Levinasian mould) would have us be. He gives Carlyle a hearing, admits his significance in the debate, but does not ask us to validate him in our public discourse. He has learned from Carlyle (and would feed the knowledge into *On Liberty*) that liberalism, when severely goaded, must remain committed to evidence-based, sceptical reasoning (as today's much-needed fact checkers are doing), but it had better not be anaemic. The last line of Mill's response to 'The Negro Question', after which his personal interactions with Carlyle were almost nil, puts aside the 'studied moderation of language' *On Liberty* would call for as, in principle, where feasible, the standard to which liberal debate should hold itself—a recommendation that would substantially and increasingly shape liberalism thereafter, not always to its advantage. He quotes an unnamed writer, with a more vivid idiom of abuse than he himself might have comfortably mustered: Carlyle 'has made himself an instrument of what an able writer in the Inquirer justly calls "a true work of the devil"' (95). Borrowed though it is, it is the note of full-hearted, angry conviction Carlyle himself wanted to hear more of in public debate, not least from Mill himself.

[96] See, for example, Michael Naas, '"Alors, qui êtes-vous?": Jacques Derrida and the Question of Hospitality', *Substance* 34/1 (2005), 6–17; Martin Hägglund and Derek Attridge, 'Ethics, Hospitality and Radical Atheism: A Dialogue' (Wadham College, University of Oxford, 2010), <https://podcasts. ox.ac.uk/ethics-hospitality-and-radical-atheism-dialogue>; Michael Marais, 'Coming into Being: J. M. Coetzee's *Slow Man* and the Aesthetic of Hospitality', *Contemporary Literature* 50/2 (2009), 273–98.

3

The Freedom of Criticism

Arnold's Cynicisms

Criticism's freedom to 'judge autonomously', as Kant and many others after him have put it, and to pursue 'truth for the benefit of all',[1] is a fundamental assumption of modern intellectual life. It has special importance for the university but wider purchase in public conceptions of the right to free speech and the democratic interest. Like freedom of self-expression generally, criticism's freedom of operation is not an unambiguous requirement: what it entails, how far public 'benefit' is its justification, what rights and interests on the part of individuals may attach to it—and what other rights and interests may take precedence over it—are all crucial questions of interpretation that can form the content, as well as the framing protocols, for critical activity.

This chapter treats an influential line of thinking about the nature, extent, and purpose of freedom in the theory and practice of cultural criticism as it emerged in the mid to late nineteenth century. Matthew Arnold's account of 'The Function of Criticism' as the 'free play of thought' (1864) retains even now a reputation as one of the most articulate formulations of how and why cultural criticism should have an active regard for the scope and seriousness of its freedom, providing legible assurances that it is not in hock to interests and purposes other than its own. I give it—and Arnold's writing more generally—dedicated space here, because he establishes some basic principles, and raises also some significant problems with respect to the definition of critical freedom, the assurances, and the relation of both to the work of public moralism. Strongly Kantian in his assumption that the one constraint on criticism was that it must be based in reason (a purely arbitrary assertion of critical will would have no validity), Arnold nevertheless took a flexible view of the styles and approaches open to rationality. Much of my argument for the function of cynicism in his thinking is an argument on the grounds of style, in which stylistic freedom becomes the first and foremost assurance that other kinds of critical freedom—moral and political—are being

---

[1] Immanuel Kant, *The Conflict of the Faculties (Der Streit der Fakultäten)*, ed. and trans. Mary J. Gregor (Lincoln, NE: University of Nebraska Press, 1992): 'the power to judge autonomously—that is, freely (according to principles of thought in general)—is called reason. [. . . T]he very *modesty* [of Philosophy's claim]—merely to be free, as it leaves others free, to discover the truth for the benefit of all [fields of knowledge]—must commend it to the government as above suspicion and, indeed, indispensable' (43–4).

The Function of Cynicism at the Present Time. Helen Small, Oxford University Press (2020). © Helen Small.
DOI: 10.1093/oso/9780198861935.001.0001

exercised. As his career progresses, however, I see the relation of the stylistic to the moral and political becoming more troublesome to Arnold, and, indeed, to discerning critics in his own time, alert to the points at which cynic freedoms may start to look more like elitist arrogance than liberal-progressivist 'free play of thought'.

Arnold's view of criticism is commonly, and not wrongly, described as norma-tive and universalist: it sets out 'norms of culture' that are, given the underpinning commitment to right reason, 'necessarily those of universal humanity', as Francis Mulhern puts it.[2] The 'necessarily' is in implied scare quotes: this is (as Mulhern reads it) Arnold's assumption, now much disputed. How strong and consistent an assumption it was for Arnold himself is a question worth asking. Some of the most revealing writing about Arnold in recent years draws out the ways in which normativity and universalism in his conception of rationality were compatible with commitment to social equality, some sensitivity to cultural pluralism, a non-prescriptive view of the proper objects of criticism, and quite a high degree of pragmatism in his thinking about the social and psychological effects, rather than intrinsic merits, of literature (especially poetry).[3] My interest in him is in line with growing interest in a more complex and flexible Arnoldianism, but it pushes somewhat against the view sometimes taken of Arnold's characteristically tactful comportment as a critic by focusing on his attraction to strongly confrontational models of reasoning and arguing—models that stretch the boundaries of conven-tional decorum in public debate in the attempt to attack habitual and convention-bound thinking. Even as Arnold sought to recommend a critical practice that placed a high theoretical value on tactful persuasion and collective commitments to culture, he demonstrated a taste and an intellectual respect for features of public debate associated, at their strongest, with cynicism: free speech, the challenging of conventions of thought and behaviour, a high tolerance for waywardness of opinion, and (crucially) an aggressive debasement of the motives that guide the conduct of others in intellectual and political life.

Arnold was not of a cynic disposition—indeed, he is one of the leading examples treated in this book of a writer unlikely to be associated with cynicism, but for whom cynicism held vivid attractions. He saw a role for cynicism as an exercise of liberty and (the potential for conflict here will be clear) an assertion of

---

[2] Francis Mulhern, *Culture/Metaculture* (London: Routledge, 2000), xvi.

[3] See esp. Amanda Anderson, *The Powers of Distance: Cosmopolitanism and the Cultivation of Detachment* (Princeton, NJ: Princeton University Press, 2001), Chapter 3, on the ways in which Arnold wrestles with the 'distinctly modern question of whether universal or impersonal value can find subjective embodiment' (108) and his cultivation of a version of critical detachment that is 'at once characterological and impersonal', its key terms seeming to 'mark the transcendence of subjectivity' even as he insists that his ideal is 'moral and psychological' and not purely 'intellectual' (114); and David Russell, *Tact: Aesthetic Liberalism and the Essay Form in Nineteenth-Century Britain* (Princeton, NJ: Princeton University Press, 2018), Chapter 3, on Arnold's concern to articulate a 'standard of judgement' for poetry that focuses on 'a poem's "pragmatic" effect on the modern mind'. Tact is also a key term in Anderson's analysis (see, esp. her concluding argument on Arnold, 11).

'force' in the defence of certain ideals not universally shared though (in his view) universally desirable. Not all of Arnold's cynicisms can be considered tactical: some have the mark of whim, or spontaneous exuberance, or (not infrequently) reaction against boredom—not least with himself and his own pieties. Like those other occasional cynics, Bertrand Russell and John Dewey (treated in Chapter 5), Arnold promoted high ideals about the progressive tendency of culture and society: both his strategic *and* his more impromptu cynicisms tend to serve the ideal of culture, and yet they also speak to a problem in reconciling the value attached to freedom with the value attached to culture as a shared good. Like Russell and Dewey, Arnold expressed a deep and fundamental commitment to freedom of individual self-realization and self-expression, and the right to exercise scepticism towards the normative values and agreements of public life. But he also recognizes freedom as the gateway to culture, its necessary support if not quite its guarantor. So, though his own incursions into the terrain of cynicism were self-limiting, he was curious about the allure and the value of a deeper scepticism than his own—looking over the fence, from time to time, (as it were) at bolder writers.

The charismatic provocations of cynicism are a minor but crucial element in his stylistic and intellectual range—employed in ways that stretch the bounds of his own liberty of expression and prevent the exercise of criticism becoming pallid or self-limitingly consensual, or stuck in a rut of reaction 'for or against' the object of its scrutiny. For that reason, much of the first section of this chapter holds cynicism at bay. Cynicism's presence at the margins of his practice (and on rare occasions at its centre) enables him to articulate a view of criticism that affirms freedom of thought as its core criterion, and looks to perceived national differences in commitment to that criterion as the ground for argument over the 'health' of a culture, its liberal credentials, its egalitarian potential.

The commitment of Arnoldian public moralism to the strong ironies, comic flair, and 'sarcastic turns'[4] of cynicism is at its subtlest and most strategic in mid-career. It is somewhat destabilized and takes on new political and cultural salience towards the end of his life, as first-hand exposure to America requires him to think harder about the generalizability of his idea of critical 'freedom'. American democratic culture, with its high valuation of 'freedom', 'frankness', and 'clear-sightedness', posed a challenge to Arnoldian criticism. His attachment to culture as a universal cause, risked (he was well aware) looking like a late-colonial projection of British national values and tastes onto a country with distinctive conceptions of culture and criticism, primed to consider Arnold himself with critical detachment. As I read it, the potential stalling of his advocacy for culture when it encounters an outlook as critical, and potentially more radical, ends not in

---

[4] Matthew Arnold, 'Heinrich Heine', in *Lectures and Essays in Criticism*, in *Complete Prose Works*, ed. R. H. Super, 11 vols. (Ann Arbor, MI: The University of Michigan Press, 1960–77), III (assisted by Sister Thomas Marion Hoctor), 107–32 (129) [hereafter, *CPW*].

Arnold's embarrassment, nor (as the standard reading of Arnold in America holds) in revelation of a narrowly nationalist and conservative core to his 'universal' culture,[5] but in a series of not-entirely satisfactory adjustments to the function of cynicism as he attempts to hold on to a critical ethos that can credibly claim flexibility of international outlook without sacrificing what he deems vital to criticism: the capacity for 'force'.

*

Culture's need of freedom—freedom of mind, freedom of expression, freedom of debate—is the central tenet of Arnoldian criticism. In his famous statement of how criticism serves culture, what is wanted is:

> disinterested love of a free play of the mind on all subjects, for its own sake,—... criticism, real criticism, is essentially the exercise of this very quality. It obeys an instinct prompting it to try to know the best that is known and thought in the world, irrespectively of practice, politics, and everything of the kind; and to value knowledge and thought as they approach this best, without the intrusion of any other considerations whatever.[6]

Harnessed though it is (vulnerable though many have thought it) to a conception of 'the best', the critical instinct, as Arnold defines it, approaches that standard by way of the play of mind, liberated from all extraneous interests and 'considerations', contingencies of 'practice', and 'politics' chief among them. He draws heavily on Kant with respect to disinterest and free play, but he goes beyond Kant when he accents the pleasure and the experiential intensity to be found in this activity of the mind. What he describes is not a critical method but a condition of possibility for critical practice: 'disinterested *love of* free play'—an ardent attachment to criticism's liberty of action that makes engagement in criticism 'vital'. Criticism so energized, so *driven* to play, gets as far as it does (and Arnold is clear that it can only '*try* to know... and to value' rightly) by committing to the widest possible view of things. Without being 'worldly' in any instrumental or ends-driven sense, it is in, and rangily of, the world—by instinct 'expansive', as Arnold puts it in the Preface to *Mixed Essays* (1879).[7]

How can we know that the exercise of criticism is genuinely free? Arnold gives a dual answer to that question. At the collective level evidenced by the national culture, we know it because the culture produces 'great works of literature and art' (260)—works that show creative power responding to the stimulus of ideas from critical thought: 'the best ideas', that is, 'on every matter which literature touches,

---

[5] See, for example, Ella Dzelzainis and Ruth Livesey (eds.), *The American Experiment and the Idea of Democracy in English Culture, 1776–1914* (Farnham: Ashgate, 2013), 7–8 (and see p. C3.P3 above).

[6] Matthew Arnold, 'The Function of Criticism at the Present Time' (1864), in *Lectures and Essays in Criticism*, 258–85 (268).

[7] In *Essays Religious and Mixed*, ed. R. H. Super, CPW VIII, 370–2 (371).

current at the time' (260). Creativity *not* nourished by such ideas cannot be 'very important or fruitful', Arnold asserts (260), and he airs some tendentious criticisms of English Romanticism on this score: Byron, Shelley, even Wordsworth (and Arnold does not want Wordsworth altered) lack, he says, the sustenance of 'a certain intellectual and spiritual atmosphere,...a certain order of ideas' (261). At the level of the individual critic, recognition of freedom is internal, intuitive, and non-ends-driven (except in the vexatious sense in which almost anything can be deemed to serve some end): we know our own mind is operating freely because 'free play' of critical ideas produces 'true happiness' (260). Arnold encourages us to think of happiness here, not as a product of critical freedom but as inherent in critical activity: criticism, rightly pursued, is 'a satisfaction in itself' (264). This second answer seems less in hock to criteria of aesthetic or other standards of judgement than the first answer—but the two ways of construing freedom are interlinked, and if creative activity remains for Arnold 'the highest function' of which human beings are capable, 'The Function of Criticism' goes a long way towards establishing free critical play of mind as the more widely available route to happiness, and an essential support to the great writer's exceptional gift.

There is, an argumentative reader may want to say at this point, some risk of false syllogism on both counts. Great works of literature and art may indeed find stimulus from the free critical play of ideas, but the existence of an intellectually liberal critical culture does not guarantee the arrival of an 'Aeschylus [or] a Shakespeare'. We could test possible counter-examples—Cicero, perhaps; Shakespeare himself; Milton?—but Arnold does not admit exceptions, taking a surprisingly tough line on the general 'currency' of critical ideas necessary to sustain great work. As to the individual critic: someone 'exercising free creative activity' (260) feels 'pleasure' and 'desire' in the unrestricted play of ideas—but 'pleasure and desire' in the act of criticism cannot themselves be *proof* of 'free creative activity' (268). Surely there are prompts to pleasure and desire other than 'disinterested free play'?—savage indignation, for example (not always, Claude Rawson reminds us, a laceration to the heart)?,[8] or resistance to oppression?, sheer countersuggestibility?, or the less meritorious, but scarcely discountable, stimulus of intellectual narcissism? When Walt Whitman, wonderfully, described Arnold as 'one of the *dudes* of literature',[9] he was pointing to an element of flamboyance in the critical style that seemed to Whitman narcissistic and, by implication, elitist—it was not an unqualified compliment.[10]

There are other answers we might give to the question of how we can know we are in the presence of a freely critical mind—answers not directly proposed in 'The

---

[8] Claude Rawson, *Swift's Angers* (Cambridge: Cambridge University Press, 2014), 243.

[9] Horace Traubel, *With Walt Whitman in Camden*, 9 vols. (Boston, MA: Small, Maynard & Co., 1906–96), I, 45.

[10] 'dude, *n.*, *adj.* (A. 1), and *int.*', *OED* 1.

Function of Criticism', but broached. We can recognize it negatively, perhaps, by its non-replicability and the difficulty of capturing it within an institutional organization (Arnold's advocacy for literary Academies notwithstanding). If we accent too heavily criticism's function in providing cultural stimulus and enhancing individual satisfaction, Arnold worries, critical activity starts to sound easy, pleasant, something your average British Philistine will have no trouble accommodating and, indeed, organizing:

> So immersed are [Philistines] in practical life, . . . that they are apt to think that truth and culture themselves can be reached by the processes of this life, . . . Away with the notion of proceeding by any other course than the course dear to the Philistines; let us have a social movement, let us organize and combine a party to pursue truth and new thought, let us call it *the liberal party*, and let us all stick to each other, and back each other up. Let us have no nonsense about independent criticism, and intellectual delicacy, and the few and the many. Don't let us trouble ourselves about foreign thought; we shall invent the whole thing for ourselves as we go along. . . . we are all liberals, we are all in pursuit of truth. In this way the pursuit of truth becomes really a social, practical, pleasurable affair, almost requiring a chairman, a secretary, and advertisements; with the excitement of an occasional scandal, with a little resistance to give the happy sense of difficulty overcome; . . .   (276)

The sarcasm makes its own point. Criticism must be tougher than standardly permitted by 'vulgar liberalism' (as Arnold often calls it).[11] Critique along complacently narrow lines, and within national boundaries, is not free: it has been incorporated, channelled to practical and instrumental ends, and it will be no less incorporated and channelled if it is clever enough to want to demonstrate that something significant is happening by allowing a little trouble-making at the margins, a frisson of 'scandal' or 'resistance' implying that the stakes are high and progress in ideas is being made. By contrast, Arnold wants criticism, including his own, to be prepared to cause upset—to be free play, not congenially liberal play.

In token of his own willingness to cause offence, Arnold recalls the upset raised by his attack, a few years earlier, on the bad science and bad theology of the Bishop

---

[11] See, for example, Letter to Jane Mary Arnold Forster, Jan. 1864, on 'stock vulgar Liberalism', and Letter to Frances Bunsen Trevenen Whately Arnold, 14 May 1865, on 'vulgar Liberals', in *The Letters of Matthew Arnold*, ed. Cecil Y. Lang, 5 vols. (Charlottesville, VA: University Press of Virginia, 1996–2001), II, 267–9 (268) and 415–16 (416); and on 'vulgar modern liberalism' in the essay on 'Joubert', in *Lectures and Essays in Criticism*, 183–211 (189). The sensed 'hardness and vulgarity of middle-class liberalism' is a core element of the description of Philistinism in *Friendship's Garland* and, more extensively, *Culture and Anarchy*: see, for example, *Culture and Anarchy, with Friendship's Garland and Some Literary Essays*, ed. R. H. Super, *CPW*, V, 107. Patrick Neal, 'Vulgar Liberalism', *Political Theory* 21/4 (1993), 623–42.

of Natal's arguments for biblical fallibility.[12] John Colenso's failings of critical intelligence, anatomized unforgivingly in two essays by Arnold, were (he wrote at the time) 'a great public act of self-humiliation' (40). Dipping down into the footnotes, added to 'The Function of Criticism' when it was reprinted in *Essays in Criticism* (1865), one finds him admitting that in the Colenso case he resorted to 'personal attack and controversy'. Others considered this bad form. He 'sincerely' prefers to avoid such methods, he says, and therefore 'abstain[s] from reprinting' the Colenso responses in *Essays in Criticism*, but he takes the opportunity 'to make here a final declaration of my sincere impenitence for having published them' (276n). Two protestations of sincerity within one footnote—eleven in the essay altogether—suggest that Trilling's distinction between sincerity and authenticity may be *à propos*: an insisted-upon 'Victorian' sincerity about one's way of acting opens a door onto the murkier territory of the 'modern' search for authenticity.[13]

As Arnold probes the function of criticism further, pleasure and happiness in exercising the function of criticism become less reliable indices of freedom. The play of critical instinct, if it is really free, must push through 'personal dislike' of aggression and controversy when occasion demands and lead the critic to state plainly where s/he sees 'confusion' and 'false estimat[ion]' in the work of others. Kick-back from his response to Colenso is a measure of how much resistance may be encountered: 'Immediately there was a cry raised: "What is this?" ... a liberal attacking a liberal' (277). Satiric ventriloquism here indicates how far Arnold was out of tune with contemporary moves to impose protocols on cultural debate: the 1860s saw increasing momentum in the transition from reviewer anonymity to 'avowal of responsibility' through signature,[14] and an increased tendency to deprecate *ad hominem* and *ad feminam* criticisms.[15] These were broadly 'liberal' reforms aimed at improving the rationality of public arguments—at some cost to freedom. Arnold was a participant, but an ambivalent one. There is no special consideration due, in 'The Function of Criticism', for subscription to free thought if the mode of subscription becomes a constraint in itself. At his most aggressive— reviewing, for example, a new and very unsatisfactory translation of Spinoza—the only difference between freedom and abuse of freedom is pantomimic excess, the performance of blatantly going over the top: 'We part from this book with sincere resentment ... a heinous literary sin committed ... another great author lost sight of ... in the hideous anarchy which is modern English literature.'[16]

---

[12] See 'The Bishop and the Philosopher', the end of 'Tractatus Theologico-Politicus', and 'Dr. Stanley's Lectures on the Jewish Church', in Matthew Arnold, *Lectures and Essays in Criticism*, 40–55, 56–64 (64), 65–82.

[13] Lionel Trilling, *Sincerity and Authenticity* (Cambridge, MA: Harvard University Press, 1971).

[14] See Elaine Hadley, *Living Liberalism: Practical Citizenship in Mid-Victorian Britain* (Chicago: University of Chicago Press, 2010), 160.

[15] For discussion, see Helen Small, 'Liberal Editing in the *Fortnightly Review* and the *Nineteenth Century*', *Publishing History* 53 (2003), 75–96.

[16] Matthew Arnold, Tractatus Theologico-Politicus', in *Lectures and Essays in Criticism*, 56–64 (64).

Some may think that muting his opposition to Colenso ('I am sincerely impenitent but I assert it in a footnote') and camping up his annoyance at a mangled Spinoza are evidence that in reality, or on an accurate reading of tone, Arnold knuckles under to the new, more restrained dispensation for criticism. To an extent, that is true. But if refusing to reprint the Colenso essay looks from one angle like inhibition, from another it is a recognition that any felt obligation to stick to a critical position becomes problematic once you define criticism as disinterested free play. Repetition of an offensive stance is especially prone to appear dogmatic: the law tends to equate repetition with aggravation, but a restaged anger on the part of a critical essayist as easily looks over-insistent, making the critic's hostility, not his or her subject's failings, the object of attention. Above all, Arnold sees that holding to the role of antagonist on any one point leads the critic down a path of predictable and entrenched opposition incompatible with freedom.

'The controversial life' is not good for us, he worries in 'The Function of Criticism' (272), and he keeps returning to the specific worry that confrontational criticism in contemporary English culture is quickly conscripted into a 'liberal' model of argument—directed, as John Stuart Mill urged it should be, into a rational contest between divergent views, out of which progress in ideas is trusted to emerge. Mill, as discussed in Chapter 2, had a tougher view than he is often credited with for what 'free and open debate' should include, but Arnold is tough in other ways. More alert than Mill to the dramatic and emotional seductions of argument, his exercise of criticism has a performative element of stylistic theatre to it—greater panache than Mill possessed in rejecting the national tendency to mistake polemic and dispute for criticism and substitute expenditure of energy ('zeal' [276]) for free play of mind. We can hear a hint of Arnold's exposure on the question of the critic's need to cut a figure as he wraps up the paragraph dealing with criticism's potential abduction by Philistines: 'The critic's duty is to refuse, or, if resistance is vain, at least to cry with Obermann: *Périssons en résistant* [Let us perish in resisting]' (276). Sloganization waits just around the corner.

Taking Arnold at his word on the duty to cause trouble, to 'refuse', but not to the point of dogmatic insistence on any position essayed, suggests a simple, potentially a cynical, and if cynical problematic, addition to the ways in which free play of mind can be recognized: you know you are doing it when other people are upset with you. If criticism is going to draw fresh ideas out 'from under the old, traditional, conventional point of view', then it must get into territory where it is going to distress those who are attached to or invested in widely agreed ways of seeing a subject—and the causing of upset will be one kind of validation (not the only one, but something to point to) of the 'scope' and 'seriousness' of the freedom being exercised.

In pursuing this line of thought, I am partly, but not entirely, at odds with one of Arnold's most sympathetic recent critics, David Russell, when he argues that

Arnold characteristically 'responds to a controversy by demonstrating an alterna-tive anti-controversial style'[17] and that the consistent aim of the writing on culture and education is to 'search for a tactful relational frame that would allow every-body the creative handling of their own experience' (96). As a description of the predominant principle, this is right, but Arnold neither dislikes nor eschews confrontation understood as part of a range of permissible critical stances. Allowing himself to overstep the bounds of 'calm confidence', 'self-control', 'tact' (all qualities he was prepared to value in criticism) was a temperamental inclination, but it was also an ineluctable corollary of following the free play of thought.

An always-tactful criticism would, as Arnold sees it, be a criticism without force or vital energy. The issue arose early in his career as a critic, during the Oxford lectures 'On Translating Homer' (1860–61), when he lambasted the work of Francis Newman, Professor of Latin at University College London, brother of John Henry Newman, and author of a punctilious translation of the *Iliad* that Arnold judged a 'conspicuous failure': correct to the point of being unreadable. Newman, much agitated, defended himself in print after the first lecture, so that Arnold found himself mid-series caught between the principle of tact and the principle of following the free play of thought wherever it led in pursuit of principles for a fresh modern English translation of Homer. The translator who tries to be even-handedly answerable to all the information and opinions out there, he states in the third lecture, will overburden his own capacity for elasticity: 'force of spirit' will be required to push through and provide something that will 'attract' and 'carry forward the reader'—the problem being that 'greater force' doesn't come just 'by wishing for it' (174–5). Looking to toughen up, he enters into unexpected rhetorical alliance with that very illiberal figure, the Duke of Wellington, quoted skewering the stupidity of 'a certain peer': '"it was a great pity his education had been so far too much for his abilities"' (175). Fortified by the Duke's waspishness, Arnold commits himself to seeing off Francis Newman: 'I agree with him; but only, I am sorry to say, up to a certain point ... in all he says he is in truth but beating the air' (175). Rhetorical flourish thrusts past embarrassment.

Many of the writers Arnold most admires have a similar lack of compunction about giving offence to 'ordinary' minds. It is a quality he finds better evidenced in other national literatures than his own. With important exceptions (Swift, cer-tainly; to an extent, Byron), the English seem to him to suffer from a want of 'original sympathy' (268) for liberty; contemporary English culture exacerbates a historical tendency, because it operates ('The Function of Criticism' argues) under an abnormal repression of free thought that has been the long national reaction to

---

[17] Russell, *Tact: Aesthetic Liberalism and the Essay Form*, 71.

revolution across the Channel. To the problem of reaction he adds the error of complacency: convinced (irrespective of party-political affiliation) that the Anglo-Saxon race is 'the best breed in the world', 'unrivalled' in its happiness, the English have lost that sense of what is not right or could be so much better that opens up the possibility of social and spiritual progress towards 'perfection' (272, 271). Seeking evidence of a better, less constrained instinct for criticism at work, he turns to other European cultures: to Germany, first and foremost (Goethe, Herder, latterly. Heine), to France (Tocqueville, Renan, de Senancour, Sand, more whimsically[18] Eugénie de Guérin—with some qualifying reservations about French sensuality and materialism); and, with poetry in his sights, to the Celtic strains within 'Englishness' itself.[19] In each of the other cultures considered, but above all in Goethe's Germany, Arnold detects a liberty of mind badly wanting in his own culture: an intellectual excitement, across 'all branches of knowledge, theology, philosophy, history, art, science', an effort 'to see the object'—whatever the branch of knowledge—'as in itself it really is' (258).[20]

German strenuousness does not always win out over less systematic critical freedoms, in these cross-cultural comparisons. One of Arnold's reasons for rescuing the French moralist Joseph Joubert from near-total obscurity to English readers is that, for all his mildness and 'tact', Joubert had 'no respect for the dominant oracle'.[21] Writing only for himself and his friends, he was at greater-than-usual liberty to try out judgements that, had they been aimed at publication, would have passed the bounds of 'permissible wrongness' (190). The French have a phrase for critical caprice on this scale, Arnold notes: *'jugements saugrenus'* (190).[22] 'Impudently absurd', is his nice translation; 'preposterous' would be less moral, and would have authority from classical rhetoric—but Arnold likes the

---

[18] The term is used by George Saintsbury, in *Matthew Arnold* (Edinburgh: William Blackwood and Sons, 1899), 84. Cavalier generalizations are 'only Mr. Arnold's way', he comments. 'I have never been able to satisfy myself whether they were deliberate paradoxes, or sincere and rather pathetic paralogisms' (86). The essays on Marcus Aurelius and Spinoza hit the right tone, for Saintsbury: there is no trace of the 'disquieting and almost dismaying jocularity which was later to invade his discussion of such things: we are still far from Bottles [and] the three Lord Shaftesburys' (94).

[19] Matthew Arnold, *On the Study of Celtic Literature* (1867), in *Lectures and Essays in Criticism*, 291–398. Anderson, *Powers of Distance*, notes the evident strain here with his universalism: Arnold 'is drawn to and wants to believe in the possibility of transformative and critical relations to what he construes as natural racial forces, but he is also haunted by the fact that such forces are starkly determining' (101). This is, she observes, an important facet of his engagement with the 'distinctly modern question of whether universal or impersonal value can find subjective embodiment' (108).

[20] On this occasion he points to David Strauss's celebrated historical investigation of the Bible, *Das Leben Jesu*, as an exemplary case of free criticism in German theology (278); other essays and lectures recognize the similarly liberated and liberating influence of Winckelmann, Lessing, and Herder in and beyond art history, dramaturgy, and philosophy. See David DeLaura, *Hebrew and Hellene in Victorian England: Newman, Arnold, and Pater* (Austin, TX: University of Texas Press, 1969), esp. Chapters 12 and 14. DeLaura rightly points out a nearer source for seeing the object 'as it really is' in 'Newman's assertion that a university training teaches a man "to see things as they are, to go right to the point"' (47).

[21] Matthew Arnold, 'Joubert', in *Lectures and Essays in Criticism*, CPW III, 183–211 (193).

[22] Arnold attributes the phrase to Charles de Rémusat.

kick of 'impudence'. In the same essay, he singles out Samuel Taylor Coleridge for his willingness to offend against conventional thought:

> that which will stand of Coleridge is this: the stimulus of his continual effort,— not a moral effort, for he had no morals,—but of his continual instinctive effort . . . to get at and to lay bare the real truth of his matter in hand, . . . ; and this in a country where at that moment such an effort was almost unknown; . . . where ordinary minds were so habituated to do without thinking altogether, . . . that any attempt to introduce within the domain of these the disturbing element of thought, they were prompt to resent as an outrage.   (189–90)

The 'as', in 'as an outrage', tells us that resentment at the disturbance of settled ideas by the free play of criticism has no justification. It is the mere protective reflex of the 'ordinary . . . habituated' mind encountering a challenge to its 'routine' and 'practical convenience'. The outrage is nevertheless of diagnostic interest and value to Arnold: it is the sign that the ideas in play are having an effect; that we may be getting closer to 'lay[ing] bare the real truth of [the] matter in hand'; that 'rich success' (189) may be within reach. (It is a question of ear whether or not one hears a sarcasm in 'rich success'—a fleeting jibe at Coleridge's pomposities. Success on what criteria? Would the really free-playing critic care for success?)

In an essay, 'In Praise of Difficult Children', Adam Phillips remarks that to 'respond well to truancy' we 'have to enjoy having truant minds [our]selves'.[23] The resentful reader of Coleridge's, or Arnold's own, freedoms is, on that reading, the one not enjoying criticism's truancy, and feeling the need or desire to rein it in. The good Arnoldian reader, by contrast, resembles Phillips's (and Winnicott's) 'good-enough' parent: relatively relaxed, s/he will take pleasure in the 'stimulus' to ideas—happy to go along with a wild proposition such as 'Coleridge had no morals at all', alert to what it would mean to curtail the freedom of expression. S/he would then have shown herself to be 'ordinary', 'habituated', set in conventional patterns of thought and valuation that are, really, ruts, too thin-skinned when the limitations of one's own tolerance are exposed. It is not a self-description most of us will want to attract.

If one way of knowing that your criticism is free is that you are upsetting people (and one way of knowing that you are a receptive reader of criticism is that you are happy to grant the latitude asked for), another is to depersonalize critical conflict by converting outward opposition into inward 'dissatisfaction'. 'Perpetual dissatisfaction' is what Arnold requires with any view of a subject that falls 'short of a high and perfect ideal' (280). Here again, conceiving of criticism as an internal, subjective activity eases the pressure on 'outward' moral and aesthetic judgement.

---

[23] *London Review of Books* 31/3 (12 February 2009), 16.

But the conversion is only partial in Arnold's criticism, and the incompleteness of the move to subjectivize free play has important repercussions for his critical style. He is famously 'frank and easy' (as he said of Joubert), willing (on occasion) to avow 'the most candid ignorance' (277), creating an atmosphere of thinking-on-the-spot, espousing lines of description and (more rarely) of judgement that sound provisional, liable to be rethought, recalibrated, even abandoned should they turn out to be wrong; but he almost never loses sight of the political and social responsibilities of criticism. The consequence, astutely identified by Amanda Anderson, is that Arnold's evocation of aesthetic play remains to a significant extent 'oblique'—an exemplary practice of freedom, that, by remaining strongly committed to certain political and social aspirations (an egalitarian state educa- tion, for example; a diminishment in religious sectarianism, but heightened appreciation of the Bible as an imaginative artefact; an enlarged role for the state in supporting public culture) leaves room for argument over whether 'disinterested' criticism in this mould is 'distinctively aesthetic'.[24] Even when the evocation of free play seems most uninhibited and most strongly concentrated on stylistics, Arnold can give the impression that 'play' is quite a serious thing—that there may be something non-negotiable about the taking of freedom, which would lead one to be dogmatic on its behalf.

*

The most telling manifestation of a cynic aspect to these questions is the about-turn in Arnold's view of Heinrich Heine in the early 1860s. When Arnold first read Heine in 1847, he objected to the scouring scepticism with which Heine undercut the high idealist strains in German Romanticism. '[H]e has thoroughly disgusted me', he wrote to his mother.[25] (Park Honan conjectures that he was, at the time, under the influence of the 'Marguerite' of Arnold's poems.)[26] In June 1863, Arnold made Heine the subject of a lecture delivered at Oxford in which he radically revised his first opinion, and worked out, more clearly than anywhere else in his writing, the relationship, as he saw it, between the advancement of political liberty, liberty of self-expression, and freedom of style.

For much of the lecture Heine is accepted at his own estimation: 'lay on my coffin a *sword*; for I was a brave soldier in the Liberation War of humanity'.[27] He was brave, but he was 'very little of a hero', Arnold warns—or tantalizes—his audience (largely composed of ladies, so he told his mother):[28] a 'brilliant' example of the literary *'genus irritabile'* (107). According to Arnold, the 'main current' of modern German literature after Goethe flows through him, and not (*contra* Thomas Carlyle) through the 'romantic school' of Tieck, Novalis, and Richter, now a 'minor current' (108). Carlyle was writing in the 1820s, Arnold concedes,

---

[24] *Powers of Distance*, 93.   [25] *Letters* I, 148.
[26] Park Honan, *Matthew Arnold: A Life* (London: Weidenfeld and Nicolson, 1981), 156–8.
[27] 'Heinrich Heine', 107.   [28] Editor's note to 'Heinrich Heine', 433.

when Heine was not yet in his prime, but Arnold is wedded to the idea that the critic's 'highest function' is to adjudicate between what has lasting cultural value and what has less (107). Making a strong case for Heine requires taking on Carlyle. The point is not that Arnold's judgement was idiosyncratic (that case was made with some ferocity by Charles D. Wright in the 1960s: Arnold is 'mostly wrong and only limitedly and inadvertently correct' on Heine as a 'Continuator of Goethe').[29] It is, rather, to draw out Arnold's greatly increased tolerance, by the early 1860s, for a style such as Heine's—and Carlyle's—that injects 'power' into the assault on routinized thinking, upheld in the modern age by 'an immense system of institutions, established facts, accredited dogmas, customs, rules' (109).

Every critic who turns to the lecture on 'Heine' quotes, as the core of it, Arnold's appreciation of Goethe's naturalism as an immense contribution to free critical thinking:

> he puts the standard, once for all, inside every man instead of outside him; when he is told, such a thing must be so, there is immense authority and custom in favour of it being so, it has been held to be so for a thousand years, he answers with Olympian politeness, 'But *is* it so? is it so *to me*?'   (110)

Few quote what comes next: an acknowledgement that, fundamentally important though Goethe's example was to 'the process of liberation', his way of working to that end was painfully 'slow' and compromised by his insider status and accepted authority. 'Olympian politeness' is not often the most winning of tones, and Arnold quotes with evident enjoyment Heine's caustic observation that Goethe lived to be over 80, labouring towards liberty, during which time the 'medieval machinery' of German institutional governance was reformed not one jot. From Heine's perspective, Goethe was an establishment liberal; from Arnold's, it has taken a younger genius, 'with all the culture of Germany, but by race a Jew', and 'warmly sympathetic' to revolutionary France, to inject the 'passion' and 'power' needed for the 'life and death battle' with convention—or as Arnold prefers to put it, 'the battle with *Philistinism*'.

Much of the lecture after this revelation of his hand takes the form of admiring quotations from Heine in Arnold's lively translation: long, brilliantly funny passages in which Heine flings his wit against *Philistinism* of the British as well as the German variety and against the want of force and clarity in most of its opponents. The great radical journalist William Cobbett is paraded as a figure of pitiful impotence: 'a chained cur, who falls with equal fury on every one whom he does not know, often bites the best friend of the house in his calves, barks incessantly, and just because of this incessantness of his barking cannot get

---

[29]   Charles D. Wright, 'Matthew Arnold on Heine as a "Continuator of Goethe"', *Studies in Philology* 65/4 (July 1968), 693–701 (693).

listened to, even when he barks at a real thief... Poor old Cobbett! England's dog!' (114) Quotation to the extent exhibited here amply demonstrates what Nicholas Dames has called the pre-professional 'protocols' of Victorian criticism: the 'long-excerpt... reproduc[ing], within the setting of the critical piece, the temporal experience of reading' the original, inviting the reader to enter it 'as co-participant with the critic'.[30] This is helpful, but if it attunes us to the quality of Arnold's engagement with Heine—which is, indeed, immersive, captivated, sympathetic—it might also help attune us to his felt need to limit the love.

Heine's exceptional stylistic and tonal richness is alluring: he is, in close concentration, jesting, pathetic, scornful, witty, at his wits' end. A master of one-liners, he exhibits a 'happy combination' of seriousness with sentimentalism, levity, and irony. He has a genius for darker dramatic effects such as 'grim innuendo' (127). Crucially, 'the sarcastic turn is never far off' (129). With this stylistic range at its command, Arnold claims, 'propagandism' for liberty of ideas takes on 'a more truly literary character'. Heine's liberalism is judged superior to Goethe's (for all the latter's impressive range and authority) because Heine retains 'a strong central idea' (119): the idea, I take it (Arnold doesn't elaborate), of the immediate and urgent need of liberty to counter social injustice and cultural complacency. Reading along these admiring lines, Arnold finds in Heine a remedy for the over-elasticity he detects in Goethe and fears in himself: a critical intelligence 'so wide, so impartial' that it needs must muscle up lest it become, as criticism, 'slack and powerless' (119).

This is compromised metaphorical terrain. Arnold's appreciation of Heine's stylistic power is shadowed by deep pity and respect for the intellectual courage of a man confined for eight years to a 'mattress-grave', subject to paroxysms of 'nervous agony', 'the use of his limbs gone... requiring, that it might be exercised, to have the palsied eyelid lifted and held up by the finger' (117). (Modern speculative diagnoses are divided between neurosyphilis and multiple sclerosis.[31]) The aristocratic libertarianism of Byron and Shelley looks more privileged than ever by comparison—condemned, not for the first time by Arnold, for 'narrowness' and 'ineffectuality'. Heine in his last years becomes, in this reading, an exemplary figure of 'absolute freedom' of ideas and expression, going well beyond anything Byron or Shelley achieved, cutting radically free of both 'stock classicism' and 'stock romanticism' (122)—only (and here Arnold's palpable reservations start) not by way of a renewed idealism. For if Heine has no truck with 'classicism' of the kind that assists a high style, he holds close company with classicism of a more rebarbative kind.

---

[30] Nicholas Dames, 'On the Protocols of Victorian Citation', *Novel: A Forum on Fiction* 42/2 (2009), 326–31 (328–9).

[31] See E. H. Jellineck, 'Heine's Illness: The Case for Multiple Sclerosis', *Journal of the Royal Society of Medicine* 83/8 (August 1990), 516–19; and Egon Stenager, 'The Course of Heinrich Heine's Illness: Diagnostic Considerations', *Journal of Medical Biography* 4/1 (February 1996), 28–32.

Increasingly, the portrait of the artist that Arnold pieces together from descriptions of Heine's physical condition and translations from excerpted prose and poetry becomes a picture of a Cynic—more exactly, a writer who strays happily and without moral compunction into the domain of Cynicism. The lecture circles, fascinated, around figures of human dogs in Heine's prose and poetry, as if Arnold is undecided quite how far the Cynic identification with the *kúōn* appeals, and how much it can promise in the way of liberation. The chained English 'cur', Cobbett, is the first in a line of constricted and brutalized canine humans—craving liberty—that are the dominant trope of the lecture. After Cobbett come the abused princes of the 'Spanish Atridæ', confined to kennels by their vengeful uncle ('The room which he has assigned to them is certainly rather small, but then it is cool in summer, and not intolerably cold in winter'; the henpecked master of the hounds often 'snatches his whip, and rushes down here, and gives it to the dogs and to the poor little boys' [127]). Then comes Prince Israel, the ironical type of the common Jew in 'Princess Sabbath' ('A dog with the desires of a dog, he wallows all the week long in the filth and refuse of life, amidst the jeers of the boys in the street, but every Friday evening, at the twilight hour, suddenly the magic passes off, and the dog becomes once more a human being' [129]).

By the time Arnold addresses Heine's exceptional combination of Hellenism and Hebraism, it is obvious that this liberator of German literature from the establishment complacencies in high Romanticism is a potential personification of modern European culture, embodying as he does its two major inheritances (it presumably helps, though Arnold does not quite say so, that Heine was a convert to Christianity).[32] The 'Hebraism/Hellenism' distinction underpinning *Culture and Anarchy* comes from Heine, '[who] has excellently pointed out how in the sixteenth century there was a double renascence,—a Hellenic renascence and a Hebrew renascence,—and how both have been great powers ever since'.[33] The taint of Cynicism is the one major qualification Arnold makes in according Heine the central importance this influence on the Arnoldian description of culture suggests. Cynicism bites at both aspects of culture, as it were: at the elements that *Culture and Anarchy* will define as a Hebraic 'habits and discipline' of moral judgement and 'energy in embracing' an inherited spiritual ideal, and at

---

[32] See Jefferson Chase, *Inciting Laughter: The Development of "Jewish Humour" in 19th Century German Culture* (Berlin: Walter de Gruyter, 2000), 4.

[33] See 'Heinrich Heine', 127. Precisely where in Heine's writings Arnold found the distinction has been a matter of dispute. Both Lionel Trilling and R. H. Super sourced it to Heine's memorial essay on Börne, but his knowledge of that essay has since been questioned. Lionel Gossman follows Ilse-Maria Tesdorpf in noting that Arnold altered the meaning of the opposition of Jews and Hellenes, as Heine had it, though he preserved the core idea that the history culture was shaped by the struggle between the forces these terms represent. See Lionel Gossman, 'Philhellenism and Anti-Semitism: Matthew Arnold and His German Models', *Comparative Literature* 46/1 (1994), 1–39 (17); citing Ilse-Maria Tesdorpf, *Die Auseinandersetzung Matthew Arnolds mit Heinrich Heine, des Kritikers mit dem Kritiker* (Frankfurt: Athenäum Verlag, 1971).

Hellenism's enlarging, ennobling sense of the beautiful.[34] In place of conventional beauty, grace, elegance, it substitutes a love of the ordinary, the ugly, the damaged; in place of high moral ideals, it offers to substitute a basic material and psychological satisfaction as sufficient for happiness.

The deeper damage is done on the Hebraic side. 'What Hebrew ever treated the things of the Hebrews like this?', Arnold asks (128), contemplating Heine's 'sarcasms' towards Judaism, and in illustration quotes at length from *Die Bäder von Lucca* (1829):

> There lives at Hamburg, in a one-roomed lodging in the Baker's Broad Walk, a man whose name is Moses Lump; all the week he goes about in wind and rain, with his pack on his back, to earn his few shillings; but when on Friday evening he comes home, he finds the candlestick with seven candles lighted, and the table covered with a fair white cloth, and he puts away from him his pack and his cares, and he sits down to table with his squinting wife and yet more squinting daughter, and eats fish with them, fish which has been dressed in beautiful white garlic sauce, sings therewith the grandest psalms of King David, rejoices with his whole heart over the deliverance of the children of Israel out of Egypt, rejoices, too, that all the wicked ones who have done the children of Israel hurt, have ended by taking themselves off; that King Pharaoh, Nebuchadnezzar, Haman, Antiochus, Titus, and all such people, are well dead, while he, Moses Lump, is yet alive, and eating fish with wife and daughter; and I can tell you, Doctor, the fish is delicate and the man is happy, he has no call to torment himself about culture, he sits contented in his religion and in his green bedgown, like Diogenes in his tub, he contemplates with satisfaction his candles, which he on no account will snuff for himself; and I can tell you, if the candles burn a little dim, and the snuffers-woman, whose business it is to snuff them, is not at hand, and Rothschild the Great were at that moment to come in, with all his brokers, bill discounters, agents, and chief clerks, with whom he conquers the world, and Rothschild were to say: 'Moses Lump, ask of me what favour you will, and it shall be granted you';—Doctor, I am convinced, Moses Lump would quietly answer: 'Snuff me those candles!' and Rothschild the Great would exclaim with admiration: 'If I were not Rothschild, I would be Moses Lump.' (175)

Hebraism takes this skew (but theologically justifiable) turn into Cynicism at the point where the impoverished street-seller finds in the ceremonial conventions of his religion the means of transforming his poverty into a sufficiency of contentment: a meagre lodging is made elegant by 'white cloth' and menorah, white fish is made 'beautiful' by 'garlic sauce', and Moses himself is made 'happy' by his small

---

[34] Preface (1869) to Matthew Arnold, *Culture and Anarchy*, in *Culture and Anarchy, with Friendship's Garland and Some Literary Essays*, ed. R. H. Super, CPW V, 231–56 (255).

comforts, by wife and daughter ('squinting' though they may be), by the singing of the Psalms, but above all by the cheering thought that so many attempts, over history, to eradicate his tribe have 'ended' in the death of the persecutors while Moses and his kind persist. As Heine interjects the thought that all that is needed for perfect contentment is the 'snuffers-woman' to snuff the candles (it is forbidden for an observant Jew to snuff the candles during Shabbat), Moses morphs fully into Diogenes, re-enacting his challenge to Alexander as a confrontation with 'Rothschild the Great': 'Stand out of my light!' 'Snuff me those candles!'

This is burlesque, but it is also, for Arnold a disturbance in the route to a higher definition of culture and its value, as a more straightforward satire on Hebraism could not be. Frank satire is the primary weapon he will himself adopt in *Culture and Anarchy* against the limiting moral dogmatism of Hebraism. Moses-as-Diogenes provides something *Culture and Anarchy* will not countenance, and that the lecture on Heine, in helping to determine the grounds of argument for that book, has to find a way of dealing with: the possibility of a relation to culture that is deliberately self-impoverishing and thereby better equipped to its own radical egalitarian purposes (though one notes the very secondary role of women here). Expressed through Moses Lump is a view of the function of criticism that is on its way to becoming radically and (for Arnold) threateningly free, willing to sacrifice dedication to the higher beauty and the best self in favour of a view of sufficient contentment in which a man has 'no call to torment himself about culture'.[35]

Radical freedom by this route still finds articulation, of course, through Heine's high cultural qualifications (the classical allusion is his, not Lump's), but Heine rattles Arnold's idealism by declining to make possession of the highest and the best in culture a generalizable aim. A glimpse opens up here of a radical Philistinism, going beyond what Arnold can address. Arnold's limited sympathy with the levelling politics of *Judenwitz* Cynicism is evident when he calls the Moses Lump passage 'Heine show[ing] us his own people by its comic side' (118). This is not wrong, but it rather misses the point of what Heine was doing. *Die Bäder von Lucca* turns a darker corner immediately after the lines quoted, delivering a scarifying attack on Heine's bugbear, Count Platen (an assault

---

[35] Arnold says nothing about *Die Bäder*'s larger picture of the aspiration to culture along these lines: the lampooning of the Jew (Gumpelino) who thinks of himself as a spokesman for culture but retains the banker's obsession with money; or Heine's initial narrative self-positioning as the 'bantering dandy' who then casts aside this fiction and tunes up the level of aggression to attack Count Platen. The hyperextension of multiple Jewish stereotypes predicts in several respects Arnold's subsequent mockery of the Philistine, but serves the purposes both of more ranging and destabilizing satire on the theme of cultural non-assimilation and of raising the *Judenwitz* of the street and theatre to a literary art. See Chase, *Inciting Laughter*, 159–64 (161). Chase argues persuasively that, though negatively charged, the Jewish wit tradition was turned by Heine to his advantage until the backlash against the *Baths of Lucca*, which largely derailed his hopes of publishing with the prestigious firm of J. G. Cotta (publishers of Goethe and Schiller) and left Heine a 'uniquely controversial' figure within the history of German literary reception (189).

notorious in German literary history for Heine's decision to fight anti-Semitism with homophobia). The occasion for the attack was Platen's latest effort to imitate Aristophanes. Aristophanes, Heine retorts in disgust, 'possessed a profound world-destroying imagination', 'no trace' of which is to be found in this effete 'troubadour of misery'.[36]

Heine felt himself to be engaged in a 'ruthless and merciless' fight for cultural self-vindication against Platen's snobbery and anti-Jewishness.[37] 'World destruction' in the face of such entitlement (both senses apply) was a form of imaginative freedom-fighting he was willing to countenance, and for which he found powerful precedents in antiquity. But for Arnold, the refusal of perfectionism as the guiding ideal presents a fatal flaw in the temper of Heine's criticism. He turns against the warrior for Liberty suddenly and fiercely. In the summary judgement with which the lecture ends, Heine's is a 'blemished name': 'with his crying faults,—his intemperate susceptibility, his unscrupulousness in passion, his inconceivable attacks on his enemies, his still more inconceivable attacks on his friends, his want of generosity, his sensuality, his incessant mocking,—how could it be otherwise?' And then, bizarrely: 'Not even the merit of his not being a Philistine' can 'make up for' his not being 'respectable' (131–2). The word is taken from Carlyle, who made it a regular term of abuse for vulgar-minded materialists (a large category, in Carlyle's book, stretching to the British Library's Principal Librarian, Anthony Panizzi).

Carlyle's reappearance makes him a framing presence in the lecture. He is there at the start as an object of disagreement for Arnold, who disputes the omission of Heine from Carlyle's account of the contemporary German literary mainstream. His return at this point strengthens a suspicion (nothing allays it) that Heine's position in German literature is analogous in Arnold's thinking to that of Carlyle, equally of the *genus irritabile*, in British literature. Arnold looks to praise Carlyle here ('no one recognises his genius more admiringly than I do' [108]), but in private and sometimes in public he deplored the collapse of the inspiring idealist into a rancorous controversialist. 'Flee Carlylese as the very Devil!' he advised Frederic Harrison; a once 'puissant voice', he wrote in the late lecture on 'Emerson', had become 'sorely strained, over-used, and mis-used since'—'very mad', as he put it more succinctly to his wife.[38] Why would Arnold, now settling his account with Heine, turn back for support to a critic who missed his significance? He does so, it seems, for the same reason he turned to the Iron Duke in 'On

---

[36] Heinrich Heine, *Pictures of Travel*, in *The Works of Heinrich Heine*, trans. Charles Godfrey Leland, Thomas Brooksbank, and Margaret Armour, 12 vols. (London: W. Heinemann, 1891–1905), II, 236.
[37] Quoted in Philip Kossoff, *Valiant Heart: A Biography of Heinrich Heine* (New York: Cornwall Books, 1983), 106.
[38] Quoted in Frederic Harrison, 'On Style in English Prose', *The Nineteenth Century* 43 (1898), 932–43 (941); Letter to Frances Lucy Wightman Arnold, 6 May 1877, in *Letters* IV, 364–5 (365).

Translating Homer', looking for an injection of 'force' to rescue himself from a dangerous elasticity.

By the end of the lecture, asserting the 'modern' importance of Heine has come to look very much like finding an acceptably offshore location for a radical debasement of literary values that Arnold is much less happy accommodating in his national literature. Heine remains, for Arnold, one of the great practitioners of liberty of self-expression and freedom of style. What he lacked is an important corollary to those goods: not 'love' (which was Goethe's complaint about Heine) but a core of moral responsibility—in Carlylean vein, 'old-fashioned, laborious, eternally needful moral deliverance' (132). None of which lessens the significance of Heine as a model for Arnold's own freelancing relationship to the literary culture of his day: bantering, adversarial, intolerant of conventional pieties, capable of tipping the scale from humour to vilification, and able, with all that, to cultivate a broad readership eager to witness the 'razor's edge' of his moralism.[39]

*

The attraction of cynicism's strong confrontationalism and abrasive critical free-doms is never as central and sustained again in Arnold's writing as in the lecture on Heine. It is, however, a persistent accompaniment to his ethical self-positioning as a critic of culture and politics. In the later 1860s strategic recourse to cynicism helps to shape the content and stylistic flexibility of a key precursor to *Culture and Anarchy*, the series of letters to the *Pall Mall Gazette* starting in 1866 and collected into the misleadingly sentimental-sounding volume *Friendship's Garland* (1871).[40] This is Arnold's most Carlylean work,[41] its stringent cultural criticisms of contemporary Britain framed as a series of communications to the *Gazette* from 'Matthew Arnold' (a pallid and defensive version of Arnold himself) and his difficult friend 'Arminius von Thunder-ten-Thronckh' (a 'harsh', 'arrogant' Prussian descended from the house of Candide—i.e., from the exemplary scepticism of Voltaire, and not without slight touches of Carlyle's Diogenes Teufelsdröckh).

Introducing Arminius, 'Arnold' explicitly regrets that we will see nothing here of the 'cynical descendant' of *Candide*'s Martin de Mabille, the 'great foe of Pangloss's optimism' (352) who was Candide's paid companion on the journey from Buenos Aires to Paris. Martin, we are told, 'has just been shut up in Paris eating rats' (352)—banished, it would seem, under the Paris Commune that had unseated Napoleon III's repressive cultural and political régime. (In the siege of Paris, 1870–71, citizens were reported to be eating rats to avoid starvation.) Without a dedicated representative, cynicism plays in and out of the rough

---

[39] This phrase is noted by Arnold in *The Yale Manuscript*, ed. and with commentary by S. O. A. Ullmann (Ann Arbor, MI: University of Michigan Press, 1989), 175 (7^r [1]).

[40] In *Culture and Anarchy*, *CPW* V, 1–72, 311–56.

[41] The debt of *Friendship's Garland* to both Heine and Carlyle was noted by Douglas Bush, *Matthew Arnold: A Survey of the Poetry and Prose* (London: Macmillan, 1971), 157.

stringencies of Arminius as he confronts 'Arnold' with the sorry truth of England's culturally impoverished 'great middle class' (38) and lack of the intelligent 'demos' necessary for the good functioning of a democracy (45). A Humboldtian progressivist, his trenchant scepticisms are rhetorically strategic, pursuing the 'victory of reason and intelligence over blind custom and prejudice', and the uniting of all liberal nations in a cosmopolitan *Geist*. His aesthetic concerns—his loathing of those 'violations of aesthetic laws' represented by modern 'Cole's truss manufactory' industrialism (43)—are matters of taste, not morality, but the gearing animus against the confidence of power and money keeps the stringencies of cynicism germane.

The principal contribution of *Friendship's Garland* to *Culture and Anarchy* lies in Arminius's attacks on Philistinism. His cynicisms here go deeper than stylistics to engage a basic scepticism in matters of motive, repeatedly tracing the debased culture of the Barbarian (aristocratic) and Philistine (middle) classes of England to a poverty of ethical concerns. The Barbarians are 'idle, self-indulgent, without mental life' (330); the Philistines are grossly complacent towards the inequalities of the class system, the inadequacies of the education system, and the want of appropriate qualifications for those who hold public office in politics, the law, magistracy, journalism. Ask what the Philistines comprehend by 'industrial development and liberty' (their avowed aims in life) and 'you find they mean getting rich and not being meddled with' (330). They have 'no great, seriously and truly conceived end' (331), they are without 'wisdom and virtue' (343). Arnold's own writing on education might encourage a view that these are failings with their basis in narrowness of education, but the castigation is nonetheless moral for that. An impoverished motive is a bad motive.

One of the ways in which it is bad is that it produces unwarranted self-satisfaction on the part of a whole social class. What most troubles 'Arnold' at the end of this series of exchanges with his Prussian counterpart is that the British middle classes have got hold of a view of themselves which is unduly self-flattering on the score of their ability to see things clearly. Reading a newspaper account of how Sir Thomas Bazley, industrialist and Liberal MP for Manchester, addressed his constituency voters (this is 1866, on the verge of the second Reform Bill), 'Arnold' warms to 'the language of clear, manly intelligence, which penetrates through sophisms, ignores commonplaces, and gives to conventional illusions their true value' (7). This is the new middle class at its best, he writes—but it is still not as clear-seeing, as 'enlightened' (5, and *passim*) as it thinks it is. The erosion of the initially flattering judgement is quick and steep: Bazley's belief that the education of the middle classes is quite fit for purpose speaks to a class confidence that is a real threat to the function of criticism: possessed of so satisfying an image of its own 'no nonsense' powers of perception, it is primed to reject cultural assistance of the practical institutional kind 'Arnold' (and Arnold) would want to see[42] (local state-funded schools, an Academy of letters, and so forth). It knows enough to resent being 'meddled with' (6, 330). It is forearmed against his perfectionism, holding itself sufficiently prepared for the future. The only answer 'Arnold' proposes in the face of such complacency is humility, keeping modestly to the slow work of 'know[ing] and understand[ing] things' and not 'intrud[ing] into a sphere' of political action 'where I have no business' (6). Given the strategic splitting of Matthew Arnold from a weakened virtual 'Arnold', we should be prepared to resist such statements. Criticism that so limits its freedom of thought and its freedom of action will (on Arnold's own view) achieve nothing; the best rescue for it will be to have 'an Arminius at [its] elbow, "trenchant" and "authoritative" and prepared to withstand "a storm of obloquy"' (31).

In direct continuity with *Friendship's Garland*, 'Culture and its Enemies' (the last of Arnold's Oxford lectures, repositioned as the Introduction and first chapter to the standard 1883 text of *Culture and Anarchy*) gives its opening sentences to quotation from a recent speech by a 'famous Liberal, Mr. [John] Bright'. Bright's role is almost identical to that of Thomas Bazley in *Friendship's Garland*, except that he takes aim directly at 'culture':

> 'People...talk about what they call *culture!*' said he contemptuously; 'by which they mean a smattering of the two dead languages of Greek and Latin.' And he went on to remark, in a strain with which modern speakers and writers have made us very familiar, how poor a thing this culture is, how little good it can do to the world, and how absurd it is for its possessors to set much store by it.   (87)

To this display of Philistine sneering, Arnold adds two more voices, not obviously of the Bright/Bazley type: Frederic Harrison, delivering a much cleverer, more 'stringent[ly]' systematic rebuttal of the 'cant about culture'; and an anonymous 'young lion' on the *Daily Telegraph* (later identified as the Liberal James Macdonell, still in his twenties)[43] who had recently attacked Arnold as an 'elegant Jeremiah', 'the high-priest of the kid-gloved persuasion', too squeamish of practical politics to sully his hands with the vulgarity of agitation for actual reform. To this formidable array of opponents—political, intellectual, journalistic—Arnold attaches a diagnosis of pervasive and weakened cynicism. Against them, he will lay

---

[42] Henry Sidgwick argues, perceptively, that the often overstated character of Arnold's advocacy for culture suggested an element of embarrassment towards the impracticality of his eloquence: 'All this criticism of action is very valuable; but it is usually given in excess, just because, I think, culture is a little sore in conscience, is uncomfortably eager to excuse its own evident incapacity for action.' Henry Sidgwick ,'The Prophet of Culture', *MacMillan's Magazine* 16 (1867), 271–80 (179–80); quoted and discussed by Matthew Bevis, *The Art of Eloquence: Byron, Dickens, Tennyson, Joyce* (Oxford: Oxford University Press, 2007), 7. Cf. Anderson, *Powers of Distance*, 91, for the argument that the primary guarantor of free play is its 'cultivated distance from the practical sphere'. Arnold's answer to the charge of inaction was simpler: that thought and judgement are forms of action.

[43] *Culture and Anarchy*, 394, n. 57: 9.

out an account of culture that has cynicism's virtues without its corrosive dangers: clear-sighted, robustly free-speaking, it is an account that claims to be not remote and idealistic but 'simple', 'real', built 'on plain grounds', and capable of offering a secure and practically efficacious basis for aiming at progress (88–9).

Culture and Anarchy takes Arnold again and again into the strategic territory of cynic confrontation—provocative free-speaking, attribution of low motives to others, hyper-sensitivity to the narrow self-interest at work beneath conventional moral claims. By way of a fierce but indicative extract, consider the following lines, in which Arnold confronts the difficulty of coming at 'the idea of a high best self' in the political sphere, where the system of representative government gives every politician a reason to pander to the self-interests of those he attempts to govern, rather than endeavour to pursue disinterested 'right' reasoning:

> it will be said, perhaps, that candidates for political influence and leadership, who thus caress the self-love of those whose suffrages they desire, know quite well that they are not saying the sheer truth as reason sees it, but that they are using a sort of conventional language, or what we call clap-trap, which is essential to the working of representative institutions. And therefore, I suppose, we ought rather to say with Figaro: *Qui est-ce qu'on trompe ici?* Now, I admit that often, but not always, when our governors say smooth things to the self-love of the class whose political support they want, they know very well that they are overstepping, by a long stride, the bounds of truth and soberness; and while they talk, they in a manner, no doubt, put their tongue in their cheek.   (152)

The passage confronts a ubiquitous expectation (one 'we' all recognize) that politics is a cynical operation. This is the philosophy of Mozart's Figaro: everyone is a cheat, we are all in on the game, the one 'moral' rule is *don't get found out*, or not so decisively that finessing a way out is impossible ... and besides, isn't the music we make, all in on the game together, pleasing ...? Insofar as engaging in cynicism of this order reassures people that they are not at fault in reaching after no higher idea of politics, it does so by appealing to their intelligence over their morality: the would-be leader gratifies the 'self-love' of the electorate, in such a way that people may recognize the blandishments offered, and take credit in knowing them for what they are. Flattery, Arnold is suggesting, is the common currency of political life: a 'sort of conventional language' that oils the workings of modern government.

Arnold mimics standard practice only to puncture it: the 'conventional language' is 'clap-trap'. Substantively, he charges that the politician who panders to another's complacent self-image is a moral victim of his own rhetoric, ensnaring and intoxicating himself with 'smooth words'; worse, he is a moral coward, failing in the obligation of leaders of culture to show the way to better ideas, and a better self-love. He is, in short, a cynic posing as an advocate for high ideals. The difference between him and the critic is that the critic puts cynicism to the service of ideals.

*

Thus far, the characterization of Arnold's cynicisms that I have been pursuing looks to fit a pattern of increasingly strategic deployment—from potential seduction by Heine's intimacy with Cynicism, through the more local and dialectical cynic scoriations of 'Arminius' vs. 'Arnold' in *Friendship's Garland*, to the more finely gauged critical positioning of *Culture and Anarchy* and (closing where I started) 'The Function of Criticism'—texts that have recourse to cynicism's strengths, but explicitly reject its corrosions. It is a description that could find support from biography: the young Arnold takes pleasure in shocking conventional persons, like the clergyman who encountered him bathing naked in the Thames and whose protests were met with an airy wave of the towel: 'Is it possible that you see anything indelicate in the human form divine?'[44] At 22, he detects in himself 'a delicate Spirit, tossed on Earth, opposumlike', and sets himself the challenge of achieving 'Force of Character' and 'fire' in lieu of the 'listless [ness]'.[45] '[H]uman nature is unspeakably ductile', he transcribes, without comment, in his Notebook (probably in his later twenties).[46] The adult Arnold was less prone to disparage ductility, more prone to worry that force is another word for arrogance. 'Only when one is young and headstrong', he writes of W. K. Clifford, 'can one . . . prefer bravado to experience, . . . '.[47]

In 'On Being Criticized', Grace Lavery suggests a strong defensive-narcissistic formation here. She reads Arnold's style of writing as a response to the conditions in which he was raised by Thomas Arnold, experiencing the father's power in terms of compulsory acknowledgement and reproof. The art of criticism, born of that relation, is a defensive-assertive response to being criticized. It makes 'a pleasure and political virtue' of 'the position of weakness', cultivating rhetorical and formal techniques that provocatively mimic the voices of authority, vocalizing his own powerlessness but fighting back (507). As readers of Arnold, we thus find ourselves (Lavery argues) in the disarming presence of the play of 'narcissistic desire', the narcissist being 'uniquely capable of treating *himself* as an object'. It is a reading that provides a handle on the irony of Arnold's advocacy for a mode of writing that, because it is secondary (commentary, not original writing), must

---

[44]   Honan, *Matthew Arnold*, 51.

[45]   Letter to Arthur Hugh Clough, [?5 March 1845], *Letters* I, 64–6 (65, 64).

[46]   *Yale Manuscript*, 203 (8r [5]). For an early indication of wariness about Force, see also the note taken in 1848, and connected by the editor with the influence of the Bhagavad Gita: 'Man's true vocation is to follow nature, however indecisive and sinuous her guidance . . . To assert one's will gives life a false and arbitrary direction and is an act of bad faith' (103, 21r²–r² [1]).

[47]   The sentence continues: ' . . . can one stand by the Sea of Time, and instead of listening to the solemn and rhythmical beat of its waves, choose to fill the air with one's own whoopings to start the echo'. Matthew Arnold, *God and the Bible*, ed. R. H. Super, CPW VII, 380–1.

'recuse itself from the privileged field of the best that is thought and known', and yet makes autoerotically charged objects, touchstones, out of other writers.[48] Not for the first time, cynicism seems to be operating in close proximity with narcissism, and it is in the nature of the 'type' (see pp. 26–37) that each seems to want to be not just the dominant explanation but the one that pulls every observer/reader into its field. So, not unlike Arnold (and she makes much of the elective identification), Lavery wants both to seduce her readers and to keep them away (or to seduce them by keeping them away): 'to date', she discloses, 'I have yet to persuade a single person that this version of him exists' (509). This in keeping with an essay that turns engagement with Arnold into an extension not just of her own declared narcissism, but the narcissism of every critic who has reached their vocation despite, or with the help of, a deep dislike of being criticized: 'The idea that criticism is written out of a condition of being criticized will feel achingly familiar', she proposes (509).[49] Arnold's cynicism, as I see it, offers no such holistic explanation, or diagnosis, of the style or of the man, and it does not present itself as the key to his concept of criticism. It is a *component* of criticism's operation that assists its expression of freedom and its clear-sightedness in pursuit of culture, but that must operate under restraint lest it go the way of Heine and admit in its company a radical Philistinism.

This last concern starts to loom larger in the later stages of Arnold's career. In one important context his use of cynicism in pursuit of critical 'free play' does not continue evenly, as a honed strategy. It takes him, late in his career, in the direction of an awkward and abrasive confrontationalism on the question of how generalizable or otherwise his model of free thinking in support of culture can be. His assumptions about the universality or otherwise of critical reason acquire new political salience and generate a less certain 'return upon himself' (to invoke his famous praise of Burke) when he lectures in America on the character of its democratic public culture and the distinctiveness or otherwise of its national claims to freedom, clear-sightedness, and frankness. His decision in the early 1880s to write and lecture repeatedly on the 'Philistine' character of American culture—the failure, as he saw it, of the world's great experiment in democracy to produce progress in culture comparable to its achievements in politics and society—provides the most striking illustrations of his willingness to affront audiences with free-speaking criticism, but also the most difficult context in which to judge the use of cynicism.

The first of these sallies, 'A Word about America', appeared in the liberal monthly, *The Nineteenth Century* in May 1882, while Arnold was in the planning

---

[48] Grace Lavery, 'On Being Criticized', *Modernism/Modernity* 25/3 (2018), 499–516 (506, 507, 512–13).

[49] See also the recurrent motif of taking her own critical licence from Arnold, e.g. 515, n. 11: 'My own evocation of the language of Marxist-feminism here takes its license from an implicit analogy, or echo, in Arnold's own prose, ...'

stages for a lecture tour of the States.[50] The timing was delicate: he had not yet set foot on US soil, and had reached his views on the basis of old reading in the classic commentators on American democracy; also some familiarity with the country's contemporary literature (most recently James's *Roderick Hudson*), regular dipping into US newspapers, and impressions gleaned from personal acquaintances—if not a null basis for comment, a very incomplete one. If he continued to hold the line against the cultural achievements of democracy in America (as he did), he was in danger of alienating people he needed to be friendly, or at least curious enough to pay for the privilege of hearing him in person. (The tour was motivated by a pressing need to replenish his finances after paying off his son's debts.) But America was an irresistible subject for Arnold: the obvious test-case for his association of class levelling with cultural deterioration. '[O]ne had to trust a great deal to one's "flair," ' he wrote to a friend once the piece was out: 'but I think my "flair" served me here pretty well.'[51] The novelty of 'flair' in English offers to ironize the boast.[52]

'A Word about America' begins by disputing a recent Boston newspaper report that Arnold has spoken of American manners as 'vulgar'.[53] He had. As early as 1848 he had warned in private of 'a wave of more than American vulgarity, moral, intellectual, and social, preparing to break over us'.[54] In *Culture and Anarchy*, he was only a little more circumspect: the 1869 Preface quotes Ernest Renan on the 'vulgarity' of American manners and judges it 'likely' he was correct—'in culture and totality, America, instead of surpassing us all, falls short'.[55] Arnold's essay on 'Democracy' (first published as the introduction to *The Popular Education of France* [1861], and reissued as a free-standing essay in 1879) had made free with the idea that the cultural threat from extension of democratic equality could be dealt with by an appeal to 'prevent the English people from becoming...*Americanised*.'[56] Now, planning his own trip across the 'big pond', Arnold insists, barefaced, that the reports are mistaken: far from looking down on the US, he writes, 'I have long accustomed myself to regard the people of America as simply "the English on the other side of the Atlantic" ... I learnt it from Burke' (2).[57] By 1882, this was a more risqué line than it had been for Burke (who delivered it to a British Parliament still largely convinced of its title over America). The implication that, when it comes to culture, the American

---

[50] See Editor's Note to 'A Word about America', in Matthew Arnold, *Philistinism in England and America*, ed. R. H. Super, *CPW* X, 410.

[51] Letter to Mountstuart Elphinstone Grant Duff, 29 July 1882, in *Letters* V, 219–21 (219). Grant Duff was currently Governor of Madras, a former Liberal MP, until recently Undersecretary of State for the Colonies.

[52] *OED* (unrevised entry) dates the first English usage of the word to 1881. 'flair, *n.* 1 (2)', *OED*.

[53] In *Philistinism in England and America*, 1–23 (1).

[54] Letter to Mary Penrose Arnold, in *Letters* I, 91–2 (91).

[55] 'Preface', in *Culture and Anarchy*, 241–2.

[56] In Matthew Arnold, *Democratic Education*, ed. R. H. Super, *CPW* II, 3–29 (16).

[57] The allusion is to Edmund Burke's 'Speech on Conciliation with the Colonies' (1775).

Revolution might as well not have happened is a startlingly pugilistic approach to transatlantic criticism from the cosmopolitan Arnold—a prima facie rejection of the cultural distinctness of the other country, coupled with cavalier homogenization of its racially diverse people under the old and never apt title 'English'.

The cultural imperialism is less defensible than deniable: sufficiently outrageous for serious intent to be disavowed. But it is more than just an *épatant* flourish to launch the essay. Arnold digs in, repeating *Culture and Anarchy*'s sharper class-articulation of the Burkean position, 'America is just ourselves, with the Barbarians [the aristocracy] quite left out, and the Populace nearly' (7).[58] It is, in short, a country where the Philistine has 'his full swing' (7). A 'livelier' sort of Philistine than one tends to find in England: more serious, industrious, energetic, and unhampered by an oppressive aristocracy.[59] This remains the core assumption of the essay. 'Let me end', Arnold concludes, 'by propounding a remedy which really it is heroic in me to propound, for people are bored to death, they say, by me with it, and every time I mention it I make new enemies and diminish the small number of friends that I have now...A higher, larger cultivation, a finer lucidity, is what is needed' (22).

Characteristically, at a late point in Arnold's career, this reaches the high notes by way of a great many lower notes: bantering self-mockery ('really it is heroic in me' to go on bleating about culture); pre-emptive negativity about the level of public interest ('people are bored to death'); avoidance, for as long as possible, of the obligation to name 'culture', substituting, when it comes to 'it', the only marginally less predictable 'cultivation'; and near the end a parodic injection of self-pity ('I make new enemies...')—recalling the last of the *Culture and Anarchy* lectures, 'Culture and Its Enemies'. The posture is that of a public man tired of his own voice, wary of grandstanding, resigned to the likelihood that his position on culture has become counterproductively familiar, an encouragement to the Philistine to shut out these nagging accents. Audience and writer are equally seen to be playing in an over-rehearsed drama ('they are bored...they say, by me with it'). The declaration of embarrassment cannot eradicate the whiff of elitism, but it can make the charge of elitism itself seem stale and critically unexamined. '[T]he worst I could say of him', Whitman wrote, alert to the challenge, '—the severest...would be, that Arnold brings coals to Newcastle—that he brings to the world what the world already has a surfeit of: his rich, hefted, lousy, reeking with delicacy, refinement, elegance, prettiness, propriety, criticism, analysis: all of them things which threaten to overwhelm us.'[60] What might still read, in a British context, as liberal 'free play' of ideas and proto-aestheticist attention to the pleasures of performativity, bringing stale habit under the gaze

---

[58] And see *Culture and Anarchy*, Ch. 3.
[59] And see Preface (1869), in *Culture and Anarchy*, 243.
[60] Traubel, *With Walt Whitman in Camden*, III, 400.

of disinterested criticism, risks revealing itself on American soil as class-ridden and complacent: the self-satisfied posturing of a man who knows what culture is and knows he has it.

Both Arnold and Whitman are on to the danger, alerting the unwary that they are in the treacherous domain of cliché ('coals to Newcastle', 'bored to death'...). But whom does Arnold think he is addressing? The converted? The unconverted? The British, clearly; Americans, potentially? *The Nineteenth-Century* had agents and subscribers across the Atlantic, and he could expect his views to make their way to a wider American audience through syndicated newspaper reporting. The essay looks, emolliently, for common ground, as though the well-worn characterological drama of the refined Englishman advocating high culture in America is at this point dispensable: 'what America wants' is also what 'we ... want', 'really good secondary schools' to raise the numbers of cultivated young people 'in circulation' by the age of 18 (23). Not that Arnold was in a position to say. His extensive first-hand study of schools and universities had not yet taken him beyond the European Continent. But it was at least a prescription few were likely to reject in principle.

Clearly, something different is happening when Arnold takes up America as a subject for more-than-passing criticism than when he writes about Germany, or Prussia, or France, or (more rarely) Russia. In all those cases his critical essays make use of non-British comparisons in order to test the health of his own intellectual culture and, more often than not, find it wanting: what is needed is the greater largeness and freedom of mind evidenced by a Goethe, Heine, Joubert, Tolstoy... In the case of America, and starting from the Burkean proposition that the United States is 'just ourselves' somewhat more democratized, the benefit of comparison to the English critic is not so clear. The reference to the 'Reconciliation' speech sets up a preliminary expectation of where Arnold may be headed: the recommendation will be some kind of reconciliation between the English prioritization of liberty and the American prioritization of equality (in effect, adjusting Tocqueville on America's combination of equality with a strong attachment to religion). Arnold is genuinely in step with Burke on the arrogance of British nationalism and the constraints of its class system—but with more than one template already in place, there is less obvious scope for the criticism's freedom.

Arnold starts from Burke's long-outdated position and makes some rhetorical trouble around the attachment to liberty. American acquaintances have been false friends, he claims:

> They kindly offered me the example of their civilisation as a help to mend ours; and I, not with any vain Anglicism, for I own our insular civilisation to be very unsatisfactory, but from a desire to get at the truth and not to deceive myself with hopes of help from a quarter where at present there is none to be found, have

inquired whether the Americans really think, on looking into the matter, that their civilisation is much more satisfactory than ours.   (22)

The tone is earnest; the attempt at naming and shedding national self-interest sounds arduous enough, but the assumptions of what is to be found on the other side of the Atlantic are cynical: America is pre-emptively judged to have made poor use, to date, of its much-vaunted freedom from the old and 'unsatisfactory' 'insular civilisation'. It has shirked the work of criticism, and contented itself with a pre-emptive and complacent view of its 'civilisation'. He (the clearer-sighted one) will not delude himself with hope of help where 'there is none to be found'.

If cosmopolitan universalism, based on an ever more generally available liberal education in 'right reason', is the overall direction of travel here, Arnold has an odd way of going about things. Patriotic jostling of a 'my culture is better and freer than your culture' sort is not the most promising route out of the narrowness of one's own national affiliations, but there was (and is) a market for it.[61] Moreover, the approach has at least the virtue of a degree of honesty about the local limitations and biases of where it speaks from. As Bruce Robbins puts it, with an eye on nationalism as a possible standpoint for criticism of global economic inequality: '[s]aying nasty things about foreign goods [here, culture] and/or the foreigners who made them does not seem a likely path toward cosmopolitanism in a significant sense of the term', but it has 'a certain heft', a 'grounded' acknow-ledgement of motivating interests.[62] In Arnold's case, that acknowledgement involves a critical element of realism, not only towards his own position but also towards the broad consensus of opinion about him in America, at the point when he began the tour. There was, as John Henry Raleigh showed in his classic study of Arnold in America, a general perception, even among more admiring critical readers, that Arnold suffered from being too English, meaning: 'priggish and artificial', over-concerned with 'correctness' in the use of the language, 'amateur-ish', and (Raleigh adds) personally dislikable on the basis of his writing ('variously pictured as the ineffectual dilettante, the cool sophisticate, or the supercilious destroyer' [66]). The antagonism he brings to the podium is, in that context, a way of acknowledging his reputation head on, playing up to the character already in circulation.

---

[61] On the generation of points of nationalist friction within the transatlantic market model, see Paul Giles, *Transatlantic Insurrections: British Culture and the Formation of American Literature, 1730–1860* (Philadelphia, PA: University of Pennsylvania Press, 2001), Introduction. Also Jessica Despain, *Nineteenth-Century Transatlantic Reprinting and the Embodied Book* (Farnham: Ashgate, 2014), esp. 77 and, for a helpful summary of the critical literature on the subject, 2–5. John Henry Raleigh's argument, in *Matthew Arnold and American Culture* (Berkeley, CA: University of California Press, 1957) identifies Arnold's 'captious[ness] about the English themselves', his complaints against English narrowness, heaviness, and provincialism, as an important element in his appeal to American audiences. Daniel Maudlin and Robin Peel (eds.), *The Materials of Exchange Between Britain and North East America, 1750–1900* (Farnham: Ashgate, 2013).

[62] Bruce Robbins, *The Beneficiary* (Durham, NC: Duke University Press, 2017), 79.

It is one thing to adopt the rhetoric of competitive nationalism as a fictitious basis for espousing the transnational value of 'culture' when the argument is theoretical, conducted on home ground, at a long distance from the comparator civilization; it is another to attempt that line of reasoning on the foreign soil in question. Arnold arrived in New York in October 1883, and spent five months touring the eastern states and southern Canada, enjoying generous hospitality from Andrew Carnegie and many others. In the course of the visit he fulfilled more than seventy speaking engagements at university colleges including Harvard, Dartmouth, Princeton, Wellesley, Smith, Vassar, and numerous public concert halls, music rooms, and civic venues. He had opportunities to observe a variety of local manners and—with hosts alert to his interests in education—a range of educational establishments, including a school for black children in Richmond, Virginia (Arnold's specific request to see segregation in action evidently discomfited his hostess).[63] He talked with several of the most famous and successful men and women in the country, and his elder daughter Lucy met in New York the aspiring lawyer who would soon become her husband.

The extensive hospitality Arnold received, press hostilities notwithstanding, might have been good reason to avoid making further accusations of 'Philistinism', but as the visit played out Arnold took large risks with his audiences' tolerance.[64] He relied on three lectures as his stock: 'Numbers; or The Majority and the Remnant', written specifically for the trip and tackling head on the dangers he perceived in the unrestrained nature of American democracy;[65] 'Literature and Science', a revised version of the 1884 Rede lecture at Cambridge in which he defended a literature-centred liberal education against T. H. Huxley's advocacy for more science and an end to the privileging of the classics;[66] and 'Emerson', also purpose-written after Emerson's death in April 1882.[67] Sitting alongside the broad liberal-educational call to culture, the two new lectures are the more striking for their enactment of a critical freedom that repeatedly oversteps the bounds of tact and politeness, but does so rather less sure-footedly than when the primary audience is imagined as British and European.

---

[63] Honan, *Matthew Arnold*, 402.

[64] Donald Stone observes a pattern of confrontation, increasingly evident in recent years. '[T]o the privileged members of the Royal Institution ("the most aristocratic and exclusive place out," as one detractor put it) ... he read [in 1878] his passionate denunciation of England's political inequality.' His talk at University College Liverpool in 1882, 'given to a group honouring its medical students' was similarly 'remarkable for its noncelebratory theme': 'Arnold cajoles his auditors to look about Liverpool and decide whether they should be praising the city for its scientific and industrial achievements or instead be lamenting the "low standard of life" practiced there'. Donald Stone, *Communications with the Future: Matthew Arnold in Dialogue* (Ann Arbor, MI: University of Michigan Press, 1997), 7.

[65] Matthew Arnold, *Philistinism in England and America*, 143–64. See *CPW*, X, 500 for the list of venues.

[66] Ibid., 53–73.   [67] Ibid., 165–86.

'As pretty a piece of anti-democratic propaganda as one could possibly find—even today'[68] was the judgement passed on 'Numbers' by one of the founding figures of twentieth-century American studies, Howard Mumford Jones, endeavouring to repurpose Arnoldian humanism to the democratic condition of American culture in the 1940s (he would take his own anti-democratic turn in reaction to 1960s radicalism).[69] Cynicism is the lecture's starting point:

> There is a characteristic saying of Dr. Johnson: 'Patriotism is the last refuge of a scoundrel.' The saying is cynical, many will even call it brutal; yet it has in it something of plain, robust sense and truth... there is undoubtedly, sheltering itself under the fine name of patriotism, a good deal of self-flattery and self-delusion which is mischievous.   (143)

It is a characteristic Arnoldian opening—at once affronting and disarming, safely high-toned (Johnson to the fore), but with a journalistic hook (why is patriotism in question? which way will it play? for or against American culture? probably against... one waits to see). The anti-patriotism is soon revealed as a double bluff: having distanced himself from the scoundrel patriot's position, with its temptations to 'self-flattery and self-delusion', Arnold rethinks. To verbalize his own strategy of address is a prime tactic here in establishing freedom from predictable narrow motives. Inadequate flattery of his own nation could be a reason why he has had so little effect on his own countrymen. Best not to repeat the 'error' in America. Adopting the responsibilities of an Englishman, he offers to bring to his analysis of America a proper sense of the greatness of England when making comparative judgements. It is, in essence, the same gambit Arnold had made in 'A Word about America', but sharper, rendering his own nationalism a source of not quite stable ironies.

Some flattery follows: America's 'numbers', in the politico-economic sense, are impressive—geographic scale, food productivity, population growth are 'very real and important ground for satisfaction' (144). But strictly quantitative argument is palpably inadequate to the purposes of Arnoldian criticism, and the statistical mode of analysis is indeed semi-parodic: an extended riff on the expansive, cumulative impulse ('bigger and better') that stereotypically gears American Philistinism, and that was already a long-standing cliché. The obvious caveat follows: big numbers are not a guarantee of quality, whether in things or, more especially, in people, and the disconnect between size of population and level of cultural and political morality is the essence of Arnold's quarrel with democracy

---

[68] Howard Mumford Jones, 'Arnold, Aristocracy, and America', *American Historical Review* 49/3 (1944), 393–409 (398).

[69] See Peter A. Brier, *Howard Mumford Jones and the Dynamics of Liberal Humanism* (Columbia, MO: University of Missouri Press, 1994), 64.

and populism alike. 'Even a popular orator, or a popular journalist,' he observes tendentiously, 'will hardly say that the multitude may be trusted to have its judgment generally just, and its action generally virtuous' (145). As evidence, Arnold points to the failures of Athenian democracy and the Old Testament Hebrew kingdoms: 'the great majority were unsound...and their state was doomed' because the critical 'remnant', the small proportion of the population with the exceptional talents required to rebuild the State, was not to be found in sufficient 'numbers' (147).

Arnold specifies no 'baseline' population size for critical mass, but invites the audience to think of the problem as scalar: there is a tipping point in the size of a community at which the function of the quasi-Socratic critic can cease to be that of an isolated agitant and start to operate within the institution of the nation state, working to the common good:

> To be a voice outside the State, speaking to mankind or to the future, perhaps shaking the actual State to pieces in doing so, one man will suffice. But to reform the State in order to save it, to preserve it by changing it, a body of workers is needed as well as a leader;—a considerable body of workers, placed at many points, and operating in many directions. (149)

The danger is that the words rebound against himself—that he stands before intelligent, educated American audiences who (unlike the American press) were remarkably willing to hear him out,[70] and looks like an arrogantly un-self-critical English intruder, his only institutional support being a profit-hungry press ('the Almighty is the only being who has the right to condescend', was the North American Review's tart observation—'except, it seems, Mr. Matthew Arnold').[71] There is no escape by way of a claim that he stands there as a representative of the British state (a latter-day Johnsonian emissary, perhaps) since he is patently there under his own steam, pursuing his own agenda. Moreover, the cynical charge flung at him by the Chicago Tribune and others that this apostle of sweetness and light was really in pursuit of 'filthy lucre' was true enough.[72] He was looking to

---

[70] Raleigh's Matthew Arnold and American Culture looks to explain how and why America fell so strongly under the influence of Arnold, from the significance of James in paving a way for that influence, through the role of William Brownell and Stuart P. Sherman in securing Arnold's influence into the twentieth century, then on to the radicalization and consolidation of Arnold's inheritance by Eliot and Trilling.

[71] CXXXVIII (May 1884), 432; quoted in E. P. Lawrence, 'An Apostle's Progress: Matthew Arnold in America', Philological Quarterly 10 (January 1931), 62–79 (79).

[72] See ibid., 65. Also David DeLaura, 'Matthew Arnold and the American "Literary Class"', Bulletin of the New York Public Library 70 (1966), 229–50, for an account sympathetic to Arnold, but situating him within a 'profoundly divided' American literary class (230) whose divisions he failed fully to apprehend: he could 'never get America right', nor America him (250). Drawing on previously unpublished materials evidencing Arnold's close relationship with Charles Eliot Norton and James Russell Lowell, DeLaura argues that Norton (then in his eighties) was almost the only member of the

claw out a profit from a country that refused to recognize British copyright, and he badly needed the income. Arnold presents the peculiar spectacle of a man plainly looking to make money from selling advocacy for the disinterested pursuit of culture, and to win a foreign audience by affronting its patriotism. He is not so much a Cynic as a satire on a Cynic—closer to Lucian than to Diogenes.

The last and most interesting of the American lectures, 'Emerson',[73] gave Arnold's audiences partial respite from confrontational stringencies and ironic urbanities on national difference, but broad trans-Atlantic comparisons rumble beneath the surface as he lays out terms for a mode of criticism that would avail itself of the best of two models: the trenchancy and 'force' of the disinterested critical spirit plus Emerson's 'invaluable virtue' of 'holding fast to happiness and hope' (182). There are obvious points of contact between Arnold and his chosen subject: both vested in the freedom of criticism; both opposed to habit and to the disciplining power of conventions; both troubled by the decay of belief;[74] both committed to a view of self-development that sees culture not as a possession but as a process of self-transformation for the better; perhaps most tellingly, in this context, both drawn to, and looking to understand better, 'the interaction between a concept and a country—about how we know a place by a name, and understand its people by their characteristics'.[75] But the differences go deep: Emerson was much the more radical thinker. His idea of self-transformation, and the critical style in which he addressed it, ask more of the self than Arnold's. As Branka Arsić and others have shown, Emerson's moralism is geared less towards progress and self-perfection, than towards willingness to leave the self behind and open oneself to fundamental reformation. In key respects, he is much closer to the spirit of the original Cynics than is Arnold. Emerson has no interest in institutions: marriage, politics, the nation state are all encouraged to admit (it may be) fundamental change (he is willing to contemplate the abandonment of marriage altogether).

---

older literary generation who accepted Arnold 'without reservations' (241). Arnold's blindness to 'the "just people" aspect of America limited his appeal for Whitman and his followers, who insisted on that element as a basis for all "higher" culture' (250). DeLaura quotes Colonel Higginson's journal entry for 28 November 1883, on showing Arnold around five Boston high schools and finding him 'very cordial and appreciative, not in the least cynical' (240)—as if cynicism were to be expected.

[73] Arnold, *Philistinism in England and America*, 165–86.
[74] See Raleigh, *Matthew Arnold and American Culture*, 8–9 (and 8–12 for his more detailed consideration of the points of sympathy between them).
[75] David La Rocca, *Emerson's English Traits and the Natural History of Metaphor* (New York: Bloomsbury Academic, 2013), 1. La Rocca gives a revealing analysis of Emerson's engagement with the idea of Englishness (and the associated 'genius' for liberty), drawing out also the more 'subversive' question that drives *English Traits* (1856), 'why America is itself and not England' (2), and the drive to go beyond and above the limitations of national characterizations. Arnold does not fall within the scope of La Rocca's argument, but Emerson's kinship with (and tolerance for) Carlyle are touched upon at several points.

Imposing nothing 'positive, dogmatic, personal',[76] he sees the willingness to be 'inconsistent', and leave old identities behind, as essential to participation in the flux of life.[77] All extraneous clutter is to be left behind. For the liberal, statist Arnold, his example is at once inspiring and upsetting.

Perhaps because there was serious competition here, Arnold's reflections on America's spokesman for self-challenging 'self-reliance' were tactless in the extreme—'heroic' (Raleigh suggests) in their intrepid trampling of the local hero (he also notes that only the 'proper Bostonians' were offended: iconoclastic as it was, the lecture 'set a stamp on Emerson criticism' until well into the twentieth century). Speaking first at Boston's Chickering Hall,[78] in sight of Boston Bay, Arnold declared himself a long-term admirer of Emerson but went on to refuse him the status of great philosopher, great poet, even great stylist. He allowed only one positive claim for his subject—that he was, like Arnold's favourite Stoic, Marcus Aurelius, 'the friend and aider of those who would live in the spirit' (177). It seems, as critics have noted, 'hardly adequate' recompense for the wash of negative criticism that comes before it.[79] For example: '"Trust thyself;" "what attracts my attention shall have it;"... With Maxims like these, we surely... run some risk of being made too well satisfied with our own actual self and state... It may be said that the common American or Englishman is more than enough disposed already to trust himself' (179).

Amanda Adams is surely correct that Emerson is 'a stand-in' for Arnold's 'own position of cultural authority', down to the habit of aphorism[80] and its attendant dangers of sloganizing. She is also right that in subjecting Emerson to hard and, many American listeners thought, untimely criticism, he was demonstrating the strenuousness of his commitment to the function of criticism: 'challenging... his own admiration for Emerson' and 'put[ting] it under critical scrutiny' (105). Criticism, if it is to be truly free and disinterested, cannot have unexamined heroes. But something more competitive and uncomfortable is also happening here: faced with a truly radical libertarianism, Arnold over-asserts his own freedoms, audibly straining to demonstrate the flexibility of tone and the capacity for force, amid flexibilities, that had been his self-imposed standard as a critic. And if you have self-imposed standards for freedom, how free are you?

The competitive element is visible around the value Arnold attaches to 'clarity'. Always a watchword for Arnold, he wrestles with the justice of applying it to Emerson, rarely doing so without supplementation or qualification. The first

---

[76] *Collected Writings* I, 204; quoted in Branka Arsić, *On Leaving: A Reading in Emerson* (Cambridge, MA: Harvard University Press, 2010), 41.
[77] See ibid., esp. Chapter 1 (on inconsistency, see 44).
[78] See headnote to 'Emerson' notes, *CPW* 10, 505.
[79] See Lawrence, 'Apostle's Progress', 68–9, citing the *Dictionary of National Biography* (first series).
[80] Amanda Adams, Performing *Authorship in the Nineteenth-Century Transatlantic Lecture Tour* (Farnham: Ashgate, 2014), 105.

recollection of Emerson is positive: a 'clear and pure voice' from 'three thousand miles away…as new and moving and unforgettable, as the strain of Newman, or Carlyle, or Goethe' (167). But then the qualifications start: two passages from the poetry are deemed 'exceptional…Excellent! But how seldom do we get from him a strain blown so clearly and firmly' (170). It seems to Arnold indicative that, familiar though Emerson is to all American readers, 'not one single passage' of his poetry 'has entered into English speech as a matter of familiar quotation' (169): the familiarity is 'national' not 'universal'. The poetry 'lacks directness; it lacks concreteness; it lacks energy'. Grammar is a problem: 'often embarrassed'; wanting 'clearly marked distinction between the subject and the object' (169–70). The prose is worse: afflicted by the unsoundness of all the transcendentalists—'a style almost impossible to a born man of letters' (172). Emerson comes right, stylistically, when exposing the political shortcomings of his own country: 'no misanthropical satirist ever saw shortcomings and absurdities more clearly' (180). And he had, at least, a proper sense of his own failure to stand comparison with the masters: 'No man could see this clearer than Emerson himself' (176).

Only when he has dealt with the opacities of the poetry, does Arnold breathe easily: 'And now I think I have cleared the ground' (177). The degree of investment in clarity (always a watchword for him, but here exceptionally agitated for) raises the question of *why* so much value is attached to it, and what it is about Emerson that particularly threatens unclarity—or, to rephrase the problem with Newman, and Arnold's strictures on Emersonian style in view, what it is about Emerson that troubles Arnold's 'grammar of assent'. The lecture is, at the end, benign towards its subject, coming to rest on a simple claim: the 'secret' of Emerson's 'effect' lies not in his insight or his truth but in his 'temper', a 'hopeful, serene, beautiful temper' (181). This is more conventionally appropriate to a memorial lecture, but it has not been the temper of Arnold's own speech, and it is disputable how good a description it is of Emerson's temper. 'Hopefulness' is right, but 'serenity' too bland. It certainly does not fit the final quotation Arnold picks out from a passage in the *Letters*: 'My whole philosophy—which is very real—teaches acquiescence and optimism. Only when I see how much work is to be done, what room for a poet—for any spiritualist—in this great, intelligent, sensual, avaricious America, I lament my fumbling fingers and stammering tongue.'[81]

Arnold is tellingly selective, jettisoning the insistence on 'reality' and the 'fumbling' and 'stammering':

I figure him as he lived, but of heightened stature and shining feature, with one hand stretched out towards the East, to our laden and labouring England; the

---

[81] Ralph Waldo Emerson and Thomas Carlyle, *The Correspondence of Emerson and Carlyle*, ed. Joseph Slater (New York: Columbia University Press, 1964), 304.

other towards the ever-growing West, to his own dearly-loved America,—'great, intelligent, sensual, avaricious America'. To us he shows for guidance his lucid freedom, his cheerfulness, and hope; to you his dignity, delicacy, serenity, elevation.   (186)

This strange figuration makes Emerson a somewhat alarming ally of Arnold's hard cultural diplomacy—a colossus of culture, achieved only by suppressing the modesty of 'fumbling fingers and stammering tongue'. It is as if Arnold, having contemplated what it would feel like to live and write, as he takes Emerson to have done, without cynicism, cannot but rush to assert that a non-cynical mind need not be a weak mind, and convert Emersonian humility back into the power of 'elevation'.

That Arnold's tough clarities were under pressure in America is discernible in the unusual level of hedging that accompanies his provocations, daring though they were, at the lecture podium. My ellipses cut a path through a sometimes clogging density of 'it may be said' and 'it could be thought'-ing that is atypical of Arnold, and reinforces the sense of being out of his normal sphere of 'clear' operation, threatened by complexities that are with difficulty held at bay. On his return from America, Arnold was at liberty to be bolder. 'A Word More about America'[82] was written immediately on his return, and sent to *The Nineteenth Century* with some trepidation. In addition to the risk of discourtesy he recognized a danger of 'impertinence' (the direct knowledge he could claim on the basis of one visit remained limited). His wife, Fanny Lucy, was on tenterhooks that a bad reception in New York would put a strain on their daughter's New York marriage as soon as it had begun. 'I often think of you', Arnold wrote to Lucy in early 1885, warning her that he was at work: 'it would be unpleasant for you if it gave offence over there; but I do not think it will. Mamma, however, is in a thousand agonies.'[83] (His relief at subsequent reassurances was clear: you have been 'sweet' about the article', he wrote on 3 March, and said the same thing again eight days later.)[84]

'A Word More about America'[85] dispatches in a few sentences the awkwardness of having told his US hosts and English friends he would not be writing about his

---

[82] This was not quite Arnold's final word on the subject. Laurel Brake rightly notes that Arnold's last essay, 'Civilization in the United States', takes a late turn back against the prospects for American culture: 'everything is against distinction in America' (in Matthew Arnold, *The Last Word*, ed. R. H. Super, CPW 11, 350–69 [360]. Brake finds the pro-Americanism of 'A Word More' 'surprising', whereas I am inclined to be more struck by the regression to the posture of the dismayed English nationalist, which I take to be explained by Arnold's specific targeting of the institution of the newspaper press for its failure (as he sees it) to provide a forum for criticism. See Laurel Brake, 'W. T. Stead and Democracy: The Americanization of the World', in Dzelzainis and Livesey (eds.), *The American Experiment*, 161–78 (165).

[83] 12 January, *Letters* VI, 3–4 (3); and see Honan, *Matthew Arnold*, 396–409 (409).

[84] *Letters* VI, 17–18 (18) and 21–3 (21).

[85] Published in *The Nineteenth Century* (February 1885); *Philistinism in England and America*, 194–217.

American experiences. The literary challenge, as Arnold now presents it, is to find a style that is not abstractly 'philosophic'. This, he confesses, was his problem reading Tocqueville on Democracy 'a long while' ago: too many abstractions, delivered in 'a style which I find trying—...cut into short paragraphs and wearing an air of rigorous scientific deduction without the reality' (194). Some of the fault no doubt lay with himself, he concedes (he implies that there is little to feel bad about): 'My debility in high speculation is well known' (194). He will perhaps try Tocqueville again one day; in the interim he is looking to adjust his pre-tour impressions in the light of experience.

Franker than his American lectures, the essay that follows is softened by Arnold turning his critical gaze as much on his own country as on the United States. He makes an important concession to experience: his pre-tour assessment failed to gauge the importance of America's institutions to the success of the democracy. He has some positive things also to say about the political benefits of American social 'homogeneity', by which he means the absence of the old class structures that hamper Britain in its attempts to gain a clear view of its political problems.

> an English country-gentleman regards himself as part of the system of nature: government and legislation have invited him so to do. If the price of wheat falls so low that his means of expenditure are greatly reduced, he tells you that if this lasts he cannot possibly go on as a country-gentleman; and every well-bred person amongst us looks sympathising and shocked. An American would say: 'Why should he?'   (201)

Never a democrat, Arnold comes close to sounding like one here, taking a dimmer view of the contributions of the landed gentry to British politics and culture than he had done in the past. The 'lively Philistinism' that enables the American to call time on the country-gentleman's inherited privileges has his approval: this is a 'healthy community' that 'sees things straight and sees them clear' (203). A major concession follows: 'I did not foresee how far [the American Philistine's] superior liveliness and naturalness of condition' would, in the absence of a constraining aristocracy, 'carry' him (203). Arnold admires the free play of mind routinely found in a society disburdened of the 'stunt[ing] and distort[ing]' pressures inherited privilege exerts against middle-class energy and enterprise in Britain. His praise for this critical clarity encourages him to the warmest endorsement he ever provides for 'the Philistine': 'in my mouth the name is hardly a reproach, so clearly do I see the Philistine's necessity, so willingly I own his merits, so much I find of him in myself' (203).

Identification with the free-speaking, American Philistine transforms for a period the basis of Arnold's rhetorical address to America. For the remainder of the essay the main target of his criticism is not America (the title is somewhat misleading) but the hide-bound, confused state of modern Britain. By contrast with the straight-seeing, straight-talking American, Arnold finds his British Philistine counterpart sadly lacking in the virtues once commonly ascribed to him by the 'Liberal newspapers'. The wording is almost identical to *Friendship's Garland*: Britain wants, and once thought it had, 'clear, manly intelligence, penetrating through sophisms, ignoring commonplaces, and giving to conventional illusions their true value' (203–4). What, Arnold now asks, would a straight-thinking, straight-proceeding American do if faced with the 'many confusions...embarrassing' British public life: the confusion of its foreign affairs, its House of Commons, its handling of Ireland. As he speculates about how the American Philistine might provide clarity, this imagined external critic becomes entirely a mouthpiece for Arnold's own liberal views: what is needed is stronger middle-class representation at the top of politics, greater devolution of power to local assemblies, substantial legislative independence for the Irish provinces and removal of control from British landlords, an elected Second Chamber of the British Parliament in place of the House of Lords.

'A Word More about America' repackages Arnoldian clarity as American bluntness, at the expense of the self-regulating relation with cynicism. The end of the essay lays out, through the adopted outlook of a straight-thinking, plain-speaking American, lines of principle and practical requirements for the reform of British culture, starting with a radical diminution in the power of the British aristocracy in favour of social and political equality: 'aristocracy now sets up in our country a false ideal, which materialises our upper class, vulgarises our middle class, brutalises our lower class. It misleads the young, makes the worldly more worldly, the limited more limited, the stationary more stationary' (213).

What, in the modern day, is the point of having an aristocracy at all—'a Duke of Norfolk or an Earl [of] Warwick, dressed in broadcloth and tweed, and going about his business or pleasure in hansom cabs and railways like the rest of us?' (213). Leave them to Shakespeare, Arnold pronounces. 'Time and circumstance' have been fatal to them; even 'artists and men of letters' will find nothing left here to provoke imaginative interest (213).

So sharp an appraisal of how antique and unfit for purpose Britain's social and political arrangements have become looks positive for America in the balance of comparative critical acuity. But Arnold ends by taking an introverting and *ad hominem* turn. Who, he asks, will now lead the needed reforms in Britain? Who has the 'lucidity and penetration' to understand the scale of change needed, and the order of importance between various reforms crying out for attention (not, for example, rushing to disestablish the Church, which Arnold considers a key institutional support for the principle of equality in England, if not Ireland, Wales or Scotland). Two men earn warm praise, for having the quality of mind and energy required: Goldwin Smith and John Morley—both major figures in the intellectual formation of Victorian liberalism. Smith, whose professorial career as a historian took him from Oxford, to Cornell, to Toronto, in the 1850s to 1870s was a key figure in the reform of the University of Oxford at mid-century, and subsequently influential in bringing English opinion to support the North in the American Civil War—a self-described 'anti-imperialist to the core'.[86] Morley is better remembered by literary critics: a hugely influential liberal journalist, editor of the *Fortnightly Review* from 1867 to 1882 and the *Pall Mall Gazette* from 1880 to 1883. Neither man can meet the need of the moment as Arnold describes it: had Goldwin Smith chosen a career in the House of Commons, he might have been 'a real power for good..., one of the leaders there'; if Morley, recently elected to Parliament, can shed the partisanship that has made him such a force in journalism, 'he will rise, he will come into office; but he will not do...what Mr. Goldwin Smith would have done' (215–16) had Smith not quit England for North America.

The dismissal of the two men Arnold thinks most capable among the current generation in their political prime leaves the essay oddly incomplete in its thinking. At this juncture, Arnold concludes, England needs someone capable of reading 'the signs of the time' (216) and effecting change through the institutions of Parliament and the press. Carlyle had died the year before, and was never the man for the liberal Arnold, but in any event a note of pessimism attaches to the function of literature ('letters'), which (Arnold argues) can no longer be the 'effective organ' for engaging the public (216). If real change is to be effected, the nation must have exceptional leaders in politics and journalism (the second a potential opening for criticism to engage with the world of practical affairs), and for Arnold the leaders must be Englishmen. Though he has found in America a great supply of free-thinking men and women, he cannot see America as a viable repository of his hope for a free play of mind in the service of the greater good. This closing assertion of English superiority over America makes for an odd reversion to prejudicial nationalism—hardly an example of the open-mindedness Arnold calls for. If it has, again, a possible justification as the kind of 'grounded' talk that admits its own motivating interests, but that doesn't do much to soften a note of cultural pugnacity in the final sentence that goes beyond owning up to one's own interests to contemplate a world too much at one's critical disposal: 'I should not like to have to own [America] to be of all countries calling themselves civilised, except Russia, the country where one would least like to live' (217).

*

'Stories about what a nation has been and should try to be', Richard Rorty writes in *Achieving Our Country* (1998), 'are not attempts at accurate representation, but rather attempts to forge a moral identity.'[87] Transnational, would-be universal

---

[86] Goldwin Smith, *Loyalty, Aristocracy, and Jingoism: Three Lectures Delivered before the Young Men's Liberal Club, Toronto* (Toronto: Hunter, Rose & CO., 1891), 30—quoting his own lecture in 1882, delivered after the passage of Gladstone's Irish Land Bill (which Smith supported 'with misgivings').

[87] Richard Rorty, *Achieving Our Country: Leftist Thought in Twentieth-Century America* (Cambridge, MA: Harvard University Press, 1998), 13.

stories of the kind Arnold wanted to tell about culture have even less to do with accuracy, and the moral positioning they undertake must struggle with the concept of 'identity'. Arnoldian criticism had, from its first formulation, aspired to a form of public speech that loosens the hold on identity, both at the personal and at the national cultural level, while endeavouring not to lose something vital to its capacity to count as criticism rather than something weaker—too capricious, less publicly efficacious, politically unmoored. Arnold, following Goethe, tended to call this quality 'force'. The word misleads if it is thought to designate the consistent keynote of Arnoldian critical style. It becomes, however, a more dominant and troublesome feature of his criticism when it crosses the Atlantic and comes under pressure from a public sphere already distinctively invested in the concept of free and frank critical speech. In that context, it becomes much harder for Arnold to have performative recourse to the kinds of cynicism that had anchored his advocacy for the cultural ideal in Britain and kept it in touch with base realities. The expectation of frankness limits the performance of freedom, cramping its style.

I am not proposing an intellectual historical line of inquiry here of the kind that would draw lines of influence from a semi-cynic Arnold to, say, the *Scrutineers* and later Cambridge critics or, perhaps more interestingly, of the kind that cross the Atlantic: through Trilling to, say, Mark Greif and the *n + 1* collective, or Dewey to Rorty, or from any and all of these to some of the more vigilant practitioners of post-critique now inclined to treat critical freedom cynically as an enabling cover-story in the critic's bid for personal and institutional power.[88] Because cynicism is a characterization, and a set of argumentative and stylistic traits, without specific ideological content, we cannot ask it to yield deeply connected stories about schools of thought. It gives us access to partial stylistic similarities, selective indebtednesses, different kinds of investment in the idea of 'freedom'.

The description of Arnold that I have been pursuing here nevertheless sets him in some very mixed political and philosophical company of his own choosing—Heine, Joubert, Burke, Carlyle, (with some strain) Emerson, Morley, Smith—the ground of connection being more stylistic than ideological: a willingness to bring a confrontational edge of free-speaking to public conversation about the values that should guide the culture. Though a less radical figure than any of the others in that grouping, I take Arnold to have still some exemplary importance in his scoping out of a serious scepticism about the motives for participation in culture—a scepticism that flirts with the astringencies of the thoroughgoing Cynic but

---

[88] For a classic articulation of this position, see Stephen Best and Sharon Marcus, 'Surface Reading: An Introduction', *Representations* 108/1 (2009), 1–21. For example, 'many of our most powerful critical models see criticism as a practice of freedom by locating autonomy, self-reflexiveness, detachment, and liberatory potential either in the artwork itself or in the valiant labor of the critic' (13).

holds back from the full self-characterization. Of all the associations that shape that scepticism, I take Emerson's radical idealism and Heine's cynicism to be the most revealing. Unlike as they are, engagement with them offers to open up a version of freedom that would thoroughly disconcert the Arnoldian vision of culture: from Emerson's side, it would deprive that vision of the aid of strong state institutions; from Heine's side, it would admit Philistinism as a serious possibility for the culture, rather than culture's 'absolute negation', as Malcolm Bull puts it.[89] Bull, indeed, reserves a place for Arnold in a 'Short History of Negation' that would open up the potential of Philistinism to loosen the higher value vested in the aesthetic. In that context he adds another to Arnold's company: Nietzsche, whose *Birth of Tragedy* was published just three years after *Culture and Anarchy*. Although the two books 'could hardly be more different', Bull observes, their 'central concern...is the same': the 'perfect freedom' that comes, for Arnold, through 'elevation' of 'higher experience' above 'ordinary' (16). The persistent and obvious difference between them is surely that we have no need of an anti-Arnoldian radical position along the lines of the anti-Nietzsche position Bull scopes out. Arnold's cynicism, unlike Nietzsche's, serves a vision of freedom that knows, and to a greater degree accepts, its own limits and those of its present day.

---

[89] Malcolm Bull, *Anti-Nietzsche* (London: Verso, 2011), 4.

4

Cosmopolitan Cynicisms

George Eliot and Ford Madox Ford

'Asked where he came from, he said, "I am a citizen of the world."'[1] When Diogenes of Sinope coined the term *kosmopolites* [κοσμοπολίτης] to claim an outlook wider than that associated with the city state, he was, some have thought, being more cagey than grandiose. This was a gambit befitting an exile, wanted back in Sinope (a flourishing Greek colony on the Black Sea) for adulteration of the local coinage.[2] For certain twentieth- and twenty-first-century political theorists, his response to the questioner was, nonetheless, the starting point of an exemplary philanthropic cosmopolitanism, a readiness to identify with the needs and interests of all humanity above those of one's place and culture of origin.

In the main, classicists have been wary of so affirmative a response to Diogenes. There are exceptions—at least one of whom raises the stakes still higher than 'species-wide'[3] humanitarianism. In embracing 'the polity of the cosmos', John Moles argues, Diogenes adopts 'a positive attitude' towards the whole of the 'natural world and all its riches (water, garlic, lupins, etc.!) as opposed to the world of the polis'; he implies 'a positive attitude to the animal world' (witness the Cynics' acceptance of their association with dogs, deflecting a term of abuse into a mark of self-respect); he does indeed make common kind with all other humans (his castigation of the unwise is what we all need to assist us on the path to wisdom), but, more boldly, he claims common habitation of the cosmos with the gods ('Diogenes', Moles reminds us, means 'Born of Zeus').[4] The last claim is the

---

[1] Diogenes Laertius, *Lives of the Eminent Philosophers*, trans. Robert Drew Hicks, rev. and reprinted edn, 2 vols. (London: William Heinemann Ltd., 1950), II, 65 (6.63); also Lucian of Samosata, 'Sale of Creeds' (8), in *The Works of Lucian of Samosata*, trans. H. W. Fowler and F. G. Fowler, 4 vols. (Oxford: Clarendon Press, 1905), I, 190–206 (193).

[2] See esp. Introduction to Bruce Robbins and Paul Lemos Horta (eds.), *Cosmopolitanisms* (New York: New York University Press, 2017), 2.

[3] Bruce Robbins, *Perpetual War: Cosmopolitanism from the Viewpoint of Violence* (Durham, NC: Duke University Press, 2012), 2.

[4] John L. Moles, 'Cynic Cosmopolitanism', in Robert Bracht Branham and Marie-Odile Goulet-Cazé (eds.), *The Cynics: The Cynic Movement in Antiquity and Its Legacy* (Berkeley, CA: University of California Press, 1996), 105–20. Other proponents of a positive Cynic cosmopolitanism (cited by Moles) include M. H. Fisch, 'Alexander and the Stoics', *American Journal of Philology* 58/1 (1937), 59–82 and 58/2 (1937), 129–51 (see esp. 130–1 for claims of Alexander's direct knowledge of Diogenes' cosmopolitanism); Ragnar Höistad, 'Cynic Hero and Cynic King: Studies in the Cynic Conception of Man' (thesis, University of Uppsala, 1948), esp. 141–3; Maurizio Buora, 'L'incontro tra Alessandro et

The Function of Cynicism at the Present Time. Helen Small, Oxford University Press (2020). © Helen Small.
DOI: 10.1093/oso/9780198861935.001.0001

most open to dispute, resting 'substantially' on the slippery syllogism attributed to Diogenes by Diogenes Laertius (*Lives of the Eminent Philosophers* 6.72): 'All things belong to the gods; the wise are friends of the gods, and friends hold things in common, therefore all things belong to the wise.'[5] Still, a bold pitch would be consistent with the Cynic character generally, and the radical commonality accords with Cynicism's reduction of 'all things' worth having to those that nature provides.

Moles's reading runs against a majority view among modern classicists that Diogenes' cosmopolitanism was 'negative' rather than 'positive' in kind; it does not, however, challenge the broad agreement that his philanthropic outlook was anti-political. When the historian Donald R. Dudley, largely responsible for the revival of popular interest in Cynicism in the twentieth century, came to the subject of cosmopolitanism, he added a cautionary note for anyone tempted to source present-day perspectives back to Diogenes:

> It is essential not to read too much into [his] profession. For us 'cosmopolitan-ism' as a conception carries an emotional colour which is the legacy of Alexander, transmitted through the Roman Empire and the Catholic Church. But...the phrase as used by Diogenes was one of negation, meaning, 'I am not a citizen of any of your Greek cities.'[6]

Diogenes' 'negative cosmopolitanism'[7] betokened, for Dudley, resistance not just to the power of the city state but to 'every kind of coercion imposed by the community on the individual'.[8] The key philosophical gearing was not *philan-thropia* but *autarkeia*—a self-sufficiency that kept studiously clear of political action and recommendation. To read into the term *kosmopolites* resistance to imperialism (military, economic, or religious) or a mission for social justice would be to mistake the remit. On this point Dudley felt the need to be emphatic: 'With the exception of Cercidas and the reform party at Megalopolis, and possibly the Cynics of Alexandria in the second century A.D., we shall not find Cynicism involving any kind of political action on behalf of social reform' (xi). Far from

Diogene: Tradizioni e significato', *Atti dell'Istituto Veneto de Scienze, Lettere ed Arti* 132 (1973–74), 243–64; and Rosa Giannattasio Andria, 'Diogene Cinico nei papyri Erconalesi', *Cronache Ercolanesi* 10 (1980), 129–51. Cf. the more standard view of 'negative cosmopolitanism' influentially articulated by (among others) G. Giannantoni (ed.), *Socratis et Socraticorum Reliquiae*, 4 vols. (Naples: Bibliopolis, 1990), IV, 537–47; Marie-Odile Goulet-Cazé, 'Un syllogisme stoïcien sur la loi dans la doxographie de Diogène le Cynique. A propos de Diogène Laërce VI 72', *Rheinisches Museum für Philologie* 125 (1982), 214–40.

[5] As translated by Moles, 'Cynic Cosmopolitanism', 114, 113.
[6] Donald R. Dudley, *A History of Cynicism* (1937), 2nd edn, Foreword and Bibliography by Miriam Griffin (Bristol: Bristol Classical Press, 2003), 35.
[7] W. D. Desmond, *Cynics* (Stocksfield: Acumen, 2008), 271.
[8] Dudley, *History of Cynicism*, 34.

being 'the philosophy of the proletariat', it took no particular critical view of the existing social order. '[O]rganiz[ing] the murder of tyrants' was not on the agenda. 'Indeed,' Dudley concluded, 'by preaching that poverty and slavery are no bar to happiness, the Cynics implied that a social revolution would be superfluous' (xi).

The topicality of a philosophical defence of anti-political self-sufficiency amid the insurgent and soon-to-be warring nationalisms of the mid-1930s invites deeper reflection—indeed, deeper political reflection—than Dudley gave it. The story of Cynicism as he presented it was one of charismatic individuals, starting with the arrival in Athens of Diogenes, 'a man of outstanding personality' (117), some quarter of a century after the death of the more scholarly Antisthenes, whose role Dudley significantly downgraded. *The History of Cynicism* takes us through the line of Diogenes' disciples to Cynicism's one period of direct political influence, in the third century BCE, when Cynic counsellors attended on kings and statesmen, and then on to its role as a kind of official 'philosophic opposition' to the Caesars (Chapter 7). With the exception of this brief spell of political consequence, Cynicism's presence is seen to be on the wane after Diogenes and Crates— philosophically absorbed into and overtaken by Stoicism, and from there sublimated into other 'life philosophies' of various kinds. Dudley sketched out some legacies in Christian asceticism, the radical sects of the Reformation, (still more remotely) modern Anarchism, and the frontier mentality of European emigrants to America, Africa, or Australia.

If there is a broad lesson on offer from *A History of Cynicism*, it is that the initial radical example of a few charismatic individuals could not sustain a distinct school of philosophic practice over time. 'The Cynic himself was becoming a familiar rather than a remarkable figure', by the end of the third century: 'his *avaideia* [shameless behaviour] ceased to shock: we now regard a communist orator as part of the furnishings of Hyde Park rather than as a forerunner of the Red Dawn' (118), Dudley observes. Politics creeps back in with that comparison. The subject has 'a melancholy significance', commented the reviewer for *The Spectator* (not a professional classicist) in March 1938: 'It is because the present is dark and the future uncertain, because governments claim citizens for their own, restrain the freedom of their bodies with concentration camps, and oppress their minds with propaganda disguised as education, that the Cynic seeks safety within the citadel of his soul.'[9] The same writer was more inclined than Dudley had been, two years earlier,[10] to worry over a growing inclination towards forms of detachment

---

[9]   C. E. M. Joad, 'Cynics Ancient and Modern', *The Spectator*, 11 March 1938, 435–6 (436). Other reviews for the most part confined themselves to the classical remit of *The History of Cynicism*—but several expressed a wish that the social conditions conducive to Cynicism's first appearance had been more extensively treated. See, for example, K. V. Fritz, 'New Books', *Mind* 47 (July 1938), 390–2; Friedrich Solmsen, *The Classical Weekly* 31/17 (1938), 163–4.

[10]   A reference to 'recent events in Spain' as an indication of Cynicism's implication in modern Anarchism is footnoted 'written in 1936'. Epilogue, 212.

reminiscent of Cynicism that, in their very hostility to politics, were having political effects: '[s]piritual vagrancy, Buchmanism, the Peace Pledge Union, the renascence of mysticism, even the cultivation of the country cottage, all these have part of their spiritual ancestry in Cynicism. For Cynicism is an expression of the eternal escapism of man' (436).

Two years had made a difference: the Peace Pledge Union, founded in 1934, launched its first manifesto and peace campaign in the same month the review appeared, and would back Chamberlain's appeasement policy at Munich a few months later; the Christian fellowship movement, formed in the 1920s by the American Lutheran Frank Buchman, had grown in strength and would adopt its more influential 'moral re-armament' identity in May 1938. Sourcing 'part of' the ancestry of these movements to Cynicism, *The Spectator* review was implicitly charging both with shirking the major political challenges of the day.

In arguing for the anti-political orientation of the Cynic *kosmopolites*, Dudley was taking a position within a then-current scholarly dispute. He drew for authority on the work of the senior independent scholar William Woodthorpe Tarn, who, in 1933, had delivered the British Academy Raleigh Lecture on the subject of 'Alexander the Great and the Unity of Mankind'.[11] Tarn's focus there was not on cosmopolitanism but on the concept of *homonoia*, the unity of mankind or 'brotherhood of man', which took hold (he argued) with Alexander's pursuit of a justificatory theory for absolute rule. Tarn distinguished *homonoia* sharply from the world citizenship of the Cynics and early Stoics: where 'cosmopolitanism' was about detached self-sufficiency, *homonoia* provided the underpinning for Alexander's military advancement of a 'civilizing' imperial project. (The depiction is in line with Plutarch but 'bears the imprint', the *Oxford DNB* observes, 'of a late Victorian British ideal of gentlemanly imperial-ism'—one that, though challenged and modified over the years, has had a lasting impact on the study of Alexander.)[12]

Push-back came four years later, around the same time as the *History of Cynicism*'s appearance, in the form of a two-part article in the *American Journal of Philology* by the non-specialist historian M. H. Fisch.[13] Insisting on a Cynic/Stoic line of influence in early ideas of the unity of mankind (and arguing that the depiction of Cynicism and Stoicism in the British Academy lecture contradicted views Tarn had himself put forward in the *Cambridge Ancient History*), Fisch depicted Alexander as a political pragmatist, turning 'from Aristotle and Isocrates to the Cynics' because Cynic ideas were more compatible with a vision of empire as a large section of humanity living under the same 'cosmic' Hellenistic law.

---

[11] William Woodthorpe Tarn, *The Raleigh Lecture on History* (London: H. Milford, 1933). For the differentiation with the Cynics, see esp. 4–5, and 30 n. 12.

[12] F. E. Adcock, rev. K. D. Reynolds, 'Tarn, Sir William Woodthorpe (1869–1957)', *Oxford Dictionary of National Biography*. Accessed 6 July 2019.

[13] Fisch, 'Alexander and the Stoics'.

'[P]hilosophic missionaries', with 'little sense of special obligation to their native cities, but with a general "philanthropy"', the Cynics provided a body of political thought tailor-made, Fisch claimed, for Greek confrontation with 'the barbarians'—emphasizing physical hardihood, the necessity that men submit to 'either reason or a halter', and worldliness (for Alexander, a political ambition as much as, or more than, an ethical perspective) (130).[14] Tarn defended himself robustly. Over 29 pages in the *American Journal of Philology*'s first issue for 1939 he laid bare errors and distortions in Fisch's argument and tightened the case for Alexander's independence of Cynic/Stoic influence. On the subject of Cynicism's world-outlook, he was scathing:

> Cynic 'cosmopolitanism' is a common cliché in books, but I have never met with any attempt to prove it, and certainly Fisch makes none. What was Cynicism? It was not a *philosophy* . . . it was a way of life, a mode of thought, and was entirely negative. . . . It never *constructed* anything, anything which affected men otherwise than as individuals; cynicism and universalism are a contradiction in terms.
>
> (42)[15]

I am less interested in the ins and outs of the philological dispute—which I take to have been won, if not absolutely put to rest, by Tarn[16]—than in the broad and, at the time, understated critical implications of drawing a line of connection from Diogenes' 'cosmopolitan' identification into modern political thought. That Tarn and, following him, Dudley should be wary of pedigree-making from Cynicism is hardly surprising. Setting aside the less attractive associations of the Cynic character, a desire to avoid anachronism haunts the philological enterprise, James

[14] Ibid., Pt. II, 130.
[15] W. W. Tarn, 'Alexander, Cynics and Stoics', *American Journal of Philology* 60/1 (1939), 41–70. He made short work of the evidence for a politically Cynic 'cosmopolitanism'. First, Diogenes' use of the word *kosmopolites/κοσμοπολίτης*: it is the remark of an 'embittered exile', scarcely used again by any Greek. '[I]t occurs twice in Philo, but he was a Jew' (43)—meaning, he was, like the whole Jewish diaspora, in exile (he had, so to speak, skin in the cosmopolitan game). Second, Diogenes Laertius 6.72: 'the one true citizenship was that in the universe' (quoted, 43). Tarn saw no reason to disagree with Epictetus: if you ask how is it possible to live without a city or a home, Diogenes is there to show you; 'no home, no city, no possessions, . . . only the earth and the sky'—this is what it means to be truly free (44). Finally, the legend that Diogenes wrote an equivalent to Plato's *Republic*, the *Diogenous Politeia/ Διογένους Πολιτέια*: what little is known of this work suggests 'not anything "cosmopolitan," but a small state within narrow limits' (44).
[16] Tim Whitmarsh lists a number of critics who subsequently followed Fisch in his opposition to Tarn: U. Wilcken, 'Die letzen Pläne Alexanders der Grossen', *Sitzungsberichte der preussische Akademie* (Berlin: Verlag der Akademie der Wissenschaften, 1937), 198–201; Truesdell S. Brown, *Onesicritus: A Study in Hellenistic Historiography* (Berkeley, CA: University of California Press, 1949), 50; E. Badian, 'Alexander the Great and the Unity of Mankind', *Historia* 7 (1958), 425–44; C. Mossé, 'Les utopies égalitaires à l'époque hellenistique', *Revue Historique* 241/2 (1969), 297–308. Tim Whitmarsh, 'Alexander's Hellenism and Plutarch's Textualism', *The Classical Quarterly* 52/1 (2002), 174–92 (179).

Turner has observed.[17] For Tarn, steeped in the German nineteenth-century scholarship on Greek antiquity, extrapolation from fourth-century BCE texts to twentieth-century politics was illegitimate, hence his passing irritation at Dudley's translation of Diogenes Laertius, notwithstanding the deference shown to himself. 'The only true commonwealth is that which is as wide as the universe' was Dudley's rewording of *Lives* 6.72 (35). This was, as Tarn saw it, simply not Greek, any more than was Fisch's rendering of kosmos [κόσμῳ] as 'world-state' (43). At the same time, it is Tarn (with four years' experience in intelligence, in the First World War), rather than the young Dudley,[18] who sounds a passing note of *realpolitik* towards political cosmopolitanism at any period: the supposed Cynic polity of the cosmos is unworkable on the grounds that 'no form of state, even world-wide, would prevent people being proud of their pedigrees' (44).

Those later political and cultural theorists who have wanted to recall Diogenes to the picture have normally had critical motives beyond fidelity to the classical sources. Most writers today assume a 'blended' conception of cosmopolitanism,[19] which has its philosophical basis in a Kantian aspiration towards rational 'detachment' from national, economic, religious, and other forms of narrow interest—combined with (and tending to dominate) an older 'ethical' cosmopolitanism associated with Stoicism. Cynicism is often silently absorbed into Stoicism in this overview, and even where critical theorists give Diogenes due credit for linguistic invention (if not a worked-out ethical position), he is frequently depicted as the nominal precursor of a more ethically respectable, or simply better-known, Stoic contribution to political thought.[20] Critics pointing to a distinctively Cynical start to cosmopolitanism are in a fairly small minority, their imperatives more political than historical. Where the explicit question for Tarn, Dudley, Fisch, and Moles was one of evidential warrant (does anything in the surviving records permit extrapolation from Diogenes to modern cosmopolitanism?), the question implicitly posed by the theorist is more permissive: to what critical use might cosmopolitanism's linguistic debt to Cynicism now be put? Would a Cynical cosmopolitanism just be a tougher-skinned ethical

---

[17] James Turner, *Philology: The Forgotten Origins of the Modern Humanities* (Princeton, NJ: Princeton University Press, 2014). I draw here also on Colin Burrow's respectful but resistant review: 'Are You a Spenserian?', *London Review of Books* 36/21 (6 November 2014), 35–7, <https://www.lrb.co.uk/v36/n21/colin-burrow/are-you-a-spenserian>. Accessed 31 May 2019.

[18] He was, at the time of writing, a Junior Research Fellow of St John's College, Cambridge.

[19] I take the word from David Held, 'Globalization, Corporate Practice and Cosmopolitan Social Standards', *Contemporary Political Theory* 1 (2002), 59–78 (64). And see Georgios Varouxakis, 'Cosmopolitan Patriotism in J. S. Mill's Political Thought and Activism', *Revue des études benthamiennes* 4 (2008), <http://journals.openedition.org/etudes-benthamiennes/188>.

[20] See, for example, Amanda Anderson, *Powers of Distance: Cosmopolitanism and the Cultivation of Detachment* (Princeton, NJ: Princeton University Press, 2001), 131; also Martha C. Nussbaum, 'Kant and Stoic Cosmopolitanism', *The Journal of Political Philosophy* 5/1 (1997), 1–25 (5–6).

cosmopolitanism (Stoicism 'plus bad manners', to echo D. J. Allan),[21] or can Diogenes be of more help in defining a critical cosmopolitanism now?

The main motive for putting Diogenes at the start of modern cosmopolitanism's political story in very recent years has been the assertion of a stronger-than-usual disposition to cast doubt on the viability of cosmopolitan ideals. The political intentions, as might be expected, vary. When Bruce Robbins and Paulo Horta start their account of the conflicting impulses of modern 'cosmopolitanisms' by suggesting that Diogenes (fleeing retribution) had good reason not to admit his Sinopean origins, they are looking to improve the real-world preparedness of those wanting to articulate versions of cosmopolitanism as accessible to the under-privileged as to the privileged.[22] Nikita Dawan is doing something methodologically similar but far less convinced of cosmopolitanism's potential for inclusiveness when she makes Diogenes part of her case for distrusting transnational solutions to ongoing economic, political, cultural, and sexual injustice under globalization.[23] The 'groundbreaking moment' at which Diogenes decoupled 'issues of political consciousness' from the concerns of 'the individual city-state' (141) provides her with a model for hardened suspicion of those who invoke cosmopolitanism as an ethical basis for humanitarianism in the early twenty-first century. Ancient Cynicism thus assists modern small-c cynicism.

Diogenes' appearance in both instances is brief—bracingly suggestive rather than historically cemented.[24] It is a gesture that has precedents, however, in nineteenth- and early twentieth-century literary writings about cosmopolitanism from which our current debates can be (and commonly are) traced.[25] Rather than

---

[21] Bruce Robbins and Paulo Horta, 'Review of Dudley, A History of Cynicism', Philosophy 13/51 (1938), 369–70 (370).

[22] I treat Arthur Rose's specifically literary treatment of cynical cosmopolitanism at p. C4.P68.

[23] Nikita Dawan, 'Coercive Cosmopolitanism and Impossible Solidarities', Qui Parle: Critical Humanities and Social Sciences 22/1 (2013), 139–66 (141, 161). Dawan starts her historical framing of cosmopolitan 'philanthropy' from Diogenes, rather than his more gregarious Stoic successor Hierocles, whose modelling of social affinity as a set of concentric circles, from self to family to tribe to nation to the whole of humanity found a warm sponsor in Martha Nussbaum. It is doubtful how well the move serves Dawan's argument that the intellectual do-gooder should step back from the 'vanguardist position' and yield the floor to the oppressed, while expressing solidarity (unless we are to take Diogenes, in his elective poverty, as the equivalent of the modern political 'tourist'). For the reference to Hierocles, see Nussbaum, 'Patriotism and Cosmopolitanism', in Thom Brooks (ed.), The Global Justice Reader (Oxford: Blackwell, 2008), 306–14; and, for critical commentary on the interpretation of the Greek, Leonidas Konstantakos, 'On Stoic Cosmopolitanism: A Response to Nussbaum's Patriotism and Cosmopolitanism', Prometeus: Filosofia em Revista 8/17 (2015), 50–60. Konstantakos argues that there is reason to be (similarly) wary of placing the Stoics at the start of cosmopolitanism's modern story, not least Hierocles' attention to the human being's 'appropriate disposition [of] self-preservation' (55).

[24] Only Arthur Rose, of the three, attends to Diogenes beyond the core statement of cosmopolitanism—examining the various interpretations of 'defacing the currency' licensed by Diogenes Laertius, and concluding that 'the first person to call himself a "cosmopolitan" believed in no cosmopolitanism'. Arthur Rose, Literary Cynics: Borges, Beckett, Coetzee (London: Bloomsbury Academic, 2017), 36.

[25] For an influential overview of the field, see Tanya Agathocleous and Jason R. Rudy, 'Victorian Cosmopolitanisms: An Introduction', Victorian Literature and Culture 38/2 (2010), 389–97; also Amanda Anderson, 'Cosmopolitanism, Universalism, and the Divided Legacies of Modernity', in

claim Diogenes as the first or most fitting sponsor of modern critical cosmopol-itanism, I am looking here to describe a commonplace but not well-recognized function for cynicism in relation to modern conceptions of world citizenship: the function of the not unsympathetic but toughly realist dissenter, ready to air ethical and political suspicions about the viability, and even the current desirability, of a primary identification with humanity on a world scale. The first target of cynicism in this context is, indeed, 'identification', insofar as any move towards identifica-tion as *solidarity* is seen, under the pressures of historical development and political immediacy, to lack feasibility. The outcome of cynicism, even so, is not ethically null. There is acceptance of heterogeneity within community, on the part of the cynic, and tenacious worldliness of interest, but the outlook is not as politically pin-downable as many proponents of cosmopolitanism would want.

In the first 'high Victorian' instance, I am focused, as before, on a tactical negativity, or testing affront (an attitudinal, not an argued, scepticism), towards cosmopolitan ideals, aimed at sharpening, not undermining, them. In this case, a Cynic cosmopolitan outlook is explicitly related to the example of Diogenes: reminders of the ancient Cynic assist a determination to make moral idealism about the shared needs and interests of humanity keep company with a truthful assessment of human tendencies to narrower forms of identification and protect-ive self-interest—patriotism prominent among them. The second instance takes us from the nineteenth to the early twentieth century, and from the high point of British globalizing confidence to the crisis of the First World War. In this context, small-c cynicism has become (or is seen to have become) a ubiquitous aspect of the public sphere, in part fuelled by a disjuncture between combatant and non-combatant experience that is undermining the common ground of political idealism and political realism alike. Militarization in this second case generates disaffection not just with British patriotism but with a wider range of supposedly shared values.

I treat two writers, George Eliot and Ford Madox Ford—both English by upbringing, their personal experience of the world confined to Britain, Continental Europe, and, latterly, in Ford's case, America. Both endorsed ideals of cosmopolitan humanism (and Ford consistently described himself as cosmo-politan), but both saw ideas of 'world citizenship' as in need of significant qualification and demurral in the face of the strength of national attachments and the political realities 'on the ground'. I argue that Eliot's challenge to the credibility of cosmopolitan ethics, given the oppression of the Jewish populations of Europe (also the Irish, Catholics, by implication others), finds its strongest

Pheng Cheah and Bruce Robbins (eds.), *Cosmopolitics: Thinking and Feeling beyond the Nation* (Minneapolis, MN: University of Minnesota Press, 1998), 265–89; Peter Van Der Veer, 'Colonial Cosmopolitanism', in Steven Vertovec and Robin Cohen (eds.), *Conceiving Cosmopolitanism: Theory, Context, Practice* (New York: Oxford University Press, 2002), 165–79.

articulation not in the humanism of the realist novels but in the Cynicism of the more experimental writings, *The Lifted Veil* (1859) and *Impressions of Theophrastus Such* (1879). Ford (whose impressionism was developed in resistance to Victorian realism generally, and Eliot's moral realism specifically) nonetheless shares important features of these writings, including a keen interest in aspects of human psychology that appear to work against a philanthropic cosmopolitanism.

In turning their attention, as both Eliot and Ford did, to human psychology rather than political institutions as the fundamental problem in the way of world citizenship, each may seem to make the predictable (some will think inadequate) novelistic choice to turn inward on the mind rather than outward to social structures for explanation and potential remedy of current political problems. Rather, both looked to the resources of literature to help close the gap between identification with one's primary culture and identification with the whole of humanity—working not through the injunctions and solicitations of high moralism but through more affronting articulations of tension between ideal aspiration and lived reality. Not the least challenging of their cynicisms, then, involves the debasement of unwarranted moral confidence about the authority of the writer, the power of literature to command attention, and its ongoing role in the cultural articulation of humanism.

The story I am telling could be taken a great deal further: the function of cynicism persists, of course, after Ford and into the present day. His cynicism and Eliot's are examples selected with an eye to establishing historical and particular objection to an ideal cosmopolitanism that are at once internalized (articulations to the self, protecting against a 'radical disappointment')[26] and projections into the world that may or may not provoke their recipients to try harder. Among the many inheritors and developers of that function can be counted, for example, Dinaw Mengestu and others now taking cynicism into the difficult territory where cosmopolitanism meets forced migration, with complex consequences for individual and collective psychology. I address Mengestu's *How to Read the Air* (2010) briefly in the Coda to this book.

Cynical Cosmopolitanism I: George Eliot, via Balzac

When George Eliot experimented, in *The Lifted Veil*, with the idea of a man for whom life has, as a matter of fact, 'no more mysteries', she was following Balzac and numerous others in the period: tapping into the familiar figure of the cosmopolitan Englishman whose Englishness was not so much a mark of cultural

---

[26] See Introduction, p. CI.P58.

'rootedness' as international shorthand for a particular way of styling oneself a 'cosmopolite'. Take, for example, Raphaël de Valentin, the protagonist of Honoré de Balzac's *La peau de chagrin* (1831), casting and losing his last sou on the roulette table of a down-at-heel Paris gambling salon: *'Il affecta l'air d'un Anglais pour qui la vie n'a plus de mystères'* ('[H]e affected the air of an Englishman for whom life holds no more mysteries').[27] It is that designation of the disenchanted-ness as peculiarly *English* that, at this temporal distance, catches the eye. Why *'un Anglais'*? Byron—filtered through Balzac's reading of Musset—was no doubt one influence (the Scottish parts of his make-up temporarily out of sight), but the figure of the young Englishman jaded with Europe, out of funds, and in exile from his own country, having overstepped the bounds of parental tolerance or English law, has too many possible models to be attributed to a single source. By the 1830s, the figure of the world-weary English was common cultural currency. Affecting to be one of them, Raphaël attempts to make light of his loss. He aims at (but does not quite carry off) an air of negligence in the face of disaster, before heading out in the direction of the Seine.

This is cultivated detachment, but any ethos projected has much more to do with isolated individualism than with egalitarian concern for the whole of human-ity or, for that matter, with nineteenth-century cosmopolitanism's antithetical relation to patriotism. The effect Raphaël aims at is world-weary cynicism; the effect of failing to pull it off is, necessarily, irony. The thin cynicism of affected 'English' detachment generates in the French novelist, and in the reader (regard-less of nationality), an ironic consciousness of how desirable it would be, at this point, to possess the self-sufficiency and the charisma of the thoroughgoing cosmopolitan Cynic.

Like *La peau de chagrin* (a novel Eliot knew and admired),[28] *The Lifted Veil* adopts a consciously incomplete orientation towards a cynical cosmopolitanism, and does so on the basis of significant alterations in the dominant literary model. The conventional model, associated with Byron, was aristocratic: decadent and/or alienated in its perspective on the world, where 'the world' meant, in the main, 'Western and Central Europe'. Balzac's protagonist is the son of an impoverished *ancien régime* Marquis failing to find a social foothold in post-Napoleonic France and attempting, *faute de mieux*, an 'air' of English aristocratic carelessness. Eliot's protagonist, Latimer, expresses an alternative displacement of the convention along class lines. His family is new aristocracy, with substantial landholdings purchased by his banker father, keen to emulate old aristocracy. Intended for Eton and Oxford, but disqualified by a fragile constitution, Latimer is privately

[27] *La peau de chagrin*, ed. Pierre Citron, in Pierre-Georges Castex and Thierry Bodin (eds.), *La Comédie humaine*, X, *Études Philosophiques* (Paris: Gallimard, 1979), 63.

[28] See 'Balzac', in John Rignall (ed.), *Oxford Reader's Companion to George Eliot* (Oxford: Oxford University Press, 2000), 11; and John Rignall, 'George Eliot, Balzac and Proust', in John Rignall (ed.), *George Eliot and Europe* (Aldershot: Scolar Press, 1997), 210–24.

tutored in England, then completes his education in Geneva; he subsequently has some wider experience of Europe, but he remains unremittingly hostile to his father's understanding of 'worldliness'. To be 'worldly', in practical terms, is to be shallow, vulgar, materialistic, ignorant, 'barren', 'dead'—above all, dead to poetic inwardness.[29]

In its geographical range, and its literary field of reference, *The Lifted Veil* was Eliot's first European story. Composed and published in 1859, it drew closely on her experiences of Geneva between 1849 and 1851 (her first taste of independence, in her late twenties) and more happily travelling with her partner G. H. Lewes from Geneva to Basle, Vienna, and Prague in 1858 (Latimer exactly repeats Eliot and Lewes's itinerary). Generically, the story's acknowledged precursors are avowedly European: the most obvious influences are French and German—Rousseau's *Rêveries* and *Confessions*, Goethe, German Romantic lyric—intermixed with elements of modern French melodrama and English and Scottish Gothic. The topos of prevision and subsequent confirmation by which the narrative achieves its main Gothic effects casts Latimer's psychological alienation as a form of old European knowledge reluctantly internalized into a modern English subjectivity: the emotional devastation of his married life is a chronicle foretold from Prague and then Vienna; symbolically, he becomes in his later years a Wandering Jew, drifting through 'foreign countries' until he returns to England, to the ironically styled 'Devonshire nest' where he awaits his foreseen death (42).

All these aspects of the novella indicate an opening out of George Eliot's literary imagination to a world beyond England, but we are a long way from the affirmative, if qualified, cosmopolitanism found in *Daniel Deronda* (1876). In recent years the single most influential contribution to critical discussion of Eliot's thinking about cosmopolitanism has been Amanda Anderson's chapter on that novel in *The Powers of Distance* (2001). Anderson concentrates much of her attention on the Jewish portions of *Daniel Deronda*, arguing persuasively that Eliot laments the 'cosmopolitan indifference' promoted by the rootless condition of the Jew, an indifference that threatens to afflict modern 'migratory Englishmen' as well; at the same time she valorizes cosmopolitan artistic culture and a reflective relation to tradition, both of which she saw as enabled by cultivated detachment as well as instructive forms of exile.[30]

The cosmopolitan distance sought is not, Anderson concludes, 'a sustained or absolute disengagement—for Eliot a destructive delusion—but rather a cultivated partiality, a reflective return to the cultural origins that one can no longer inhabit in any unthinking manner'.[31] The reconciliation of modernity and cultural inheritance thus achieved 'verges', for Anderson (I take it there is a shade of scepticism

---

[29] George Eliot, *The Lifted Veil* and *Brother Jacob*, ed. Helen Small (Oxford: Oxford University Press, 1999), 32, 35; also 30. References hereafter in main text.
[30] *Powers of Distance*, 64.   [31] Ibid., 120.

here) on 'a prescriptive ideal': a 'cultivated partiality' that will combine the best features of inhabited tradition and critical distance. This hint of suspicion before the prescriptivism of *Daniel Deronda*'s cosmopolitanism is worth keeping in view, but I want to approach it via the question of what *The Lifted Veil* says about Eliot's earlier thinking on the subject of cosmopolitanism, given its position as her first extended imaginative engagement with the idea of 'English' ethical detachment in a European context.

It is a commonplace of George Eliot criticism that *The Lifted Veil* is an admission, within limits, of scepticism about the viability of a humanism based on non-discriminatory sympathy. Given insight into other minds and hearts, would we really care more deeply, and more equitably, for the rest of humanity? It would be in keeping with that interpretation to see the story as a comparable admission, similarly delimited, of scepticism about the ethical claims often attached to cosmopolitanism: deliberately standing back from the belief or hope that wider experience of the world will foster a more egalitarian allegiance to humanity beyond the proximate claims of family and nation. But such a reading produces a problem of intellectual historical sequence: nothing Eliot had written before 1859 suggests that she had as yet developed views we could be justified in calling 'cosmopolitan idealism', and she would write nothing really sustained in that vein until *Daniel Deronda* seventeen years later. Accepting Anderson's description of *Daniel Deronda*, the effect of putting it in company with *The Lifted Veil* is to suggest that if Eliot was verging on 'prescriptive' cosmopolitan idealism by the mid-1870s, she had reached that point by *way* of Cynicism: that is, by consciously testing out the Cynic's 'debasing' assumption that a primary driver of human morality is not sympathetic identification but a narrower self-concern.

To widen the critical lens from the 'moral realism' of Eliot's major novels to her less studied, more experimentally risk-taking work, is to find the near-prescriptive cosmopolitanism of *Daniel Deronda*, and the more 'attenuated cosmopolitanism' of *Middlemarch*,[32] framed by two strikingly Cynical reflections on cosmopolitanism: *The Lifted Veil* on the early side, and, on the later, *Impressions of Theophrastus Such* (1879). Rather than treat *The Lifted Veil*, then, as an idiosyncratic, even perverse first take, or mis-take, on cosmopolitanism, I propose to read it as a companion piece with *Impressions*: a serious and not an isolated inquiry into the ethical claims of Cynicism as a historically significant and still intellectually provocative starting point for a credible cosmopolitanism ethics.

---

[32] By 'attenuated cosmopolitanism' (a phrase borrowed from Carlyle), I mean to describe the European passages of the novel (primarily, Ladislaw's dilettante wanderings through what he casually refers to as 'the entire area of Europe', and Dorothea's blighted Roman honeymoon) which put a temporary distance (historical, critical, and aesthetic) on the priority of what Carlyle called 'the old insular home feeling', but do not seem to me fundamentally to challenge it. See George Eliot, *Middlemarch*, ed. David Carroll (Oxford: Clarendon Press, 1986), 81; Thomas Carlyle, 'Burns' (1828), in *Critical and Miscellaneous Essays* I, *The Works of Thomas Carlyle*, Centenary Edition, 30 vols. (London: Chapman and Hall, 1896–9), XXVI, 258–318 (287–8).

George Eliot may seem a non-obvious case for sustained interest in Cynicism. We know, however, from her letters and *Notebooks* that she had, all her adult life, an affection for Diogenes of Sinope. 'You will think', she wrote, aged 18, to her former teacher Miss Lewis, that 'I need nothing but a tub for my habitation to make me a perfect female Diogenes, and I plead guilty to occasional misanthropical thoughts, but not to the indulgence of them.'[33] Like Arnold, she seems to have found the contemplation of the Cynic performance a kind of relief from the exacting demands of her own ideals. She plainly enjoyed Diogenes' reputed willingness to thumb his nose at conventional behaviour as well as conventional morality. (A transcription from Rabelais, in one of her *Notebooks* from the mid-1870s reads: 'Diogenes rolls his tub because he does not like to be idle among people so busy.')[34] She was probably still a schoolgirl when she first read the other Diogenes (Laertius)'s *Lives of the Eminent Philosophers*: the work is referenced in her *Notebooks* and quoted on several occasions in the novels.

The most immediately relevant allusion to Diogenes of Sinope comes in a letter written to John Blackwood in February 1859 as Eliot was beginning work on *The Lifted Veil*. She writes to share with him a letter from Jane Carlyle, warmly praising *Adam Bede*:

> Mrs. Carlyle's ardent letter will interest and amuse you. I reckon it among my best triumphs that she found herself 'in charity with the whole human race' when she laid the book down. I want the philosopher [that is Carlyle] himself to read it, because the *pre*-philosophic period—the childhood and poetry of his life—lay among the furrowed fields and pious peasantry. If he *could* be urged to read a novel! I should like, if possible, to give him the same sort of pleasure he has given me in the early chapters of 'Sartor', where he describes little Diogenes eating his porridge on the wall in sight of the sunset, and gaining deep wisdom from the contemplation of the pigs and other 'higher animals' of *Entepfuhl*.[35]

In the context it is not absolutely clear what Eliot takes to be the thrust of the passage describing the 'little Diogenes' Teufelsdröck's pastoral suppers, though she evidently enjoys the Cynic's cheerful elevation of the pigs. Carlyle plays havoc with the pastoral mode, and leavens his own Cynicism, by caustically implying

---

[33] Letter to Maria Lewis, August 1838, in George Eliot, *The George Eliot Letters*, ed. Gordon S. Haight, 9 vols. (New Haven, CT: Yale University Press, 1954–78), I, 5–8 (6).

[34] Undated note in Holograph Notebook 711, in William Baker, *Some George Eliot Notebooks: An Edition of the Carl H. Pforzheimer Library's George Eliot Holograph Notebooks MSS 707, 708, 709, 710, 711*, 3 vols. (Salzburg: Institut für Anglistik und Amerikanistik, 1976–80), 83; reproduced in *The Notebooks and Library of George Eliot*, 6 vols., electronic edition (Charlottesville, VA: InteLex Corporation, 2003), III, fol. 85. Eliot is quoting (and translating) Rabelais, 'Prologue de l'auteur', *Le tiers livre des faicts et dicts héroïques du noble Pantagruel*. She owned the *Œuvres de François Rabelais*, 5 vols. in 2 (Paris: Bibliothèque Nationale, 1870–73). See *Notebooks and Library*, III, 94 and 220n. Notebook 711 as a whole is dated by William Baker to 1874–75. See *Notebooks* I: MS 707, 16–18.

[35] Letter to John Blackwood, 24 February 1859, in *Letters* III, 23–4 (23).

that, however beautiful the sunsets, the young philosopher's education will progress somewhat haphazardly if left to nature alone. (The chapter 'Idyllic' is thus both in tune with Cynicism's animal-like indifference to social convention, and sceptical of any claims that would press that indifference—or that Romanticism—all the way to anti-intellectualism.)[36] It is possible that Eliot's own attachment to the idea of an idyllic '*pre*-philosophic period' in childhood, so important to *The Mill on the Floss* (1859–60), softened her reading of *Sartor* a little at this point. Even if that were the case, it is clear that the Cynic tradition, both in its classical form and as revived for the nineteenth century by Carlyle, was attractive to her and in her mind when she first conceived of the narrator of *The Lifted Veil*.

The peculiar disease of consciousness that afflicts Latimer with accurate prevision of the future and unwanted insight into the banality of other minds is, from one perspective, a study in a degraded philosophical cynicism, now functioning only as a narcissistic pathology of mind. But Latimer's cynicism has this peculiarity: that it appears to have the stamp of external justification, his caustic insights repeatedly finding validation from the world in ways that (apparently) exceed the distortions of his subjectivity. Latimer does not merely anticipate the disappointment of his own romantic hopes through the selfishness of others; he knows, with second sight as empirically valid (to him) as normal ocular experience, that the future holds disillusionment and death. The story draws on the language of empirical scientific observation to underwrite its psychological and moral claims:

> I began to be aware of a phase in my abnormal sensibility, to which ... I had not been alive before. This was the obtrusion on my mind of the mental process going forward in first one person, and then another, with whom I happened to be in contact: the vagrant, frivolous ideas and emotions of some uninteresting acquaintance ... would force themselves on my consciousness like an importunate, ill-played musical instrument, or the loud activity of an imprisoned insect ... I might have believed this importunate insight to be merely a diseased activity of the imagination, but that my prevision of incalculable words and actions proved it to have a fixed relation to the mental process in other minds. But this superadded consciousness, wearying and annoying enough when it urged on me the trivial experience of indifferent people, became an intense pain and grief when it seemed to be opening to me the souls of those who were in a close relation to me—when the rational talk, the graceful attentions, the wittily-turned phrases, and the kindly deeds, which used to make the web of their characters, were seen as if thrust asunder by a microscopic vision, that showed all

---

[36] The pigs of *Sartor* anticipate Carlyle's later extensive lashing of the 'Pig Philosophy' (*Schwein'sche Weltansicht*) of an age obsessed by material progress and economic gain. See esp. 'Jesuitism', the last of the *Latter-Day Pamphlets*. Thomas Carlyle, *Latter-Day Pamphlets* (London: Chapman and Hall, 1850), 249–86 (268–70).

the intermediate frivolities, all the suppressed egoism, all the struggling chaos of puerilities, meanness, vague capricious memories, and indolent make-shift thoughts, from which human words and deeds emerge like leaflets covering a fermenting heap.   (13–14)

Eliot's earlier fiction had encouraged the reader to see 'the poetry and pathos, the tragedy and comedy' of human life as our common psychological experience, that commonness then underpinning the case for humanitarian compassion towards all 'ordinary' human beings. Latimer, by blunt negation, sees the content of other minds as unformed and so without dignity: the inner mental workings that force themselves upon his own consciousness are 'vagrant, frivolous ... uninteresting', but no less 'obtrusive' for that. Irrational, banal, 'egois[tic]', they are nonetheless 'importunate[ly]' real. In its degrading alertness to the material base of the human condition (immorality, and amorality, under the microscope), and its pervasive disgust at the pretence of rationality and idealism with which most people 'grace' their mental life, Latimer's narrative stands intransigently at odds with the ethos of imaginative sympathy that was the foundation of Eliot's humanism.

The debasing 'realism' that characterizes his dealings with individuals characterizes also his dealings with culture. His anti-idealism is articulated along sightlines that mock the ostensible ethical effects of cosmopolitan distance. So, the actual experience of Prague that confirms his pathological power of prevision is expressed as an induction into knowledge of the true tendencies of cultural history, overturning and annulling any assumption of liberal progress:

as I stood under the blackened, groined arches of th[e] old synagogue, made dimly visible by the seven thin candles in the sacred lamp, while our Jewish cicerone reached down the Book of the Law, and read to us in its ancient tongue—I felt a shuddering impression that this strange building, with its shrunken lights, this surviving withered remnant of medieval Judaism, was of a piece with my vision. Those darkened dusty Christian saints, with their loftier arches and their larger candles, needed the consolatory scorn with which they might point to a more shrivelled death-in-life than their own.   (22)

In the eyes of the cosmopolitan Cynic, history turns in on itself: the 'Christian saints' find meagre consolation for their loss of cultural authority in scorning the 'withered remnant of medieval Judaism'. Both forms of faith reduce to blackened cultural and linguistic survivals. Recognizing the synagogue's mockery of liberal Enlightenment history, Latimer and his party themselves start to take on the aspect of *mittel*-European Jews: they are the audience of the ancient Book of the Law, read to them in Hebrew by the *cicerone*; as they leave the place Latimer reaches out for a Judaic phrase—'the elders of our party wished to return to the hotel' (22); the precise confirmation of his second sight, when it comes, is a compacted symbol of Old Testament lore—a 'patch of rainbow light on the pavement transmitted through a lamp in the shape of a star' (23).

In all these respects, Latimer's narrative seems to bespeak a very reduced cynical cosmopolitanism. We are certainly a long way from the Cynic's claimed self-sufficiency. Though Latimer despises others, he is only reluctantly 'non-attached'. He longs for human fellowship, but the 'very dogs shun[ned him]', he reports (casting himself as Richard III):[37] they 'fawned on the happier people about me' (25). As he bitterly reflects, his lot is to have possessed the poet's sensibility without the poet's powers of expression. 'This disposition of mine was not favourable to the formation of intimate friendships' (7); more self-pityingly, a 'dumb passion' makes for 'a fatal solitude of soul in the society of one's fellow-men' (7). Latimer yearns after, but is denied, the softening influence of the idealism he believes himself temperamentally inclined to until the change in his consciousness.

By his own reckoning, the true cynic in his story is Bertha, his brother's fiancée, and after his brother's death his own wife, whose 'prematur[e] cynic[ism]' disturbs him, not least when she directs it against the German lyrics that are his 'pet literature' at the time of their meeting (15). When she tells him that she would prefer not to love the man she marries ('I should be jealous of him; our ménage would be conducted in a very ill-bred manner. A little quiet contempt contributes greatly to the elegance of life'), he is dismayed (26). The older Latimer would, presumably, agree, but for the younger Latimer there is no pleasure in having one's ideals knocked out of one 'prematurely'. The sole act of compassion he is capable of, in these years, is to feel for his father, who encounters disappointment too late in life to have many resources against it: 'Perhaps the tragedy of disappointed youth and passion is less piteous than the tragedy of disappointed age and worldliness' (28). Certainly Latimer does not stop to wonder why cynical detachment might recommend itself to an orphaned young woman dependent, as he is not, on the marriage market for her future comfort. As he sees it, the difference between himself and Bertha is that her detachment is cultivated, ironizingly post-Byronic ('my small Tasso' is her mocking soubriquet for Latimer [26]), and serves her self-interest; his is unwilling, and costs him everything that might have made life emotionally pleasurable and morally sustainable.

Latimer is, on closer scrutiny, not so much Diogenes as a man who embodies the fundamental problem exposed by a mid-nineteenth-century cynic cosmopolitanism: that of finding the appropriate ethical distance on the rest of humanity. Given the apparent accuracy of his insight into the moral life of those around him, there seems to be no adequate resolution in his case: proximity breeds a level of insight corrosive of affection and respect; distance breeds despair. And what is

---

[37] '...dogs bark at me as I halt by them' (I.i).

true of his personal affective life is also true of his response to the world. The problem of the cynic and the problem of the cosmopolitan are here made to look the same, and they come together in Latimer's despairing sense that his own impending death is only a personal image of the inevitable death of all human culture:

> All that was personal in me seemed to be suffering a gradual death...It was as if the relation between me and my fellow-men was more and more deadened, and my relation to what we call the inanimate was quickened into new life. The more I lived apart from society,...the more frequent and vivid became such visions as that I had had of Prague—of strange cities, of sandy plains, of gigantic ruins, of midnight skies with strange bright constellations, of mountain-passes, of grassy nooks flecked with the afternoon sunshine through the boughs: I was in the midst of such scenes, and in all of them one presence seemed to weigh on me in all these mighty shapes—the presence of something unknown and pitiless...to the utterly miserable—the unloving and the unloved—there is no religion possible...   (35–6)

This is no more the ethical detachment of Diogenes than it is the ethical 'partial detachment' of Daniel Deronda. It is closer to (and is surely meant to recall) the 'last man' trope of so much late Romanticism: Shelley's 'Ozymandias', Byron's 'Hell', Mary Shelley's *The Last Man*. It is also, plainly, the point at which Eliot's story moves to marshal our resistance to Latimer, if it hasn't done enough to ensure that already. Always a difficult candidate for sympathy, or for the kind of indulgence a more flamboyantly performative Cynicism might command, he is too obviously teetering here on the edge of pastiche. What the story (what Eliot) wants out of its readers, as it nears its conclusion, is a renewed commitment to that element of idealism requisite to the functioning of human sympathy—which is perhaps why Latimer is not permitted to tip over entirely into pastiche, or to match Bertha in his cynicism. It is undoubtedly why Eliot added to the 1878 Cabinet Edition the directive motto, requiring us to read *The Lifted Veil* as a monitory exploration of how damaging it will be to human fellowship to turn too mercilessly revealing a light on human nature:

> Give me no light, great Heaven, but such as turns
> To energy of human fellowship;
> No powers beyond the growing heritage
> That makes completer manhood.

It is a matter of record that Eliot quickly came to be dissatisfied with the *jeu de melancholie* that was *The Lifted Veil*. She turned down an opportunity to reprint it in 1873 while at work on *Daniel Deronda*, insisting nevertheless that 'I care for the idea which it embodies and which justifies its painfulness. There are many things in it which I would willingly say over again, and I shall never put them in any other form. But we must wait a little.'[38] She waited five more years, until 1878 when, in the same year that she agreed to republication of *The Lifted Veil*, she composed her last complete work, *Impressions of Theophrastus Such*. This strange, demanding text, more social critique than fiction, is closer in temper to *The Lifted Veil* than to anything else in Eliot's oeuvre. But where the cynicism of *The Lifted Veil* was represented as pathological—reluctantly entertained by its narrator, carefully contained by its author—the cynicism of *Impressions of Theophrastus Such* (1879) is fully embraced, stylistically and (by way of experiment) ethically.

The emboldening of Cynicism has much to do with the choice of literary vehicle. *The Lifted Veil* offers, as I have described it, a kind of prejudicially cynical psychological realism—filtering its narrative through an account of human psychological interiority that makes self-centredness and irrationality (or weak rationality) the common denominators of social interaction. It thus mounts an aggressively 'realist' psychological objection to sympathy as a moral basis for humanism. *Impressions* adopts an older literary model, downgrading interiority in favour of external characterizations of human behaviour. The 'characters' of the original Theophrastus, student of Aristotle, are given a modern reinterpretation, but some underlying assumptions are continuous.

Character-delineation, as Aristotle practised it, was a rhetorical training exercise. It identified 'the linguistic behaviour to be expected' from certain categories of speaker whom the rhetorician sought to understand and mimic.[39] Eliot updates the focus on rhetoric, concentrating on her contemporary literary culture and its associated institutions: authorship, print, reviewing, reading.[40] She also inflects the form with developments in psychology (S. Pearl Brilmyer makes a strong case for the influence of natural history as it helps Eliot to put pressure back against contemporary psychologists' association of character with individual mental development, and to re-accent the conditioning effects of 'bodily frameworks and habitual responses'.)[41] The 'impressions' are angular, satiric takes on the habits of mind and practice that prevent her present-day culture achieving or sustaining the value it might otherwise have for humanity: the man so convinced that the high points of human intellectual achievement are in the past that he is in

[38] Letter to John Blackwood, 2 February 1873, in *Letters* V, 380–1 (380).

[39] The description is taken from M. S. Silk, 'Nestor, Amphitryon, Philocleon, Cephalus: The Language of Old Men in Greek Literature from Homer to Menander', in Francesco de Martino and Alan H. Sommerstein (eds.), *Lo Spettacollo delle Voci* (Bari: Levante, 1995), 165–214 (178).

[40] Nancy Henry notes that the word 'impression' combines multiple meanings: the imprint made by experience on the writer's mind; the act of impersonation; the functioning of the printing press. Introduction to George Eliot, *Impressions of Theophrastus Such*, ed. Nancy Henry (Iowa City: University of Iowa Press, 1994), xv–ix.

[41] See S. Pearl Brilmyer, '"The Natural History of My Inward Self": Sensing Character in George Eliot's *Impressions of Theophrastus Such*', *PMLA* 129/1 (2014), 35–51 (36).

'voluntary' moral 'exile' from the modern world (Chapter II; 26); the pedant, lost to normal social functioning because he is desperate to triumph in intellectual controversy (Chapter III); the contrarian, who unreasonably expects all excesses to be forgiven (Chapter VI); the man out of his moral element, having lost contact with the values that first motivated him (Chapter IX). And so forth. A final two 'impressions' take a wider sceptical view of two supposedly general cultural tendencies: towards increased dependence on artificial intelligence,[42] and towards cosmopolitanism.

Constructed as a *series* of impressions, the text can correct, up to a point, for its own selectivity. There are women as well as men in the picture (though not many). The greater the range of types portrayed, the fuller the collective depiction, in theory—but a collective depiction of what? However plural the portraits the modern Theophrastus sketches, the gallery does not, and could not, add up to, an account either of a fully rounded psyche or of a culture, for the simple reason that he is so caustic in his assessment of human motives. In Aristotle's *Rhetoric* the range of attention was not ungenerous: it included friendly as well as hostile or self-serving dispositions. But the *Impressions*, like the sketches of the first Theophrastus, filter Aristotelian rhetorical technique through the influence of Greek new comedy and, with it, the long literary inheritances of Cynicism and its contributions to satire (Menander is a key intermediary). The comic-Cynic impulse disregards virtues to concentrate on 'the ludicrous elements of weak, eccentric or faulty personalities', yielding nothing like a balanced picture of dispositions;[43] rather, a set of close variations on vanity, self-regard, and self-delusion—and, running through them all, the intrusive, judgemental, waspish (but self-mocking, somewhat vulnerable) presence of Theophrastus himself.

Theophrastus is just socially situated and psychologically developed enough to count as a 'realistic' character and not merely a mouthpiece for satire (like Eliot, he spent his early years in the rural Midlands but is now a settled 'town bird'), but he owes a heavy debt to the Cynic type. Strongly biased towards detecting self-interest as a primary explanator of human behaviour, he makes it his mission to expose bad moral reasoning; his *philanthropia*, like that of Diogenes, is shown in his goading other men and women towards a more accurate view of themselves, challenging the superfluity of material desires and social pretensions. Unlike Diogenes, he operates at a distance, in print, and he is preoccupied by a problem to which Diogenes gave little thought.

---

[42] She has in view the arrival of more and more refined machines, like those weighing coins at the Bank of England; and 'I am told of micrometers and thermopiles and tasimeters which deal physically with the invisible, the impalpable, and the unimaginable; of cunning wires and wheels and pointing needles which will register your and my quickness so as to exclude flattering opinion' (138).

[43] See Introduction to *The Characters of Theophrastus*. Theophrastus, *The Characters of Theophrastus*, trans. with an introduction by Charles E. Bennett and William A. Hammond (London: Longmans, Green and Co., 1902), xxxiv.

It is the same dilemma *The Lifted Veil* had addressed, but from which in the end it retreated: what to do with the ineradicable presence of one's self—however 'typical'—in one's ethical philosophy. The trouble with the Cynic's cosmopolitan detachment, for Theophrastus, is that achieving a cultivated distance on one's society is very much harder than simply claiming to be cosmopolitan might suggest. He, like all of us, has particular attachments and investments in his own portion of the Earth. Initially this realization is vexatious to him: he sees it as limiting his capacity to achieve a sufficiently philosophical objectivity about the human condition. 'May there not be at least a partial release', he asks in the first chapter of *Impressions* ('Looking Inward'), from the imprisoning verdict that 'a man's philosophy is the formula of his personality?' Imagining the world to be like a book: in theory, 'an attention fixed on the main theme or various matter of the book would deliver us from [our] slavish subjection to our own self-importance. And I had the mighty volume of the world in front of me. Was there no escape here from this stupidity of a murmuring self-occupation?'[44]

Not yet, was his verdict. It has been the attempt of this would-be cosmopolitan character's life thus far to cultivate detachment, and with it a proper concentration on matters outside himself (the 'main' theme of the book of the world), but 'self-occupation' has kept obtruding in the form of asking himself the question, 'have I done with self-occupation yet?':

> the habit of getting interested in the experience of others has been continually gathering strength, and I am really at the point of finding that this world would be worth living in without any lot of one's own. Is it not possible for me to enjoy the scenery of the earth without saying to myself, I have a cabbage garden in it?
>
> (10–11)

What Theophrastus means by the 'self' here is not to be mistaken for irreducible psychological individuality. The appeal of the cabbage garden is idiosyncratic, quirkily self-ironizing, but not really particular. It conjures a hypothetical individuality—a man possessed of a modest 'lot of his own', 'a cabbage garden'—rather than a fully imagined individuality.

In keeping with this sense of an insistent but not a unique particularity to his (and all human) experience, the style of Theophrastus's *Impressions* aims at a level of address between the personal and the impersonal, that can avoid the errors of mere subjectivism, on the one hand, and a false or premature universalism, on the other. This is not a prose that makes any use of that familiar vertical shift, in Eliot's writing, from third person narrative to first person plural ethical reflection; nor does it employ the lyricism commonly and characteristically associated with her as

---

[44] *Impressions*, 10.

a moral writer. Like *Sartor*, it adopts a tonally unstable and destabilizing mode of address—one that can express decidedness and undecidedness in equal measure, that deals in tolerance and exasperation, self-interest and self-mockery, mixing philosophical speculation with a demotic, levelling causticity, and an insistent self-concern. It has a quality Eliot admired in Balzac, 'who dares to be thoroughly colloquial, in spite of French strait-lacing'.[45]

Like the original Theophrastus, Eliot does not make her speaker's Cynicism the subject of study in its own right. She does, however, dedicate Chapter X, 'Debasing the Moral Currency', to small-c cynicism as a common vulgarizing cultural tendency. Here Theophrastus addresses two related worries: that crude wit and a popular appetite for satire and ridicule are eroding serious morality; and that superficial engagement with the ideas and texts handed down from the past is undermining the education of the young, reducing the 'time of studious preparation for life to the moral imbecility of an inward giggle' (84). Up to a point the direction of travel is that of *The Lifted Veil*: asserting the need to protect ideal standards against a tendency to debase 'the ideal stamp' with the irreverence of comedy. Clowning, burlesque, parody are everywhere 'lower[ing] the value of every inspiring fact and tradition', Theophrastus complains, 'so that it will command less and less of the spiritual products, the generous motives which sustain the charm and elevation of our social existence' (84). That is the overt message; but there is a limit to how seriously we can take the threat to 'inspiring fact and tradition', especially when expressed through the intellectually demanding vehicle that is the *Impressions* overall. Theophrastus may profess to fear that the Socratic education of the next generation will not survive early exposure to 'a burlesque Socrates, with swollen legs, dying in the utterance of cockney puns' (85), but Eliot knows, and we know, that Socrates will survive, and that it may sometimes be the function of popular cynicism, as well as a more calculated Cynicism, to hold idealism—and pomposity (its stylistic partner here)—down to earth.

Theophrastus's own cultural criticism is, in the way of cynicism, totalizing—detecting only low motives on all sides: the producers of culture just want to bring in the money; the consumers put their own pleasure ahead of education. The extravagance of his alarm should be its own warning against unquestioning agreement with his outlook on contemporary culture: 'This is the impoverishment that threatens our posterity', he protests, somewhat in the fashion of Carlyle: '—a new Famine, a meagre fiend with lewd grin and clumsy hoof, is breathing a moral mildew over the harvest of our human sentiments' (85), but in context it is, plainly, a line he has used before, his cynicism on this count being a well-worked routine.

---

[45] Letter to François D'Albert-Durade, 29 January 1861, in *Letters* III, 374.

Superficially the idea of world citizenship comes out of this cynic performance in poor shape. Theophrastus's recourse to Sainte-Beuve is *à propos*—so to speak. The chapter has a great deal of fun at the expense of the superficial cosmopolitanism that consists in displaying one's knowledge of the French language, a temptation Eliot had learned over the years to rein in herself (one of the revisions she made to *The Lifted Veil* when she permitted its reprinting in 1878 was to alter much of the French-in-passing to English). Chapter X starts with a sizeable quotation from La Bruyère on the proper objects of ridicule, then moves into a wordy reflection on 'that enhancement of ideas when presented in a foreign tongue, that glamour of unfamiliarity conferring a dignity on the foreign names of very common things, of which even a philosopher like Dugald Stewart confesses the influence' (81). But there is, of course, a deeper cosmopolitanism of learning at work throughout *Impressions*, in the homage paid to Theophrastus and his later imitators (La Bruyère and Sainte-Beuve included),[46] and in the updating of the purpose of the character sketch to admit a more modern set of concerns, including the concerns of modern psychology.

In her Introduction to *Impressions*, Nancy Henry argues that Chapter X is a 'transitional chapter marking Theophrastus's increasing anxiety about the '"dissolution" of civilization' (xxiii). If that is right, it is a subtle transition, not easily legible in the structure of the book. Had Eliot wanted to show up the limitations of Cynicism and its more casualized modern derivatives, this would be the point at which Theophrastus might step away from his interest in human failings to take a more redemptive or holistic view. That is not what happens. More cynically-reductive sketches follow: the casual plagiarist (a too-ready writer, boosting his own authority by opining that all ideas belong to a common cultural pool and there is no such thing as originality) (Chapter XI); the man who likes to think of himself as an exceptionally young achiever (Chapter XII); the writer who massively inflates her own achievements based on one not-very-important book (Chapter XV). But in Chapters XIII and XIV, Eliot breaks with the character sketch as her form of choice, turning Theophrastus's attention back to the problem of the self, considering how it is that we can persist in such false ideas of ourselves, and then asking how far the failings represented by the types he has put before us are failings he too must own. All, in some degree, Theophrastus decides. Only that is too cheap a moral to rest content with. The worry, as Theophrastus frames it now, is that if we judge others by ourselves, we are likely *either* to make the Cynic's mistake of reducing everything too low (being alert to our own failings, we will see them everywhere around us), or we will estimate the general moral tendency too high (human beings really are far from perfect; the

---

[46] Sainte-Beuve provided the Introduction to a new edition of La Bruyere's *Les Caractères, ou Les Mœurs de ce Siècle* (Paris: Morizot, 1864); Charles Augustin Sainte-Beuve, *Portraits contemporains et divers*, 3 vols. (Paris: Didier, 1846–47) are lightly indebted to the model.

Cynic has some truth on his side and we should attend to it). But if we put the invitation the other way around and judge ourselves by what we see in others, we will be differently inhibited from good judgement—and Theophrastus is inclined to think this the greater risk.

These are arguments that pave the way for the book's concluding consideration of how to respond to the human actions that stand in the way of a cosmopolitan humanism. Too much 'impartiality and keenness of discernment...has a laming effect', Theophrastus opines, 'enfeebling the energies of indignation and scorn, which are the proper scourges of wrong-doing and meanness' (105). We need 'the horsewhip', and we will not help anyone if we are inhibited in its use by worrying too much about our own moral standing. What is wanted at the point of action is less comparative assessment of ourselves with others and more quick discrimination and 'active heroism' to combat wrong-doing. Initially he directs the fruits of his decision towards specific challenges facing the writer as moralist. The most credible moral writing, he argues, keeps in view a clear and sane distinction between word and action, ideas and lived reality. It is a capacity he recognizes in Dante and in Cervantes: a 'sanity of expectation' (111) that recognizes and portrays everyday illusion and error but still gives imaginative form to the motivating ideal. A more pointed Cynicism is in operation here than in what went before, looking to calibrate itself by an accurate sense of how far the society in which it operates is capable of improvement. Cynicism, so targeted, steers clear of any pretence that a writer is somehow in a position to (or could honestly wish to) rise above the concerns and attachments that limit its outlook on the world. As Eliot outlines its purposes, in Chapter XVI ('Moral Swindlers'), it aims at combating the degradation of morality by putting people's professed ideals in the same frame with their lived practice of morality. We should put an end, 'Moral Swindlers' argues, to the 'radical, irreconcilable opposition' that too often exists 'between intellect and morality' (134); what is wanted is a proper 'use of the word morals', that does not 'shu[t] out from its meaning half those actions of a man's life which tell momentously on the wellbeing of his fellow-citizens' (133).

The final chapter takes up the challenge for those wanting to see the advancement of cosmopolitan ideals.[47] It completes a logical progression (perhaps not the clearest, but this is not a tidy or easy book) from problems of the self, to the debasement of English culture, to considerations of the cultural, political, and ethical future of humanity. 'The Modern Hep! Hep! Hep!' is the one section of

---

[47] Two final portraits of literary types focus on the too-prolific, intellectually lazy writer [XIV]; then the under-productive but immensely complacent writer [XV]. They are followed by the first of two largely self-standing essays, 'Shadows of the Coming Race', which must fall outside my ambit here, though its prescience (and cynicism) on the subject of artificial intelligence are remarkable. See Henry, Introduction, xxviii, on reasons why the original placement of 'Shadows of the Coming Race' after 'The Modern Hep! Hep! Hep!' made the logic of *Impressions* clearer. I treat 'Shadows' in a forthcoming essay for *19* (special issue on George Eliot, eds. Isobel Armstrong and Carolyn Burdett).

Impressions well known to many non-specialist students of Eliot today—frequently extracted and read in tandem with *Daniel Deronda*. In that context it provides a concentrated theoretical expression of Eliot's sense that the idea of a common humanity is 'not yet enough' to feed the human cultural and political imagination: 'The time is not come for cosmopolitanism to be highly virtuous, any more than for communism to suffice for social energy' (147). The reasons given are bracingly realistic, both on political grounds—human cultures remain too distinct, and too precious in their distinctness, to be dissolved into some more universal idea of culture—and on psychological grounds: what is close to us quite properly has primary importance for us. 'I am not bound to feel for a Chinaman as I feel for my fellow-countryman', Eliot writes (147), with Rousseau and Balzac in her sights.[48] It may sound like a defiant reassertion of narrow prejudices, but it is a claim based on a psychologically realistic, normative view of the workings of human morality.[49]

Two, not seamlessly logical, political moves follow: the first is Theophrastus's moral case for Zionism; the second, his defence of English nationalism. The 'ground of... distinction' between the English and the Jewish peoples is a 'deeper affinity', he argues (148), founded on shared tenets of religion, history, and experience of oppression. Shared resistance to Roman imperialism is made to do a lot of work in support of this claim to under-recognized affinity—but the reader is then asked to consider how much English imperialism has done to thwart it, having had comparable effects to early Roman imperialism in its persecution of other 'nations' (she uses the term broadly to include diasporic communities). The Irish, Catholics, Jews, have all suffered and continue to suffer, and Theophrastus is inclined to forgive the zealotry of conservative Jews when he considers their long history of oppression. *Despite* the ill the English have done, 'The Modern Hep!' asserts, there is a rightness to English patriotism (and by extension all patriotisms, including some without a recognized *patria*) as long as the bond of fellow-feeling among the population sustains it. Our overall historical 'tendency', Eliot assumes, 'is towards the quicker or slower fusion of races' (160), and she takes that tendency to be unstoppable. But the essay seeks to 'moderate' a too-rapid endorsement of cosmopolitanism that would fail to recognize the strength of identitarian attachments; it puts its trust in critical 'discrimination' to tell us when the strength of our own attachments is leading us awry.

---

[48] 'Have you read Rousseau?', asks Rastignac in *Le Père Goriot* (1834). 'Do you remember the passage where he asks the reader what he would do if he could make a fortune by killing an old mandarin in China just by exerting his will, without stirring from Paris?... if it were proved to you that the thing was possible and you only needed to nod your head, would you do it?' Trans. [as *Old Goriot*] by Marion Ayton Crawford (London: Penguin, 1951), 157. For discussion, see Helen Small, *The Long Life* (Oxford: Oxford University Press, 2007), 149.

[49] For discussion, see Introduction, pp. CI.P45, CI.P68.

The strain of argument here is considerable, and it shows in the unstable role accorded to cynicism which—playing a somewhat erratic second fiddle to the essay's progressivism—risks derailing it altogether. The overall direction of travel is ameliorative and gradualist but the intensity of the demand for critical distance on cosmopolitan liberalism and on nationalism alike in 'The Modern Hep! Hep! Hep!' is challengingly acerbic. The shade of Carlyle is never closer, for example— or under sharper scrutiny—than when the essay figures the failure of human 'sympathy with the injured and oppressed' by returning us to the starkest failings of empire: 'There is understood to be a peculiar odour from the negro body, and we know that some persons, too rationalistic to feel bound by the curse on Ham [looking to Old Testament authority for oppression of another race], used to hint very strongly that this odour determined the question on the side of negro slavery' (161). Carlyle is, surely, a model here, as much as a target. This is Eliot wielding the moral whip, scorning the complacent irrationality of attitudes that enable racism, and with it much of the active evil in the world: she wants the energy and panache of Carlyle's cynicisms. The errors of the past are, after all, ongoing ('There is', not 'There was'). But she does not want the relentless causticity of 'The Negro Question'. As Eliot mobilizes cynicism, in this last, most demanding of her books, it has largely left the individualism of the Cynic behind. Perhaps this is the root of the problem with 'The Modern Hep!': its confrontationalism now floats free of Theophrastus, who is barely if at all discernible in the last two essays, his authority in effect merging with Eliot's (pseudonymous) authority. The function of cynicism remains, in theory, the same: it is there to support the general intelligence, serving advocacy for ideals pitched at a level where they can be credible and (once credible) genuinely desirable. But the execution, at the end, seems less secure, less certain of its ground, than when it inhabited the stabilizing parameters of the Theophrastan character sketch.

Cynical Cosmopolitanism II: Ford Madox Ford

One reason why Ford had little time for Victorian realism generally, and Eliot particularly, was that he reacted against what the critic Robert Green calls the 'sentimental altruism' of the last century—that persistent strain of Romanticism 'in Hulme's sense, ... concerned ... with making "humanist" generalisations about life and erecting a moral system'.[50] On that ground, Ford convicted Eliot of having failed to hold her audience over time: 'George Eliot was ... a great figure. She was great enough to impose herself upon her day; ... Taking herself with an enormous seriousness, she dilated upon sin and its results, and so found the easy success of

---

[50] Robert Green, *Ford Madox Ford: Prose and Politics* (Cambridge: Cambridge University Press, 1981), 66.

the popular preacher who deals in horrors. She desired that is to say, to be an influence.'[51] But 'popularity' of this order does not last:

> to the great bulk of educated criticism of to-day, George Eliot has become a writer unreadable in herself and negligible as a critical illustration. Her character-drawing appears to be singularly wooden: her books without any form, her style entirely pedestrian and her solemnity intolerable. And it was this very solemnity that gave to her works all the qualities that make them to men in touch with the life of to-day so entirely unreadable.   (55–6)

This is harsh, and there is much more in the same vein, in *The Critical Attitude* (1911), Ford's collected editorial writings from the *English Review*, the magazine through which he did so much to change the temper and style of contemporary literature. The accusations of vulgar populism (she 'found the easy success of a popular preacher who deals in horrors'... 'another Frankenstein... evolving obedient monsters') are, a cynic might say, directed at securing a distinctive success for himself in modernism's marketplace: success by way of *épatant* educated, conventional literary taste.

The counter-popular, anti-literary-establishment hyperbole goes nonetheless seriously to the nub of how Ford differentiated his own literary and critical practice from high Victorianism. Whatever a modern artist may seek to be, he or she should, for Ford, avoid the lure of 'being an influence'. Undercutting one's own solemnity is essential to attaining what he takes to be the goal of criticism (Arnold's accent on freedom still has force here, though his, and Eliot's, attachment to the term *discrimination* is starting to look old-fashioned). What is needed, now, is 'a broad catholicity and great powers of self-abnegation in the realms of taste' (55), Ford asserts. It is a motto borne out by development of his much-cited theory of 'Impressionism': a frank expression of personality' in order to produce 'an illusion of reality'. This means being 'alive' to the way in which the mind (one's own; anyone's) wanders, is distracted, and has to have its attention 'seized' by the artist. Sustained argument asks too much of us, Ford claims, and the essayistic wanderings and jokes and indulgent detours of 'On Impressionism' enact the message to the artist: the picture needs to 'come out of its frame'.[52]

The resulting combination of dogmatic self-assertion ('The Impressionist must always exaggerate' [36]) and relaxed open-mindedness is a constant of Ford's prose style, with little distinction in voice between the public correspondence (to the newspaper editor, or government official) and private communications: both are, or seem, unguarded, freely demotic to the point of vulgarizing, quick and

---

[51] Ford Madox Ford, *The Critical Attitude* (London: Duckworth & Co., 1911), 55.

[52] Ford Madox Hueffer, 'On Impressionism', in *Critical Writings of Ford Madox Ford*, ed. Frank MacShane (Lincoln, NE: University of Nebraska Press, [1914] 1964), 33–55 (36, 44, 48).

unsparing in their judgements while making no claims for their own final authority. '[T]here is not enough vinegar in the salad', complains one early letter, in response to a novel by John Galsworthy: 'You are too kind...to your characters; you haven't enough contempt.'[53] The subject of Anthony Bertram's latest novel is 'too provincially Middle Class English', he tells Bertram himself: 'You *must* shake that off...'.[54] He was, predictably, unseduced by academia though grateful for a visiting lectureship at Olivet College, Michigan, at a time of financial difficulty: 'is it really advisable to put my LLD which is really a D.Litt on the title page of Provence[?]', he asked his publisher late in his life, 'considering my long and strenuous anti-academic career'.[55] It should be unsurprising, then, that the forms of cynicism that engaged Ford have little to do with literary-historical allusion to ancient philosophy and much more with psychological internalization and the disruptive outward effects of the Cynic's debasing challenge to moral ideals.[56]

There is occasion to regret that Ford did not (the evidence suggests) know Eliot's writing beyond the 'major novels', for the cynical cosmopolitanism of her early experimental vein and the later testing of a more explicit Cynic cosmopolitanism within the frame of the psychological 'Impression' find a telling counterpart in his efforts to rethink the scope of literary impressionism amid the experience of war. (He would have been hyperalert to how far a strategic cynicism enabled her to widen the range of her pulpits; the counterclaim is that a tactical cynicism brings his own writing as close as it comes to the moralizing it despises.) In the early years of the war, Ford saw an important moderating role for cynicism in relation to cosmopolitan idealism as it confronted the rise of militant nationalisms. Looking for a viable cosmopolitanism idealism (his own included), a controlled cynicism protects the idea of '*homo europeaus sapiens*' (Ford's quaintly dignifying description of Conrad)[57] at a time when violence, politics, and war ('these frightfulnesses', as he puts it semi-ironically in the essay 'Preparedness' [71]) seemed to have made casual cynicism the too-easy resort of the majority. In the texts on which I concentrate, the *War Prose* and (with necessary compaction) the great tetralogy *Parade's End* (1924–28), the pressures on the cosmopolitan Englishman are multiple. They are, as with Balzac, financial (Ford, like Balzac, was all too familiar with chronic want of money); as in *The Lifted Veil*, they have much

---

[53] [?] October 1900, Ford Madox Ford, *Letters of Ford Madox Ford*, ed. Richard M. Ludwig (Princeton, NJ: Princeton University Press, 1965), 10–14 (12).

[54] 15 October 1935, ibid., 245–7 (245).

[55] Letter to Stanley Unwin, 4 August 1938, ibid., 298–9 (299).

[56] Diogenes makes only two appearances in Ford's writing, as far as I have discovered: the first is in keeping with the form of the historical romance: in *The Fifth Queen Crowned* (London: Eveleigh Nash, 1908) old Lady Rochford, invited by the Queen always to speak her mind in private, responds archly: 'Before Heaven,...shall I have the office of such a one as Diogenes who derided Alexander the Emperor? Then must my old husband live with me in a tub!' (93). The second reference, in *Parade's End*, is discussed below.

[57] Ford Madox Ford, *Joseph Conrad: A Personal Remembrance* (London: Duckworth & Co., 1924), 18.

to do with bad judgement in love and misery in marriage; but they are also specific to the cultural effects of the 'European struggle'.[58]

Ford's cosmopolitanism is undoubtedly negative rather than positive in its relation to politics. Moreover, Fordian impressionism resists the ethical descriptions often given to modernist cosmopolitanisms as they experiment with new formal expressions, which may be why he has largely escaped attention in comparative accounts of the subject, despite a now extensive specialist literature on his own practice here.[59] His is not, as I read it, a cosmopolitan perspective that can be captured, as recent criticism has sought to capture some other modernist examples, by attention to 'tropic patterns', rhythms, or even distinctive preoccupations.[60] Nor does it fit with Arthur Rose's account of a taste for cynicism among writers of subsequent generations (Borges, Beckett, Coetzee), who look, Rose suggests, to deface the currency of their own authority in a marketplace that capitalizes (economically, culturally, sometimes politically) on their cosmopolitan status.[61] It is, rather, a psychological habitat, subject to fluxes of attitude, mood, temperament. Moreover, it is important to my argument here that for Ford, by comparison with Eliot, to take a literary-critical distance on the nation state and its politics requires treating psychology beyond its involvement in morality—that is, his cosmopolitanism becomes a matter of morality when the mode of attention to it is moral. This broadening of the perspective on cosmopolitan ethics is consistent with the long-held animus against Victorian 'moralism'. But concentration on individual psychology, and aversion to 'influence', do not remove—but often enhance—the ethical import of the writing, reminding us of how much of what passes for moral thought in our lives is (without the grief Latimer brought to the

---

[58] Ibid., 119. Alternatively, 'European vicissitudes'. Ibid., 43.

[59] There is a large and rightly admiring literature on Ford's cosmopolitan humanism. In addition to extensive treatment in Saunders's biography, see esp. Douglas Goldring, *South Lodge: Reminiscences of Violet Hunt, Ford Madox Ford and the English Review Circle* (London: Constable & Co., 1943), Chapter 16 ('The Standard of Values')—a paean to Ford's role in America as a kind 'watchtower' for European humanism amid the demoralizing effects of Communism and Fascism; and Andrzej Gasiorek, 'Ford among the Aliens', in Dennis Brown and Jenny Plaistow (eds.), *Ford Madox Ford and Englishness* (Amsterdam: Rodopi, 2006), 63–82. An important effort to extend the scope of 'worldliness' is made by Nicholas Brown, who reads Ford comparatively with Chinua Achebe to cast light on their contrasting modes of utopian resistance to history. See Nicholas Brown,*Utopian Generations: The Political Horizon of Twentieth-Century Literature* (Princeton, NJ: Princeton University Press, 2005), Part 2.

[60] See esp. Rebecca L. Walkowitz, *Cosmopolitan Style: Modernism beyond the Nation* (New York: Columbia University Press, 2006); Melba Cuddy-Keane, 'Modernism, Geopolitics, Globalization', *Modernism/Modernity* 10/3 (2003), 539–58, and Melba Cuddy-Keane, 'Global Modernisms', in David Bradshaw and Kevin J. H. Dettmar (eds.), *A Companion to Modernist Literature and Culture* (Oxford: Blackwell, 2006), 558–64; Susan Stanford Friedman, *Planetary Modernism: Provocations on Modernity across Time* (Oxford: Oxford University Press, 2016).

[61] Much of Rose's argument is confined to the literary (cynicism is a way of reclaiming 'esteem' on something like the writer's own terms, he argues). But he also identifies effects of cynicism that he both does and doesn't want to call political: these writers challenge 'the scale on which this society self-identifies' geographically, linguistically, politically, defacing abstract and idealistic claims of world-belonging. See Rose, *Literary Cynics*, 36–7.

observation) 'vagrant'. This is especially the case in *Parade's End*, which has at its heart the portrait of a man, cosmopolitan in his education and outlook, attempting, under immense psychological pressure, to do what the nation requires in wartime and to withstand a near-ubiquitous cynicism towards his philanthropic 'decency'. His self-sufficiency and his humanism are both, as I shall argue, assisted by (but not reducible to) his exercise of tactical cynicism.

By Ford's own account, his early-acquired multilingualism enabled him to feel 'at home' across much of Europe. 'For as long as I can remember', he wrote in 1915, 'I have been accustomed to think indifferently in French, in German, or in English, and I am indeed conscious that whilst I was writing this sentence in my mind, since I am writing with extreme care, I began to phrase it in French before committing myself to its final form.'[62]

Approaching different forms of writing via different languages was an engrained habit: care in writing prose required a first articulation in French, or 'more rarely' Latin, we are told, then translation into English. When writing poetry, by contrast, Ford went at once to colloquial English. Speaking or writing about the pleasures of the table required German. Multilingualism of this kind has little to do with intellectual display, nothing at all with 'academicism' (the Latin notwithstanding). Ford tended to make less display of his linguistic competences than Eliot (even late Eliot, but we are to understand that they enable his 'European' outlook). Minimal German, or French, or Latin makes it on to the page. Language choice, as he represents it, is just a question of psychological 'fit'. More confident than Eliot, perhaps, in the possession of languages acquired at the knee of parents and grandparents (this was a boy sufficiently negligent of German language studies to assail his German master, in front of the class, in protest at being set *Indem ich faulenzte* ['On Idling'] as a test piece),[63] Ford dwells on the feeling of being at home anywhere in Western Europe: '[it] has never, for me, seemed to be a matter of travelling; it has been merely a change of abode, as it were, from one country to another'.[64]

When war came, he was nonetheless content to put aside any idea of impartiality and assist the national fight-back against Prussian aggression. Enlisting in the summer of 1915, and posted to Rouen in July 1916 as an officer in the Transportation Corp,[65] he was, he later assured an American readership, no

---

[62] Ford Madox Ford, *When Blood Is Their Argument: An Analysis of Prussian Culture* (London: Hodder and Stoughton, 1915), viii. Cf. Ford's description of comparable discrimination in Conrad's use of Polish, French, and English. Ford, *Joseph Conrad*, 37.

[63] Max Saunders, *Ford Madox Ford: A Dual Life*, 2 vols. (Oxford: Oxford University Press, 1996), I, 40—quoting Ford's memoir, Ford Madox Ford, *Ancient Lights and Certain Reflections: Being the Memories of a Young Man* (London: Chapman and Hall Ltd, 1911).

[64] Ford, *When Blood*, iii.

[65] Ford enlisted in the summer of 1915. An officer in the Transportation Corp, he was posted to Rouen on 13 July 1916, joining the 9th Welch Battalion, which formed part of the 58th Infantry Brigade of the 19th Division. See James Longenbach, 'Ford Madox Ford: The Novelist as Historian', *The*

'old-fashioned, peace-at-any-price pacifist of the wool-next-the-skin, vegetarian type': he was 'personally happier... somewhere in France between August 1914, and November 11, 1918, than I ever was previously' (a significant stretching at both ends of his time in service). 'I like soldiers and soldiering', he insisted: 'I like to make men jump to it and dress by the left and number off from the right.' He professed a sincere admiration for the institution of the army: 'I have long said... that the British regular army is one of the two most perfect organizations that humanity has produced.' He declined to name the other, beyond clarifying that he did not mean the US army ('too infernally strict')—not wanting to 'poke [him]self into' American political problems.[66] The reference was, surely, to the League of Nations.[67] All the more significant, then, that the 'Allied cause' with which he identified was not 'British' (his biographer Max Saunders notes) but 'European and transatlantic', his allegiances, even in wartime, 'cosmopolitan and complex'.[68]

It is a distinctive aspect of Ford's two contributions to C. F. G. Masterman's War Propaganda Bureau, *When Blood Is Their Argument: An Analysis of Prussian Culture* and *Between St. Dennis and St. George: A Sketch of Three Civilizations*[69] (both published in 1915 under the name Ford Madox Hueffer) that he sources his engagement with the Allied war effort to his polyglot multicultural upbringing. As described in *When Blood Is Their Argument*, inherited cosmopolitanism came with pronounced partialities. From a South German Catholic father and a French grandfather, he acquired 'a deep hatred of Prussianism' and its associations ('materialism', 'academicism', 'pedagogism', 'purely economic views of the values of life') plus an ardent attachment to 'French learning, arts, habits of mind, lucidity... and that form of imagination which implies a sympathetic comprehension of the hopes, fears, and ideals of one's fellow men' (vii). The warrant, then, for taking up literary, as well as actual, arms against the Prussian aggressor is not 'English' nationalism but a cross-Channel affiliation with 'French' cosmopolitan habits of mind. (Ford would add a French epilogue to *Between St. Dennis and St. George* in 1916 and take pleasure in the book 'really rather booming along

Princeton University Library Chronicle, 45/2 (January 1984), 150–66 (154); and Saunders, *Dual Life*, I, 486ff.

[66] Ford Madox Ford, 'Preparedness', *New York Herald Tribune Books*, 6 November 1927; reprinted in Ford Madox Ford, *War Prose*, ed. Max Saunders (Manchester: Carcanet, 1999), 69–74 (70–1).

[67] See Susan Pedersen, *The Guardians: The League of Nations and the Crisis of Empire* (Oxford: Oxford University Press, 2015), Chapter 7. America, having declined to join the League, was moving towards agreement of the Kellogg-Briand Pact (the General Treaty for Renunciation of War as an Instrument of National Policy), signed in 1928, with opponents in the American Senate arguing that it would mean a modification of the Constitution, valid in perpetuity, limiting the war-making power of Congress. See Oona A. Hathaway and Scott J. Shapiro, *The Internationalists and Their Plan to Outlaw War* (London: Allen Lane, 2017), 121–9 (esp. 125).

[68] Introduction to *War Prose*, 2.

[69] Ford Madox Ford, *Between St. Dennis and St. George: A Sketch of Three Civilizations* (London: Hodder and Stoughton, 1915).

among the lit. gents & official world of Paris'.[70]) His claim to be able to represent continuation of the cosmopolitan ideal—'Sympathetic comprehension of the hopes, fears, and ideals of one's fellow men'—has credibility, he claims, because he can regard the German people, 'at any rate South Germans' (a deft qualifier), as 'ordinary human beings' (viii).

As a propagandist, Ford necessarily 'argues'; but he remains as faithful as he can be to impressionism's insistence on the personal perspective and its reluctance to generalize. Contrasting himself with the German military historian Hans Delbrück, he urges declaration of 'personal' considerations as a method of resistance to the impersonal arguments of the 'paid official of the Prussian state'. Delbrück has 'ransacked history' for 'incidents and precedents' that serve Prussia's purpose, suppressing evidence of first-person 'inclination', 'conscientious belief', and 'self-interest', including identification with his 'national interest'—and concealing, Ford tells us, earlier opposition to the state which earned him a 500-mark fine. The evident partiality of the empirical historian turned 'special pleader' for his country should leave us feeling badly let down, not because it *is* partiality but because the partiality is not admitted (x). What Ford most objects to, in the practice of propagandists on both sides of the conflict (Benjamin Doty points out), is the attempt to create 'unanimity': unanimity can only be impersonal, and to sacrifice personality is to lose credibility. Persuasive propaganda should strive rather to 'satisfy' than to 'influence'.[71] The way through is a politicized impressionism: put the first person to the fore, make no attempt to conceal—instead put on show—the shaping consciousness behind the writing, and admit voices of dissent. Not least, the propagandist should be 'utterly unafraid of alienating a reader', accepting that some readers must be of the opposing view (176–80, 180).

Ford wrote trenchant propaganda, but it was propaganda of a non-standard hue, quick to retreat from 'breathless attack upon that Prussia who is "L'ennemi"' to contemplate the nature of enmity itself. 'How does one get oneself hated?...How should one act when one discovers that some one person—or some large body of persons—is actively desiring one's humiliation, death, imprisonment, or silencing?'[72] To ask such questions in the middle of war (those last sentences were written a few months before Ford enlisted) is to undertake a more than usually taxing version of the dual demand for national attachment and cosmopolitan critical detachment—something other than the rational-argumentative scrutinizing of one's own opinions urged under Mill's liberalism.

---

[70] Letter to C. F. G. Masterman, 13 September 1916, in *Letters*, 76.

[71] Benjamin Doty, '"As a Mass, a Phenomenon so Hideous": Crowd Psychology, Impressionism, and Ford Madox Ford's Propaganda', *Journal of War & Culture Studies* 6/2 (May 2013), 169–82 (174, 177).

[72] Ford Madox Ford, 'Literary Portraits—LXXI. Enemies', *Outlook* 35 (16 January 1915), 79–80; excerpted in *War Prose*, 212–14 (212).

It sets the tone for what was to become a key element of Ford's literary modernism during and after the war: a seeking out, from the personalized perspective, of conflicting views on oneself as a representative of one's nation—including or especially views that are hostile, entrenched, not readily displaced. The effect is to decentre assumptions of privilege on the part of the male, educated, geographically mobile Englishman, but without claiming that the act of decentring itself has the power to produce change.

As might be expected, the undercutting of first-person authority is more thoroughgoing, and psychologically more complex, in the non-propaganda writing where the propagandist's obligation to argue no longer applies. A short piece entitled 'Epilogue' takes as its theme the destabilization in wartime of the cosmopolitan's 'sympathetic comprehension'. It has the same antipathy to coerced unanimity expressed in the propaganda, but the antipathy is partly overtaken by a concern with how far the war has corroded shared moral ground, so that cosmopolitanism has altered (and, in effect, shrunk) the scope of its expression to the experience of those at the Front, who forge bonds of solidarity briefly, and *in extremis*. Written at some point between 1 March 1917 and 7 January 1919, the date on which Ford was gazetted out of the army, 'Epilogue' was probably intended for Ezra Pound's *Little Review*, where it would have followed Ford's series of impressionist pieces, *Women & Men*, but it remained unpublished until discovered among Pound's papers in the 1980s.[73] Starting out as a diary-like record of personal experience, it announces an intention to describe the courage of two individuals (Rosalie Martin and Emil Vanderkerckhoven)[74] near the northeastern French border with Belgium in September 1916, but in the event only mentions Rosalie. Emil's non-appearance may be inadvertent—an oversight on the part of a writer struggling to hold concentration and sanity together—but it is in keeping with the dominant subject matter of 'Epilogue': the near total disappearance of men from the domestic life of the war zone.

Rosalie is a refugee from the village of Ploegsteert to nearby Nieppe, where she occupies a house abandoned by its owners after the start of the war. 'Chaplains to

---

[73] Max Saunders, header note to 'Epilogue', in Ford, *War Prose*, 52–63 (52). And see Longenbach, 'Ford Madox Ford'. I have accepted Saunders's reading (in *War Prose*) of the MS over Longenbach's, but the latter's commentary has been helpful. One can see why Pound might have rejected 'Epilogue': *Women & Men* was conceived as 'an antidote to the oppressive, patriarchal Victorian Great' who had 'loomed over' Ford's recent book *Ancient Lights and Certain Reflections* (1911). It is a performative series of first person reflections tilting at the long nineteenth-century tradition of theoretical writing about the woman question and relations between the sexes—'Weininger, Schopenhauer, Ruskin, John Stuart Mill, Mr. Bernard Shaw, and Solomon the author of the proverbs', 22. Generalizations about essential or characterological differences between men and women dissolve under the corrosive force of Ford's witty anecdotalism, and chatty elaboration of individual cases he has known.

[74] Speculatively, this may be the 'Emile' who is one of the dedicatees of *When Blood Is Their Argument*, referred to there as having 'disappeared from the knowledge of the world' on 3 August 1914, but whose surname Ford does not give on that occasion 'lest the inscription ensure . . . the final culture of death'.

the Forces and stray officers' are billeted with her and she makes a 4d profit per day supplying them with food. Ford (nothing suggests that this is not autobiography) pays her to mend the frayed cuffs of his shirt sleeves—an employment that soothes his nerves, badly rattled by information just received. In conversation with his regimental quartermaster he has learned that his battalion sustained sixty casualties the day before, a 'whole company' worth. That information has subsequently been corrected—the dead belonged to the Wiltshires not Ford's Welch regiment—but his mind stalls at the number of deaths and the substitutability of those who died. Rosalie's 'opportunist domesticity' provides an oasis of normality amid chaos (the 'coffee in a saucepan on the stove' bubbles and occasionally jumps when shells fall into the churchyard [57]). While she sews, she tells 'Ford' her story (presumably in French, but perhaps in Flemish—Ford spoke both)[75] and he relays the gist in English without reference to his role as translator. She has lost her husband and both sons since December 1914. The fate of her two daughters is unclear, but the loss of the sons weighs more heavily: she laboured harder than with the daughters to bring them into the world and keep them alive. 'One's male children are gone', she concludes (58), and the phrase seizes Ford's attention.

It implies to him a forced change in 'mentality' for the writer taking Europe as a subject. (French is close to the surface of Ford's English here).

> If, before the War, one had any function it was that of historian. Basing, as it were, one's mentality on the Europe of Charlemagne as modified by the Europe of Napoleon I, one had something to go upon. One could approach with composure the Lex Allemannica, the Feudal System, problems of Aerial Flight, the price of wheat or the relations of the Sexes. But now, it seems to me, we have no method of approach to any of these problems.
>
> We *don't know how many men have been killed* .... One is always too close or too remote. (59)

Neither the quantitative tools of the social historian (the too-round 'sixty' casualties of the quartermaster) nor the personal testimony of a Rosalie provides the right focal length on what is happening to 'Europe'. Ford wants to see history as a continuity (this is 'no doubt how it went in Marathon and Thermopylae and how it went and goes on at Mont St Jean and Codford and West Point—and Potsdam'

---

[75] For his competence in Flemish, see Letter to Lucy Masterman, 23 August 1916, complaining of being overworked on the Belgian Front 'because I talk Flemish. So I have to buy straw and pacify infuriated farmers', in *Letters*, 68–70 (68). Patrick McGuinness observes (email communication) that a woman in Rosalie's location and social position would have spoken French as well as (perhaps) Dutch. Ploegsteert is to all intents and purposes Wallonia, but the bourgeoisie, even if 100 per cent Flemish, would have communicated in French as the language of educated society, the courts, media, etc. Lower-class Flemish people and country folk might speak no French or very bad French, but Rosalie, with her French name (Rosalie Prudent), and now living in Nieppe on the French side of the border, is presumably a native speaker.

[56]), but when he contemplates 'counted millions of men moving million against million' 'from the Somme up to the Belgian coast', the assumption collapses. No 'composed' historical overview will serve, but nor will any single experience of loss. One of Rosalie's daughters is thought to have taken refuge in a convent on the Isle of Wight. This is too specific. She cannot be representative even if stories like hers accumulate. 'You think of Armageddon', he observes (twice) (59, 60) and the recourse of the struggling mind to that word, with its pre-made symbolic loading, crystallizes the danger to the writer of (as he later warned Bertram) falling back on the 'vieux jeu', 'going slack all over the shop'.[76]

Ford already had a low tolerance for 'social speculations'[77] and for the kind of historical writing that deals in them (the early, pre-Impressionist sequence of *Fifth Queen* novels already shows a commitment to realizing the lived drama of history without recourse to 'authoritative' fact or theoretic abstraction[78]). But the dilemma as he presents it in 1917 is new: a complete divide in experience between those in the inner theatre of war and those protected by distance, occupation, and, to a degree, gender, so that it is unclear what 'reality' the historian might aim to capture. In that divide, popular cynicism finds its inlet. It is a cynicism that goes a long way towards corroding the ideal of 'identification' with others, even where identification supposedly starts, 'at home':

> Out there, in the Somme, or in Belgium, you and your fighting comrades seem to be the whole world...But go to London or to Birmingham or to Manchester— and you hear no talk but of the sufferings, composures, heroisms and endurances—of the Civilian Population. But one does not discern that the Civilian Population has at all a bad time...In one's capacity of returned and crocked up warrior one is pushed off buses, swindled by shopkeepers who take advantage of one's necessity for specialized clothes and accoutrements; one is used as a pawn in one woman's social game or another's love affair; one is sweated and swindled by the authorities in the interests of the taxpayer, till the sinister thought surges up in the mind that all these people would *like* the war to go on—and other wars supervene, for the sake of the fun and the talk and the moneymaking... (60-1)

This is another version of Theophrastus's concern with the right relation between the personal and the general, but recast as a problem of perception and reason, not a moral problem of self. The schism between 'warrior' and 'civilian' blocks

---

[76] 15 October 1935, *Letters*, 245–7 (245).
[77] Letter to H. G. Wells, 1 August 1920, *Letters*, 119–22 (121).
[78] William Gass's excellent account of the *Fifth Queen* series captures the pursuit of a style that could capture what eludes the historian: 'gossip, slander, hearsay, anecdote, lies. He wants to recreate the past, not understand it.' William Gass, 'The Neglect of *The Fifth Queen*', in Sondra J. Stang (ed.), *The Presence of Ford Madox Ford* (Philadelphia, PA: University of Pennsylvania Press, 1981), 25–43 (27).

humane sympathy. The 'theatre' of European war is 'very tiny', modestly cosmo-politan in composition and ethos: men, hitherto strangers, from across England, Wales, Scotland, France, Belgium, are posted 'say to the Italian border', then 'on leave to Paris, to London, into the Shires' (60). They bond quickly, but it is in the nature of war that the bonds are often broken. The common language of the soldiery—second-person toughened sentimentalism—finds a way of respecting particularity amid the sameness of loss: 'You will find another pal, but never quite the same' (62). For those wounded, not killed, everything goes wrong on return home: the 'you' becomes a depersonalized 'one', subject to subtle hostilities. In 'London or...Birmingham or...Manchester' (no differentiation), the 'Civilian Population' pursues its self-interested way, happily profiteering at the expense of the injured returnee whose 'specialized' needs offer a whole new market to the enterprising salesman.

It would be easy—Ford makes it easy—to seize on the 'sinister thought' that civilian populations have an investment in war continuing. But having voiced the cynicism 'Epilogue' moves to reject it as a prime example of false generalization: 'just as the cataclysm has swept over Europe, blotting out alike the Europe of Charlemagne and the Europe of Napoleon I, so a cataclysm of the author's intelligence has swept over this book. The sense of values has changed completely...' (61).

The point is not that the cynical observation is mistaken: that returnees did not experience exploitation and lack of sympathy. British social historians tell us there were many such cases,[79] but Ford shifts the focus of attention off the reports to the cynic's error of too-totalizing judgement, the slip of a 'tired brain' still just capable of recognizing the 'cataclysm' that has befallen its own understanding. It is a move away from the ground of public morality (seen as treacherous) to the ground of reasoning (more within the individual's control) that repeatedly shapes *Parade's End*'s representation of the European war's effect on the viability of ideals gener-ally, and the cosmopolitan ideal specifically.

A scene from the second volume of the tetralogy, *No More Parades* (1925) can illustrate the series' immersive depiction of a mind struggling to locate and maintain credible ideals in a context where the political and the personal refuse compartmentalization. Leading a unit at the Front, exhausted, battling cold and wind, and in pyjama bottoms (his 'slacks' are at the tailor's), Christopher Tietjens[80] inspects a returning draft of men who want only to go to their tents.

---

[79] See esp. Adrian Gregory, *The Last Great War: British Society and the First World War* (Cambridge: Cambridge University Press, 2008), 264ff.

[80] To the best of my knowledge, Tietjens' cynicism has not been the subject of close critical discussion. It is acknowledged, occasionally, but the point is not developed. (See, for example, an insightful passing comment by Saunders: '*Parade's End* is often discussed as if its centre is the change in Tietjens from being one of the ones who "do not" to someone who can accept happiness for himself despite social convention. But that's also Valentine's story. Even more so, since she starts from a less cynical place than Tietjens.' Max Saunders, '"Sex Ferocity" and the "Sadistic Lusts of Certain

This is a man no less cosmopolitan than Ford himself: Yorkshire-born but intimate with several of the languages and many of the cultures of the Continent—Russia included. War requires him to act on the demands of patriotism, but the mind is vagrant. He finds his attention taken by a rose growing against a brigade hut:

> He staggered, his knees wooden-stiff with the cold, and the cold more intense now the wall of men no longer sheltered him from the wind, out along the brink of the plateau to the other lines. It gave him satisfaction to observe that he had got his men into their lines seventy-five per cent. quicker than the best of the N.C. O.'s who had had charge of the other lines. Nevertheless, he swore bitingly at the sergeants: their men were in knots round the entrance to the alleys of ghost-pyramids . . . Then there were no more, and he drifted with regret across the plain towards his country street of huts. One of them had a coarse evergreen rose growing over it. He picked a leaf, pressed it to his lips and threw it up into the wind . . . . 'That's for Valentine,' he said meditatively. 'Why did I do that? . . . Or perhaps it's for England . . . .' He said: 'Damn it all, this is patriotism? . . . *This* is patriotism . . .' It wasn't what you took patriotism as a rule to be. There were supposed to be more parades, about that job! . . . But this was just a broke to the wide, wheezy, half-frozen Yorkshireman, who despised every one in England not a Yorkshireman, or from more to the North, at two in the morning picking a leaf from a rose-tree and slobbering over it, without knowing what he was doing. And then discovering that it was half for a pug-nosed girl whom he presumed, but didn't know, to smell like a primrose; and half for . . . England! . . . [81]

Motive does not precede action here. It arises as matter for speculation, after unreflective action. Having kissed the rose leaf and cast it to the wind, Tietjens asks himself 'Why did I do that?' The first ellipsis registers the drift of the mind towards the poetic explanation it favours ('. . . "That's for Valentine"'); the second registers a gap in which he tests an alternative possibility, also poetic ('Or perhaps it's for England'). Thoroughly conventional, both explanations carry an edge of self-mockery. The process is characteristic of Tietjens' way of operating mentally, and of Ford's impressionistic method generally: embodied experience has a kind of phenomenological priority,[82] but that doesn't mean that it anchors or even

Novelists": Sexuality, Sadomasochism and Suppression in *Parade's End*, in Ashley Chantler and Rob Hawkes (eds.), *War and the Mind: Ford Madox Ford's* Parade's End, *Modernism, and Psychology* (Edinburgh: Edinburgh University Press, 2015), 17–34 (22).

[81] Ford Madox Ford, *The Bodley Head Ford Madox Ford*, ed. Graham Greene, 5 vols. (London: The Bodley Head, 1963), IV, 96.
[82] See esp. Max Saunders, 'Modernism, Impressionism, and Ford Madox Ford's *The Good Soldier*', *Etudes Anglaises* 57/4 (2004), 421–37; Eve Sorum, 'Empathy, Trauma, and the Space of War in *Parade's End*', and Meghan Marie Hammond, 'Fellow Feeling in Ford's *Last Post*: Modernist Empathy and the

provides the conditions of self-perception: rather, a kind of deliberative self-scrutiny follows from what the body has done, challenging, probing, looking for clarity in circumstances that prohibit it.[83] Barbara Farmworth may well be right that self-analysis on such lines indicates engagement with William James's theories of 'selective consciousness and free will', replicating James's exercise of intelligent introspection to understand and impose a measure of control over one's own mental life[84] but supplanting James's interest in morality by a concern with personal freedom. Tietjens is not blind to unconscious factors: various psycho-analytic ideas are referenced in the tetralogy (repression, obsession, sadism, inhibition),[85] but they retain the status of theories, held out for consideration by a mind vigilant against its own potential weaknesses. This is a competitive intelligence, silently scoring points for efficiency against 'the N.C.O.'s who had had charge of the other lines', but it is also a humane intelligence: Tietjens alone seems to recognize the desperation of his men to be in bed.

There is plenty of vinegar in his salad. Tietjens finds his way to affirmation of ideals ('patriotism', romantic love) by way of preliminary acquiescence in all the factors that tell against them: the cold, the wind, the shortfalls in military discipline, the absence of the kind of military show that once assisted patriotism, the 'pug-nosed' nature and unseemly youth of the 'girl'. He knows, and is quick to remind himself, where imagination takes over from knowledge: Valentine Wannop may smell nothing like primroses; and how unlikely an object of desire she is for a 'wide, wheezy half-frozen Yorkshireman' predisposed to sneer on all soft Southerners.[86] The last is self-caricature: 'wide', 'wheezy' (lungs damaged by gas), and 'half-frozen' are all accurate (if blunt) descriptors, but the appeal to Yorkshire origins is, as with his brother Mark, a sign that an especially strong dose of reality is wanted (a Yorkshireman 'speaks as he finds'). It is a tactical gambit leavened by humour—aimed at repositioning ideals at a level where they are

---

Eighteenth-Century Man', both in Chantler and Hawkes (eds.), *War and the Mind*, 50–62, 63–75; and, on the phenomenology of reading as a 'constitutive element' of Ford's modernism, see Max Saunders, 'Impressions of War: Ford Madox Ford, Reading, and *Parade's End*', in Shafquat Towheed and Edmund G. C. King (eds.), *Reading and the First World War: Readers, Texts, Archives* (Basingstoke: Palgrave Macmillan, 2015), 63–77.

[83] Isabelle Brasme offers a similar perspective on this method, but concentrated on self-editing as a form of linguistic expression of mental control: see Isabelle Brasme, ' "A Caricature of His Own Voice": Ford and Self-Editing in *Parade's End*', in Jason Harding (ed.), *Ford Madox Ford, Modernist Magazines and Editing*, International Ford Madox Ford Studies 9 (Amsterdam: Rodopi, 2010), 243–52.

[84] 'Barbara Farmworth, 'The Self-Analysis of Christopher Tietjens', in Chantler and Hawkes (eds.), *War and the Mind*, 77–91.

[85] See Saunders, ' "Sex Ferocity" ', 18–19; and see Richard A. Cassell, *Ford Madox Ford: A Study of His Novels* (Baltimore, MD: Johns Hopkins University Press, 1962), 223–41.

[86] A broke is, I take it, a Yorkshire regional term, perhaps vulgar (one recorded meaning is a hernia of the animal scrotum), but none of the standard dictionaries records a usage that quite fits Tietjens' deployment of it here. Perhaps 'a minor vexation'. See Joseph Wright (ed.), *The English Dialect Dictionary. Being the Complete Vocabulary of All Dialect Words Still in Use, or Known to Have Been in Use in the Last Two Hundred Years*, 6 vols. (London: Henry Frowde, 1898–1905), I (A–C), 412.

sustainable under inhospitable circumstances: an improbable love not likely to find social sanction; a patriotism survivable, 'At two in the morning with the thermometer at ten degrees below zero' (96).

Patriotism requires such assistance from cynicism primarily because it is a restriction on Tietjens' habits of mind thus far. He has, we are told, 'elected' to be 'peculiarly English in habits', rather than French, Prussian, Italian, or American, on the grounds that Englishness offered the best chance of 'materially ... modify [ing] his automatic habits' (*Some Do Not*, 223). (The English empiricism that so annoyed Nietzsche asserts itself again here.)[87] But this is not (as Virginia Woolf famously ventured) 'an ordinary mind'. One sign of the exceptional intelligence that makes Tietjens indispensable to many, admirable to a few, enraging to his wife Sylvia, is an analytic command of history, current political events and economic and social data, assisted by personal knowledge of European cultures, that enables him to predict the coming conflict with Prussia and see that 'Victorian' ideals of heroism will be of little help. Sylvia is the beneficiary of a pragmatism that, in wartime, looks identical to cynicism. It has secured her a desirable residence in Gray's Inn, before the large house in Mayfair became a tax burden and unsustainable without servants (now engaged in the war effort). Tietjens guides what political *nous* she shows, warning (without moralizing) that flirtations with Austrian officers will draw opprobrium once the countries are at war. He alone is capable of appeasing a 'savagely careworn' French duchess agitated by the price of coal, offering to supply her hothouses from his own mines, at 'pit-head price ... *livrable au prix de l'houillemaigre dans l'enceinte des puits de ma campagne*'. Much to the satisfaction of the duchess, who knew all about prices (*NMP* 151), Tietjens' French is fantastically old-fashioned ('like hearing Chateaubriand talk', Sylvia thinks, '—if Chateaubriand had been brought up in an English hunting country' [*NMP* 150]), but to the duchess's ears, it is also gratifyingly true to type as she conceives of the English type. This is cross-Channel mutual cynicism as a form of wartime diplomacy: pit prices, escalating in wartime, can be undercut to mutual advantage. She gets to keep her greenhouses flourishing; he secures her signature on a marriage settlement with his Colonel, appeasing the higher brass. Byron, via Balzac, hovers once again behind the scenes, as she responds with an *anglicisme* of her own: 'just what she would have expected of a *milor Anglais. ... Avec* un spleen *tel que vous l'avez!*' (*NMP* 150 [my emphasis]).[88]

---

[87] It is a description that anticipates Ford's later protest against Frieda Lawrence's description of him as of 'Russian descent' but 'prefer[ring] to be an Englishman': 'I have been called in my time French, English, German, Polish, Welsh, Scotch, and Galician Ruthenian, and more often than anything, American, but never, oh never, Russian.' Englishness 'I could not help. I was born in England. One does not preside at the destiny of one's birth.' See letter to the Editor of the *American Mercury*, 19 January 1937, in *Letters*, 269–70 (269).

[88] 'Spleen est un anglicisme qui désigne l'ennui de toutes choses, une mélancolie profonde, voire un certain dégoût de la vie.' *L'Encyclopédie Française*, <http://www.encyclopedie.fr/definition/spleen>.

It is a consistent feature of Tietjens' depiction that he knows ('purely by instinct' as it seems to Sylvia) the difference between the true worth of things and the price they will fetch at any given time (the brilliant Section IV of *Some Do Not* is largely devoted to Sylvia's meditations on the similarity between his genius with the antique furniture market and her ability to control the price of her attentions to men). It is, then, a blackly comic irony that his personal endeavour to sustain English patriotism alongside his deep European cosmopolitanism is publicly undermined by her thinly cynical cosmopolitanism. The farce of their marriage has been played out across the Continent in the years leading up to the war: Paris, Brittany, Lobscheid, Kiev, and at some point there have been those flirtations in Austria. Her private conviction is that the 'immoralities' of most Englishwomen are a fiction, and that English men reserve their 'amours' for politics:[89] the destructive passion of her first affair thus makes her the exception, her Catholicism underwriting an idea of virtue that has force for her primarily as it is violated. Tietjens, by contrast, blames John Stuart Mill and George Eliot: 'What's the sense of all these attempts to justify fornication? England's mad about it. Well, you've got your John Stuart Mills and your George Eliots for the high-class thing [free, that is, to stretch conventional *mores* on marital fidelity]. Leave the furniture out! [he has in view the 'fetid' excesses of the Pre-Raphaelites] Or leave me out at least' (*SDN*, 27–8, 28). His prescription is the same for himself, for her, and for the country and it goes by way of cynicism:[90] lower the level of heroism looked for and 'we' will 'behave' better because there will be less to rebuke ourselves with.

When Graham Greene looked back on the Tietjens series as 'that appalling examination of how private malice goes on during public disaster—no escape even in the trenches from the secret gossip and the lawyers' papers',[91] he was capturing the most upsetting aspect of Ford's narrative: its intimate interweaving of public and private aggression. Taken at her own word, Sylvia looks like thoroughly Greenean material: a Catholic willing to court damnation because she cannot bear an unassailable goodness. But her cynicism, like Tietjens', goes hand in hand with a dangerous empathy. She knows that his decency, in private and in public, rests more on reason than on morality: '*you*! ... without a brain!', she will mock, as he struggles in his damaged state to recall the word 'Metternich' (*SDN*, 211, 209). Her fiercest charges against him are that there is a 'simple, sheer immorality' to his being always in the right, and that decency of this kind rests on a large measure of

[89]   Ford Madox Ford, *Parade's End: Part I, Some Do Not* (1924), in *The Bodley Head Ford Madox Ford*, ed. Greene, III.

[90]   He has just learned that his banker, eager to marry Sylvia should there be a divorce, has cancelled his overdraft so that his cheque has been denied at his club. '"To please you?"' he asks with scrupulous neutrality: '"Do bankers do that? It's a new light on British society ...!"'

[91]   Graham Greene, 'Ford Madox Ford', *The Spectator* 163 (7 July 1939), 11; reprinted in Frank MacShane (ed.), *Ford Madox Ford: The Critical Heritage* (London: Routledge and Kegan Paul, 1972), 212–15 (214).

egoism: he is 'so appallingly competent, so appallingly always in the centre of his own picture' (*SDN*, 39). She is not alone in that cynicism. Others, too, are driven to it: Ethel Duchemin, lover then wife of his closest friend Macmaster, increasingly sees his generosity as latent bribery; his own father credits stories that he is 'a bloody pimp living on women'; even Valentine Wannop vents her frustration in cynicism ('he did himself proud! With women!' [*SDN*, 337]). Only Sylvia fully sees the psychological effort required to follow his chosen behavioural code (he declines to call it moral and has a hawk eye for the conventionality of all moralities, liberal as much as conservative, most glaringly evident towards sex.)[92]

Read at the level of psychology, the first three volumes of *Parade's End* depict a strenuous effort at asserting sanity under such extreme conditions of political and sexual hostility, and if some modern psychologists will detect defensive narcissism here, it has to be said that Tietjens has a lot to be defended against. As registered at the level of style, the effect is best described by D. H. Lawrence (responding to Ford's characteristic mode of letter writing) as 'an ironical cynicism'.[93] Lawrence saw through the cynicism and implied that others might be expected to do the same:

> Mr Hueffer is really such a lot better fellow tha[n] he thinks he ought to be, to belong to this shabby frame of things. So he daubs his dove-grey kindliness with a villainous selfish tar, and hops forth a very rook among rooks: but his eyes, after all, remain, like the Shulamites, doves eyes. He makes me jolly mad. I think the ironic attitude, consistently adopted, is about as tiresome as the infant's bib which he says I wear for my mewling and puking... Some things are jolly bad, and while we're afflicted, the best thing to do is to howl to the ever-attentive heavens...[94]

Cynicism, on this reading, is a disguise for humane decency ('kindliness') allowing the Cynic to appear to himself as 'selfish' as everyone else while, in reality, looking on the world with dovish gentleness. Much as Lawrence professes to prefer the honest howl of the infant, his own response is anything but innocent (saturated by the Bible and Shakespeare) and hardly free of irony: to view the generality of humanity as villainous, selfish, full of 'rooks', is to be so thoroughly cynical—or, in Ford's case, to aspire to being so thoroughly cynical ('he ought to be')—that there will be no visible difference between oneself and the real 'rooks'. Neither ironic cynicism nor Lawrence's own (ostensibly) naïve sincerity escapes a charge of 'tiresome[ness]' that is itself a mannerism (one that recalls the world-weariness

---

[92] See esp. his strictures to MacMaster against 'sham sexual morality' of the liberal sort, and his acute reading of Mrs Duchemin's 'Higher Morality'. *SDN*, 29 and 201.

[93] Letter to Violet Hunt, 3 February 1911, in D. H. Lawrence, *The Letters of D. H. Lawrence*, gen. ed. James T. Boulton, 8 vols. (Cambridge: Cambridge University Press, 1979–2000), I, 226–8 (227).

[94] Ibid., 227.

of the established English cynic type). What Ford and Lawrence can agree on, says Lawrence, is that the state of affliction in the world requires a response ('Some things are jolly bad') and that silent stoicism is not an option.

There is a touch of naivety about the early reference to Tietjens' 'good-natured cynicism' as we see it from Valentine's perspective in volume 1 (*SDN*, 311).[95] When she makes the association between Tietjens and cynicism again, on the other side of the war, she is more alert to the effort and to the stylistic anachronism. It is Armistice Day and she is approaching Tietjens' house with the intention of giving herself to him, in defiance of her mother's Victorian scruples. In her jagged state of mind the Georgian square alarms her ('houses...so eighteenth-century and silver-grey and rigid and serene that they ought all to be empty too and contain dead, mad men' [*A Man Could Stand Up*, 435]), but it softens in her perception once she runs into Tietjens himself, large, clumsy, now partially grey, his face 'too pink and too white' for health, his grey uniform unbecoming (436). Waiting in the empty house for him to complete an errand, she considers that he is like his house—'*He* was eighteenth-century...The only century that never went mad. Until the French Revolution. And that was either not mad or not eighteenth century' (437). The thought takes sharper form: 'friendly...Eighteenth-century. Cynical, but not malignant' (444). The guarded externality of the description is acute, on her part: this is character delineation confined fiercely to outward appearance, historical affiliation, and the discerning judgements of a critic intimate with her subject's formal requirements. Her preservation of distance admits love, tenderness (the tolerance of the modern young for what is ostensibly outmoded), but above all respect and admiration.

It is a view of Tietjens that accords with his sense of himself as psychologically out of time: a man cut somewhat after the cloth of an Enlightenment empiricist—'a perfect encyclopaedia of exact material knowledge' (*SDN*, 13). His aesthetic tastes have the same bias: a 'great white drawing-room, with fixings that [Sylvia] knew were eighteenth century and to be respected' (*SDN*, 191); his respect for Mrs Wannop stems from her having written, in his view, 'the only novel worth reading since the eighteenth century' (not George Eliot, then) (*SDN*, 96). Cast in this light, his cynicism suggests a desired return to, or persistence in, a 'mentality' that now registers even to himself as outdated: one that prizes intellectual clarity over the false generalizations of Victorian 'moralizing' or the equally generalizing revelations of Freud. Certainly the strategic cynicisms by which Tietjens tries to keep command of his sanity can read like a privatization of the Enlightenment

---

[95] She is observing his amusement when the expected pecking order at Edith Duchemin's celebrity party is upset by Sylvia (easily the most beautiful woman in the room) introducing herself to the isolated Mrs Wannop, drawing a crowd of watchers after her. Sylvia already suspects Christopher of interest in Valentine, so what reads to the girl as a gesture of 'goodness' to her mother is in fact self-interested: Valentine thus hears the cynicism in Tietjens' remark, 'it seems to have upset some apple-carts', but doesn't quite get the range of cynicism's application (*SDN*, 311–12).

philosophes' aspirations as Louisa Shea has described them—desiring to 'shape' and critique the common intellectual life by an effort of the intelligence. Eighteenth-century French cynicism thereby rendered the Cynicism of antiquity 'virtually unrecognizable', she argues: a 'clean-shaven' Diogenes no longer poses a serious threat to the common moral currency.[96]

Tietjens is not a clean-shaven figure, however. He is, for all his efforts at rationality, untidy. The critical literature on *Parade's End* has, understandably, paid close attention to the fiction of Englishness he represents. Helpful commentary by Andrzej Gasiorek and others, for example, has elaborated the peculiarities of Tietjens' political self-description as an eighteenth-century Tory radical, and the ways in which it does and does not coincide with Ford's own intermittent self-presentation. Gasiorek describes a radicalism emanating imaginatively from the political right, 'humanitarian, anti-capitalist, anti-centralist' and by instinct 'feudal'[97]—looking back to a time when alliance between landed gentry and workers against factory owner and central state might have made more political sense. In the context of early twentieth-century battling for the future of the Conservative Party, he points out, nostalgia of this ilk was less eccentric than it may appear: a mode of resistance to contemporary efforts at strengthening the party's association with business and industry.[98]

Criticism that brings so much political theory to bear on *Parade's End* is adding a great deal to what is on the novelistic page, in danger of creating a Tietjens (and, behind him, a Ford Madox Ford) too much in the image of J. W. Burrow. It ignores those many moments at which Tietjens appears not an eighteenth-century figure but an earlier or later one, his imaginative moorings slipping around according to his mood and the moods of those who observe him: playing Chateaubriand to the duchess, he also feels the pull of an earlier period in English history ('One ought to be a seventeenth-century parson' [*NMP*, 256]), but then he appeals to a thoroughly Victorian element in his make-up ('the belief Arnold forced upon Rugby that the vilest of sins—the vilest of all sins—is to preach to the head master! That's me, sir' [248]).

[96] Shea describes 'a desire . . . to shape the emergent figure of the public intellectual and a willingness to grapple with the social and political difficulties raised by what Diderot called the impulse to "change the common way of thinking"'. Louisa Shea, *The Cynic Enlightenment: Diogenes in the Salon* (Baltimore, MD: Johns Hopkins University Press, 2010), xii–xiii.

[97] Robert Stewart, *The Foundation of the Conservative Party, 1830–1867* (London: Longman, 1978), 170, quoted in Andrzej Gasiorek, 'The Politics of Cultural Nostalgia: History and Tradition in Ford Madox Ford's *Parade's End*', *Literature & History*, 3rd ser. 11/2 (2002), 52–77 (57). See also Gene M. Moore, 'The Tory in a Time of Change: Social Aspects of Ford Madox Ford's *Parade's End*', *Twentieth Century Literature* 28/1 (1982), 49–68.

[98] See Gasiorek, 'Politics of Cultural Nostalgia', esp. 56–70. Gasiorek extends the political portrait drawn by Saunders in his (now the standard) biography, *Ford Madox Ford*. Though the detail does not bear closely on the current reading, I also depart from Gasiorek's reading in that I take Tietjens to have given up on land-holding long before he gives the Groby estate over to Sylvia and their young son. (He knows she has no love of the place, and her cutting down of Groby's great tree, though intensely painful to him, comes too late to be decisive in the critical distance he takes on his own 'nostalgia'.)

The cynically sustained negative cosmopolitan of *Parade's End* is, by the same token, not a matter of political theory and it makes no claims to philosophical consistency. It would be a mistake to interpret it as *The Spectator* reviewer was inclined to read all modern derivations of cynicism: as evidence of the 'eternal escapism' of man. The difference between a cynicism that takes one out of the world and a cynicism that, detaching itself from the business of politics, remains in and of the world and inescapably political in its implications is, indeed, the principal focus of the tetralogy's final volume. *The Last Post* (1928)[99] treats the post-war experience of the tetralogy's characters, with Christopher, Valentine, Mark and Mark's French wife, living in Christopher's country retreat in West Sussex—a small landholding where Marie Léonie keeps pigs and chickens, brews cider, and nurses her husband. Ford draws on his own spell living on the land after the war, in something close to the ironized pastoral simplicity of *Sartor* (the pigs misbehaved and bit the postman).[100]

The Last Post filters much of its action through Mark Tietjens, felled by a stroke on Armistice Day: a man who has 'done with' the world, and watches its action, unmoving and unspeaking, from his pallet bed like a latter-day Heine. In his manner of life thus far Mark has been at least as cosmopolitan as his brother: exposed to French culture as a boy ('Dijon! For my French!' [*SDN*, 265]), keeping, for years, a French mistress, in 'constant intimacy', through her gossip, 'with the life and point of view of individuals of the French *petite bourgeoisie*' (*LP*, 130). But his professional life as a senior Whitehall civil servant has put him at odds with a government that deals 'treacherously' with its Continental allies (*LP*, 130): only a conviction that he is indispensable to the war effort has kept him in post. England's national interest has been Mark's professional business, but he falls ill after making the case to Valentine that Germany, having lost, must be politically punished—English symbols of triumph hung in the squares of Berlin. Even as he argues the case, he concedes that European jostling for position on this model is (a nice thought) a thing of the past: 'England is necessary to the world.... To my world.... Well, make it your world and it may go to rack and ruin how it will. I am done with it' (*LP* , 185).

As Max Saunders and others have pointed out, there is a pan-European and trans-Atlantic scope to *The Last Post* that chimes with 'the post-Versailles world and the founding of the League of Nations'.[101] Silencing the assertive-English side of Mark's disposition, it is a novel about relenting on past hatreds for the sake of the next generation, Sylvia's truce with Christopher making a clear analogy with

---

[99] Ford Madox Ford, *The Last Post* (London: Duckworth, 1928).

[100] Letter to F. S. Flint, 12 May 1921, in *Letters*, 131.

[101] Saunders, *Dual Life* II, 255. See also Paul Skinner, 'The Painful Process of Reconstruction: History in *No Enemy* and *Last Post*', in Joseph Wiesenfarth (ed.), *History and Representation in Ford Madox Ford's Writings* (Amsterdam: Rodopi, 2004), 65–75; and Gene M. Moore, 'Peace of Mind in *Parade's End*', in Chantler and Hawkes (eds.), *War and the Mind*, 159–69.

the Allies' reluctance to pursue the enemy.[102] But it is also a novel alert to the uncertainty of American commitment to the new international solidarities aimed at preventing further wars, and wary of American 'avidity' (LP, 39). Christopher's cynicisms are now side-lined: he has turned his cosmopolitan experience to practical ends, and works away in the background of The Last Post with a Jewish American business partner (a man of German extraction, forced into the Prussian army on a badly timed visit to Berlin, then encountered by Christopher as a POW). Together they now scrape a living finding European antiques for the trans-Atlantic market. Having 'predicted the American mopping up of the world's gold supply and the consequent stripping of European houses of old stuff' (LP, 128–9), he has no nostalgia to spare for the smaller 'world' that has gone. The cynic debasements of his own sentimental ideals that kept him sane through the first three books are, presumably, still at work inside him, and acknowledged in the Preface to The Last Post to the extent that Ford recalls the character of the man—'slightly contemptuous—and sentimental in his human contacts' (vii)—on whom Tietjens' personality was based, but they are no longer the primary focalization of the narrative.

The concentration is on the silenced brother and his garrulous French mistress. There is no naivety about either. When Sylvia sends up the white flag, at last, by sending her young son Mark to plead on her behalf with his uncle, the motives in play are clear to Mark, as they are to Marie Léonie. Why has Sylvia not come herself?, he thinks:

> Of course, the results of venereal disease are not pleasant to contemplate, and, no doubt, Sylvia, having invented the disease for him, had not liked to contemplate the resultant symptoms. At any rate, that boy did not know—and neither did Mrs. de Bray Pape—that he did not speak. Not to them, not to anybody. He was finished with the world. He perceived the trend of its actions, listened to its aspirations, and even to its prayers, but he would never again stir lip or finger. It was like being dead—or being God.   (99–100)

This locked-in but (in its judgements) undiluted cynicism, would be remorseless—a quality Ford claimed to believe there was not nearly enough of in English literature[103]—were it not for the leavening effect of a mind watching its

---

[102] Saunders, Dual Life, II, 250; and see Charles G. Hoffmann, Ford Madox Ford (1967), updated edn (Boston: Twayne Publishers, 1990), 97. The strongest case is made by Robert Green, who argues that Ford's purpose in writing Parade's End was to prevent all future wars. Ford Madox Ford, 130–1. And see Hoffmann, 99.

[103] 'England . . . has hardly ever produced a remorseless novelist. Smollett is perhaps the one example that she can show, and for one lover of Smollett in the land, Sterne, who wilfully and even cynically sentimentalised over human vicissitudes, can show ten thousand. England has practically never produced a remorseless statesman. Thomas Cromwell is almost the only example that she can show.' Ford, Critical Attitude, 15.

own performance, on the lookout for self-pity ('dead') and pomposity ('God'). The cynicism ends only on the last page of the novel, when, dying, Mark breaks his peace, exerting himself to plead gently, humorously, not with Sylvia but with a careworn, pregnant Valentine, not to judge Christopher harshly: 'A good man!' (*LP*, 291). If anything is to be made, in this context, of Ford's much-cited ambivalence towards *The Last Post*,[104] it would be to observe that a cynicism so consciously rescinded runs the risk, however gracefully it is styled, of precisely the coercive sentimentalism he associated with Eliot.

Ford would continue, through the 1920s and 1930s, to try to live and to represent a sustainable cosmopolitanism, frugal ('material comfort deadens one's interest in life'),[105] unillusioned, and at a remove from England (first, in the States, then in Provence, where the deep cosmopolitanism of the old Great Trade route appealed to the historical romanticist in him). The critical distance on England was firm, and ironically belligerent at times: 'Why should a London public like my work? My constatations of life have dubious international backgrounds;... they are "machined" with a Franco-American modernity that must be disagreeable to the inhabitants of, say, Cheltenham.'[106] 'You live apparently amongst the middle-class Left in England', he wrote to his daughter Julia in 1935: 'I live about the world with no politics at all except the belief—which I share with Lenin—that the only thing that can save the world is the abolition of all national feelings.'[107] Characteristically, he casts the claim to apoliticism in political terms. He saw clearly enough what was coming: 'the national feeling, like a dog to its vomit, has returned to the vaguenesses and self-deceptions of the Teutonic strain. That is natural and can't be helped'.[108] It might sound like cynicism, but in context it was realism.

*

To set Ford Madox Ford next to George Eliot as two kinds of exercise in a Cynically-assisted cosmopolitanism is to tell a critical story—one that goes from high Victorian moralism at its most experimental to a modernist critical rejection of moralism as not the business of literature at all. It is to treat two ways of conceiving of cynicism as a subject of psychology, the first holding an understanding of mind to be a needed component in the moralist's armoury,[109] the

---

[104] See Saunders, *Dual Life*, II, 253 on Graham Greene's 'controversial' omission of the novel from the Bodley Head edition of *Parade's End*. Ford himself vacillated, as Saunders notes: in 1930, he expressed a strong wish to omit it from the edition, but then he 'backtracked, saying that the was "ready to be guided by Duckworth"' (254).

[105] Letter to Julia Ford, 11 September 1935, in *Letters*, 237–42 (239).

[106] Letter to Gerald Bullett, 24 August 1933, in *Letters*, 221–3 (222). For discussion, see Julian Barnes, 'The Saddest Story', *The Guardian*, 7 June 2008, <https://www.theguardian.com/books/2008/jun/07/fiction.julianbarnes>. Accessed 3 September 2019.

[107] Letter to Ford, in *Letters*, 238.   [108] Letter to Ford, in *Letters*, 238–9.

[109] See Introduction for an account of the long and uneven process by which modern psychology consolidated a view of the cynic temperament as defensive narcissism.

second regarding moral attachments as one aspect of a larger psychological picture. The story is indicative rather than representative. It is in keeping with critical histories of cynicism that see the late nineteenth and early twentieth centuries ushering in a privatization or internalization of Cynicism usually understood to sever its association with any seriously challenging philosophical enterprise, though it does not offer to refine the explanation of how we got from one to the other. It does *not* condemn the cynic to apoliticism, rather offering to cast some light on how deeply politically attuned the negativity of modern cynic cosmopolitanism may be.

What ties Eliot and Ford together, finally, is their shared sense that if cosmopolitan sympathy is to be viable as an ideal in the world, it requires something beyond the motivational 'good will' Kant associated with duty or the Stoics' belief in the 'community of human argument and aspiration'.[110] What cynicism offers for each of them is an exercise of the intelligence—outwardly didactic in Eliot's case, inwardly defensive in Ford's—in conditions where intelligence understands itself to be imperilled and limited in its powers to effect change. Within those limits it nevertheless looks to improve the fit between the world imagined and the world inhabited. For both, this is a critical as well as a literary practice. From the vantage point of the early twenty-first century, it is a reminder that, historically, some of cosmopolitan humanism's strongest literary advocates have sought protection against casual cynicism from a controlled Cynic realism.

---

[110] For the connection between the two, see Nussbaum, 'Kant and Stoic Cosmopolitanism', 6.

5

In Praise of Idleness?

Cynicism and the Humanities

Bertrand Russell, John Dewey, and Laura Kipnis

Cinematic portrayals of university Humanities departments, I am not the first to observe, can be a gauge of changing public perceptions. A striking pair of American movies in 2008, *Smart People* and *The Visitor*, led one critic to note a cultural shift away from a trope that William Deresiewicz had observed dominating the American college movie genre in the late 1990s to the mid-2000s: the middle-aged, male English professor and failed writer who sleeps with his students, neglects his wife, and bullies his children.[1] The 2008 films were different enough, Bruce Robbins observed, 'to look like a deliberate refutation'. 'Again the professor is crabby, misanthropic, affectively stunted. But this time he has an excuse. In both films . . . the professor is acting the way he is because his wife has died, and he's in mourning for her.' 'My speculation', he went on,

> is that the dead wives are Hollywood's figure for the subject matter of the humanities. That is, they're a figure for art and ideas that in the public's eyes are genuinely beautiful and worthy to be adored, as we academic humanists adore them, but that are also lost forever. By this theory, Hollywood would supply the deadwood professors with dead wives in a surprisingly good-faith attempt to penetrate the mystery of what it is that humanists *do*, and the answer would be: the remembering of beloved but now distant things.[2]

If 2014's thinner revisitation of the genre, *The Rewrite*,[3] is any indication, things have moved on again. The teaching culture of the Humanities still has an opening

---

[1] William Deresiewicz, reflecting on *The Squid and the Whale* (2005), *One True Thing* (1998), *Wonder Boys* (2000). 'Love on Campus', *The American Scholar*, 1 June 2007, <https://theamericanscholar.org/love-on-campus/#.XXuGVy2ZM3E>; cited in Bruce Robbins, 'Deadwood: Freedom and *Smart People*', *South Atlantic Quarterly* 108/4 (2009), 741–9.
[2] Ibid., 742.
[3] Written and directed by Marc Lawrence (Castle Rock Entertainment, 2014). Many other recent films might serve my argument equally well here. For a brief consideration of Woody Allen's *Irrational Man* (Sony Pictures Classics, 2015), in an earlier version of this opening argument, see <https://talkinghumanities.blogs.sas.ac.uk/2016/03/10/professor-helen-small-discusses-the-value-of-humanities/>. Accessed 9 May 2018.

The Function of Cynicism at the Present Time. Helen Small, Oxford University Press (2020). © Helen Small.
DOI: 10.1093/oso/9780198861935.001.0001

for the deadwood professor, but he is visible to everyone (himself included) as a cliché. He is less institutionally secure than he once was. Middle-aged, crabby, misanthropic, affectively stunted, he is now divorced, his former wife meriting only a brief and fractious phone call at the start of the movie. He is out of contact with his child; and he is an adjunct, not a tenured employee. Driven into college teaching by financial desperation, he assumes that a semester directing Creative Writing will be jammy money—a salary for very little work, and his pick of the attractive young women applying for the course. The drama, such as it is, now attaches less to the potential erotics of the encounter between teacher and student than to the interplay between the would-be deadwood professor and an institution far less tolerant of misbehaviour than it was in the past.

To that end, *The Rewrite* gives the university an alternative representative: the professor's line manager. A Jane Austen scholar who, in his unreformed view, has sold out and become an institutional functionary (head of the Ethics Committee), she is the disciplined sceptic who will need placating if he is to perform his role as educator in a way the other staff, the students, and the hypothetical tax- and fee-paying public might find at once tolerable and charismatic. It is not irrelevant that she is played by Allison Janney, better known as the White House Press Secretary in *The West Wing*. The ideal higher education institution of 2010 onwards allows for both, it would seem: the professional overseer of ethics who does Austenian irony, at the top; the imperfectly professionalized teacher who prefers *Clueless* to Austen straight, giving her a disciplinary job to do.

Regrettably, not much frisson is generated by this particular version of institutionally assisted *Bildung*, and if one were to rewrite *The Rewrite* with a view to improving matters, Janney's exasperatedly acidic Chair of Ethics looks a more promising place to start than Hugh Grant's adjunct 'creative'. The ethical requirements of the workplace have normative force here, but they are not presented as meriting much reflection and they are not open for debate. They entail basic procedural and moral rules, not higher intellectual commitments: do your preparation, turn up, pay attention, don't abuse your power. Things might have been more interesting, dramatically, if the professor had tested the limits a little harder. The philosopher protagonist of Woody Allen's *Irrational Man* (2015) comes to mind—also in the deadwood mould, but too burdened by anomie to be called crabby, and sexually impotent; his blood only starts pumping again when he is struck by the bright existentialist thought that he might commit a perfect murder. Comparatively bland though it is, *The Rewrite* has its finger more on the pulse of contemporary academic culture. Not least, the re-gearing of the renegade professor *topos* as a narrative of professional 'taming' suggests that, three years before the downfall of Harvey Weinstein, some in Hollywood were taking a critical interest in the ethos of Humanities departments in parallel with the formation, or deformation, of the film industry itself.[4]

---

[4] Weinstein studied for a degree in English at SUNY Buffalo, though he did not complete it and the university withdrew his honorary degree in 2017.

This partial refurbishing of an old but not quite defunct typology of the Humanities professor offers a way in to an aspect of cynicism that connects the primarily historical focus of *The Function of Cynicism* to current dilemmas facing the liberal university generally and the Humanities especially. If the starting premise of the deadwood trope, even in revised form, sounds more like casual cynicism than critique, anyone who has tried to represent 'what it is that the Humanities *do*' to the world beyond the academy will recognize in it a confrontational scepticism, not confined to 'anti-humanists' or those more broadly sceptical of the value of higher education: a scepticism that must be faced, ideally overcome, or at least worked with, if one is to make the case. In the main (as in *The Rewrite*), scepticism of the kind that interests me here presents as a low-level, casual, semi-humorous cynicism, though more hardened and antagonistic forms are not difficult to find. Behind the casual variety one can often discern as much affection as resentment. Cynicism, in those cases, can provide a cover for forms of nostalgia—self-ironizing, to a degree—either towards the relative freedoms of one's own university experiences by contrast with what came later, or (more questionably) for a world in which the Humanities are thought to have exercised greater or more direct power in public life. Casual or serious, soft or hard, cynicism on this subject operates in taut relation with idealism about the value and purpose of the Humanities. It has, I will suggest, the potential to be more-helpful-than-not to Humanities advocates in their current state of need.

Typically, cynicism towards the university generally, the Humanities particularly, attaches to two points of ostensible dispute: (i) whether, or in what way, the daily business of the professors and students counts as 'work'; and (ii) what the motives of the professors are for staying in the academy. (I am setting to one side, for now, that further form of cynicism regarding the social value of the Humanities' objects of study.) The public moralism of Bertrand Russell will be central to my development of a case for recognizing a constructive role in cynicism. His thinking about the status and rationale for the work of the university offers another example of a style of public moralism that has been the subject of much of this book's attention: stringently cynical towards certain aspects of conventional moral thinking, adopting testing freedoms of thought and attributions of low motive as part of a wider and more varied effort to safeguard and strengthen idealism. Like Carlyle, Arnold, Eliot, and Williams, Rorty after him, Russell is alert to the risk that rationality, left to itself on these matters, will lack the necessary 'spirit' to inspire the 'energy and ardour' that drive social change.[5] And, as in those cases, the alertness produces a peculiar relation to the authority of his own moral ideals: a tendency to assert an ideal and cynically to abuse that ideal within the scope of the same rhetorical performance.

---

[5] The phrases are taken from Bertrand Russell, *Why Men Fight: A Method of Abolishing the International Duel*, introduction by Richard A. Remple (London: Routledge, [1916] 2010), 146–7, but the general position is consistent across Russell's public moralism.

I turn first to the 1935 essay 'In Praise of Idleness' for what Russell has to say there in locally cynical but, in the end, near-utopian fashion about the reasons for holding on to an idea of the university as an institution requiring special freedoms if it is to fulfil its role of advancing the nation's intellectual life. Russell's cynicisms about the nature and value of intellectual work, as against other kinds of work, are, I argue, a way of exposing and scrutinizing commonplace assumptions about the purpose of the university, and the liberty it has in the past afforded and still to a degree affords its academics, relative to workers in most other sections of the modern economy. The extent of that liberty for college and university teachers and researchers today is significantly diminished from what it was for academics of Russell's generation, but it is worth remembering that the general trajectory of UK government policy at the time he was writing, and for several subsequent decades, was away from state interference in the university and towards actively strengthening legal and administrative protections on its freedoms. (The same was true, albeit less evenly, in the USA, where the founding in 1915 of the American Association of University Professors [AAUP] played a crucial role in establishing and defending principles of academic freedom and tenure, and advocating for faculty involvement in governance.)[6]

Russell's cynicisms towards the freedom of academic work were and are thought-provoking and critically astringent. They were and are unlikely to give much offence, given the institutional, historic, and depersonalized nature of his reflections. The next part of the argument shows Russell in a more provocative guise: as a moral controversialist whose views on sexual morality (which are well known) and on intergenerational conflict (rather less well known) made him an individual test case for academic freedom a few years after he wrote 'In Praise of Idleness'. In 1940, the New York Supreme Court moved to vacate Russell's appointment as Professor of Philosophy at the City College of New York on the grounds that he was 'an alien' (British, not American) 'and an advocate of sexual immorality' in danger of corrupting the young.[7] I look in greater detail at the text largely responsible for the fracas, *Marriage and Morals* (1929), and at the defence offered for it and its author by John Dewey, whose essays 'The Case for Bertrand Russell' (1940)[8] and 'Social Realities versus Police Court Fictions' (1941)[9] became

---

[6] See Stanley Aronowitz, *The Last Good Job in America: Work and Education in the New Global Technoculture* (Lanham, MD: Rowman & Littlefield, 2001), 33–4; Larry G. Gerber, 'College and University Governance', *Academe* 101/1 (January–February 2015), 31–7; and Paul Strohm (ed.), '75 Years: A Retrospective on the Occasion of the Seventy-Fifth Annual Meeting', *Academe* 75/3 (May–June 1989), 1–33.

[7] John Dewey, The Collected Works of John Dewey, 1882–1953, ed. Jo Ann Boydston, 37 vols. (Carbondale, IL: Southern Illinois University Press, 1972–85), XIV, 467. Hereafter cited as *CW*.

[8] Nation 150 (15 June 1940), 732–3.

[9] First published in John Dewey and Horace M. Kallen (eds.), *The Bertrand Russell Case* (New York: Viking Press, 1941), 55–74.

key documents in attempts by civil liberties groups to overturn the Supreme Court decision.

The Russell case and its aftermath turn a sharper light on the principle of academic freedom as an ideal vital to the work of the university. I am interested here in what the case can tell us, at a relatively early stage in the development of formal institutional protections on academic freedom, about its rationale and its permissible extent as it enters the terrain of moral controversialism—a persistent and difficult ethical concern for the modern university, often in tension with other forms of freedom (the freedom of students from harm, for example; or the freedom some may claim from 'offence'). The primary question raised by Dewey, a founding figure of the AAUP, was whether mid-twentieth-century America was willing to protect the wide latitude for critical thought that he, like Matthew Arnold (a writer he held in high regard), considered requisite to a progressive democratic culture with the university at its intellectual heart. In teasing out Dewey's views on this subject, I draw on the (revised) 1932 version of his *Ethics*, where he provides his most explicit theoretical justification for moral controversialism, drawing a line, like Michel Foucault after him, between the ancient Cynics and Cyrenaics' historic challenges to conventional thinking and the robust tolerance required if modern 'intelligent' individualism is to flourish amid institutions of education and research dedicated to the common good. Dewey, importantly, had greater reservations about the contribution of the Cynics than Foucault expresses, and those reservations have a bearing on the ways in which he seeks to give controversialism a purpose along with its licence, and a licence only insofar as it has that purpose.

The Russell case is historic, but the concerns it raises, and the defence it prompted from Dewey—in effect, a *normative* defence of the university professor's right to model and to test *anti*-normative lines of thought and speech in the service of the common good—have ongoing relevance, and are, at the time of writing, subject to renewed and intense debate. The final section of this chapter looks at the response to one much more recent work of moral controversialism, Laura Kipnis's *Unwanted Advances: Sexual Paranoia Comes to Campus* (2017). Again, the immediate context is American, but the issues are debated transatlantically and, indeed, now globally. I treat Kipnis as a litmus test for the willingness of the university to go on making the kind of space it has historically agreed to make for sometimes-cynical freedoms of speech that breach normative constraints on debate about sexual morality within and about the academy. Other kinds of case might serve the broad purpose here (No-Platforming disputes, for example, focused on the political views of the speaker—say, Steve Bannon at Berkeley and Chicago), but the less obviously tribal nature of arguments around free speech about sexual misconduct on campus, and the continuity with the old (and not yet dead) stimuli to casual cynicism about the Humanities (professors supposedly more interested in bedding their students than advancing the state of knowledge), give *Unwanted Advances* special salience.

In Praise of Idleness? The Work of the Humanities

'In Praise of Idleness' is a short theoretical essay on modern labour conditions that takes a significant detour into the special labour conditions of the university. In it, Bertrand Russell argues that one of the aims of modern civilization should be to release as many people as possible from the burden of alienated labour and afford them the benefits of a 'wise use of leisure'. His claims are broad-stroke, speculative, at times capricious—conscious of (perhaps embarrassed by) the mismatch between their author's career and the work prospects of younger generations. Not well known outside the specialist field of Russell studies, the essay occupies a minor place (a prominent niche, as it were) in a long line of writing, predominantly but not exclusively from the left/liberal end of the political spectrum, that has challenged the rightness of the dominant work ethic. In its twentieth- and twenty-first-century forms, that line of thinking runs from Keynes's 'Economic Possibilities for Our Grandchildren' (1930), through Karel Čapek's *In Praise of Idleness* (translated into English in the same year Russell's essay appeared), to Clive Jenkins and Barrie Sherman's *The Collapse of Work* (1979), André Gorz's *Farewell to the Working Class* (1980), Jeremy Rifkin's *The End of Work* (1995), Stanley Aronowitz's *The Last Good Job in America* (2001), and Tim Jackson's *Prosperity Without Growth* (2009) to Kate Soper's series of journalistic essays, written at the start of the latest economic downturn, outlining how Humanities departments might assist an 'alternative hedonism'—'a shift to a more materially reproductive way of living, . . . a low- or no-growth economic model rooted in an expansion of leisure time and rather different conceptions of social flourishing and human wellbeing'.[10]

Not the smallest hazard of praise for productive 'idleness', still on occasion issuing from the academy,[11] is that in defending the value and virtue of unalienated labour to non-academic publics the philosopher-critic will seem primarily to be justifying their own privileged position as an employee of an institution whose work may appear to others, and perhaps also to themselves, suspiciously like

---

[10] Parts of this genealogy are given in 'The Persistence of Work', *The Current Moment*, 25 February 2013, <https://thecurrentmoment.wordpress.com/2013/02/25/the-persistence-of-work/>. Accessed 28 March 2014. See also Kate Soper, 'Humanities Can Promote Alternative "Good Life"', *The Guardian*, 30 November 2010, <http://www.theguardian.com/commentisfree/2010/nov/30/humanities-promote-alternative-good-life>. Accessed 27 March 2013.

[11] Most of the writers just listed were employees of higher education institutions. Further examples, not confined to the university, would include Robert Sidelsky and Edward Sidelsky, *How Much Is Enough?: Money and the Good Life* (London: Penguin, 2012), 12, who draw on Russell and (for literary models), Oscar Wilde, Robert Louis Stevenson, Thomas Mann, and Karel Čapek.

pleasure. Orwell's '*rentier*-intellectuals' cast a long shadow: enjoying freedoms made possible by money they have not directly earned, all too often 'convicted of a too Olympian attitude, a too great readiness to wash their hands of the immediate practical problem'.[12] Those phrases from 'Inside the Whale' (1940) are anticipated in the final pages of Russell's essay, privileged class background in both cases perhaps sharpening the political antennae for the subject. Having made a case for decreasing the quantity of mechanical or procedural work done, and improving the kinds and quality of leisure to be enjoyed, Russell ruminates on the as-yet very partially democratized condition of the intelligentsia:

> In the past, there was a small leisure class and a larger working class. The leisure class enjoyed advantages for which there was no basis in social justice; this necessarily made it oppressive, limited its sympathies, and caused it to invent theories to justify its privileges. These facts greatly diminished its excellence, but in spite of this it contributed nearly the whole of what we call civilization. It cultivated the arts and discovered the sciences; it wrote the books ... [13]

A defence of the leisured class's existence by way of its cultural productivity must be an inadequate justification, Russell reflects, given how 'extraordinarily wasteful' the model proved: 'one Darwin' for every 'tens of thousands of country gentlemen who never thought of anything more intelligent than fox-hunting and punishing poachers'. By 1935, in contrast, 'the universities [we]re supposed to provide, in a more systematic way, what the leisure class provided accidentally and as a by-product' (13).

The most pressing challenges for the modern university, as Russell saw them, were, first, that enlarged access to the privileged conditions of academic work had not of itself done much to close the gap between 'the occupations and problems of ordinary men and women' and the occupations of the few who earn a salary for intellectual labour. In other words, democratization of access to the university had not yet ushered in a more democratic conception of what university work should be about, and whom it should be for. Russell presumably does not mean to suggest that universities should become more receptive to popular culture, though his views are, on this occasion, tacit (he was no Raymond Williams or Stuart Hall, and in other contexts bemoaned the downward slide of culture towards the popular).[14] Second, the academic institutions of the 1930s were, in Russell's view, too

---

[12] George Orwell, 'Inside the Whale', in George Orwell, Essays, ed. John Carey (London: Everyman, [1940] 2002), 211–49 (228). The phrase 'idle rich' is from George Orwell, 'The Lion and the Unicorn: Socialism and the English Genius' (London: Searchlight Books, 1941), 291–348 (306).

[13] Bertrand Russell, *In Praise of Idleness, and Other Essays*, with a new preface by Anthony Gottlieb, introduction by Howard Woodhouse (London: Routledge, 1996), 13.

[14] See Bertrand Russell, 'Some Prospects: Cheerful and Otherwise', in *Sceptical Essays*, with a new preface by John Gray (London: Routledge, [1928] 1996), 202–17 (214).

utilitarian, too instrumental in their conceptions of teaching and research, for really original minds to flourish in them. The benefits of intellectual freedom had not, in that respect, kept pace with advances in social justice—though whether he is diagnosing a fault of institutional systems, or making a vaguer complaint about the dearth of originality at all levels of society, is never entirely clear.[15]

On both points, Russell is inclined again to point the finger at an unhealthy disjunction between the freedoms of the university and the constraints of the world beyond the university. Close that gap, and the work of the university will improve, he suggests. For a start, academics will want to write more accessibly, 'without the academic detachment that makes the work of [say] university economists often seem lacking in reality', and with a view to engaging a 'general public' now equipped with the leisure to take an interest in what they have to say. As things stand,

> University life is so different from life in the world at large that men who live in an academic *milieu* tend to be unaware of the preoccupations and problems of ordinary men and women; moreover their ways of expressing themselves are usually such as to rob their opinions of the influence that they ought to have upon the general public...
>
> In a world where no one is compelled to work more than four hours a day, every person possessed of scientific curiosity will be able to indulge it, and every painter will be able to paint without starving,...   (13–14)

Egalitarian access to leisure (a lot of leisure) is here presumed to drive equality of opportunity for engagement in intellectual culture, with general social benefits having priority over any predictable rise in the level of culture. If the paintings done in the young painter's spare time turn out not to be of the highest calibre, just as the young university economist's work is not always as original as it might be, then *tant pis* (to echo Russell's fondness for borrowed French *élan*): at least there will be less cause for the painter to resent the special privileges that make the academic's underachievement and his/her incomprehensibility to the man and woman in the street look like a waste of public resources, while the non-academic worker's creative potential simply goes untested. We will, in short, have fewer mute inglorious Miltons weighing on our collective conscience.

In the new world of equitably shared leisure, 'There will be happiness and joy of life', *In Praise of Idleness* concludes, 'instead of frayed nerves, weariness, and dyspepsia. The work exacted will be enough to make leisure delightful, but not enough to produce exhaustion. Ordinary men and women...will become more kindly and less persecuting and less inclined to view others with suspicion. The

---

[15] Russell, *In Praise of Idleness*, 13–14.

taste for war will die out', partly for this reason, and partly because war will start to look too much like hard work (14–15). 'Good nature' will abound (15). The 'elderly pundi[t]' (14), as Russell appears to denominate himself at the end, is in fantasy land by this point, and at some risk, perhaps, of eliciting low-level cynicism in lieu of the energized optimism he looks for.

The serio-comic air of 'In Praise of Idleness' has led at least one recent critic to identify it as, indeed, a modern exercise in cynic provocation[16]—challenging the normative assumption that work is a necessity, but ducking the 'next step' of proposing a serious political programme for social reform (I expand on a brief critical hint). Cynicism, on this reading, would be doing what it has always done philosophically: debasing the moral currency—in this case, the conventional moral currency of labour, but also, and (it may be) more provokingly in the eyes of advocates for the modern university, the currency of intellectual freedom, with the observation that most of what it gives rise to does not justify—though it may warrant—the special privileges required to produce it.

Russell, it is important to note, did not conceive of himself as a cynic, but his exposure to the charge lends additional interest to 'On Youthful Cynicism', one of the make-weight pieces added to 'In Praise of Idleness' for the volume's publication (121–9). Russell here explicitly identifies cynicism as a condition or illness afflicting 'the intelligent young' in 'the Universities of the Western world' and in need of 'cure' (121). Its main cause, he argues, is 'always comfort without power. The holders of power are not cynical, since they are able to enforce their ideals. Victims of oppression are not cynical, since they are filled with hate, and hate, like any other strong passion, brings with it a train of attendant beliefs' (127). This leaves cynicism the domain of the exposed middle—those intellectually equipped to recognize the collapse of religious faith, the danger of patriotism as a guiding ideal, the narrow basis of claims to 'progress', the inadequacy of 'beauty' as a salve for a divided and harsh world, the cumulative damage done by many philosophical assaults on 'truth' with no compensatory guidance towards alternative ideals (123–6).

Cynicism is institutionally nourished in the West, Russell argues, by the ease of obtaining and keeping an academic job—a claim that looks wildly archaic now and was not true even then (as he knew from personal experience). He is, himself, happy to wax cynical on the demoralization encouraged by security: the 'aims' of the institutional employer 'probably seem absurd, if not pernicious' to the young intellectual, he pronounces. Cynicism becomes a way of 'adjust[ing]' (127). It is an argument that might more plausibly run the other way—institutional *in*security exacerbating the scenario in which an educated capacity for critical scepticism undermines the ability to foster ideals strong enough to withstand that scepticism,

---

[16] W. D. Desmond, *Cynics* (Stocksfield: Acumen, 2008), 126–7.

or even take force from it. In any case, Russell discriminates between the academic divisions of the university. The man of science will be all right, able still to pursue 'wholly admirable' work to the general public benefit. Far more vulnerable is the 'literary intellectual':

> if a man's education has been literary, as is still too often the case, he finds himself at the age of twenty-two with a considerable skill that he cannot exercise in any manner that appears important to himself... If this diagnosis is right, modern cynicism cannot be cured merely by preaching, or by putting better ideals before the young than those that their pastors and masters fish out from the rusty armoury of outworn superstitions. The cure will only come when intellectuals can find a career that embodies their creative impulses. I do not see any prescription except the old one advocated by Disraeli: 'Educate our masters.'
>
> (127–8)

'Youth' and 'literary intellectualism' have, in effect, blended here in a composite image of what it means to be educated but without the social or economic power to act upon the consequences of one's own finely tuned intelligence.

And if the diagnosis is correct, what is Russell himself? An enlightened educator, helpfully close to the 'masters'? A man, privileged by dint of age, inherited position, and institutional affiliations, who has found in public moralism and essay journalism an outlet for his own idealism and creativity? Or a man increasingly drawn to the humanistic and socially engaged aspects of philosophy, but too well-versed in scepticism and cognizant of the limits of his own power and institutional security (notwithstanding his age, social status, and institutional advantages) to peddle any simple idealism; a man for whom, as much as for the young, cynicism is a way of 'adjust[ing]' aspiration to the cramping conditions of possibility?

The Public Intellectual as Moral Controversialist

Moral controversialism is hardly co-extensive with the exercise of intellectual freedom, and one can be a moral controversialist with few if any pretensions to intellectualism, but where the two functions coincide, they amplify a structural tension endemic (as Stefan Collini observes) to the role of public intellectual.[17] Contesting norms of belief, or agreed standards of conduct, on general questions of public morality, the intellectual controversialist can expect to trigger protests that he or she has overstepped the bounds of expertise. Russell's peculiarly volatile

---

[17] Stefan Collini, *Absent Minds: Intellectuals in Britain* (Oxford: Oxford University Press, 2006), 57–8.

stylistic performances in the role of public moralist—crisp dispatching of matters of logic is frequently interrupted by provocative, funny, sometimes waspish barbs and causticities against the arrogance and complacencies of the current moral climate and those it empowers—are, I take it, indicative of a recognition that there is more than one kind of problem here. There is the common problem detected when an individual proficient in one domain of academia (namely, philosophy of mathematics) takes up a public position on matters of common interest, outside the legitimate scope of that expertise; there is a more basic problem of whether *anyone* can hope 'calmly' and 'quietly' to assert the authority of reason with respect to norms of morality that are not matters of logic or objective assessment but of social agreement or, as he prefers to put it, 'opinion'.[18] (Clearly he had limited expectations of social-scientific data.)

The difference between epistemological and moral scepticism, as Russell sets it out in the *Sceptical Essays* (1928), is that, in matters of epistemology, expert consensus and plain 'common sense' can play a large role in guiding us; in matters of morality, often 'no sufficient ground for a positive opinion exist[s]' (2); unhelp-fully, beliefs tend to be held with a strength and passion almost inversely propor-tional to their warrant in reason. He is by no means a pure relativist or an out-and-out denier of the importance of ethical rules and standards: he is clear on the viciousness of permitting children to swallow pins, for example.[19] What is at issue is not whether there should be 'an element' of moral restraint on behaviour, an assertion of 'discipline and authority', but what is to be the agreed 'amount of it', how it is 'to be exercised', and how best to secure advances in liberalism that will take society beyond the medieval (and even pre-medieval) ways of thinking about matters of high importance, including war and sex (157).

One work more than any other made Russell's peculiar combination of thor-oughgoing moral scepticism and utopian moral idealism the focus of public debate about the proper scope and tenor of academic freedom.[20] *Marriage and Morals* (1929) was his most widely controversial and commercially successful attempt to further the cause of sexual liberation. As he saw it, the sexual morality of Western societies in the late 1920s was the product of two principal historic forces: the 'desire for certainty as to fatherhood', and an 'ascetic' (largely Pauline) belief that sex, other than for purposes of procreation, is wicked (185). Both influences, in Russell's view, possessed no warrant to guide belief and action in the modern age. The assurance of paternity, once an advantage to families and communities in turbulent states of society, had been rendered increasingly unnecessary by expansion of the role of the state. Once the state offers to safeguard the child's health, education, and well-being,

---

[18] Bertrand Russell, *Marriage and Morals* (London: Routledge, [1929] 2009), 160.

[19] Bertrand Russell, 'Freedom versus Authority in Education', in *Sceptical Essays*, 157–72 (157).

[20] Though his writing against conscription and in defence of conscientious objection had, famously, lost him his academic position at Trinity College, Cambridge, in 1916 (he was offered reinstatement in 1919), the war texts attracted less intense controversy, and sold much less well, than *Marriage and Morals*.

Russell argues, one can 'expect a complete breakdown of traditional morality, since there will no longer be any reason why a mother should wish the paternity of her child to be indubitable' (5). Statism is a benign force in this argument; not so the power of the Church, which takes the brunt of Russell's anger for centuries of moral tyranny, unfounded in reason or virtue.

Marriage and Morals is written with reformist zeal, but it is also a scholarly work, drawing on the comparative cultural perspectives of ethnography, and (with reservations) the insights of psychology. On that basis, rather than his own libertarian sentiments (though the latter are evident), Russell reasons that sexual ethics are customary, not natural, and that recent advances in the invention of contraception, more effective treatments for sexual disease, and, crucially, the emancipation of women have made changes 'desirable both from a private and public point of view'. He recommends:

- an end to the taboo on sexual knowledge (ignorance does harm, and deliberately withholding or misrepresenting facts undermines trust between generations);
- revision of the laws on obscenity to permit intelligent discussion of the case for reform;
- (in line with *In Praise of Idleness*), the overthrow of the 'gospel of modern work and economic success' to make possible individual and familial happiness of a kind unsustainable amid the 'money-making struggle';
- a new ethic with children at its centre. Where there is conflict between the needs of children and the adult claims of 'passionate love', children take precedence. Divorce should be made easier, but where children are involved, all desirable efforts should be made to protect the stability of marriage.
- husbands and wives must cease to regard themselves as one another's 'policemen', and 'learn to understand that whatever the law may say, in their private lives they must be free'.

The arguments are rational, and directed at an ideal balance between liberty of personal conduct and responsibility to minors; the style of reasoning is frequently cynical and nowhere more so than in the handling of motive. In principle, Russell took a hard line against attribution of motive in the course of arguments about morality, both in the interests of truth (how can we know other people's motives?) and in the service of advancing progressive ideals (getting bogged down in questions of individual and collective motive does little to help us identify more rational and socially beneficial moral agreements, he thought). By way of antidote against unwarranted assumptions, *Marriage and Morals* (1929) warmly recommends a practice found in Jeremy Bentham:

Bentham made a table of the springs of action, where every human desire was named in three parallel columns, according as men wish to praise it, to blame it, or to treat it neutrally. Thus we find in one column 'gluttony', and opposite it, in the next column, 'love of the pleasures of the social board'. And again, we find in the column giving eulogistic names to impulses, 'public spirit', and opposite to it, in the next column, we find 'spite'. I recommend anybody who wishes to think clearly on any ethical topic to imitate Bentham in this particular, and after accustoming himself to the fact that almost every word conveying blame has a synonym conveying praise, to acquire a habit of using words that convey neither praise nor blame. (36)

The attractions of such quasi-mathematical habits of thought, the plus and the minus term offering to cancel one other out, suggest a natural alliance between the founding father of utilitarianism and the logician turned public moralist and political activist. But to read *Marriage and Morals* in the light of Russell's 'neutrality' precept is to find him repeatedly, and deliberately, falling foul of it.

Far from avoiding speculation on what drives those standing in the way of liberalization, Russell is quick to discern in them the same motivation that he finds at work behind the conservatism of the churches: preservation of their own power at all costs.

> If...the old morality is to be re-established, certain things are essential;.... The first...is that the education of girls should be such as to make them stupid and superstitious and ignorant; this requisite is already fulfilled in schools over which the Churches have any control. The next requisite is a very severe censorship upon all books giving information on sex subjects;.... These conditions,...since they exist already, are clearly insufficient. The only thing that will suffice is to remove from young women all opportunity of being alone with men: girls must be forbidden to earn their living by work outside the home; they must never be allowed an outing unless accompanied by their mother or an aunt...It must be illegal for an unmarried woman under fifty to possess a motor-car, and perhaps it would be wise to subject all unmarried women once a month to medical examination by police doctors, and to send to a penitentiary all such as were found to be not virgins... [A]ll policemen and all medical men should be castrated. Perhaps it would be wise to carry this policy a step farther,... [M]oralists would be well advised to advocate that all men should be castrated, with the exception of ministers of religion. (Note:...I have begun to feel that even this exception is perhaps not quite wise.)

One slight hypothecating 'if' launches a flood of satire against a hypothecated conservatism that assumes all women are potential sluts (but also that all women are weak, therefore controllable sluts) and all men inherently depraved (but also strong, so carceral measures will not be enough to contain them). In question is not whether the process of liberation can be stopped (cynical assumption number one is that supporters of the 'old' morality are too complacent to have observed that it is already well under way), but what it would take to put it into reverse (cynical assumption number two is that the forces of reaction and self-interest will support any extremity of response).

The greatest danger Russell perceives is that failure to accept the need for liberalization will create intergenerational conflict around the extent of individual sexual freedom permitted by society. In other words, a dangerous cynicism on the part of those vested in maintaining the status quo will drive a wedge between young and old, and (to a lesser extent) women and men. How far the young—especially young women—might go in defence of their freedoms Russell was not prepared to guess. 'This whole [feminist-egalitarian] movement is as yet in a very early phase,' he observes, 'and it is impossible to say how it will develop. Its adherents and practitioners as yet are mostly quite young. They have very few champions among persons of weight and importance.' Given the imbalance of power between old and young, this situation seemed to him quite 'unstable'. One of two things will happen, he predicts: 'either the old will become aware of the facts and will set to work to deprive the young of their new-won freedom, or the young, growing up, will themselves acquire positions of dignity and importance, which will make it possible to give the sanction of authority to the new morality' (53).

Marriage and Morals had been in wide circulation for over a decade when the City College of New York announced in early 1940 that it was appointing Russell to a seventeen-month visiting professorship of philosophy, starting 1 February 1941. The letter of appointment from the Chairman of the New York Board of Higher Education, Ordway Tead, was 'a little odd' (Russell's biographer, Ray Monk notes), looking forward to Russell 'deepening and extending the interest of the College in the philosophic bases of human living'—wording that suggests an expectation that the college would capitalize on his popularity as a moral controversialist, though the professorial offer related only to teaching courses on logic and on the philosophy of mathematics and science.[21] Opposition came speedily, led by Dr William T. Manning, Episcopal Bishop of New York, whose fulminations against 'a man who is a recognized propagandist against both religion and morality, and who specifically defends adultery' were printed in all the New York newspapers and reported widely across the United States.[22] An 'extraordinary campaign of vilification' followed, led by the religious press but quickly gaining traction with politicians and elements of the public. On 15 March, the City Council of New York (CCNY) lined up with Russell's antagonists and passed a resolution calling upon the Board of Higher Education to revoke the appointment.[23]

[21] Ray Monk, *Bertrand Russell, 1921–70: The Ghost of Madness* (London: Jonathan Cape, 2000), 231.
[22] Ibid., 232.   [23] Ibid., 233.

The Deweyan Defence of Moral Controversialism

That John Dewey would come to the defence of Russell in this crisis was not necessarily to be expected. The two had met in 1920, when they coincided on visits to China. Dewey disliked Russell's apparent 'insensitiveness to other people's feelings', on that occasion.[24] He had no hesitation, however, and plentiful support, in defending Russell's appointment: the CCNY Philosophy department, the Committee for Cultural Freedom, and much of the wider American philosophical community joined in protesting on behalf of Russell's right to say what he had said on the subject of sexual morality, even if many (Dewey certainly) had reservations about the manner of arguing.

'The Case for Bertrand Russell' stands out from the substantial literature generated by this subject for the clarity with which Dewey distinguishes between three kinds of freedom at stake: (i) the institutional freedom of the City College of New York to make appointments to academic positions without legal interference; (ii) the intellectual freedom of any appointee to an academic post to address other 'adults' on 'matters of social importance' (that is, to act in the capacity of a public intellectual); and then (iii) the more particular kind of freedom asserted by a moral controversialist.

The institutional point is straightforward. Dewey is satisfied with stating the legal fact, and the predictable repercussions of contradicting it: to challenge the independence of university appointments is potentially to throw all such processes into time-consuming and costly legal 'uncertainty'; in the long term, such interference will strip 'responsibility as well as ... power' from educational administrators (a point to come back to). As to Russell's freedom of intellectual self-expression on matters of general public interest: his opponents, as Dewey presents them (not without a cynical edge of his own) are driven by a sinister interpretation of Russell's motives, according to which he uses academic freedom as a 'cloak' to promote 'popularization in the minds of adolescents of acts forbidden by the Penal Law' (236). He is, in short, a self-serving pervert: or, in the preferred lexicon of his attackers, 'lecherous, salacious, libidinous, lustful, venerous, erotomaniac, aphrodisiac, atheistic, irreverent, narrow-minded, untruthful, and bereft of moral fiber' (236). Dewey does not describe this response as 'hysteria', nor does he refer to 'witch hunts' or 'Salem'. He ventures a more neutral and generalizable psychological explanation. Moral disturbance of this kind is a symptom of 'cultural lag'

---

[24] Ray Monk, *Bertrand Russell: The Spirit of Solitude* (London: Jonathan Cape, 1996), 591. After the CCNY fracas was over, Russell would indeed show himself uninhibited in his antagonism to Dewey's 'instrumentalism'—though, many years earlier, he had told Lady Ottoline Morrell that Dewey's was 'the only mind of real quality' he encountered in America (Monk, *Ghost of Madness*, 276). See Jay Martin, *The Education of John Dewey: A Biography* (New York: Columbia University Press, 2002), 253.

nowhere more evident than in the discrepancy existing between the conclusions of specialists in anthropology, medicine, psychology, and so on upon general matters of ethical theory—not just special matters of sexual ethics—and popular beliefs, which, when they have not been received from some dogmatic institutional source, have usually been picked up from the flotsam and jetsam of old traditions. Because of this discrepancy any public discussion based upon results reached by scientific investigators but couched in words that can be understood by those without specialized technical training is bound to be disturbing, and even shocking. (232)

The individual who interprets 'the conclusions of specialists' to the wider public is, in this reading, almost 'bound' to appear to those without his 'technical training' as a moral controversialist. The motive, then, for challenging existing norms (the 'actual' motive, not whatever dark purpose is ascribed by those defending existing mores) is vital to any decision about the rightness or wrongness of his or her intervention.

To find what Dewey has to say about the justification for moral controversialism it is necessary to look back a few years before his intervention in the Russell Case, to Part II of the revised *Ethics* (1932), the 'Theory of the Moral Life'.[25] Moral life emerges, for Dewey, out of the conflict between 'the urgent claims of developing personality' (felt as 'intelligence and desire') and 'the authority of the group, embodied in custom and institutions' (97). A long view of the history of morality is brought to bear here. The special contribution of the Greeks in the development of ethics, Dewey claims, was to make self-development increasingly understood as 'a civic and not merely an individual' process (97). The 'new' theoretical views put forward by 'Socrates, Plato, Aristotle, Cynics, Cyrenaics, Epicureans, and Stoics' (98) encouraged a way of thinking that did not simply set the individual adrift from community and culture—'a stick of wood', as it were, 'spatially and numerically separate'—but perceived her/him as 'an individual *because of and in relations with others*' (227, my emphasis). This reading of the ancient texts is consistent with Dewey's career-long effort to present intelligence not as a given but as the product of education and experience, and to enrich and improve a concept of democracy that, in America, looked to him to have produced 'little more than a leveling of individuals and "messy confusion"'.[26]

The Cynics are only one group in the line-up of Greek schools contributing to an increasingly holistic view of individualism in the ancient world, but they mark an important point of intellectual return for Dewey. Cynicism, as he reads it (again, conventionally enough) toughens the edges of conflict between individual

---

[25] In *The Later Works of John Dewey, 1925–1953*, CW VII.

[26] Martin, *Education*, 359—reflecting on Dewey's three important books of the 1920s: *Human Nature and Conduct* (1922), *Experience and Nature* (1925), and *The Quest for Certainty* (1929).

ideas of the 'right' and the established views of the community. 'The principle of right has . . . a natural basis and inevitable role' deriving from 'the social claims which attend human relations' (228–9). In other words, Dewey, like Russell to this extent, understands morality to be produced and sufficiently secured through social agreements. 'Any *particular* claim' to define the good and the proper ends of life, however, 'is open to examination and criticism. Is it entitled to claim the authority of right for itself? Is it truly rightful?' (229).

Confronted with the conflict between individual and social, Dewey observes, the Cynics chose individualism, 'with the emphasis on independence from wants' (109). 'Society, they held, is artificial. Its so-called goods, on the one hand, and its restrictions on the other, are to be rejected unless they favor the individual's happiness' (110). The *problems* with Cynicism emerge from how Antisthenes, Diogenes, and their followers interpreted 'the state of nature' in opposition to the artifice of custom. Helpful though they were in putting particular ideas of 'right' to the test, they erred, Dewey argues, in espousing a reductive view of 'nature', associating it with 'primitive beginnings' instead of 'the fullest development' of life. Their limitation of pleasure to the satisfaction of the barest 'natural' wants involves, he implies, a risible turning of their backs on the advances of civilization. In sum: 'the state of nature was opposed to the State' (110). More expansively, Dewey quotes Wilhelm Windeland's *History of Philosophy* (1898) (translated by his close friend, James Hayden Tufts):[27] 'Art and science, family and native land, were indifferent. Wealth and refinement, fame and honor'—and, one might add, friendship and the pleasures of scholarship—'seemed as superfluous as those enjoyments of the senses which went beyond the satisfaction of the natural wants of hunger and sex' (110).

In essence, Dewey follows the Platonic and Aristotelian response to the Cynics, here, defending a conception of nature that looks to its 'complete development', and laying the foundations of his political philosophy on that basis: the State is 'a natural institution', as Aristotle put it in *Politics* I.ii (quoted by Dewey, 112); whatever the individual's development is to be follows from the associations the State makes possible or prohibits—including what it admits in the way of the individual's ability to challenge 'all society's laws and standards and bring them to the bar of knowledge' (118). It is an argument for the symbiosis of individual and society, but it is also, more directively, an argument for the logical and moral priority of the group: 'In the order of nature the State is prior to the household or individual. For the whole must needs be prior to its part' (112).

What Dewey has to say, subsequently, about the justification for moral conformity follows from these premises. Indeed, the perception that moral non-conformity *requires* a justification, and is not simply to be defended in itself, or

---

[27] Jane M. Dewey, 'Biography of John Dewey', in Paul Arthur Schilpp (ed.), *The Philosophy of John Dewey* (New York: Tudor Publishing Co., 1939), 3–45 (24).

for its own sake, is of a piece with his insistence that there is no such thing as an individual apart from the social whole. 'The justification of the moral non-conformist is that when he denies the rightfulness of a particular claim he is doing so not for the sake of private advantage, but for the sake of an object which will serve more amply and consistently the welfare of all. The burden of proof is upon him' (230).

This is not a licence to cause trouble. The non-conformist has a right to assert his or her own judgement that what is currently thought 'right' or 'obligatory' should not be thought so—but public spiritedness is required. Moral non-conformity makes 'a social claim', and that claim cannot rest solely on the authority of the individual who enacts the challenge: it has to be 'tested and confirmed by further trial by others'. And when that happens, what one asks of the non-conformist is that s/he 'suffe[r] the consequences' of having initiated a disturbance in the status quo: 'patience, cheerfulness, freedom from conceit, self-display, and self-pity are demanded', with the corollary that conformists, or would-be conformists, have in their turn a 'duty of toleration' (231).

This is a normative (or would-be normative) view of non-conformity—one that risks, and presumably knows that it risks, taking the edge and much of the fun out of trouble-making. No-one gets to throw their toys out of the pram on a whim, in this way of looking at things. Which makes the tone and temperature of Dewey's intervention in the Russell case the more interesting: angrier, more agitated, more urgent than the theoretical ethicist of 1932 had envisaged might be required in the way of defending moral controversialism—and not quite sure what to do with that anger other than repeatedly to admit it, then put it to one side while advancing the defence. 'I shall not even raise a question that is of great social importance', he asserts (indicatively), only to spell it out: 'How and why is it that in eleven short years there has been such a growth of intolerance and bigotry? My part in this volume of record and protest is to point out the immense difference between the realities of the case . . . and the opinion' (237).

Dewey is not in every respect a good reader of Russell. *Marriage and Morals* is a much more feminist book than Dewey allows. It is a book that puts the potential non-alignment of generational interests to the fore, where Dewey prefers to think of 'welfare' as a general good, shared by 'all', even though he admits that the balancing of priorities for individual against social development is itself subject to generational changes in perception.[28] Not least, it is a book of confrontational and sometimes savage humour almost unrecognizable in Dewey's defensive description of an 'argument, based upon facts', reflecting 'the attitude of scientific students', and 'serious in spite of an occasional regrettable asperity of tone' (233). It is a regrettable note of regret (and perhaps he sees the book more clearly

[28] See esp. John Dewey, 'The Theory of the Chicago Experiment', in *The Dewey School*, Appendix 2, in *The Later Works*, 202–16 (204).

than he admits), but it sets the tone for a common kind of ambivalence and, more than ambivalence, a reluctance to let the cynic, qua moral controversialist, have the floor—even as the critic defends in principle his or her right to be there.

Which brings me to today, and to Laura Kipnis.

'A Cynic Might Say...': Laura Kipnis and the Idea of the University

Unwanted Advances: Sexual Paranoia Comes to Campus by Laura Kipnis (2017) is—within Deweyan limits—a cynic text for our times. The immediate point of discussion is narrowly American: recent institutional interpretations of Title IX, the 1972 amendment to the US Higher Education Act that affirms a student's right to be free from sexual discrimination.[29] Federal funding for higher education has, since 2011, been dependent upon an institution responding satisfactorily to complaints, taking 'immediate and effective steps to end sexual harassment and sexual violence'.[30] Its national legal focus notwithstanding, *Unwanted Advances* explores cultural tensions between libertarianism and identitarianism, between free speech and regulatory protection from harm, that are widely in evidence on university campuses around the globe at present—in Britain, Canada, India, Australia, New Zealand, and elsewhere.

Kipnis comes to Title IX with a track record of controversial writing about contemporary sexual morality. The subjects she has taken on in the past include the pleasures of adultery, the liberatory aspects of pornography, and (most saliently) the degree to which women themselves can be held responsible for the incoherence of contemporary attitudes towards female sexual agency, ostensibly 'the vanguard class when it comes to gender progress', yet '*fettered* in so many traditionally feminine ways'—now 'entirely self-imposed'.[31] Kipnis's teaching specialism is in film studies, but her public moralism exhibits wide cultural range and a keen interest in the dynamics of sexual transgression and sexual fantasy as they play out in the distinct but not separate worlds of academia and 'beyond'. The faux tentative self-positioning of *Against Love* is germane: 'Might we entertain the possibility that posing philosophical questions [about love and liberty] isn't restricted to university campuses and learned tomes, that it's

---

[29] United States Department of Justice, 'Overview of Title IX of the Education Amendments of 1972, 20, U.S.C. A§ 1681 Et. Seq.', updated 7 August 2015', <https://www.justice.gov/crt/overview-title-ix-education-amendments-1972-20-usc-1681-et-seq>. Accessed 28 June 2018.

[30] United States Department of Education, 'Title IX and Sex Discrimination', revised April 2015, <https://www2.ed.gov/about/offices/list/ocr/docs/tix_dis.html>.

[31] Laura Kipnis, *The Female Thing: Dirt, Envy, Sex, Vulnerability* (London: Serpent's Tail, 2007), xiv. See also Laura Kipnis, *Against Love: A Polemic* (New York: Pantheon Books, 2003); Laura Kipnis, *Bound and Gagged: Pornography and the Politics of Fantasy in America* (Durham, NC: Duke University Press, 1996).

something everyone does in the course of everyday life—if not always in an entirely knowing fashion?' (28). Closed minds get short shrift from Kipnis, on either side of the specialist/non-specialist divide: 'I don't care if my students buy the Freudian line', she writes in *Unwanted Advances*, describing her route into class discussion of how desire relates to prohibition: 'it's a heuristic, not a set of unassailable truths' (29). Willingness to tolerate humour is crucial: she is naughtily funny, more than a little fond of so-called 'harmless joke[s]' (35) that tap knowingly into the Freudian understanding of the tendentious joke as an assault on institutional power, 'open[ing] up sources of pleasure that have become inaccessible' (see Introduction, p. CI.P49).

Kipnis's stated intention, on this occasion, is to call attention to administrative interpretations of sexual equality law that have infringed other core legal rights within higher education, including intellectual freedom and freedom of expression. She details several cases, references many more, in which a 'culture of sexual panic' (44) has led to allegations of misconduct being handled without due process, without transparency, and with serious punitive consequences (loss of employment; expulsion from a course of study; professional and personal reputational damage). *Unwanted Advances* takes aim at a 'feminist paternalist' university management culture that she sees as failing in honesty about 'the sexual realities and ambivalences hidden behind the notion of "rape culture"'; it identifies a broader target in 'the covert sexual conservatism of hookup culture', and 'the institutionalized backlash of holding men alone responsible for mutually drunken sex' (jacket blurb). Ambivalence towards sex rather goes with the terrain, Kipnis observes—sexual desire is 'leaky', 'idio[tic]', 'messy'[32]—but she objects strenuously to a recent pattern of reinterpreting ambivalence in hindsight as ground for accusations of assault or rape.

Four Title IX complaints were made against Kipnis, in the course of writing *Unwanted Advances*—writing about Title IX accusations generating more Title IX accusations which generate more writing, . . . and so on. The melodramatic circularity befits an analysis alert to the melodramatic aspects of 'complaint culture': its 'theatricalized dissent' (in Elaine Hadley's nice description); the reliance on 'polarities of good and evil'; the particular (but not exclusive) focus on 'scripts devoted to the moral plight of women'.[33] Broadly, the charges against Kipnis have been that, in publishing an article in *The Chronicle of Higher Education* and a subsequent tweet about Northwestern's response to a Title IX accusation against a colleague in Philosophy, she had '"a chilling effect" on students' ability to report

---

[32] On leakiness and idiocy, see Christine Smallwood interview, 'Laura Kipnis's Battle against Vulnerability', *The New Yorker* 2 April 2017, <https://www.newyorker.com/culture/persons-of-interest/laura-kipniss-battle-against-vulnerability>. Accessed 28 June 2018; on messiness, Laura Kipnis, *Unwanted Advances: Sexual Paranoia Comes to Campus* (New York: Harper, 2017), 43 and *passim*.

[33] Elaine Hadley, *Melodramatic Tactics: Theatricalized Dissent in the English Marketplace, 1800–1885* (Stanford, CA: Stanford University Press, 1995), title, 110, 133.

sexual misconduct'; that she 'made deliberate mistakes' when describing one case, in 'violation of the norms of academic integrity' (148); that she breached the faculty's 'non-retaliation policy' and thus created a 'hostile environment' for students wanting to exercise their right to complain (137); and, finally, that she was 'potentially involve[d] in/or approv[ed] of' statements made by her own Faculty support person in the university's Faculty Senate (148). Not all the complaints have been first-hand: one was made on behalf of another student, deemed by the complainant to have been potentially harmed. At the time of writing, at least one lawsuit against Kipnis and her publishers (for public disclosure of private facts, false-light invasion of privacy, defamation, and intentional infliction of emotional distress)[34] is in process.

Unwanted Advances asks to be understood as a work of intellectual, over and above moral, provocation. The two are linked: you cannot think clearly about moral norms if you are not prepared to entertain questions about their validity—though the performative zest with which Kipnis undertakes that task is in part what marks the approach out as strategically cynic. 'I like stirring up trouble', she announces on p. 1:

> Despite being a feminist, something in me hates a slogan, even well-intentioned ones like "rape culture". Worse, I tend to be ironic—I *like* irony; it helps you think because it gives you critical distance on a thing. Irony doesn't sit very well in the current climate, especially when it comes to irony *about* the current climate. Critical distance itself is out of fashion—not exactly a plus when it comes to intellectual life (or education itself). Feelings are what's in fashion. I'm all for feelings; I'm a standard-issue female, after all. But this cult has an authoritarian underbelly...   (1–2)

There is something curious, even awry, about a work of 'irony' that has to announce itself as such. As the book proceeds, irony does, indeed, become the lost, or displaced, term—the preferred mode of a critical intelligence that discerns little room, in the present climate, for irony's characteristic wash of uncertainty, and perforce adopts a more explicit confrontationalism. The interpretation of 'critical distance' that Kipnis espouses here, and that she would have her reader

---

[34] Allyson Chiu and Matthew Choi, 'In Focus: Graduate Student Sues Professor for Invasion of Privacy, Defamation Following Book Release', *Daily Northwestern*, 22 May 2017, <https://dailynorthwestern.com/2017/05/22/campus/northwestern-graduate-student-sues-professor-for-invasion-of-privacy-defamation-following-book-release/>; and see Danuta Kean, 'Study of "Sexual Paranoia" on US Campuses Draws Lawsuit from Student', *The Guardian*, 18 May 2017, <https://www.theguardian.com/books/2017/may/18/study-of-sexual-paranoia-us-campuses-lawsuit-from-student-laura-kipnis>; Jane O'Grady *Unwanted Advances*, *Times Higher Education*, 22 June 2017, <https://www.timeshighereducation.com/books/review-unwanted-advances-laura-kipnis-harper-collins>. Accessed 2 July 2018. Maddie Burakoff, 'Kipnis Lawsuit Moves Forward [...]', *The Daily Northwestern* 9 March 2018, <https://dailynorthwestern.com/2018/03/09/campus/kipnis-lawsuit-moves-forward-as-judge-declines-motion-to-dismiss-the-case/>. Accessed 28 June 2018.

recognize as vital to 'intellectual life' (or, lowering the pitch, just 'education'), rests on clarity not obliquity. Framed in classic Cynic terms: she tests the moral norms of today's campus, 'forestall[ing] easy moralizing' (28) and challenging a 'cultural script' whereby sex is increasingly cognate with 'danger', not 'pleasure' (218). 'Contrarian, free-spoken', this is an image of cultural criticism unconstrained by current 'fashions', unimpressed by cheap 'slogans', and alert to the coercive aspect of the political mobilization of feeling (its 'cultish' and 'authoritarian' power).

In espousing the role of provocateur, Kipnis could hope to pass the Deweyan test for justified moral controversialism with little difficulty: this is cynicism explicitly directed towards restoring the university's commitment to freedom of critical inquiry and free critical speech (not everyone will accept the starting assumption that these freedoms have been lost); also towards shoring up sexual liberty, though Kipnis places limits on what is acceptable speech and acceptable sex on campus. The brunt of her criticism is directed at new codes prohibiting 'all dating, romantic or sexual relations between undergraduates and faculty members, consensual or not' and looking to regulate faculty relationships with graduate students (20). Longer-standing codes banning non-consensual sexual professor-student dating are repeatedly affirmed. She acknowledges, many times over, that sexual assault is a reality and a crime; and by way of evidencing her empathy for those who have experienced or had reason to fear rape, she details late in the book her undergraduate terror (and its long after-effects) at having an intruder break into her apartment in the middle of a night. She is performatively affronting—'"Confidentiality?" "Conduct befitting a professor?" Kiss my ass' (34). She is clearly having fun; and yet this is also a mode of criticism audibly on the defensive. Were it not for that note of defensiveness, cynicism would consistently be the term of art for what it is doing, but it is an identification Kipnis evidently finds worrying as well as appealing.

The allure of the cynic confrontation with power is strongest with respect to university administrators. Contemplating the feminism of today's campuses, deploying Title IX 'to remedy sexual ambivalences or awkward sexual experiences, and to adjudicate relationship disputes post-breakup', Kipnis concludes: 'this feminism is broken. It has exactly nothing to do with gender equality or emancipating women—*a cynic might say* it actually has more to do with extending the reach of campus bureaucracy into everyone's lives' (17; my emphasis). Though this keeps the name of cynic at arm's length, the tactical alliance is clear. Elsewhere, cynicism appears as a self-characterization hitherto readily accessible, by implication widely if not generally understood in its function, but newly under threat in a system more and more resistant to critical challenge. Going through a Title IX process on her own behalf, Kipnis suggests, has made her 'a little mad...transformed from a harmless ironist [just doing her critical job, nothing more] into an aspiring whistleblower. High-flown terms like *due process* now spout from my cynic's lips' (34). Ethical and psychological consistency, then, requires her to resist co-optation into the current ethos and go on confronting the arrogance of power in the modern university—even as she recognizes that external political pressures on the university (including increased right-wing hostility) have played a part in creating a more defended, less flexible liberalism.

On the growth in power of the administration under Title IX, Kipnis is almost unwaveringly confrontational. The germ of *Unwanted Advances* was the 2015 essay in *The Chronicle*, arguing that 'the implementers of new campus codes' were overseeing the shaping of a landscape in which 'sexual panic rules. Slippery slopes abound. Gropers become rapists and accusers become survivors.'[35] *Unwanted Advances* takes further that line of resistance to the campus code—and it is salient that the role of the administrator looms larger in the book than in the article.[36] 'Teams of campus administrators' have been needed, the book now observes, to ensure Title IX compliance (16); the 'irony about this insistence on student vulnerability is how successful it's been as a tactic for accruing administrative power. Encouraging students' sense of fragility is swelling the ranks of potentially jobless professors while bolstering the power of administrations over faculty.' (25) To a degree, it is a line of cynicism that shows its (and Kipnis's) age: a beneficiary of, and participant in, earlier decades of anti-conformist advocacy for sexual liberation, she is, she remarks at one point, 'dispirit[ed] to find student activists, all assiduously pro-sex and genderqueer (at least sporting a lot of piercings and other insignias of nonconformity), joining arms with campus bureaucrats to demand wider prosecutorial nets for professorial sex offenders' (23). 'Benevolent officialdom' is, in one of her most potently cynical claims, a 'fiction'. A counterview (not aired) would recognize benign aspirations at work at a federal level here, however uneven the institutional enactment, and might also acknowledge that the financial scale and operational complexity of modern universities, and the demands upon them for legal compliance, necessitate some—though not necessarily all—of that administrative expansion. (Complaining about the expansion of administration is easy; identifying which parts are needed and which are superfluous is much less so, especially when fee-paying parents, and students themselves, start mounting legal challenges against the institution.)

Beyond the cynic scenting out of self-interest in administrators growing their power base, higher education administrators fall foul of a wider scepticism towards the university, depicted as a corporation that will do anything to protect its reputation and, thus, its revenue streams: 'there's no adequate method for

---

[35] Laura Kipnis, 'Sexual Paranoia Strikes Academe', The Chronicle Review, *The Chronicle of Higher Education*, 27 February 2015, <https://www.chronicle.com/article/Sexual-Paranoia-Strikes/190351>. Accessed 28 June 2018.

[36] 'I'd argued', she explains (3), 'that the new codes infantilized students and ramped up the climate of accusation'—this much is a correct summary of the original article—'while vastly increasing the power of university administrators over all our lives'—which is considerably stronger than the original claims.

sorting legitimate from specious claims... It's not in administrators' interests *to sort* them: a campus's success in "combatting sexual assault" is measured in increased accusations' (30). A late footnote indicates that more might be said, if time allowed for the gathering of evidence. It records the insight Kipnis gained from attendance at the 2016 Association of Title IX Administrators convention in Philadelphia. This is, literally, a cynicism in and of the marketplace. Walking past the exhibitor booths, crammed with 'assault prevention "products"', from smart-phone apps to training courses, she hears a salesman say 'smarmily to a potential customer: "Are you guys in one of those three-to-five-year contracts that everyone is in?"' There is, she concludes, 'an investigative story to be written about the revenues being generated by the expanding definitions of sexual assault, and what part of the educational pie is shrinking to cover it' (220). That's for another cynic day.

Only a few concessions to the administrative wing of the university soften the criticism: some Title IX officers spoke to Kipnis off the record, acknowledging that the universities' stance was 'incoherent and that everyone's left trying to figure out how to comply with insufficient and wildly contradictory directives' (140); indi-vidual administrators sometimes expressed concern about the underdefined, inadequately delimited powers given to them; and, since the book's publication, Kipnis has observed (in response to criticisms published by the feminist journal *Signs*) that, 'Title IX officers themselves have started acknowledging they've gone too far; see the recent white paper "Due Process and the Sex Police" (from NCHERM, one of the major Title IX consulting firms).'[37] It is a reference worth pursuing, since Kipnis's need of institutional allies at this point in the critical and prosecutorial follow-up to *Unwanted Advances* seems to hold her back from further criticism of the institution here, at a point where she could have found plenty more to work with.

NCHERM is a legal consultancy group specializing in higher education litiga-tion and risk management. Risk assessors, external advisors not direct employees of the university, sit in close relation with the administration, being the defensive avant-garde for challenges to the institution's interpretation of the law. The 2017 report alerts Title IX officers that a change in behaviour is urgently required to 'advance the commitment of the field to due process' (17) and afford 'the full measure of their rights' to responding parties (4). Where 'yesterday's environ-ment' required scepticism towards the professoriate and an active concern for victims, today's demands a reprioritization to due process and makes advisable

---

[37] Jaclyn Friedman, Kelly Oliver, Claire Potter, Aishah Shahidah Simmons, Lisa Wade, and Laura Kipnis, 'Short Takes: Laura Kipnis' *Unwanted Advances*', Short Takes: Provocations on Public Feminism, *SIGNS: Journal of Women in Culture and Society* (July 2017), <http://signsjournal. org/unwanted-advances/>. Accessed 28 June 2018. Citing The NCHERM Group, LLC, *The 2017 NCHERM Group White Paper: Due Process and the Sex Police*, <https://www.ncherm.org/wp-content/ uploads/2017/04/TNG-Whitepaper-Final-Electronic-Version.pdf>. Accessed 4 July 2018.

clear separation between sympathy for victims and victim-favouring (a still more scrupulously self-critical document would have referred to 'complainant-favoring'). A sharply confrontational section entitled 'Some of You Have Become the Sex Police' reads: 'we want you to know that The NCHERM Group condemns what you are doing in the strongest possible terms and entreats you to change your thinking and your practices' (4). A 'Note about Tone' anticipates objections:

> There are some readers who might perceive this publication to be less victim-centered than our previous body of work. We'd suggest that perception is only accurate in comparison to the tone of our past work, which was needed at the time we wrote it, to catalyze an important shift needed in the field at that time. Now, the tone of this publication is appropriate to the environment in which we are writing today. As times change, our guidance has to as well. We intend this publication to build on the strong foundation of victim-centered (not victim-favoring) work we have done, rather than to weaken it.   (14)

If attention to negativity in tone can be, as Sianne Ngai has argued,[38] an entry point for political criticism, this looks like a missed opportunity: 'condemnation' goes well beyond the normal tonal remit of an advisory document, but the opportunity for self-reflection on the risk advisors' own contribution to disciplinary excess is rapidly closed down. Unambiguous castigation is, apparently, 'appropriate' to the dangers now evident ahead. One short, clichéd subordinate clause—'As times change...'—says a lot about the motive, here, for reform. This is not a political agenda driven by concern for rights, though the authors have the obligation to protect rights firmly in their sights: it is risk advice to the university administration, drafted with a canny eye on shifting patterns of litigation. But Kipnis, surprisingly, says nothing about the presumptive interest of administrative officers in changing the agenda and managing shifting perspectives on its own actions.

These late elements of restraint aside, Title IX administrators, their employers, and their advisors are (collectively and, in some cases, individually) proper targets for Kipnis's cynicism in the absence of a satisfactory legal framework, but they are also easy targets. The tougher questions arise in what is due from the university to students, where the power differentials between parties are prima facie more uneven. Not surprisingly, when it comes to the potential empowerment of students under Title IX, the cynicism of *Unwanted Advances* becomes more guarded, caustic asides on the conformity of new queer sexualities notwithstanding. This element of caution has not been much noted (her critics to the left would have liked much more of it), but on a comparative analysis with the book's treatment of university officers, there is a clear difference in the tenor of the scepticism. Testing

---

[38] Sianne Ngai, *Ugly Feelings* (Cambridge, MA: Harvard University Press, 2005), esp. Chapter 1.

the respective credibility of her former Philosophy colleague and one of the student complainants against him, Kipnis asks:

> Is it inconceivable that a professionally ambitious young woman, after spending months emailing her famous professor..., finds herself in his company and decides to test the waters? Let's go further: if we're cynical enough to think [Prof] Ludlow offered to promote Cho's career in exchange for sex or romance, why aren't we cynical enough to think that Cho spotted a potential gravy train and decided to play it for all she could get?   (85)[39]

Mixed metaphors (in what waters does Cho spot a gravy train for the testing?) suggest some discomfort with, even partial disavowal of, a speculatively dark reading of motive, but the point of principle here requires persistence in the line of thought. Did this young undergraduate see an opportunity to get close to a high-profile professor and boost her own profile/performance/marks/future career? Did she, having gained some intimacy with him, see an opportunity to milk Title IX 'for all she could get'?

Cynicism gives a name to a tough, if uneasy, speculative scepticism that consciously goes beyond the evidence base. Kipnis wants to see such testing readiness to imagine self-interested motives, already apparent in the institution's response to Ludlow, operating even-handedly towards accuser and respondent. Being 'cynical enough'—sufficiently cynical—requires taking a critical distance of a kind that should (and in law, would) subject the claims of all parties to the same stringency of assessment, scouting out the possibility of base self-interest at work on both sides. The first effect of a more evenly distributed cynicism, Kipnis wants us to understand, would be to allow that not all the power, potentially very little of it, lies with the professor accused of breaking the university's recently ramped-up ethical code. A more balanced approach would allow that 'power' may not be the most relevant differential in the situation: the relevant interests, surely, stem as much from perceptions of who has most to lose.

A major reason why *Unwanted Advances* has upset and angered a great many readers is that it declines to make this an abstract matter. Unlike more measured participants in the Title IX debate (Jennifer Doyle's *Campus Sex, Campus Security* [2015] stands out for its intelligence), Kipnis repeatedly crosses the line between testing critical scepticisms of the kind practised in an intellectually demanding seminar or tutorial ('Let's go further' with this line of critical inquiry) into commentary on individual cases. Or rather, she explicitly disputes that there can be a clear line between the general principle and the individual case until or unless

---

[39] See also 235, on Cho's later willingness to look for 'a peaceful, restorative, universal resolution': 'A cynical reading might be that having effectively bankrupted Ludlow, she thought she had a better chance of getting money out of the university.'

'due process' is established. In its absence, the working out of the individual case is the only means by which operative assumptions become legible. She emphatically declines to stay within the procedural frame that her own institution was looking to place around Title IX complaints circa 2015: confidential, 'in-house', bound by formal agreements administrators thought fit to propose, self-protection being, in Kipnis's cynic reading, their paramount concern. Transparency, under such murky circumstances, trumps confidentiality—though, again, there are declared limits. The names of complainants and respondents are concealed unless they were already in the public domain, or the person was acting in an official capacity, or permission was given. Kipnis's own case seemed to her to require no such caution: publication of the full narrative (complainant names redacted; and in any case not known to her until late in the process) is a security measure—a shot across the bows of an administration that had yet to define satisfactorily, and make known, the understood scope of its powers and obligations.

Critics have not been slow to argue that, concealment of identities notwith-standing, there is a power imbalance in Kipnis's relationship to student complain-ants about which she is either blind or naïve or disingenuous. Unlike the students she investigates, she had little reason to be fearful, Anne McClintock argues: she had published an essay in the leading general journal of higher education; she had not slept with or been in a compromising personal situation with a student. 'She confesses she had complete confidence she would win and that "academic free-dom would prevail".' Then, with some scorn: 'And she indeed won. All charges were dropped. Freedom of speech prevailed.'[40] True—importantly true—but the quotation is selective: Kipnis states that she was 'fairly', not 'completely', confident that she would not be fired, but adds that some form of censure 'didn't seem unlikely'—'sensitivity training or some other humiliation' (143). Another provo-cation there, to the feminist paternalist campus, but the point is not null: these are in-house disciplinary measures that carry a punitive edge and have predictable repercussions for career advancement and professional reputation.

McClintock and several others, cynical in their turn,[41] have been quick to locate self-interest at work in Unwanted Advances. In commercial terms, the book has presumably been a profitable addition to Kipnis's publications list (though legal fees must be making a dent). Copyright lies with her; the risks and costs of litigation are shared with HarperCollins publishers, and The Chronicle of Higher Education. And she has not been without institutional allies: the

---

[40] Anne McClintock, 'Who's Afraid of Title IX?', *Jacobin*, 24 October 2017, <https://jacobinmag.com/2017/10/title-ix-betsy-devos-doe-colleges-assault-dear-colleague>. Accessed 4 July 2018.

[41] It is worth noting that key elements that McClintock and others do not like in Kipnis's critical stance—the confrontational projection of her own individual critical agency, the unflinching and sometimes *ad personam* calling to account—are strikingly replicated in their own stance as reviewers. This is not in and of itself a criticism: the reviews column remains a space for critical confrontation in which toughly sceptical things get said, often resting on cynical attributes of motive to the text or writer under review.

'Acknowledgments' page duly pays tribute to Jean Tamarin (Senior Editor at *The Chronicle*) and her boss, Evan Goldstein (Managing Editor), 'an intrepid duo' (241). Other professional gains (and protections) might be counted in. The critical reception—predictably split—has certainly heightened Kipnis's public profile. *Unwanted Advances* will no doubt appear in the 'Scholarly Publications' and 'Public Engagement' sections of her CV, and count towards her fulfilment of the expectations upon her as a scholar.

One can grant that self-interest is, in all these ways, at work, but then no critical position can be free of it—and free of the question of it. Recall Epictetus: self-interest does not exclude other-interest (Introduction, p. 25). Every public respondent to Kipnis's views has their own interests to defend, and, for most, self-interest sits in continuity with strongly avowed commitment to others. No-one is safe from being seen as a 'virtue-monger', as Kipnis puts it, flirting with a right-of-centre perspective on herself.[42] She 'fancies herself a provocateur', Jaclyn Friedman writes, rebukingly, in the *Signs* Forum:

> so no doubt my criticisms will only convince her of her virtue and effectiveness. That's fine; Kipnis's self-regard is not my concern. What does worry me is how many people in power will be seduced by her tempting fiction that most rape is just bad sex that hypersensitive women exaggerate, and that campus adminis-trators (and the rest of us) should relax and do less about it.[43]

Jacqueline Rose is similarly unhappy, her dislike of Kipnis's *modus operandi* if anything more emphatic:

> You could argue that she is trying to redress the balance, but that is a term I have always considered corrupt in an unbalanced world... Each [case she examines] opens a door into the murky world of sexuality, where all bets are off, where desire can flare up and be followed by a change of heart in the space of a single breath. Such moments may indeed give us pause. But it is the elation with which they are seized on, the unseemly haste with which they are used to bludgeon the complainant's case, that I find chilling.[44]

---

[42] See 25 for Kipnis's core objections to the climate created by administrative overreach on campus: 'Had you been there to witness my reaction to a recent memo sent to the faculty in my department by one of our undergraduate majors, imploring us to "be conscious of the vocabulary and discourse used in your classroom" and "to challenge ideas of gender, rape culture, whiteness and heteronormativity" in the teaching of your classes, you'd understand what I mean. Why does the purgatory of the nice place have to entail so many empty slogans?, I fumed silently. There I was, huffing and puffing like some bow-tied neocon: this isn't intellect, I snorted (to myself), it's virtue-mongering.'

[43] 'Short Takes'.

[44] Jacqueline Rose, 'I Am a Knife', five reviews, *London Review of Books* 40/4 (22 February 2018), 3–11, <https://www.lrb.co.uk/v40/n04/jacqueline-rose/i-am-a-knife>. Accessed 28 June 2018.

The adoption of that emotive last term, used by one of the complainants in her allegations against Kipnis (she has had 'a "chilling effect" on students' ability to report sexual misconduct' [137]), is, I assume, knowing. It makes a choice, in a field of argument where participants have opted into strongly polarized political and emotional identifications—men vs. women, professoriate vs. students, perpetrators vs. victims—to identify with the female student complainant.[45] More than that, it identifies with the subjective experience of victimization. Kipnis is not wrong on the lure of melodrama, though others rightly observe that she does not push the point as far as it might go: melodrama does not confine itself to fantasies of powerful men threatening vulnerable women.

Most of these accusations say as much or more about the respondents than about Kipnis, whose cynicism is nothing if not self-conscious, though it is not and does not try to be equally attentive or even fair to all parties concerned. (Doyle is far more alert to the role of race and sexuality in Title IX infringements and complaints, though Kipnis has elaborated her position in subsequent discussions of the book.) The primary concern of *Unwanted Advances* is, in the end, with the quality of the intellectual life on campus, for which Kipnis, like so many others, takes the liberty or otherwise of sexual and social arrangements to be a critical indicator. She discounts, at least rhetorically, perspectives that would recognize that not everyone, even now, has the same access to liberty. Disparities of age and of social and institutional advantage matter to her argument largely insofar as the institution's efforts to rectify their effects seem to make it harder to keep in view the old idea of the liberal university. One version of that ideal looks particularly, worryingly, vulnerable to her: 'the traditional ideal of the university', in her words, 'as a refuge for complexity, a setting for the free exchange of ideas' (5). 'After I published an account of my Title IX case,' she records, 'my email account quickly became an overflowing archive of bitterness, cynicism, and fury' from students, parents, professors 'whose lives had been thrown under a great wrecking ball' (159). For all these people, the university has fallen a long way short in its delivery of the promised goods of freedom and intellectual complexity.

Even as she flexes her own independence of view, and looks to model a practice of criticism that rests on a strong assertion of individual agency, Kipnis (like Russell before her) expresses a recurrent concern that students will fall prey to the casual, counterproductive cynicism that results when educated scepticism towards moral ideals leaves the possessor unable to discern better ways of proceeding. Making a point of conversing with her own students about sexual assault on campus, she finds them 'uniformly cynical about the institutional measures meant to combat the sexual targeting of freshmen women' (191). None recalls their practical training in self-defence. In their experience, measures to discipline

---

[45] Her stated feminist allegiances and purposes notwithstanding, Rose argues, 'Kipnis's strongest identifications' seem to be with men, 'especially with those she feels have been victims of injustice'.

students on campus simply shifted unwanted behaviour a few miles down the road, off university premises. This is admittedly a select group of interviewees: 'mostly women students I knew fairly well, and sometimes friends they suggested I speak to'. Canvassing views from them was 'in no way a systematic endeavour': '(...our campus may not be typical. Students tell me it's not much of a party school and that the drinking is actually less intense than at other places.) My students may not be typical either, though what students are?' (190).

In principle, the full picture would be welcome—only that last phrase seems to renege on the idea in ways consistent with cynicism, which has always looked to the specificity of the individual case over the blurred abstractions of typology and 'typicality'.

In its final pages, *Unwanted Advances* unambiguously puts its strategic cynicism to one side in order to advocate positive reform. The final chapter of the book is a constructive manifesto for the future, offering practical proposals for improving campus culture: mandatory training for all freshers in 'interpersonal violence prevention' and self-defence; educating women to 'hold themselves responsible' for their use of alcohol; emboldening women and men to 'say no' to sex (and to alcohol) when sex (and/or alcohol) are not positively wanted.[46] With respect to students, administrators, and the tenured professoriate, the justification for moral controversialism is amply clear. But one constituency of the university looks less readily incorporated into this calculated injection of cynicism in the name of protecting critical freedom, and with it a long-standing ideal of the university. Writing in *Heterodox Academy*,[47] James Anderson suggests an alternative way of reading *Unwanted Advances*. An adjunct professor, self-described as 'from Illinois but now tr[ying] each semester to cobble together classes to teach at various campuses in Southern California', Anderson picks up on Kipnis's exploration of how far graduate students, 'aspiring academics' with greatly diminished academic employment opportunities, may have found in Title IX a means of revenging

[46] Commentators have responded to the book accordingly, as a more or (for some) less compelling mix of the 'disturbing' and the 'pragmatic' (Terry Castle, back jacket); 'provocateur[ship]' and 'wry, pragmatic analysis' (Charlotte Shane, 'Title Bouts': review of Kipnis, *Unwanted Advances*, *Book Forum* April/May 2017, <https://www.bookforum.com/inprint/024_01/17547>. Accessed 28 June 2018); the 'practical and hyperbolic...and maybe a dozen other neurotically contradictory things' (Joan Senior, '*Unwanted Advances* Tackles Sexual Politics in Academia': review of Kipnis, *Unwanted Advances*, *The New York Times*, 5 April 2017, <https://www.nytimes.com/2017/04/05/books/review-laura-kipnis-unwanted-advances.html>. Accessed 28 June 2018); a book that 'pushes [its] argument beyond the reasonable' in part 'for professorial aims—to force readers to really consider their position and to see if they can fully defend it, or at least to think beyond feminist platitudes' (Jill Filipovic, 'Two Books Explore the Furor Over Rape on Campus': review of Kipnis, *Unwanted Advances* and K. C. Johnson and Stuart Taylor Jr, *The Campus Rape Frenzy: The Attack on Due Process at America's Universities*, *New York Times*, 4 July 2007, <https://www.nytimes.com/2017/04/07/books/review/two-books-explore-the-furor-over-rape-on-campus.html>. Accessed 3 July 2018.).
[47] James Anderson, 'Book Summary' of Kipnis, *Unwanted Advances*, *Heterodox Academy*, 21 July 2017, <https://heterodoxacademy.org/book-review-unwanted-advances-sexual-paranoia-comes-to-campus/>. Accessed 28 June 2018.

themselves against the tenured professoriate. 'There's a reality to academic privilege', *Unwanted Advances* indeed concedes: '—old people have the few remaining
good jobs, we're not ready to give them up, and a lot of younger people feel eaten
alive in the academic marketplace, which is more brutal these days than ever' (84).
Kipnis 'completely concur[s]' with the 'someone' (Stanley Aronowitz) who 'once
referred to being a professor as the last good job in America' (34).

Anderson perceives the scope for political embarrassment here, the uncomfortable awareness on the part of an established member of the professoriate that
someone in her position, with the relative security of tenure and long employment, may be an understandable, if not legitimate, target for revenge:

> a reader has to wonder to what extent this assertion is the repressed compunction
> of a tenured scholar becoming manifest. Does the stunning acuity of her psy-
> choanalysis sidestep the discussion of the complicity of tenured professors in a
> two-tiered academic system benefiting a few at the expense of the many adjuncts
> comprising the new faculty majority? It's plausible her analysis is like the
> contrite, near-genius neo-Freudian response to the critique leveled by the 2016
> Truman Capote Award for Literary Criticism, Kevin Birmingham, of the rela-
> tively privileged tenured and tenure-track professors who both 'function as the
> instrument and the direct beneficiary of exploitation.'
>
> Let's just call it a competing hypothesis which need not negate the insights of the
> original.

It is a striking departure from other cynic speculations ventured by Kipnis, or
directed back at her by provoked readers. The tone is markedly unstable: hyper-re-
spectful—ironically respectful?—proffering a suspicious reading, but then stepping
back from the judgement its hard scepticism suggests ('Let's just call it a competing
hypothesis'). This insecurity befits a disparity in the structural freedom to occupy the
role of moral controversialist. It is hard to conceive of an answering cynicism that
would look credible as a response to it, unless to say that any adjunct would jump at a
tenured position if offered one (and that might be a cynicism too far if only because
self-interest at that level is necessary, or—risking tautology—entirely proper). No
self-interest attributable to the adjunct would justify even the most sceptical of
observers in disputing the description of a 'two-tiered academic system' today.

The self-deflected cynicism of the adjunct generates a line of argument for
which the ground has been well prepared, of late. Reflecting, in 2012, on the
growth of the precariat, Andrew Ross remarked that 'A cynic might well conclude
that "working for nothing" is the latest high-growth jobs sector, and a substantial
portion of that economic activity might be classified as cultural in nature.'[48]

---

[48] Andrew Ross, 'Theorizing Cultural Work: An Interview with the Editors', in Mark Banks,
Rosalind Gill, and Stephanie Taylor (eds.), *Theorizing Cultural Work: Labour, Continuity and
Change in the Cultural and Creative Industries* (London: Routledge, 2012), 175–82 (176).

Bridget Conor, in the same volume, describes cynicism as the compensatory 'confidence, even egotism' of intellectual workers aware of the limits of their authority before 'more powerful elites' (48; 52). The screenwriter is her chosen example, but it is not hard to see the relevance of her logic to the situation of the university. 'Working for nothing', or precariously next-to-nothing, imperils, and will eventually deform, the value of the profession in question—because a profession sustained by labour it does not fully recognize or remunerate is abusing (and at last will forfeit) its title as a profession (as distinct from, say, a charitable vocation of an ascetically self-denying kind). If cynicism can be an inflated, compensatory rhetorical claim to agency under such circumstances, it is also, plainly, a 'defensive posture',[49] and one that threatens to feed rather than counter the sense of a 'crisis of the humanities'. The *muting* of that posture is the point at which the institution should be really worried.

Spotting a new tendency on the part of some labour activists to arraign tenured Faculty for their failure to 'identify with . . . fellow workers, and organize across the tenure-adjunct divide', two observers of the ongoing adjunct crisis, Michael Bérubé and Jennifer Ruth, demur:

> Only very rarely [Ruth observes] do I run anymore into the stock character who thinks adjuncts are there to pick up the scraps that fall off his table. I talk regularly, however, with tenured faculty members who complain bitterly about slave-driving administrators but do not know—and, more to the point, give every appearance of not wanting to know—how many adjuncts their own departments employ and what it pays them . . . We are in danger of embracing the identity of labor so that we absolve ourselves of responsibility for having poorly managed our affairs and generated our own underclass.[50]

Get practical, in short, and get specific: work out the numbers, work '*with* administrators' (82)—often the people best placed to help adjuncts. It is an argument that starts by acknowledging the toughly sceptical position of the cynic but then looks to arrest cynicism in favour of a more engaged politics. The rhetorical move is, in other words, strikingly similar to Kipnis's, and classically Deweyan in the justification it provides to a strategic cynicism from today's advocate for the university.

Not the least timely cynicism Bérubé and Ruth acknowledge, in the course of their arguments for internal reform of the professoriate, is directed towards the role being played in the adjunct debate by appeals to the protection of academic freedom. Freedom to speak one's critical mind on intellectual matters, including

---

[49] Aronowitz, *Last Good Job*, 44.

[50] Michael Bérubé and Jennifer Ruth, 'Slow Death and Painful Labours', in Michael Bérubé and Jennifer Ruth, *The Humanities, Higher Education, and Academic Freedom: Three Necessary Arguments* (Basingstoke: Palgrave Macmillan, 2015), 57–86 (82).

matters pertaining to the political condition of higher education, is not, they remind us, the same thing as 'freedom of speech'. It is an additional and more specific form of freedom accorded to the professoriate in order to safeguard its work as a 'self-regulating group'.[51] In this reading, identifying 'academic freedom' as the primary ideal under alleged threat at this point in contemporary history risks mistaking the relevant issue, the thing most under threat, which is not the valuation normatively placed on the principle of academic freedom but the active effort required to realize its necessary conditions through employment practices. Kipnis, for all her tough-mindedness about what intellectual freedom requires, is not immune to this line of criticism: 'What's the point of having a freedom you're afraid to use?', she asks near the end of *Unwanted Advances*, before dangling the image of herself 'being led off campus by security guards as you read this' (157). There are, one hopes, sufficient protections in current employment law to see her safely through the immediate threat. Her recourse to irony, rather than system, rather implies some security. Whether her tentatively cynical adjunct reviewer could play the controversialist with equivalent security is a more open question, one that it is incumbent on the profession—on her—to answer.

Arguably the toughest criticism Kipnis, like any strategic cynic, has to answer to is that there is a time for cynicism and a time for constructive action. Anne McClintock puts the point more fiercely than most, but she is not alone in thinking that Kipnis's timing is badly off—that she has taken aim against the 'infantilization' of students at precisely the point when they are engaging in concerted political action of a kind sorely missed in recent decades:

Kipnis accuses female students of abandoning agency, 'joining arms with campus administrators as the fast track to empowerment.' But they've done exactly the opposite. Furious with administrators for protecting their institutional reputations instead of their students' rights, survivors bypassed obstructionist deans, invented new strategies of collaboration, taught themselves Title IX, and with unprecedented clout brought over two hundred universities under federal investigation.

Anti-rape activist groups like Know Your IX, EVOC, SurvJustice, and FAR burgeoned. Men's groups joined up. The One Billion Rising movement began.... Lady Gaga's video 'Til It Happens to You' has forty million views and counting. I call that historic. Kipnis calls it 'hysterical.'[52]

[51]   Michael Bérubé and Jennifer Ruth, 'From Professionalism to Patronage', in Michael Bérubé and Jennifer Ruth, *Humanities, Higher Education, and Academic Freedom* (Basingstoke: Palgrave Macmillan, 2015), 87–120 (105).

[52]   McClintock, 'Who's Afraid of Title IX?'. For Kipnis's reply to McClintock, see 'The Other Side of Title IX', *Jacobin*, 24 October 2017, <https://jacobinmag.com/2017/10/title-ix-laura-kipnis-response-mcclintock>. Accessed 13 July 2018.

Once again, the point is not null: *Unwanted Advances* is markedly out of align-ment with a collective will to advance reforms of a university and wider social system that have historically failed to take sexual assault seriously, and (in the case of the Church and many other institutions) fallen dismally short of the duty to protect minors from harm. This is recent and ongoing mass action, putting the size of its crowds to the fore (One Billion Rising, 40 million and counting). Opposing so broad-based a reform movement leaves the function of Kipnis's targeted cynicisms exposed to a different kind of criticism than arises when the cynic speaks against long-settled conventionalities or complacencies. She might defend herself on the grounds that *any* mass political agreement stands to benefit from hearing the cynic's dissent (much as Arnold had recourse to cynicism as a token of criticism's regard for its own freedom). A more nuanced Deweyan defence would allow the circumstances of the cynic's speech greater consideration—but even then the door may not close on cynicism entirely. Part of the cynic's contrarian offer is to have an eye not only to the present but to the future, keeping the debate cognizant of how quickly power can shift its ground.

Coda

Last and First Things

Dinaw Mengestu's novel *How to Read the Air* (2010) has an unsettling narrator. Ten years out from his English literature degree, and still harbouring thoughts of enrolling for a PhD 'with a focus on American poetry',[1] Jonas Woldemariam has spent the better part of the last decade working in temporary low-paid jobs before being taken on at an immigration centre. There his role is to read the statements of refugees seeking permanent residency in the United States. Early on he is simply required to divide the cases between 'the persecuted and not so persecuted' (23). Over time, his role expands.

> I was given the job of editing out the less credible or unnecessary parts of some of the narratives, while at the same time pointing out places where some stories could be expanded upon or magnified for greater narrative effect. . . . I took half-page statements of a coarse and often brutal nature and supplied them with the details that made them real for the immigration officer who would some day be reading them. (16)

In short, he sexes up the dossiers. Initially content with minor expansion on the facts ('They came at night' becomes 'We had all gone to sleep for the evening, my wife, mother, and two children. All the fires in the village had already been put out, but there was a bright moon . . . That's why they attacked that night' [26]), he soon cuts free altogether. A family who 'flew business class straight to Dubai' is instead 'forced to take shelter for weeks in a church while outside a militia stood waiting for them'. '[O]ne of my more dramatic and better efforts', as he thinks (27).

If we are to call this cynicism (and I will be giving reasons to draw back), it would be cynicism of what this book has tended to describe as the philosophically 'thin' but 'corrosive', or indeed, corroded sort. A sharp enough judge of the system in which he operates, and to which he brings his training as a writer, Jonas has nothing publicly critical or politically constructive to add. He can see perfectly well

---

[1] Dinaw Mengestu, *How to Read the Air* (London: Vintage, 2012), 19. I am grateful to Grace A. Musila whose paper, 'The Narrative Pressures of Migrant Precarity in Dinaw Mengestu's *How to Read the Air*', delivered at a colloquium on 'Architectures of the Novel' (University of Oxford, 21 June 2019), first drew my attention to cynicism in this novel.

The Function of Cynicism at the Present Time. Helen Small, Oxford University Press (2020). © Helen Small.
DOI: 10.1093/oso/9780198861935.001.0001

that bare statements of fact do not work for the lawyers representing these clients in court, and that the firm is 'losing all the time': clients are abruptly disappearing, 'on a weekly if not daily basis', either deported or disappearing quietly into anonymity before judgement can be given against them. He knows, too, that his interventions, though they have some initial success, in a short while make no difference: even enhanced stories become standard fare in a context where there are too many 'poor' from 'distant, foreign countries' desperate for a new start (27). How deep Jonas's sympathy goes is never quite clear: indeed, his perception that what the refugee needs is not sympathy but 'respect' sounds, briefly, like a serious moral position—until that, too, is undermined as not securely his perspective (perhaps he is trying to sound more serious) (27). Lying 'comes naturally to him', and, as a student of English literature, he takes some pride in doing it well. When he says 'brutal', there is reason to fear that he means 'lacking stylistic polish' more than he means 'testifying to brutality suffered'.

It is increasingly evident that the term 'cynic' applies more robustly to his employer, Bill, who instructed him to lie, and Jonas's wife, Angela. Both are human rights lawyers, with experience (in Bill's case decades of it) trying to beat odds that, even when better than average, cannot be 'good enough' for people who have lost everything. Bill and Angela know 'how to temper that loss with an appreciation of reality'. Hence Bill's willingness to sanction pious lies (in the old Jesuitical phrase). His regular joke is that the centre exists 'to give people enough time to learn how the system worked before they vanished' (22). This is a tougher, more pointed cynicism, comparable to the cosmopolitan cynicisms explored in Chapter 4, but adapted to the 'forced humanitarian migration' challenges (in then new UN parlance) of c.2008. Rather than corroding the moral idealism of people who spend their days trying to change lives for the better, Bill and Angela seek to brace that idealism with cynicism, turning repeated disappointment in the direction of the salving witticism and creative endeavour at subverting the system, in lieu of the 'cold hard pragmatism' Jonas thinks he sees in the majority of the centre's employees (24).

The peculiar difficulty of reading Mengestu's novel lies in assessing what moral and political force Bill and Angela's 'strong' cynicism can possess in a work of fiction that repeatedly undermines imaginative sympathy as the ground of humanitarian connection between people (Bill's strategy is short-lived because sympathy fails, wears thin, grows tired, has to hear about more and worse suffering to get it going) and yet whose *narrator* seems to want to believe that sympathy may still be the answer to our collective difficulties. When the refugee centre's money runs out, and Bill lays him off, Jonas takes a post teaching English at an academy. Instead of delivering the syllabus, he spends his class time telling students the story of his father's long, and near fatal, journey from Addis Ababa, to a Sudan prison, then from the Sudan port to Italy, France, Spain, and at last America. How much of that story, and of the accompanying tale of his parents' unhappy and violent marriage, is 'true' is undecidable. It is ultimately all Mengestu's fiction, of course. *How to Read the Air* at one and the same time sends its reader down a (by now rather tired) *mise-en-abyme* of fictitiousness and delivers a memorably realistic representation of migrant life *in extremis*. The price of that double act is that its central protagonist is not only untrustworthy but, to return to my starting point, unsettling: Is he badly damaged?—cynical 'before his time', as the cynical phrase goes? Or just not there?—a formal front for a series of provocations to mull over the limits of sympathy and the case for cynicism? Possibly too much of both and too little of either.

Cynicism's power to disturb is not a simple power. In some contexts, the affront, and it may be offence, of a robust cynicism has an almost curative property. In that role it may be wanted, even needed, though the judgement call there is likely to be disputed. The danger of a weak cynicism is that it merely unsettles and offers (for the moralist) nothing consequential as the payoff of the unsettlement. In focusing on texts from the Victorian and modern periods through to today, I have chosen to get into terrain where the formal frameworks that held cynicism's stronger meanings and effects substantially in place are very much looser than they were in classical antiquity and even in the high period of Cynicism's revival, the seventeenth and eighteenth centuries. Dispersively part of our everyday psychological vocabulary, cynicism nevertheless remains capable (as all my writers understood—and understand) of retrieving earlier, sharper forms. When it does that, it is taking on a formal and stylistic 'hard'-ness (as Nietzsche put it), a 'character' that permits it to become *functional*, whether serving the aims of radical philosophizing about morality, or the purposes of political rhetoric for Carlyle, Russell, Kipnis, or the assertive critical freedom of Arnold, or the fictive psychological 'impressionism' of Eliot and Ford. 'Hard'-ness need not mean lacking subtlety or discretion (as Nietzsche saw, there may be sophistication in the deployment of the crude). When that functional quality is not present, and the cynicism in question is of the more casualized and corrosive kind seen in Mengestu's narrator, the lack of serious affront, or its repression, becomes itself the problem under scrutiny. Hence the claims, from Foucault, Sloterdijk, and some others in their wake that a radical theory might reanimate the stronger, older form.

My view is different: it is that declarations of cynicism's viability on such terms mistake its place and the basis of its power, which can only function within a larger discourse or system. There, it can, indeed, provide a moment of pressure or leverage, or create a stage during which a certain clearing-away of received notions takes place; but built into any use of cynicism's strengths must inevitably be an awareness of its weaknesses. Its peculiar challenge as it does the various things it has done in this book—sounding the basis of our attachment to morality, assisting the articulation of more than one idea of freedom, puncturing the complacency of morality in the field of politics, helping calibrate a credible level for certain important ideals—is that it must carry with it some obvious limitations which are historical, psychological, and formal. For Nietzsche, the modern Cynic must necessarily be extravagant to make an impression, since the rhetorical schema out of which s/he emerges no longer has authority. The excess of the performance is a kind of honesty about the limits of its legitimacy. The corollary of that claim is that this strong character has, throughout, existed in relation to a psychological cynicism that is weaker: not a character but, as it were, a failure of character (though the phrase risks sounding too little like Theophrastus and too much like a Victorian headmaster). Strong and weak articulations of the character alike exist not in isolation from other psychological and social factors, and not in some oddly purified form of dialectic, but as part of the larger set of discourses in which they become audible. This seems to me to have been fairly consistently so across the period in question, and was neither generated nor negated by the arrival of Victorianism, or modernism, or postmodernism (about which I have, purposely, had little to say). The psychological vocabularies for describing cynicism are enriched somewhat in that period, primarily thanks to Freud, but they do not fundamentally alter a pre-existing sense that cynicism is a formal concentration of attitude and effect—one that comes and goes.

It is in the nature of fiction, and vividly so with *How to Read the Air*, that *settling* questions of cynicism's legitimacy in the particular context will not always be pertinent (though for some literary critics, especially the politically driven, they will be). A novelist may reasonably claim that s/he is under no obligation to be clear or cogent about the 'uses' made of its debasing affronts, or its stylistic goads. Those are part of a general repertoire available to the imaginative writer; they are likely to be filtered through and made more complex by narrative voice. The critic may disagree (and in Mengestu's case, I have taken the novel's engagement with the politics of migration to be reason to demur over both the weakened cynicism and the voice it is given). The moral philosopher who enters this terrain is likely to feel under a less negotiable obligation to be clear about their purposes.

I acknowledged briefly in the Preface to this book that it found one of its promptings in Williams's observation that most contemporary moral philosophy is 'surprisingly lacking' in a 'genuinely disturbing moral scepticism'. In focusing on cynicism (ancient and modern), I have given more weight to the question of what constitutes a 'genuine disturbance' in thinking and writing about morality than to scepticism, which has come in and out of the frame as my selections of writers and texts required. (An important element in the readings of Nietzsche, Mill vs. Carlyle, and Russell, scepticism was less so in responding to Arnold, Eliot, Ford, Dewey, Kipnis.) My principal concern has been to elaborate the function of cynicism in relation to moral ideals. This has meant attending to advocacy for new and higher ideals (above 'morality') (Nietzsche), reanimation of old ones (Carlyle, Arnold, and Eliot, the writers on the university), and the more internal activity of self-orientation towards inherited ideals now under pressure from contemporary circumstance (pre-eminently Ford's terrain, but in some degree common to all these writers, Mengestu included). Williams has not featured prominently, here, beyond some moments in the reading of Nietzsche, but I give him space in his own right in these closing pages as I consider the implications of *The Function of Cynicism* at the present time.

In his last completed book, Williams gave the question of distinction between a 'serious' and a non-serious scepticism its fullest articulation, and did so with an eye not just on the dangers of a weak and indiscriminate cynicism within philosophy but also within the Humanities as a whole. *Truth and Truthfulness: An Essay in Genealogy* (2002)[2] looks to defend truth and its importance to humanity both against those who were (he thought) professing to undervalue it, even denying its possibility altogether (Richard Rorty, Jürgen Habermas, Hayden White are prominent among those targeted);[3] and against those inclined, more traditionally, to overvalue it. To these ends, he drew extensively on Nietzsche. At the methodological centre of the book is a genealogy of truthfulness that revises the terrain of the genealogy of morality in ways that restrict the scope for cynicism. The genealogy's narrative structure and broad philosophical purposes remain intact. Here again, and more explicitly than in Nietzsche, the genealogy is an imaginative story, though with elements of history. And again, it is a story that takes us back to a point of origin, or as Williams clarifyingly rephrases matters, to a basic level of 'abstraction' (40 and *passim*): the 'State of Nature'. The purpose is:

> [to] represen[t] as functional a concept, reason, motivation, or other aspect of human thought and behaviour, where that item was perhaps not previously seen as functional; the explanation of the function is unmysterious, because in par-ticular it does not appeal to intentions or deliberations or (in this respect) already purposive thought; and the motivations that are invoked in the explanation are ones that are agreed to exist anyway.   (34)

In keeping with Nietzsche's purposes, Williams looks to genealogy to achieve what could not be done by isolating function synchronically, looking at what 'truthful-ness' contributes to human life and its social organization. But Williams makes one important change in the basic assumption about human 'motivations': where Nietzsche (and before him Hume, even more so) told a story about base egoism and self-interest driving recognition of a distinction between good and evil, and

---

[2] Bernard Williams, *Truth and Truthfulness: An Essay in Genealogy* (Princeton, NJ: Princeton University Press, 2002).

[3] For Rorty's response, see Richard Rorty, 'To the Sunlit Uplands', review of Williams, *Truth and Truthfulness*, *London Review of Books*, 24/21 (31 October 2002), 13–15, <https://www.lrb.co.uk/v24/n21/richard-rorty/to-the-sunlit-uplands>. Several reviewers have suggested that Williams also has Foucault in his sights. I see little evidence of that, and if the criticisms apply to the early Foucault, it is much less clear that they are pertinent to the later work.

subsequent finer articulations of morality such as the interpretation of 'justice', Williams rejects, or at least demotes the prominence of, self-interest. He puts cooperation at the start of human communication, and thus the human disposition to value truth and truthfulness. Everyone, he observes, 'is at various times and with respect to different pieces of information, at an advantage or disadvantage...in relation to one another. What they need, in fact, is to pool information...' (42–3). In effect, he puts a *cordon sanitaire* around egoism, and hence around the scenarios of primitive battling for position between the self and others, of the kind that were part of the tactically cynical argumentative gearing of the *Genealogy of Morality*.[4]

I necessarily short-change the detail of Williams's argument, isolating what is, with regard to the study of cynicism, the essential point: that, along with the stylistic and formal resources it brings with it, modern cynicism imports an assumption about the dominance of self-interest. This is its debasing note of 'realism' with respect to psychology. In some contexts (a challenge to conventional morality) there has been, and may still be, positive scope for a strategic cynicism on those terms: put crudely, on the subject of morality there has not, historically, been enough cynicism around. In a defence of truth and truthfulness the debasing note is without the same critical warrant. Not that cynicism had no formal or stylistic attraction for Williams. Elsewhere, he was keenly interested in its disruptive possibilities for both ancient and modern cynicism, and that interest went beyond his reading of Nietzsche.[5] He had been, as is well known, attentive to the importance of egoism in certain moral contexts, looking to correct the inadequate understanding of human motives in much deontological ethics by identifying cases where 'the moral agent's attention [is] confined to egoistic projects, [and] moral critics would agree that it is legitimately so confined.'[6] What concerned him in *Truth and Truthfulness*, writing at a point where the late twentieth-century confrontations between traditionalism and post-structuralism were receding (and 'common sense', he thought, coming more to the fore), was his perception that correction in another direction was needed. If the waning of hostilities between the two camps signalled a loss of investment in questions of truth and truthfulness, he worried, the decline might 'do no more than register *an inert cynicism*, the

---

[4] That those scenarios were gearing, and *not* truth claims, is a perhaps a necessary repetition if this Coda is read in isolation. See Chapter 1.

[5] See, for example, the review of Martha Nussbaum's *The Therapy of Desire* (1994), regretting (as she had done herself) that she found no space for the Cynics in discussing the Hellenistic philosophers' contributions to the redress of human misery. 'She may be right in saying that we know too little of th[e] Cynics', he comments; but there is a hint also of their potential attraction: 'ill-behaved malcontents', who might have challenged or complicated the portfolio of ancient therapeutic philosophies. Bernard Williams, *Essays and Reviews, 1959–2002*, 339–45 (339). And, for the most sustained consideration of cynicism in the arts, Bernard Williams, 'Passion and Cynicism: Remarks on *Così fan tutte*' (1973), in *Essays and Reviews*, 363–4.

[6] Bernard Williams, 'Moral Luck', in *Moral Luck: Philosophical Papers, 1973–1980* (Cambridge: Cambridge University Press, 1981), 31.

kind of calm that in personal relations can follow a series of hysterical rows' [my emphasis]. In that case, 'the study of the humanities runs a risk of sliding from professional seriousness, through professionalization, to a finally disenchanted careerism' (3).

Twenty years old though these reflections are now, they seem prescient about the rise of 'disenchanted careerism'—though the causes explored in Chapter 5 were not confined to intellectual detachment from truthfulness and its associated virtues. Williams could not have anticipated changes in the wider political and cultural climate that have made defence of truth and truthfulness a much higher priority for many, certainly a more charged subject matter for most, and (I think) lessened the amount of 'inert cynicism' in the university. I remarked briefly in Chapter 2 that it is a measure of how quick and how worrying some of the changes are that the arguments preoccupying many literary critics, historians, and political theorists, as well as moral philosophers, today are less about the need to agree on normative ethical dimensions for our work, but are more about differentiating between agreements that are vital and those that are not, and between the frames in which a radical testing of *even* the basic agreements can have value and those in which it is (more or less recklessly) trivializing. *The Function of Cynicism* belongs to that context of debate.

My starting assumption, that there is enough self-interest in human psychology to make the Cynic's challenge 'realistic' and able to find argumentative traction, was not an assumption that self-interest dominates human psychology. It was an assumption that the amount of self-interest in human make-up gives the writer drawn to cynic styles and strategies something to work with, permitting a provisional, or strategic, or licensed operation of cynicism to be 'useful' to Nietzsche and others before and after him in the articulation and calibration of morality and other shared ideas. The fact that this was already old terrain in the nineteenth century is what makes the strategic use possible, isolatable as a technique (though not necessarily under control). My first epigraph, at the start of the book, Nietzsche's performatively cavalier claim 'One should not hesitate to pursue a vice if it is the means to a worthy end', is not cynicism, though it sounds like it. It is a claim, improvisatory in style, that the writer may have special reason to loosen the ground under morality and, to that end, pursue the kind of strategizing after his or her own ends that we routinely, or conventionally, call cynicism. Behind it can be heard La Rochefoucauld's only slightly more constrained 'Vices have a place in the composition of virtues', and before both Epicurus. My other epigraph, from Louis MacNeice's *Autumn Journal* (1939), section XXII, offers a literary counterpart to the philosopher and the moralist when they are in declarative moral-strategizing mode with cynicism. MacNeice goes to the heart of the cynic self-presentation: to be a cynic is to deal in 'overstatements'—but there is scope here for art and not just for coarsening. Overstatement, as he puts it, may be an 'achieve[ment]'. To *read* cynicism right requires subtlety in its turn, MacNeice suggests. Facing the onset of war, he knows the dangerous lure of cynicism, but he knows also its pleasures ('How I enjoy this bout of cynical self-indulgence, / Of glittering and hard-boiled make-believe'), and there is a witty self-reflexivity at work when he urges attention to what may be going on beneath the surface: 'if you are going to read the testaments of cynics, / You must read between the lines' (XVII). The cynic (not interested in argument) declines to be his or her own reader, stopping at the overstatement; it is up to the reader to probe the effect. If grandstanding or retreating were all modern cynicism could offer, time would have run out on the function of cynicism, and its capacity to attract keen-eyed readers, long ago. But in the play between its strategies and its styles, its moral content and its expression as character, its strengths and its weaknesses, it has more than enough energy for ongoing renewal.

Bibliography

Adams, Amanda. *Performing Authorship in the Nineteenth-Century Transatlantic Lecture Tour* (Farnham: Ashgate, 2014).

Adams, James Eli. *A History of Victorian Literature* (Chichester: Wiley-Blackwell, 2012).

Adams, Matthew. *Teaching Classics in English Schools, 1500–1840* (Newcastle upon Tyne: Cambridge Scholars Publishing, 2015).

Allan, D. J. 'Review of Dudley, *A History of Cynicism*', *Philosophy* 13/51 (1938), 369–70.

Allen, Woody. *Irrational Man* (Sony Pictures Classics, 2015).

American Psychiatric Association. *Diagnostic and Statistical Manual of Mental Disorders: DSM-IV-TR*. 4th edn, text revision (Washington, DC: American Psychiatric Association, 2000).

Anderson, Amanda. *The Powers of Distance: Cosmopolitanism and the Cultivation of Detachment* (Princeton, NJ: Princeton University Press, 2001).

Anderson, Amanda. *The Way We Argue Now: A Study in the Cultures of Theory* (Princeton, NJ: Princeton University Press, 2006).

Anderson, Amanda. *Bleak Liberalism* (Chicago: University of Chicago Press, 2016).

Anderson, James. 'Book Summary of Kipnis, *Unwanted Advances*', *Heterodox Academy* 21 July 2017. <https://heterodoxacademy.org/book-review-unwanted-advances-sexual-paranoia-comes-to-campus/>.

Ansell-Pearson, Keith. *An Introduction to Nietzsche as Political Thinker: The Perfect Nihilist* (Cambridge: Cambridge University Press, 1994).

Appiah, Kwame Anthony. *Cosmopolitanism: Ethics in a World of Strangers* (New York: W. W. Norton, 2006).

Arehart-Treichel, Joan. 'Cynical Hostility Personality Trait Strongly Predicts Depressed Mood', *Psychiatric News* 7 May 2010. <https://psychnews.psychiatryonline.org/doi/10.1176/pn.45.9.psychnews_45_9_028>.

Arnold, Matthew. *The Complete Prose Works of Matthew Arnold*, ed. R. H. Super, 11 vols. (Ann Arbor, MI: University of Michigan Press, 1960–77).

Arnold, Matthew. *The Yale Manuscript*, ed. with commentary by S. O. A. Ullmann (Ann Arbor, MI: University of Michigan Press, 1989).

Arnold, Matthew. *The Letters of Matthew Arnold*, ed. Cecil Y. Lang, 5 vols. (Charlottesville, VA: University Press of Virginia, 1996–2001).

Aronowitz, Stanley. *The Last Good Job in America: Work and Education in the New Global Technoculture* (Lanham, MD: Rowman and Littlefield, 2001).

Arsić, Branka. *On Leaving: A Reading in Emerson* (Cambridge, MA: Harvard University Press, 2010).

Aschheim, Steven E. *The Nietzsche Legacy in Germany 1890–1990* (Berkeley, CA: University of California Press, 1992).

Aschheim, Steven E. 'Max Nordau, Friedrich Nietzsche and *Degeneration*', *Journal of Contemporary History* 28/4 (1993), 643–57.

Babich, Barbara, 'Sloterdijk's Cynicism: Diogenes in the Marketplace', in Stuart Elden (ed.), *Sloterdijk Now* (Cambridge: Polity, 2011), 17–36.

Badian, E. 'Alexander the Great and the Unity of Mankind', *Historia* 7 (1958), 425–44.

Bair, Deirdre. *Jung: A Biography* (London: Little Brown, 2004).

Balzac, Honoré de. *Old Goriot*, trans. Marion Ayton Crawford (London: Penguin, 1951).

Balzac, Honoré de. *La peau de chagrin*, ed. Pierre Citron, in Pierre-Georges Castex and Thierry Bodin (eds.), *La Comédie humaine*, X, *Études Philosophiques* (Paris: Gallimard, 1979).

Barnes, Jonathan. 'Nietzsche and Diogenes Laertius', *Nietzsche-Studien* 15/1 (1986), 16–40.

Barnes, Julian. 'The Saddest Story', *The Guardian* 7 June 2008. <https://www.theguardian.com/books/2008/jun/07/fiction.julianbarnes>.

Baumgarten, Murray. 'Carlyle and "Spiritual Optics"', *Victorian Studies* 11/4 (1968), 502–33.

Bentley, Eric. *A Century of Hero-Worship: A Study of the Idea of Heroism in Carlyle and Nietzsche, with Notes on Wagner, Spengler, Stefan George, and D. H. Lawrence*, 2nd edn (Boston: Beacon Press, 1957).

Bergler, Edmund. 'On the Psychology of the Cynic', in Edmund Bergler, *Selected Papers, 1933–1961* (New York: Grune & Stratton, 1969), 846–8.

Bérubé, Michael and Jennifer Ruth. *The Humanities, Higher Education, and Academic Freedom: Three Necessary Arguments* (Basingstoke: Palgrave Macmillan, 2015).

Best, Stephen and Sharon Marcus. 'Surface Reading: An Introduction', *Representations* 108/1 (2009), 1–21.

Betz, Hans Dieter. 'Jesus and the Cynics: Survey and Analysis of a Hypothesis', *The Journal of Religion* 74/4 (October 1994), 453–75.

Bevis, Matthew. *The Art of Eloquence: Byron, Dickens, Tennyson, Joyce* (Oxford: Oxford University Press, 2007).

Bewes, Timothy. *Cynicism and Postmodernity* (London: Verso, 1997).

Bishop, Paul. *The Dionysian Self: C. G. Jung's Reception of Friedrich Nietzsche* (Berlin: Walter de Gruyter, 1995).

Bishop, Paul. (ed.). *Nietzsche and Antiquity: His Reaction and Response to the Classical Tradition* (Rochester, NY: Camden House, 2004).

Blake, Robert. 'A History of *The Spectator*', *The Spectator* 23 September 1978, 30. <http://archive.spectator.co.uk/article/23rd-september-1978/30/a-history-of-the-spectator>.

Bloom, Harold. *Essayists and Prophets*, Bloom's Literary Criticism 20th Anniversary Collection (Philadelphia, PA: Chelsea House Publications, 2005).

Brake, Laurel. 'W. T. Stead and Democracy: The Americanization of the World', in Ella Dzelzainisand Ruth Livesey (eds.). *The American Experiment and the Idea of Democracy in British Culture, 1776–1914* (Farnham: Ashgate, 2013) 161–78.

Branham, Robert Bracht. 'Cynics', in Edward Craig (gen. ed), *Routledge Encyclopaedia of Philosophy*, 10 vols. (London: Routledge, 1998), 753–9.

Branham, Robert Bracht. 'Nietzsche's Cynicism: Upper or Lowercase?', in Paul Bishop (ed.), *Nietzsche and Antiquity* (Rochester, NY: Camden House, 2004), 170–81.

Branham, Robert Bracht and Marie-Odile Goulet-Cazé (eds.). *The Cynics: The Cynic Movement in Antiquity and Its Legacy* (Berkeley: University of California Press, 1996).

Brasme, Isabelle. '"A Caricature of His Own Voice": Ford and Self-Editing in *Parade's End*', in Jason Harding (ed.), *Ford Madox Ford, Modernist Magazines and Editing*, International Ford Madox Ford Studies 9 (Amsterdam: Rodopi, 2010), 243–52.

Brennan, Geoffrey, Lisa Eriksson, Robert E. Goodin and Nicholas Southwood, *Explaining Norms* (Oxford: Oxford University Press, 2013).

Brier, Peter A. *Howard Mumford Jones and the Dynamics of Liberal Humanism* (Columbia, MO: University of Missouri Press, 1994).

Briggs Myers, Isabel. *Introduction to Type: A Guide to Understanding Your Results on the Myers-Briggs Type Indicator*, rev. Linda K. Kirby and Katharine D. Myers, 6th edn (Oxford: Oxford Psychologists Press Ltd, 2000).

Brilmyer, S. Pearl '"The Natural History of My Inward Self": Sensing Character in George Eliot's *Impressions of Theophrastus Such*', *PMLA* 129/1 (2014), 35–51.

Brobjer, Thomas H. *Nietzsche's Philosophical Context: An Intellectual Biography* (Urbana, IL: University of Illinois Press, 2008).

Brobjer, Thomas H. *Nietzsche and Science* (London: Routledge, 2017).

Brown, Dennisand Jenny Plaistow (eds.). *Ford Madox Ford and Englishness* (Amsterdam: Rodopi, 2006).

Brown, Nicholas. *Utopian Generations: The Political Horizon of Twentieth-Century Literature* (Princeton, NJ: Princeton University Press, 2005).

Brown, Truesdell S. *Onesicritus: A Study in Hellenistic Historiography* (Berkeley, CA: University of California Press, 1949).

Bull, Malcolm. *Anti-Nietzsche* (London: Verso, 2011).

Buora, Maurizio. 'L'incontro tra Alessandro et Diogene: Tradizioni e significato', *Atti dell'Istituto Veneto de Scienze, Lettere ed Arti* 132 (1973–4), 243–64.

Burakoff, Maddie. 'Kipnis Lawsuit Moves Forward [. . .]', *The Daily Northwestern* 9 March 2018. <https://dailynorthwestern.com/2018/03/09/campus/kipnis-lawsuit-moves-forward-as-judge-declines-motion-to-dismiss-the-case/>.

Burrow, Colin. 'Are You a Spenserian?', review of Turner, *Philology, London Review of Books* 36/21 (6 November 2014), 35–7. <https://www.lrb.co.uk/v36/n21/colin-burrow/are-you-a-spenserian>.

Bush, Douglas. *Matthew Arnold: A Survey of the Poetry and Prose* (Lonredon: Macmillan, 1971).

Campbell, Ian M. 'Carlyle's Religion: The Scottish Background', in John Clubbe (ed.), *Carlyle and His Contemporaries: Essays in Honor of Charles Richard Sanders* (Durham, NC: Duke University Press, 1974), 3–20.

Campbell, Ian M. 'David Masson and Thomas Carlyle', *Studies in Scottish Literature* 40/1 (2014), 134–45.

Campioni, G. et al. (eds.), *Nietzsches Persönliche Bibliothek, Supplementa Mietzscheana* VI (Berlin: Walter de Gruyter, 2003).

Carlyle, Thomas. 'Occasional Discourse on the Negro Question', *Fraser's Magazine for Town and Country* XL (December 1849), 670–9.

Carlyle, Thomas. *Latter-Day Pamphlets* (London: Chapman and Hall, 1850).

Carlyle, Thomas. *The Works of Thomas Carlyle*, Centenary Edition, 30 vols. (London: Chapman and Hall, 1896–69).

Carlyle, Thomas and Jane Carlyle. *The Collected Letters of Thomas and Jane Welsh Carlyle*, eds. Ian Campbell, Aileen Christianson and David R. Sorensen, 47 vols. (Durham, NC: Duke University Press, 1970–). <https://carlyleletters.dukeupress.edu/home>.

Carlyle, Thomas and Jane Carlyle. *The Carlyle Letters Online: A Victorian Cultural Reference* (Durham, NC: Duke University Press, 2007). <http://carlyleletters.dukeupress.edu>.

Cassell, Richard A. *Ford Madox Ford: A Study of His Novels* (Baltimore, MD: Johns Hopkins University Press, 1962).

Cavell, Stanley. *The Claim of Reason: Wittgenstein, Skepticism, Morality, and Tragedy* (1979), new edn (New York: Oxford University Press, 1999).

Chaloupka, William. *Everybody Knows: Cynicism in America* (Minneapolis, MN: University of Minnesota Press, 1999).

Chantler, Ashley and Rob Hawkes(eds.). *War and the Mind: Ford Madox Ford's Parade's End, Modernism, and Psychology* (Edinburgh: Edinburgh University Press, 2015).

Chase, Jefferson. *Inciting Laughter: The Development of 'Jewish Humor' in 19th Century German Culture* (Berlin: Walter de Gruyter, 2000).

Cheah, Phengand Bruce Robbins (eds.). *Cosmopolitics: Thinking and Feeling beyond the Nation* (Minneapolis, MN: University of Minnesota Press, 1998).

Chiu, Allyson and Matthew Choi. 'In Focus: Graduate Student Sues Professor for Invasion of Privacy, Defamation Following Book Release', *Daily Northwestern* 22 May 2017. <https://dailynorthwestern.com/2017/05/22/campus/northwestern-graduate-student-sues-professor-for-invasion-of-privacy-defamation-following-book-release/>.

Clarke, M. L. *Greek Studies in England, 1700–1830* (Cambridge: Cambridge University Press, 1945).

Clarke, M. L. *Classical Education in Britain, 1500–1900* (Cambridge: Cambridge University Press, 1959).

Colclough, David. '*Parrhesia*: The Rhetoric of Free Speech in Early Modern England', *Rhetorica* 17/2 (1999), 177–212.

Collini, Stefan. *Absent Minds: Intellectuals in Britain* (Oxford: Oxford University Press, 2006).

Collini, Stefan. '"What, Ultimately, For?" The Elusive Goal of Cultural Criticism', *Raritan* 33/2 (2013), 4–26.

Corning, Peter A. 'Evolution and Ethics... An Idea Whose Time Has Come? Part Two: Review of Wright, *The Moral Animal*', *Journal of Social and Evolutionary Systems* 20/3 (1997), 323–31.

Corsini, Ray. *The Dictionary of Psychology* (London: Routledge, 2016).

cruel.org. 'The Carlyle-Mill "Negro Question" Debate'. <https://cruel.org/econthought/texts/carlyle/negroquest.html>.

Cuddy-Keane, Melba. 'Modernism, Geopolitics, Globalization', *Modernism/Modernity* 10/3 (2003), 539–58.

Cuddy-Keane, Melba. 'Global Modernisms', in David Bradshaw and Kevin J. H. Dettmar (eds.), *A Companion to Modernist Literature and Culture* (Oxford: Blackwell, 2006), 558–64.

Cutler, Ian. *Cynicism from Diogenes to Dilbert* (Jefferson, NC: McFarland & Co., 2005).

Dames, Nicholas. 'On the Protocols of Victorian Citation', *Novel: A Forum on Fiction* 42/2 (2009), 326–31.

Davenport, Guy. *Eclogues: Eight Stories* (San Francisco: North Point Press, 1981).

Davenport, Guy. 'Guy Davenport, The Art of Fiction No. 174', interviewed by John Jeremiah Sullivan, *The Paris Review* 163 (Fall 2002). <https://www.theparisreview.org/interviews/355/guy-davenport-the-art-of-fiction-no-174-guy-davenport>.

Dawan, Nikita. 'Coercive Cosmopolitanism and Impossible Solidarities', *Qui Parle: Critical Humanities and Social Sciences* 22/1 (2013), 139–66.

de Certeau, Michel. *The Practice of Everyday Life*, trans. Steven Rendall (Berkeley, CA: University of California Press, 1984).

Decleva Caizzi, Fernanda. 'τύφος. Contributo alla storia di un concetto', *Sandalion* 3 (1980), 53–66.

DeLaura, David. 'Matthew Arnold and the American "Literary Class"', *Bulletin of the New York Public Library* 70 (1966), 229–50.

DeLaura, David. *Hebrew and Hellene in Victorian England: Newman, Arnold, and Pater* (Austin, TX: University of Texas Press, 1969).

Deresiewicz, William. 'Love on Campus', *The American Scholar* 1 June 2007. <https://theamericanscholar.org/love-on-campus/#.XXuGVy2ZM3E>.

Desch, Michael C. 'America's Liberal Illiberalism: The Ideological Origins of Overreaction in U.S. Foreign Policy', *International Security* 32/3 (2007/8), 7–43.

Desmond, W. D. *The Greek Praise of Poverty: The Origins of Ancient Cynicism* (Notre Dame, IN: University of Notre Dame Press, 2006).

Desmond, W. D. *Cynics* (Stocksfield: Acumen, 2008).

Despain, Jessica. *Nineteenth-Century Transatlantic Reprinting and the Embodied Book* (Farnham: Ashgate, 2014).

Dewey, Jane M. 'Biography of John Dewey', in Paul Arthur Schilpp (ed.), *The Philosophy of John Dewey* (New York: Tudor Publishing Co., 1939), 3–45.

Dewey, John. 'The Case for Bertrand Russell', *Nation* 150 (15 June 1940), 732–3.

Dewey, John. 'Social Realities *versus* Police Court Fictions', in John Dewey and Horace M. Kallen (eds.), *The Bertrand Russell Case* (New York: Viking Press, 1941), 55–74.

Dewey, John. *The Collected Works of John Dewey, 1882–1953*, ed. Jo Ann Boydston, 37 vols. (Carbondale: Southern Illinois University Press, 1972–85).

Dewey, John and Horace M. Kallen (eds.). *The Bertrand Russell Case* (New York: Viking Press, 1941).

Dickerson, Vanessa D. *Dark Victorians* (Urbana, IL: University of Illinois Press, 2008).

Diogenes the Cynic. *Sayings and Anecdotes: with Other Popular Moralists*, trans. Robin Hard (Oxford: Oxford University Press, 2012).

Diogenes Laertius. *Lives of the Eminent Philosophers*, trans. Robert Drew Hicks, rev. and reprinted edn, 2 vols. (London: William Heinemann Ltd, 1950).

Diogenes Laertius *Lives of the Eminent Philosophers*, ed. with introduction by Tiziano Dorandi (Cambridge: Cambridge University Press, 2013).

Diogenes Laertius *Lives of the Eminent Philosophers*, ed. James Miller, trans. Pamela Mensch (Oxford: Oxford University Press, 2018).

Donnellan, Brendan. 'Nietzsche and La Rochefoucauld', *The German Quarterly* 52/3 (May 1979), 303–18.

Doty, Benjamin. '"As a Mass, a Phenomenon so Hideous": Crowd Psychology, Impressionism, and Ford Madox Ford's Propaganda', *Journal of War & Culture Studies* 6/2 (May 2013), 169–82.

Drochon, Hugo. *Nietzsche's Great Politics* (Princeton, NJ: Princeton University Press, 2016).

Du Bois, W. E. B. *Black Reconstruction in America, 1860–1880* (1935), with an Introduction by David Levering Lewis (New York: Free Press, 1998).

Du Bois, W. E. B. *The Souls of Black Folk* (1903), with an Introduction and Chronology by Jonathan Scott Holloway (New Haven, CT: Yale University Press, 2015).

Dudley, Donald R. *A History of Cynicism* (1937), 2nd edn, Foreword and Bibliography by Miriam Griffin (Bristol: Bristol Classical Press, 2003).

Duff, The Right Hon. Sir Mountstuart E. Grant, *Notes from a Diary, 1851–1872* (London: John Murray, 1897).

Durkheim, Emile. *Les Règles de la méthode sociologique* (1895), trans. W. D. Halls, *The Rules of Sociological Method*, ed. with an Introduction by Stephen Lukes (New York: Free Press, 1982).

Dzelzainis, Ella and Ruth Livesey (eds.). *The American Experiment and the Idea of Democracy in British Culture, 1776–1914* (Farnham: Ashgate, 2013).

Eiguer, Alberto. 'Cynicism: Its Function in the Perversions', trans. Philip Slotkin, *International Journal of Psycho-Analysis* 80/4 (1999), 671–84.

Eiguer, Alberto. 'Docteur Alberto Eiguer'. <http://alberto-eiguer-psy.fr>.

Elden, Stuart (ed.). *Sloterdijk Now* (Cambridge: Polity, 2011).

Eliot, George. *The George Eliot Letters*, ed. Gordon S. Haight, 9 vols. (New Haven: Yale University Press, 1954–78).

Eliot, George. *Middlemarch*, ed. David Carroll (Oxford: Clarendon Press, 1986).

Eliot, George. *Impressions of Theophrastus Such*, ed. Nancy Henry (Iowa City: University of Iowa Press, 1994).

Eliot, George. *The Lifted Veil* and *Brother Jacob*, ed. Helen Small (Oxford: Oxford University Press, 1999).

Eliot, George. *The Notebooks and Library of George Eliot*, 6 vols., electronic edn (Charlottesville, VA: InteLex Corporation, 2003).

Emden, Christian J. *Nietzsche's Naturalism: Philosophy and the Life Sciences in the Nineteenth Century* (Cambridge: Cambridge University Press, 2014).

Emerson, Ralph Waldo and Thomas Carlyle, *The Correspondence of Emerson and Carlyle*, ed. Joseph Slater (New York: Columbia University Press, 1964).

Emre, Merve. *What's Your Type?: The Strange History of Myers-Briggs and the Birth of Personality Testing* (London: William Collins, 2018).

Epictetus. *The Discourses of Epictetus*, ed. Christopher Gill, trans. Robin Hard (London: Dent, 1995).

Epictetus. *Discourses and Selected Writings*, ed. and trans. Robert Dobbin (London: Penguin, 2008).

Faber, Marion. 'The Metamorphosis of the French Aphorism: La Rochefoucauld and Nietzsche', *Comparative Literature Studies* 23/3 (Fall 1986), 205–17.

Farmworth, Barbara. 'The Self-Analysis of Christopher Tietjens', in Ashley Chantler and Rob Hawkes (eds.), *War and the Mind: Ford Madox Ford's* Parade's End*, Modernism, and Psychology* (Edinburgh: Edinburgh University Press, 2015), 77–91.

Farrell, John P. *Revolution as Tragedy: The Dilemma of the Moderate from Scott to Arnold* (Ithaca, NY: Cornell University Press, 1980).

Ferguson, Frances. 'What Should I Do and What Was I Thinking?: Philosophical Examples and the Uses of the Literary', *boundary 2: An International Journal of Literature and Culture* 40/2 (2013), 9–23.

Fermanis, Porscha and John Regan(eds.). *Rethinking British Romantic History, 1770–1845* (Oxford: Oxford University Press, 2014).

Filipovic, Jill. 'Two Books Explore the Furor Over Rape on Campius: Review of Kipnis, *Unwanted Advances* and K. C. Johnson and Stuart Taylor Jr, *The Campus Rape Frenzy: The Attack on Due Process at America's Universities*', *New York Times* 4 July 2007. <https://www.nytimes.com/2017/04/07/books/review/two-books-explore-the-furor-over-rape-on-campus.html>.

Fisch, M. H. 'Alexander and the Stoics', *American Journal of Philology* 58/1 (1937), 59–82, and 58/2 (1937), 129–51.

Flint, Kate (ed.). *The Cambridge History of Victorian Literature* (Cambridge: Cambridge University Press, 2012).

Ford, Ford Madox. *When Blood Is Their Argument: An Analysis of Prussian Culture* (London: Hodder and Stoughton, 1915).

Ford, Ford Madox. *Women & Men* (Paris: Contact Editions, 1923).

Ford, Ford Madox. *Joseph Conrad: A Personal Remembrance* (London: Duckworth & Co., 1924).

Ford, Ford Madox. *Last Post* (London: Duckworth, 1928).

Ford, Ford Madox. *Parade's End: Part I, Some Do Not* (1924), *Part II, No More Parades* (1925) and *Part III, A Man Could Stand Up* (1926), in *The Bodley Head Ford Madox Ford*, ed. Graham Greene, 5 vols. (London: The Bodley Head, 1963), vols. III–IV.

Ford, Ford Madox. *Letters of Ford Madox Ford*, ed. Richard M. Ludwig (Princeton, NJ: Princeton University Press, 1965).

Ford, Ford Madox. *War Prose*, ed. Max Saunders (Manchester: Carcanet, 1999).

Förster-Nietzsche, Elizabeth. *Der einsame Nietzsche* (1914) (Bremen: Unikum, 2012).

Foucault, Michel. *Remarks On Marx: Conversations with Duccio Trombadori*, trans. R. James Goldstein and James Cascaito (New York: Semiotext(e), 1991).

Foucault, Michel. *Foucault Live: Interviews, 1961–1984*, eds. Sylvère Lotringer, Lysa Hochroth, and John Johnston (New York: Semiotext(e), 1996).

Foucault, Michel. *Le courage de la vérité: Le gouvernement de soi et des autres II: Cours au Collège de France (1983–1984)*, ed. Frédéric Gros, gen. eds. François Ewaldand Alessandro Fontana (Paris: Seuil/Gallimard, 2009).

Foucault, Michel. *The Government of Self and Others: Lectures at the Collège de France, 1982–1983*, ed. Frédéric Gros, gen. eds. François Ewaldand Alessandro Fontana, English ser. ed. Arnold I. Davidson, trans. Graham Burchell (London: Palgrave Macmillan, 2010).

Foucault, Michel. *The Courage of Truth (The Government of Self and Others II): Lectures at the Collège de France 1983–1984*, ed. Frédéric Gros, gen. eds. François Ewaldand Alessandro Fontana, English ser. ed. Arnold I. Davidson, trans. Graham Burchell (London: Palgrave Macmillan, 2011).

Frankel, Oz. 'Blue Books and the Victorian Reader', *Victorian Studies* 46/2 (2004), 308–18.

Freud, Sigmund. *The Standard Edition of the Complete Works of Sigmund Freud*, gen. ed. and trans. James Stracheyin collaboration with Anna Freud, assisted by Alix Strachey, Alan Tyson and Angela Richards, 24 vols. (London: Hogarth Press and the Institute of Psycho-Analysis, 1953–79).

Freud, Sigmund. *Jokes and Their Relation to the Unconcious*, trans. Joyce Crick, Introduction by John Carey (London: Penguin Books, 2002).

Friedman, Jaclyn, Kelly Oliver, Claire Potter, Aishah Shahidah Simmons, Lisa Wade, and Laura Kipnis. 'Short Takes: Laura Kipnis' *Unwanted Advances*', Short Takes: Provocations on Public Feminism, *SIGNS: Journal of Women in Culture and Society* (July 2017). <http://signsjournal.org/unwanted-advances/>.

Friedman, Susan Stanford. *Planetary Modernisms: Provocations on Modernity across Time* (Oxford: Oxford University Press, 2016).

Fritz, K. V. 'New Books: Review of Dudley, *A History of Cynicism*', *Mind* 47 (July 1938), 390–92.

Froude, James Anthony. *Froude's Life of Carlyle*, ed. John Clubbe (Columbus, OH: Ohio State University Press, 1979).

Frye, Northrop. *Anatomy of Criticism: Four Essays* (Princeton, NJ: Princeton University Press, 1957).

Fulton, Richard. '*The Spectator* in Alien Hands', *Victorian Periodicals Review* 24/4 (Winter 1991), 187–96.

Furlani, Andre. *Guy Davenport: Postmodernism and After* (Evanston, IL: Northwestern University Press, 2007).

Garton Ash, Timothy. *Free Speech: Ten Principles for a Connected* World (London: Atlantic Books, 2016).

Gasiorek, Andrzej. 'The Politics of Cultural Nostalgia: History and Tradition in Ford Madox Ford's *Parade's End*', *Literature & History*, 3rd ser. 11/2 (2002), 52–77.

Gasiorek, Andrzej. 'Ford among the Aliens', in Dennis Brown and Jenny Plaistow (eds.), *Ford Madox Ford and Englishness* (Amsterdam: Rodopi, 2006).63–82.

Gass, William. 'The Neglect of *The Fifth Queen*', in Sondra J. Stang (ed.), *The Presence of Ford Madox Ford* (Philadelphia, PA: University of Pennsylvania Press, 1981), 25–43.

Gates Jr, Henry Louis and Cornel West. *The Future of the Race* (New York: Alfred A. Knopf, 1993).

Gerber, Larry G. 'College and University Governance', *Academe* 101/1 (January–February 2015), 31–7.

Ghosh, Ranjan. *Transcultural Poetics and the Concept of the Poet: From Philip Sidney to T. S. Eliot* (London: Routledge, 2016).

Giannantoni, G. *Socratis et Socraticorum Reliquiae*, 4 vols. (Naples: Bibliopolis, 1990).

Giannattasio Andria, Rosa. 'Diogene Cinico nei papyri Ercolanesi', *Cronache Ercolanesi* 10 (1980), 129–51.

Gibbs, Jenna M. *Performing the Temple of Liberty: Slavery, Theatre, and Popular Culture in London and Philadelphia, 1760–1850* (Baltimore, MD: Johns Hopkins University Press, 2014).

Giles, Paul. *Transatlantic Insurrections: British Culture and the Formation of American Literature, 1730–1860* (Philadelphia, PA: University of Pennsylvania Press, 2001).

Gilroy, Paul. *The Black Atlantic: Modernity and Double Consciousness* (Cambridge, MA: Harvard University Press, 1993).

Gilroy, Paul. *Cynicism and Passion* (Saratoga, CA: Anma Libri, 1995).

Glucksmann, André. *Cynisme et Passion* (Paris: Grasset, 1981).

Goldberg, David Theo. 'Liberalism's Limits: Carlyle and Mill on "The Negro Question"', *Nineteenth-Century Contexts* 22/2 (2000), 203–16.

Goldring, Douglas. *South Lodge: Reminiscences of Violet Hunt, Ford Madox Ford and the English Review Circle* (London: Constable & Co., 1943).

Gooch, Todd. 'Atheism', in Michael N. Forster and Kristin Giesdal (eds.), *The Oxford Handbook of German Philosophy in the Nineteenth Century* (Oxford: Oxford University Press, 2015), 829–51.

Goodlad, Lauren M. E. *The Victorian Geopolitical Aesthetic: Realism, Sovereignty, and Transnational Experience* (Oxford: Oxford University Press, 2015).

Gossman, Lionel. 'Philhellenism and Anti-Semitism: Matthew Arnold and His German Models', *Comparative Literature* 46/1 (1994), 1–39.

Goulet-Cazé, Marie-Odile. 'Un syllogisme stoïcien sur la loi dans la doxographie de Diogène le Cynique. A propos de Diogène Laërce VI 72', *Rheinisches Museum für Philologie* 125 (1982), 214–40.

Goulet-Cazé, Marie-Odile. *L'Ascèse cynique: Un commentaire de Diogène Laërce, VI. 70–71* (Paris: Vrin, 1986).

Goulet-Cazé, Marie-Odile and Richard Goulet (eds.). *Le Cynisme ancien et ses pronlongements: Actes du colloque international du CNRS (Paris, 22–25 juillet 1991)* (Paris: Presses universitaires de France, 1993).

Grafton, Anthony. 'Diogenes Laertius: From Inspiration to Annoyance (and Back)', in Diogenes Laertius, *Lives of the Eminent Philosophers*, ed. James Miller, trans. Pamela Mensch (Oxford: Oxford University Press, 2018), 546–54.

Green, Robert. *Ford Madox Ford: Prose and Politics* (Cambridge: Cambridge University Press, 1981).

Greene, Graham. 'Ford Madox Ford', *The Spectator* 163 (7 July 1939), 11.

Gregory, Adrian. *The Last Great War: British Society and the First World War* (Cambridge: Cambridge University Press, 2008).

Greif, Mark. 'Living Against Everything: An Interview with Mark Greif', interviewed by Chris Townsend and Johannes Lenhard, King's Review 1 June 2017. <http://kingsreview.co.uk/articles/greif-interview/>.

Grey, Henry George, 3rd Earl Grey. *The Colonial Policy of Lord John Russell's Administration*, 2 vols. (London: Richard Bentley, 1853).

Gros, Frédéric (ed.) *Foucault: Le courage de la verité* (Paris: Presses Universitaires de France, 2002).

Gros, Frédéric. 'La *parrhesia* chez Foucault (1982–1984)', in Frédéric Gros (ed.), *Foucault: Le courage de la verité* (Paris: Presses Universitaires de France, 2002), 155–66.

Hadley, Elaine. *Melodramatic Tactics: Theatricalized Dissent in the English Marketplace, 1800–1885* (Stanford, CA: Stanford University Press, 1995).

Hadley, Elaine. *Living Liberalism: Practical Citizenship in Mid-Victorian Britain* (Chicago: University of Chicago Press, 2010).

Hägglund, Martin and Derek Attridge. 'Ethics, Hospitality and Radical Atheism: A Dialogue' (Wadham College, University of Oxford, 2010). <https://podcasts.ox.ac.uk/ethics-hospitality-and-radical-atheism-dialogue>.

Hakulinen, Christian, Markus Jokela, Liisa Keltikangas-Järvinen, Päivi Merjonen, Olli T. Raitakari and Mirka Hintsanen. 'Longitudinal Measurement Invariance, Stability and Change of Anger and Cynicism', *Journal of Behavioral Medicine* 37/3 (June 2014), 434–44.

Hammond, Meghan Marie. 'Fellow Feeling in Ford's *Last Post*: Modernist Empathy and the Eighteenth-Century Man', in Ashley Chantler and Rob Hawkes (eds.), *War and the Mind: Ford Madox Ford's* Parade's End, *Modernism, and Psychology* (Edinburgh: Edinburgh University Press, 2015), 63–75.

Harcourt, Edward. 'Nietzsche and the "Aesthetics of Character", in Simon May (ed.), *Nietzsche's* On the Genealogy of Morality: *A Critical Guide* (Cambridge: Cambridge University Press, 2011), 279–81.

Harcourt, Edward. 'Nietzsche and the Virtues', in Lorraine Besser-Jones and Michael A. Slote (eds.), *The Routledge Companion to Virtue Ethics* (New York: Routledge, 2015), 165–79.

Harrison, Frederic. 'On Style in English Prose', *The Nineteenth Century* 43 (1898), 932–43.

Hartman, Geoffrey H. *Criticism in the Wilderness: The Study of Literature Today*, 2nd edn (New Haven, CT: Yale University Press, 2007).

Hatab, Lawrence. *Nietzsche's* On the Genealogy of Morality: *An Introduction* (Cambridge: Cambridge University Press, 2008).

Hathaway, Oona A. and Scott J. Shapiro. *The Internationalists and Their Plan to Outlaw War* (London: Allen Lane, 2017).

Haynes, Kenneth, 'Eccentric Classics: The Fiction of Guy Davenport', in Kenneth Haynes (ed.), *The Oxford History of Classical Reception*, vol. 5: *After 1880* (Oxford: Oxford University Press, 2019), 549–75.

Heine, Heinrich. *Pictures of Travel*, in *The Works of Heinrich Heine*, trans. Charles Godfrey Leland, Thomas Brooksbank and Margaret Armour, 12 vols. (London: W. Heinemann, 1891–1905), vol. II.

Held, David, 'Globalization, Corporate Practice and Cosmopolitan Social Standards', *Contemporary Political Theory* 1 (2002), 59–78.

Henderson, Jeffrey. *The Maculate Muse: Obscene Language in Attic Comedy*, 2nd edn (Oxford: Oxford University Press, 1991).

Hitchens, Christopher. 'Why Women Aren't Funny', *Vanity Fair* 1 January 2007. <http://www.vanityfair.com/culture/2007/01/hitchens200701>.

Hoelker, Florentine. 'Menippean Satire as a Genre: Tradition, Form and Function in the 17th and 18th Centuries' (PhD thesis, Loyola University of Chicago, 2003), ProQuest dissertation no. 3114131.

Hoffmann, Charles G. *Ford Madox Ford* (1967), updated edn (Boston: Twayne Publishers, 1990).

Höistad, Ragnar. 'Cynic Hero and Cynic King: Studies in the Cynic Conception of Man' (thesis, University of Uppsala, 1948).

Holowchak, Mark. *The Stoics: A Guide for the Perplexed* (New York: Continuum, 2008).

Honan, Park. *Matthew Arnold: A Life* (London: Weidenfeld and Nicolson, 1981).

Hueffer, Ford Madox. *The Fifth Queen Crowned* (London: Eveleigh Nash, 1908).

Hueffer, Ford Madox. *Ancient Lights and Certain Reflections: Being the Memories of a Young Man* (London: Chapman and Hall Ltd, 1911).

Hueffer, Ford Madox. *The Critical Attitude* (London: Duckworth & Co., 1911).

Hueffer, Ford Madox. *Between St. Dennis and St. George: A Sketch of Three Civilizations* (London: Hodder and Stoughton, 1915a).

Hueffer, Ford Madox. 'Literary Portraits—LXXI. Enemies', *Outlook* 35 (16 January 1915b), 79–80.

Hueffer, Ford Madox. 'On Impressionism', in Frank MacShane (ed.) *Critical Writings of Ford Madox Ford* (Lincoln, NE: University of Nebraska Press, [1914] 1964), 33–55.

Illingworth, Dustin. 'An Intellectual Love Affair: Guy Davenport and Hugh Kenner', *The Paris Review* 14 November 2018. <https://www.theparisreview.org/blog/2018/11/14/an-intellectual-love-affair-guy-davenport-and-hugh-kenner/>.

Janaway, Christopher. *Beyond Selflessness: Reading Nietzsche's* Genealogy (Oxford: Clarendon Press, 2007).

Janz, Curt Paul. *Friedrich Nietzsche: Biographie*, 3 vols. (München: Hanzer, 1978–79).

'Jehu Junior'. 'Men of the Day. No. 12. Thomas Carlyle', *Vanity Fair* 22 October 1870, in *The Vanity Fair Album: A Show of Sovereigns, Statesmen, Judges, and Men of the Day; with Biographical and Critical Notices by Jehu Junior*, 2 vols. (London: "Vanity Fair" Office, 1870), no pag. (image no. 103).

Jellineck, E. H. 'Heine's Illness: The Case for Multiple Sclerosis', *Journal of the Royal Society of Medicine* 83/8 (August 1990), 516–19.

Jensen, Anthony K. 'Nietzsche's Unpublished Fragments on Ancient Cynicism: The First Night of Diogenes', in Paul Bishop (ed.), *Nietzsche and Antiquity* (Rochester, NY: Camden House, 2004), 182–91.

Joad, C. E. M. 'Cynics Ancient and Modern', *The Spectator* 11 March 1938, 435–6.

Jones, Howard Mumford. 'Arnold, Aristocracy, and America', *American Historical Review* 49/3 (1944), 393–409.

Jordan, Alexander. 'That Scotch Diogenes: Thomas Carlyle and Cynicism', *International Journal of the Classical Tradition* 26/3 (September 2019), 295–318.

Jung, C. G. *Jung's Seminar on Nietzsche's* Zarathustra, ed. James L. Jarrett, abridged edn (Princeton, NJ: Princeton University Press, 2004).

Jung, C. G. *Psychological Types*, rev. R. F. C. Hull, trans. H. G. Baynes, with a new foreword by John Beebe (London: Routledge, 2017).

Kant, Immanuel. *The Conflict of the Faculties (Der Streit der Fakultäten)*, ed. and trans. Mary J. Gregor (Lincoln, NE: University of Nebraska Press, 1992).

Kanter, Donald L. and Philip H. Mirvis. *The Cynical Americans: Living and Working in an Age of Discontent and Disillusion* (San Francisco: Jossey-Bass Publishers, 1989).

Kean, Danuta. 'Study of "Sexual Paranoia" on US Campuses Draws Lawsuit from Student', *The Guardian* 18 May 2017 <https://www.theguardian.com/books/2017/may/18/study-of-sexual-paranoia-us-campuses-lawsuit-from-student-laura-kipnis>.

Keenan, Thomas. 'Fables of Responsibility', in Alexander Gelley (ed.), *Unruly Examples: On the Rhetoric of Exemplarity* (Stanford, CA: Stanford University Press, 1995), 121–41.

Kennedy, Randall. *N——: The Strange Career of a Troublesome Word* (New York: Vintage, 2002).

Kerry, Paul and Marylu Hill (eds.). *Thomas Carlyle Resartus: Reappraising Carlyle's Contribution to the Philosophy of History, Political Theory, and Cultural Criticism* (Madison, NJ: Farleigh Dickinson University Press, 2010).

Kipnis, Laura. *Bound and Gagged: Pornography and the Politics of Fantasy in America* (Durham, NC: Duke University Press, 1996).

Kipnis, Laura. *Against Love: A Polemic* (New York: Pantheon Books, 2003).

Kipnis, Laura. *The Female Thing: Dirt, Sex, Envy, Vulnerability* (London: Serpent's Tail, 2007).

Kipnis, Laura. 'Sexual Paranoia Strikes Academe', The Chronicle Review, *The Chronicle of Higher Education* 27 February 2015. <https://www.chronicle.com/article/Sexual-Paranoia-Strikes/190351>.

Kipnis, Laura. 'The Other Side of Title IX: Response to Anne McClintock', *Jacobin* 24 October 2017. <https://jacobinmag.com/2017/10/title-ix-laura-kipnis-response-mcclintock>.

Kipnis, Laura. *Unwanted Advances: Sexual Paranoia Comes to Campus* (New York: Harper, 2017).

Kirk, E. P. *Menippean Satire: An Annotated Catalogue of Texts and Criticism* (New York: Garland, 1980).

Kofman, Sarah. *Nietzsche and Metaphor*, trans. with an Introduction, Additional Notes, and a Bibliography by Duncan Large (London: Athlone Press, 1993).

Konstantakos, Leonidas. 'On Stoic Cosmopolitanism: A Response to Nussbaum's *Patriotism* and *Cosmopolitanism*', *Prometeus: Filosofia em Revista* 8/17 (2015), 50–60.

Kossoff, Philip. *Valiant Heart: A Biography of Heinrich Heine* (New York: Cornwall Books, 1983).

La Bruyère, Jean de. *Les Caractères, ou Les Mœurs de ce Siècle* (Paris: Morizot, 1864).

Landau, Sidney I. *Dictionaries: The Art and Craft of Lexicography*, 2nd edn (Cambridge: Cambridge University Press, 2001).

Lande, Joel B. *Persistence of Folly: On the Origins of German Dramatic Literature* (Ithaca, NY: Cornell University Press, 2018).

Largier, Niklaus. *Diogenes der Kyniker: Exempel, Erzählung, Geschichte in Mittelalter und früher Neuzeit; mit einem Essay zur der Figur des Diogenes zwischen Kynismus, Narrentum und postmoderner Kritik* (Tübingen: M. Niemeyer, 1997).

La Rochefoucauld, François de. *Collected Maxims and Other Reflections*, ed. and trans. E. H. Blackmore, A. M. Blackmore, and Francine Giguère (Oxford: Oxford University Press, 2007).

La Rocca, David. *Emerson's English Traits and the Natural History of Metaphor* (New York: Bloomsbury Academic, 2013).

LaValley, Albert J. *Carlyle and the Idea of the Modern: Studies in Carlyle's Prophetic Literature and Its Relation to Blake, Nietzsche, Marx and Others* (New Haven, CT: Yale University Press, 1968).

Lavery, Grace. 'On Being Criticized', *Modernism/Modernity* 25/3 (2018), 499–516.

Lawrence, D. H. *The Letters of D. H. Lawrence*, gen. ed. James T. Boulton, 8 vols. (Cambridge: Cambridge University Press, 1979–2000).

Lawrence, E. P. 'An Apostle's Progress: Matthew Arnold in America', *Philological Quarterly* 10 (January 1931), 62–79.

Lawrence, Marc. *The Rewrite* (Castle Rock Entertainment, 2014).

Le Dœuff, Michèle. *Hipparchia's Choice: An Essay Concepting Women, Philosophy, etc.* (1991), 2nd edn, trans. Trista Selous (New York: Columbia University Press, 2007).

Ledgister, F. S. J. 'Racist Rantings: Travelers' Tales, and a Creole Counterblast: Thomas Carlyle, John Stuart Mill, J. A. Froude, and J. J. Thomas on British Rule in the West Indies', in Paul Kerry and Marylu Hill (eds.), *Thomas Carlyle Resartus: Reappraising Carlyle's Contribution to the Philosophy of History, Political Theory, and Cultural Criticism* (Madison, NJ: Farleigh Dickinson University Press, 2010), 106–32.

Lehmann-Haupt, Christopher. 'Guy Davenport Dies at 77; Prolific Author and Illustrator', *New York Times* 7 January 2005. <https://www.nytimes.com/2005/01/07/books/guy-davenport-dies-at-77-prolific-author-and-illustrator.html>.

Lehrer, Ronald. 'Freud and Nietzsche, 1892–1895', in Jacob Golomb, Weaver Santaniello, and Ronald L. Lehrer (eds.), *Nietzsche and Depth Psychology* (Albany, NY: State University of New York Press, 1999), 181–204.

Leiter, Brian. *Routledge Philosophy Guidebook to Nietzsche on Morality* (London: Routledge, 2002).

Lewis, David Levering. *W. E. B. Du Bois: Biography of a Race, 1868–1919* (New York: Henry Holt and Company, 1993).

Lewis, David Levering. *W. E. B. Du Bois: The Fight for Equality and the American Century, 1919–1963* (New York: Henry Holt and Company, 2000).

Liddle, Rod. 'The Spectator Has Gone Soft – Prisons Should Be Much Nastier Places', *The Spectator* 26 November 2016. <https://www.spectator.co.uk/2016/11/the-spectator-has-gone-soft-prisons-should-be-much-nastier-places/>.

Liddle, Rod. 'What I Did on International Women's Day', *The Spectator* 11 March 2017. <https://www.spectator.co.uk/2017/03/what-i-did-on-international-womens-day/>.

Liddle, Rod. 'Don't Judge a Play by Its Audience', *The Spectator* 13 October 2018.

Liddle, Rod. 'Bercow the Brazen', *The Spectator* 23 March 2019.

Long, A. A. *Epictetus: A Stoic and Socratic Guide to Life* (Oxford: Clarendon Press, 2002).

Longenbach, James. 'Ford Madox Ford: The Novelist as Historian', *The Princeton University Library Chronicle* 45/2 (January 1984), 150–66.

Lucian of Samosata. *The Works of Lucian of Samosata*, trans. H. W. Fowler and F. G. Fowler, 4 vols. (Oxford: Clarendon Press, 1905).

MacNeice, Louis. *Autumn Journal*, in *Collected Poems*, ed. Peter McDonald (London: Faber and Faber, [1939] 2007), 99–164.

MacShane, Frank (ed.). *Ford Madox Ford: The Critical Heritage* (London: Routledge and Kegan Paul, 1972).

Malecka, Joanna Aleksandra. 'Between Herder and Luther: Carlyle's Literary Battles with the Devil in his Jean Paul Richter Essays (1827, 1827, 1830), and in *Sartor Resartus* (1833–34)' (MPhil(R) thesis, University of Glasgow, 2013). <http://theses.gla.ac.uk/4343/>.

Mansfeld, J. and D. T. Runia. *Aëtiana: The Method and Intellectual Context of a Doxographer,* vol. I: *The Sources* (Leiden: Brill, 1997).

Marais, Michael. 'Coming into Being: J. M. Coetzee's *Slow Man* and the Aesthetic of Hospitality', *Contemporary Literature* 50/2 (2009), 273–98.

Martin, Jay. *The Education of John Dewey: A Biography* (New York: Columbia University Press, 2002).

Maudlin, Daniel and Robin Peel (eds.). *The Materials of Exchange Between Britain and North East America, 1750–1900* (Farnham: Ashgate, 2013).

May, Simon (ed.) *Nietzsche's On the Genealogy of Morality: A Critical Guide* (Cambridge: Cambridge University Press, 2011).

May, Simon. 'Why Nietzsche is Still in the Morality Game', in Simon May (ed.), *Nietzsche's On the Genealogy of Morality: A Critical Guide* (Cambridge: Cambridge University Press, 2011), 78–100.

Mazella, David. *The Making of Modern Cynicism* (Charlottesville, VA: The University of Virginia Press, 2007).

McClintock, Anne. 'Who's Afraid of Title IX?', *Jacobin* 24 October 2017. <https://jacobinmag.com/2017/10/title-ix-betsy-devos-doe-colleges-assault-dear-colleague>.

McLuhan, Eric. *Cynic Satire* (Newcastle upon Tyne: Cambridge Scholars Publishing, 2015).

Meakins, William. 'Nietzsche, Carlyle, and Perfectionism', *Journal of Nietzsche Studies* 45/3 (November 2014), 258–78.

Mehta, Uday Singh. *Liberalism and Empire: A Study in Nineteenth-Century British Liberal Thought* (Chicago: University of Chicago Press, 1999).

Mengestu, Dinaw. *How to Read the Air* (London: Vintage, 2012).

Meredith, George. *Letters of George Meredith*, ed. C. L. Cline, 3 vols. (Oxford: Clarendon Press, 1970).

Meyer, Susan. *Imperialism at Home: Race and Victorian Women's Fiction* (Ithaca, NY: Cornell University Press, 1996).

Mill, John Stuart. 'The Negro Question', *Fraser's Magazine for Town and Country* XLI (January 1850), 25–31.

Mill, John Stuart. *Essays on Politics and Society, Part I (On Liberty)*, in *The Collected Works of John Stuart Mill*, gen. ed. John M. Robson, 33 vols. (Toronto: University of Toronto Press; London: Routledge and Kegan Paul, 1963–91), vol. XVIII.

Moles, John L. 'The Cynics and Politics', in André Laks and Malcolm Schofield (eds.), *Justice and Generosity: Studies in Hellenistic Social and Political Philosophy: Proceedings of the Sixth Symposium Hellenisticum* (Cambridge: Cambridge University Press, 1995), 129–58.

Moles, John L. 'Cynic Cosmopolitanism', in Robert Bracht Branham and Marie-Odile Goulet-Cazé (eds.), *The Cynics: The Cynic Movement in Antiquity and Its Legacy* (Berkeley, CA: University of California Press, 1996), 105–20.

Moles, John L. 'The Cynics', in C. J. Rowe and Malcolm Schofield (eds.), *The Cambridge History of Greek and Roman Political Thought* (Cambridge: Cambridge University Press, 2000), 415–34.

Money-Kyrle, Roger E. *The Collected Papers of Roger Money-Kyrle*, ed. Donald Meltzer, assisted by Edna O'Shaughnessy (London: Karnac, 2015).

Monk, Ray. *Bertrand Russell: The Spirit of Solitude* (London: Jonathan Cape, 1996).

Monk, Ray. *Bertrand Russell, 1921–70: The Ghost of Madness* (London: Jonathan Cape, 2000).

Moore, Gene M. 'The Tory in a Time of Change: Social Aspects of Ford Madox Ford's *Parade's End*', *Twentieth Century Literature* 28/1 (April 1982), 49–68.

Moore, Gene M. 'Peace of Mind in *Parade's End*', in Ashley Chantler and Rob Hawkes (eds.), *War and the Mind: Ford Madox Ford's* Parade's End, *Modernism, and Psychology* (Edinburgh: Edinburgh University Press, 2015), 159–69.

Moore, Gregory and Thomas H. Brobjer. *Nietzsche and Science* (Aldershot: Ashgate, 2004).

Morrow, John. 'Thomas Carlyle, "Young Ireland" and "The Condition of the Ireland Questions", *The Historical Journal* 51/3 (2008), 643–67.

Mossé, Claude. 'Les utopies égalitaires à l'époque hellénistique', *Revue Historique* 241/2 (1969), 297–308.

Mothersill, Mary. 'Book Reviews: Review of Three Works by Stanley Cavell', *The Journal of Philosophy* 72/3 (January 1975), 27–48.

Mulhern, Francis. *Culture/Metaculture* (London: Routledge, 2000).

Murdoch, Iris. *A Fairly Honourable Defeat* (London: Chatto & Windus, 1970).

Musila, Grace A. 'The Narrative Pressures of Migrant Precarity in Dinaw Mengestu's *How to Read the Air*', paper delivered at a colloquium on 'Architectures of the Novel' (University of Oxford, 21 June 2019).

Naas, Michael. '"Alors, qui êtes-vous?": Jacques Derrida and the Question of Hospitality', *Substance* 34/1 (2005), 6–17.

Navia, Luis E. *Classical Cynicism: A Critical Study* (Westport, CT: Greenwood Press, 1996).

Navia, Luis E. *Diogenes of Sinope: The Man in the Tub* (Westport, CT: Greenwood Press, 1998).

NCHERM Group, LLC. 'The 2017 NCHERM Group White Paper: Due Process and the Sex Police'. <https://www.ncherm.org/wp-content/uploads/2017/04/TNG-Whitepaper-Final-Electronic-Version.pdf>.

Neal, Patrick. 'Vulgar Liberalism', *Political Theory* 21/4 (November 1993), 623–42.

Nehamas, Alexander. *Nietzsche: Life as Literature* (Cambridge, MA: Harvard University Press, 1985).

Nelson, Fraser. 'We're the Magazine for the Queen and the Scaffolder', interviewed by Emily Hill, *Spiked* 13 September 2019. <https://www.spiked-online.com/2019/09/13/were-the-magazine-for-the-queen-and-the-scaffolder/>.

Ngai, Sianne. *Ugly Feelings* (Cambridge, MA: Harvard University Press, 2005).

Niehues-Pröbsting, Heinrich. *Der Kynismus des Diogenes und der Begriff des Zynismus* (Frankfurt: Suhrkamp, 1988).

Niehues-Pröbsting, Heinrich. 'Die Kynismus-Rezeption der Moderne: Diogenes in der Aufklärung', *Deutsche Zeitschrift für Philosophie* 40/7 (1992), 709–34.

Niehues-Pröbsting, Heinrich. 'Diogenes at the Enlightenment: The Modern Reception of Cynicism', in Robert Bracht Branham and Marie-Odile Goulet-Cazé (eds.), *The Cynics: The Cynic Movement in Antiquity and Its Legacy* (Berkeley, CA: University of California Press, 1996), 329–65.

Nierenberg, A. A., S. N. Ghaemi, K. Clancy-Colecchi, J. F. Rosenbaum and M. Fava. 'Cynicism, Hostility, and Suicidal Ideation in Depressed Outpatients', *The Journal of Nervous and Mental Disease* 184/10 (1996), 607–10.

Nietzsche, Friedrich. *Beyond Good and Evil: Prelude to a Philosophy of the Future*, trans. Helen Zimmern (London: T. N. Foulis, 1907).

Nietzsche, Friedrich. *Thus Spake Zarathustra: A Book for All and None*, ed. and trans. Thomas Common (Edinburgh: T. N. Foulis, 1909).

Nietzsche, Friedrich. *The Birth of Tragedy, or Hellenism and Pessimism*, ed. and trans. W. M. A. Haussmann (Edinburgh: Foulis, 1910).

Nietzsche, Friedrich. *The Joyful Wisdom*, trans. Thomas Common, poetry rendered by Paul V. Cohn and Maud D. Petre, in *The Complete Works of Friedrich Nietzsche*, gen. ed. Oscar Levy, 18 vols. (London: T. N. Foulis, 1910–13), vol. X.

Nietzsche, Friedrich. *Historisch-kritische Gesamtausgabe*, ed. Hans Joachim Mette, 9 vols. (Munich: C. H. Beck, 1934–40).

Nietzsche, Friedrich. *Kritische Gesamtausgabe*, gen. eds. Giorgio Colli and Mazzino Montinari (Berlin: Walter de Gruyter, 1967–).

Nietzsche, Friedrich. *The Genealogy of Morals*, trans. Walter Kaufmann and R. J. Hollingdale (New York: Vintage Books, 1969).

Nietzsche, Friedrich. *The Portable Nietzsche*, selected and translated, with an Introduction, prefaces and notes by Walter Kaufmann (London: Chatto & Windus, 1971).

Nietzsche, Friedrich. *Daybreak: Thoughts on the Prejudices of Morality*, trans. R. J. Hollingdale, introduction by Tony Tanner (Cambridge: Cambridge University Press, 1982).

Nietzsche, Friedrich. *Human, All Too Human: A Book for Free Spirits*, trans. R. J. Hollingdale, introduction by Erich Heller (Cambridge: Cambridge University Press, 1986).

Nietzsche, Friedrich. '*Human, All Too Human* II and *Unpublished Fragments* from the Period of *Human, All Too Human* II (Spring 1878–Fall 1879)', trans. with afterword by

Gary Handwerk, in *The Complete Works of Friedrich Nietzsche*, gen. eds. Alan D. Schrift, Duncan Large, and Adrian del Caro, 19 vols. (Stanford: Stanford University Press, 1995–), vol. IV.

Nietzsche, Friedrich. *Human, All Too Human: A Book for Free Spirits*, trans. R. J. Hollingdale, introduction by Richard Schacht (Cambridge: Cambridge University Press, 1996).

Nietzsche, Friedrich. *Untimely Meditations*, ed. Daniel Brezeale, trans. R. J. Hollingdale (Cambridge: Cambridge University Press, 1997).

Nietzsche, Friedrich. *The Gay Science: With a Prelude in German Rhymes and an Appendix of Songs*, ed. Bernard Williams, trans. Josefine Nauckhoff and Adrian del Caro (Cambridge: Cambridge University Press, 2001).

Nietzsche, Friedrich. *Beyond Good and Evil: Prelude to a Philosophy of the Future*, eds. Rolf-Peter Horstmann and Judith Norman, trans. Judith Norman (Cambridge: Cambridge University Press, 2002).

Nietzsche, Friedrich. *The Anti-Christ, Ecce Homo, Twilight of the Idols, and Other Writings*, eds. Aaron Ridley and Judith Norman, trans. Judith Norman (Cambridge: Cambridge University Press, 2005).

Nietzsche, Friedrich. *The Pre-Platonic Philosophers*, ed. and trans. Greg Whitlock (Urbana, IL: University of Illinois Press, 2006).

Nietzsche, Friedrich. *Thus Spoke Zarathustra*, eds. Adrian del Caro and Robert Pippin, trans. Adrian del Caro (Cambridge: Cambridge University Press, 2006).

Nietzsche, Friedrich. *Beyond Good and Evil/On the Genealogy of Morality*, trans. Adrian del Caro (Stanford, CA: Stanford University Press, 2014).

Nietzsche, Friedrich. *On the Genealogy of Morality and Other Writings*, ed. Keith Ansell-Pearson, trans. Carol Diethe, 3rd edn (Cambridge: Cambridge University Press, 2017).

Nozick, Robert. *The Nature of Rationality* (Princeton, NJ: Princeton University Press, 1993).

Nussbaum, Martha C. 'Kant and Stoic Cosmopolitanism', *The Journal of Political Philosophy* 5/1 (1997), 1–25.

Nussbaum, Martha C. 'Patriotism and Cosmopolitanism', in Thom Brooks (ed.), *The Global Justice Reader* (Oxford: Blackwell, 2008), 306–14.

OED Online (Oxford: Oxford University Press, 2019). <https://www.oed.com/>.

Oehler, Max (ed.), *Nietzsches Bibliothek* (Weimar: Nietzsche-Archives, 1942).

O'Grady, Jane. 'Review of Kipnis, Unwanted Advances', *Times Higher Education* 22 June 2017. <https://www.timeshighereducation.com/books/review-unwanted-advances-laura-kipnis-harper-collins>.

Orwell, George. *Essays*, ed. John Carey (London: Everyman, 2002).

Osborne, Peter. 'Disguised as a Dog', in Peter Osborne, *The Postconceptual Condition: Critical Essays* (London: Verso, 2018), 73–89.

Oxford Dictionary of National Biography (Oxford: Oxford University Press, 2019). online version <https://www.oxforddnb.com/>.

Patterson, Orlando. *The Ordeal of Integration: Progress and Resentment in America's 'Racial' Crisis* (Washington, DC: Civitas/Counterpoint, 1997).

Pedersen, Susan. *The Guardians: The League of Nations and the Crisis of Empire* (Oxford: Oxford University Press, 2015).

Phillips, Adam. 'In Praise of Difficult Children', *London Review of Books* 31/3 (12 February 2009), 16. <https://www.lrb.co.uk/v31/n03/adam-phillips/in-praise-of-difficult-children>.

Picker, John M. 'The Soundproof Study: Victorian Professionals, Work Space, and Urban Noise', *Victorian Studies* 42/3 (April 1999), 427–53.

Pippin, Robert B. 'How to Overcome Oneself: Nietzsche on Freedom', in Ken Gemes and Simon May (eds.), *Nietzsche on Freedom and Autonomy* (Oxford: Oxford University Press, 2009), 69–87.

Pippin, Robert B. *Nietzsche, Psychology, & First Philosophy* (Chicago: University of Chicago Press, 2010).

Pippin, Robert B. 'Figurative Philosophy in Nietzsche's *Beyond Good and Evil*' (13 May 2017). <https://www.youtube.com/watch?v=j_1OSwcS37M>.

Plantz, Diane M. 'Cynicism, with Consequences', *The Hastings Center Report* 41/2 (2011), 12–13.

Plotz, John. 'Crowd Power: Chartism, Carlyle, and the Victorian Public Sphere', *Representations* 70 (Spring 2000), 87–114.

Porter, James I. *Nietzsche and the Philology of the Future* (Stanford, CA: Stanford University Press, 2002).

Prince, Susan Hukill. *Antisthenes of Athens: Texts, Translations and Commentary* (Ann Arbor, MI: University of Michigan Press, 2015).

Rabelais, François. 'Prologue de l'auteur', in *Le tiers livre des faicts et dicts héroïques du noble Pantagruel*. In *Œuvres de François Rabelais*, 5 vols. in 2 (Paris: Bibliothèque Nationale 1870–73).

Raleigh, John Henry. *Matthew Arnold and American Culture* (Berkeley, CA: University of California Press, 1957).

Rawson, Claude J. *Swift's Angers* (Cambridge: Cambridge University Press, 2014).

Reik, Theodor. 'Psychoanalytische Bemerkungen über den zynischen Witz', *Imago: Zeitschrift für Anwendung der Psychoanalyse auf die Geisteswissenschaften* 2 (1913), 573–88.

Reik, Theodor. *Jewish Wit* (New York: Gamut, 1962).

Relihan, Joel C. *Ancient Menippean Satire* (Baltimore, MD: Johns Hopkins University Press, 1993).

Relihan, Joel C. 'Late Arrivals, Julian and Boethius', in Kirk Freudenberg (ed.), *The Cambridge Companion to Roman Satire* (Cambridge: Cambridge University Press, 2005).

Remhof, Justin Marc. 'Nietzsche's Reconception of Science: Overcoming Nihilism' (PhD thesis, University of Illinois at Urbana-Champaign, 2013), ProQuest dissertation no. 3614687/Proquest document ID 1518142896.

Rignall, John. 'George Eliot, Balzac and Proust', in John Rignall (ed.), *George Eliot and Europe* (Aldershot: Scolar Press, 1996), 210–24.

Rignall, John. (ed.). *Oxford Reader's Companion to George Eliot* (Oxford: Oxford University Press, 2000).

Robbins, Bruce. 'On Amanda Anderson's *The Way We Argue Now*', *Criticism* 48/2 (2006), 265–71.

Robbins, Bruce. 'Cosmopolitanism: New and Newer', *boundary 2: An International Journal of Literature and Culture* 34/3 (2007), 47–60.

Robbins, Bruce. 'Deadwood: Academic Freedom and *Smart People*', *South Atlantic Quarterly* 108/4 (2009), 741–9.

Robbins, Bruce. *Perpetual War: Cosmopolitanism from the Viewpoint of Violence* (Durham, NC: Duke University Press, 2012).

Robbins, Bruce. 'On the Non-Representation of Atrocity', *b2o* [*boundary2 online*] 7 October 2016. <http://www.boundary2.org/2016/10/bruce-robbins-on-the-non-representation-of-atrocity/>.

Robbins, Bruce. *The Beneficiary* (Durham, NC: Duke University Press, 2017).

Robbins, Bruce and Paulo Lemos Horta (eds.). *Cosmopolitanisms* (New York: New York University Press, 2017).

Robinson, Peter. '(Further Work on) Pissarro's Dream ... Or ... When Camille Pissarro the Impressionist Painter and Anarchist Met Diogenes of Sinope the Performance Artist and Cynic Philosopher...', *Peter Robinson artist painter* 31 March 2017, Wordpress. <https://peterrobinsonartist.com/2017/03/31/further-work-on-pissarros-dream-or-when-camille-pissarro-the-impressionist-painter-and-anarchist-met-diogenes-of-sinope-the-performance-artist-and-cynic-philosopher/>.

Rorty, Richard. *Achieving Our Country: Leftist Thought in Twentieth-Century America* (Cambridge, MA: Harvard University Press, 1998).

Rorty, Richard. 'To the Sunlit Uplands: Review of Williams, *Truth and Truthfulness*', *London Review of Books* 24/21 (31 October 2002), 13–15. <https://www.lrb.co.uk/v24/n21/richard-rorty/to-the-sunlit-uplands>.

Rose, Arthur. *Literary Cynics: Borges, Beckett, Coetzee* (London: Bloomsbury Academic, 2017).

Rose, Jacqueline. 'I Am a Knife': five reviews, *London Review of Books* 40/4 (22 February 2018), 3–11. <https://www.lrb.co.uk/v40/n04/jacqueline-rose/i-am-a-knife>.

Ross, Andrew. 'Theorizing Cultural Work: An Interview with the Editors', in Mark Banks, Rosalind Taylor, and Stephanie Taylor (eds.), *Theorizing Cultural Work: Labour, Continuity and Change in the Cultural and Creative Industries* (London: Routledge, 2012), 175–82.

Russell, Bertrand. *In Praise of Idleness and Other Essays* (1935), with a new preface by Anthony Gottlieb, introduction by Howard Woodhouse (London: Routledge, 2004).

Russell, Bertrand. *Sceptical Essays* (1928), with a new preface by John Gray (London: Routledge, 2004).

Russell, Bertrand. *Marriage and Morals* (London: Routledge, [1929] 2009).

Russell, Bertrand. *Why Men Fight: A Method of Abolishing the International Duel*, introduction by Richard A. Remple (London: Routledge, [1916] 2010).

Russell, David. *Tact: Aesthetic Liberalism and the Essay Form in Nineteenth-Century Britain* (Princeton, NJ: Princeton University Press, 2018).

Ryals, Clyde de L. 'Thomas Carlyle and the Squire Forgeries', *Victorian Studies* 30/4 (Summer 1987), 495–518.

Sainte-Beuve, Charles A. *Portraits contemporains et divers*, 3 vols. (Paris: Didier, 1846–47).

Saintsbury, George. *Matthew Arnold* (Edinburgh: William Blackwood and Sons, 1899).

Saunders, Max. *Ford Madox Ford: A Dual Life*, 2 vols. (Oxford: Oxford University Press, 1996).

Saunders, Max. 'Moderism, Impressionism, and Ford Madox Ford's *The Good Soldier*', *Etudes Anglaises* 57/4 (2004), 421–37.

Saunders, Max. 'Impressions of War: Ford Madox Ford, Reading, and *Parade's End*', in Shafquat Towheed and Edmund G. C. King (eds.), *Reading and the First World War: Readers, Texts, Archives* (Basingstoke: Palgrave Macmillan, 2015), 63–77.

Saunders, Max. '"Sex Ferocity" and the "Sadistic Lusts of Certain Novelists": Sexuality, Sadomasochism and Suppression in *Parade's End*', in Ashley Chantler and Rob Hawkes (eds.), *War and the Mind: Ford Madox Ford's* Parade's End, *Modernism, and Psychology* (Edinburgh: Edinburgh University Press, 2015), 17–34.

Savage, Barbara Diane. 'W. E. B. Du Bois and "The Negro Church"', *The Annals of the American Academy of Political and Social Science* 568 (March 2000), 235–49.

Schacht, Richard. *Nietzsche* (London: Routledge, 1983).

Schreier, Benjamin. *The Power of Negative Thinking: Cynicism and the History of Modern American Literature* (Charlottesville, VA: University of Virginia Press, 2009).

Self, Will. 'Why Is He So Angry?: Review of Rod Liddle, *Selfish Whining Monkeys*', *The Guardian* 22 May 2014. <https://www.theguardian.com/books/2014/may/22/selfish-whining-monkeys-rod-liddle-review>.

Senior, Joan. '*Unwanted Advances* Tackles Sexual Politics in Academia: Review of Kipnis, *Unwanted Advances*,'. *The New York Times* 5 April 2017. <https://www.nytimes.com/2017/04/05/books/review-laura-kipnis-unwanted-advances.html>.

Shane, Charlotte. 'Title Bouts: Review of Kipnis, *Unwanted Advances*', *Book Forum* April/May 2017. <https://www.bookforum.com/inprint/024_01/17547>.

Shaw, Tamsin. *Nietzsche's Political Scepticism* (Princeton, NJ, Princeton University Press, 2007).

Shea, Louisa. *The Cynic Enlightenment: Diogenes in the Salon* (Baltimore, MD: Johns Hopkins University Press, 2010).

Shea, Victor and William Whitla (eds.). *Victorian Literature: An Anthology* (Chichester: Wiley-Blackwell, 2015).

Sidelsky, Edward. 'State of Nature: Rreview of Williams, *Truth and Truthfulness*', *New Statesman* 18 November 2002. <https://www.newstatesman.com/node/156669>.

Sidelsky, Robert and Edward Sidelsky. *How Much is Enough?: Money and the Good Life* (London: Penguin, 2012).

Sidgwick, Henry. 'The Prophet of Culture', *MacMillan's Magazine* 16 (August 1867), 271–80.

Silk, M. S. 'Nestor, Amphitryon, Philocleon, Cephalus: The Language of Old Men in Greek Literature from Homer to Menander', in Francesco de Martino and Alan H. Sommerstein (eds.), *Lo Spettacollo delle Voci* (Bari: Levante, 1995), 165–214.

Simmel, Georg. 'Bergson und der deutsche "Zynismus"', in *Georg Simmel Gesamtausgabe*, 24 vols. (Frankfurt: Suhrkamp, [1914] 1989–2016), vol. XVII, 121–3.

Skinner, Paul. 'The Painful Process of Reconstruction: History in *No Enemy* and *Last Post*', in Joseph Wiesenfarth (ed.), *History and Representation in Ford Madox Ford's Writings* (Amsterdam: Rodopi, 2004), 65–75.

Sloterdijk, Peter. *Kritik der zynischen Vernunft* (Frankfurt: Suhrkamp, 1983).

Sloterdijk, Peter. *The Critique of Cynical Reason*, trans. Michael Eldred (London: Verso, 1988).

Small, Helen. 'Liberal Editing in the *Fortnightly Review* and the *Nineteenth Century*', *Publishing History* 53 (2003), 75–96.

Small, Helen. *The Long Life* (Oxford: Oxford University Press, 2007).

Small, Helen. 'Does Self-Identity Persist into Old Age?', in Geoffrey Scarre (ed.), *The Palgrave Handbook of the Philosophy of Aging* (London: Palgrave Macmillan, 2016), 248–81.

Small, Helen. 'The Liberal University and Its Enemies', John Stuart Mill Lecture delivered at the University of St Andrews, 3 February 2017.

Smallwood, Christine. 'Laura Kipnis's Battle against Vulnerability', *The New Yorker* 2 April 2017. <https://www.newyorker.com/culture/persons-of-interest/laura-kipniss-battle-against-vulnerability>.

Smith, Goldwin. *Loyalty, Aristocracy, and Jingoism: Three Lectures Delivered before the Young Men's Liberal Club, Toronto* (Toronto: Hunter, Rose & Co., 1891).

Solmsen, Friedrich. 'Review of Dudley, *A History of Cynicism*', *The Classical Weekly* 31/17 (March 1938), 163–4.

Soper, Kate. 'Humanities Can Promote Alternative "Good Life"', *The Guardian* 30 November 2010. <http://www.theguardian.com/commentisfree/2010/nov/30/humanities-promote-alternative-good-life>.

Sorabji, Richard. *Gandhi and the Stoics: Modern Experiments on Ancient Values* (Oxford: Oxford University Press, 2012).

Sorum, Eve. 'Empathy, Trauma, and the Space of War in *Parade's End*', in Ashley Chantler and Rob Hawkes (eds.), *War and the Mind: Ford Madox Ford's* Parade's End, *Modernism, and Psychology* (Edinburgh: Edinburgh University Press, 2015), 50–62.

Srinivasan, Amia. 'The Archimedean Urge', *Philosophical Perspectives* 29/1 (December 2015), 325–62.

Stang, Sondra J. (ed.). *The Presence of Ford Madox Ford: A Memorial Volume of Essays, Poems, and Memoirs* (Philadelphia, PA: University of Pennsylvania Press, 1981), 25–43.

Stanley, Sharon. 'Retreat from Politics: The Cynic in Modern Times', *Polity* 39/3 (2007), 384–407.

Stanley, Sharon. *The French Enlightenment and the Emergence of Modern Cynicism* (New York: Cambridge University Press, 2012).

Staten, Henry. *Nietzsche's Voice* (Ithaca, NY: Cornell University Press, 1990).

Steiner, Greorge. 'Rare Bird', in Robert Boyers (ed.), *George Steiner at the New Yorker* (New York: New Directions, 2009), 148–56.

Stenager, Egon. 'The Course of Heinrich Heine's Illness: Diagnostic Considerations', *Journal of Medical Biography* 4/1 (February 1996), 28–32.

Stewart, John. *The Stable Book; Being a Treatise on the Management of Horses* (1855), American edn (New York: A. O. Moore, 1858).

Stewart, Robert. *The Foundation of the Conservative Party, 1830–1867* (London: Longman, 1978).

Stone, Donald D. *Communications with the Future: Matthew Arnold in Dialogue* (Ann Arbor, MI: University of Michigan Press, 1997).

Strohm, Paul (ed.). '75 Years: A Retrospective on the Occasion of the Seventy-Fifth Annual Meeting', *Academe* 75/3 (May–June 1989), 1–33.

Swanger, Daniel Anthony Ignatius. *Diogenes Throwing Away His Bowl*, painting (2014). <https://www.saatchiart.com/art/Painting-Diogenes-Throwing-Away-His-Bowl/330609/2022719/view>.

Tamarkin, Eliza. 'Why Forgive Carlyle?', *Representations* 134/1 (Spring 2016), 64–92.

Tambling, Jeremy. 'Carlyle through Nietzsche: Reading *Sartor Resartus*', *Modern Language Review* 102/2 (April 2007), 326–40.

Tarn, W. W. 'Alexander the Great and the Unity of Mankind', The Raleigh Lecture on History (London: H. Milford, 1933).

Tarn, W. W. 'Alexander, Cynics and Stoics', *American Journal of Philology* 60/1 (1939), 41–70.

Tennyson, G. B. *Sartor Called Resartus: The Genesis, Structure, and Style of Thomas Carlyle's First Major Work* (Princeton, NJ: Princeton University Press, 1965).

Tesdorpf, Ilse-Maria. *Die Auseinandersetzung Matthew Arnolds mit Heinrich Heine, des Kritikers mit dem Kritiker* (Frankfurt: Athenäum Verlag, 1971).

The Current Moment. 'The Persistence of Work', *The Current Moment* 25 February 2013, Wordpress. <https://thecurrentmoment.wordpress.com/2013/02/25/the-persistence-of-work/>.

Theophrastus. *The Characters of Theophrastus*, trans. with an introduction by Charles E. Bennett and William A. Hammond (London: Longmans, Green and Co., 1902).

Thomas, R. Hinton. *Nietzsche in German Politics and Society, 1890–1918* (Manchester: Manchester University Press, 1986).

Thompson, Mark. *Enough Said: What's Gone Wrong with the Language of Politics* (London: The Bodley Head, 2016).

Thompson, Mark. 'Trump, Brexit, and the Broken Language of Politics', lecture delivered at Hertford College, University of Oxford, 17 March 2017. <https://www.hertford.ox.ac.uk/alumni/hertford-today/john-donne-lectures/mark-thompson>.

Thorne, Christian. *The Dialectic of Counter-Enlightenment* (Cambridge, MA: Harvard University Press, 2009).

Timko, Michael. 'Carlyle, Sterling, and the Scavenger Age', *Studies in Scottish Literature* 20/1 (1985), 11–33.

TORCH [The Oxford Research Centre for the Humanities]. 'Recovering the Hidden Carlyle', conference held at the University of Oxford, 6–8 July 2016. <http://www.torch.ox.ac.uk/cfp-recovering-hidden-carlyle>.

Traubel, Horace. *With Walt Whitman in Camden*, 9 vols. (Boston, MA: Small, Maynard & Co., 1906–96).

Trilling, Lionel. *Sincerity and Authenticity* (Cambridge, MA: Harvard University Press, 1971).

Turner, James. *Philology: The Forgotten Origins of the Modern Humanities* (Princeton, NJ: Princeton University Press, 2014).

United States Department of Education, 'Title IX and Sex Discrimination', rev. April 2015. <https://www2.ed.gov/about/offices/list/ocr/docs/tix_dis.html>.

United States Department of Justice. 'Overview of Title IX of the Education Amendments of 1972, 20, U.S.C. A§ 1681 Et. Seq.', updated 7 August 2015. <https://www.justice.gov/crt/overview-title-ix-education-amendments-1972-20-usc-1681-et-seq>.

Van Der Veer, Peter. 'Colonial Cosmopolitanism', in Steven Vertovec and Robin Cohen (eds.), *Conceiving Cosmopolitanism: Theory, Context, Practice* (New York: Oxford University Press, 2002), 165–79.

Varouxakis, Georgios. 'Cosmopolitan Patriotism in J. S. Mill's Political Thought and Activism', *Revue d'études benthamiennes* 4 (2008). <http://journals.openedition.org/etudes-benthamiennes/188>.

Virtanen, Reino. 'The Spectre of Solipsism in Western Literature', *The Journal of the Midwest Modern Language Association* 19/1 (Spring 1986), 59–76.

Waddy, Frederick. *Cartoon Portraits and Biographical Sketches of Men of the Day* (London: Tinsley Brothers, 1873).

Walkowitz, Rebecca L. *Cosmopolitan Style: Modernism beyond the Nation* (New York: Columbia University Press, 2006).

Warren, Mark. *Nietzsche and Political Thought* (Cambridge, MA: MIT Press, 1988).

Weinbrot, Howard D. *Menippean Satire Reconsidered: From Antiquity to the Eighteenth Century* (Baltimore, MD: Johns Hopkins University Press, 2005).

Whitmarsh, Tim. 'Alexander's Hellenism and Plutarch's Textualism', *The Classical Quarterly* 52/1 (2002), 174–92.

Wilcken, U. 'Die letzten Pläne Alexanders der Grossen', in *Sitzungsberichte der preussische Akademie* (Berlin: Verlag der Akademie der Wissenschaften, 1937).

Williams, Bernard. *Problems of the Self: Philosophical Papers, 1956–1972* (Cambridge: Cambridge University Press, 1973).

Williams, Bernard. *Moral Luck: Philosophical Papers, 1973–1980* (Cambridge: Cambridge University Press, 1981).

Williams, Bernard. *Truth and Truthfulness: An Essay in Genealogy* (Princeton, NJ: Princeton University Press, 2002).

Williams, Bernard. *The Sense of the Past: Essays in the History of Philosophy*, ed. with intro. by Myles Burnyeat (Princeton, NJ: Princeton University Press, 2006).

Williams, Bernard. *Essays and Reviews, 1959–2002* (Princeton, NJ: Princeton University Press, 2014).

Williams, Bernard. 'The Need to be Sceptical', in Bernard Williams, *Essays and Reviews, 1959-2002* (Princeton, NJ: Princeton University Press, 2014), 312-18.

Wright, Charles D. 'Matthew Arnold on Heine as a "Continuator of Goethe"', *Studies in Philology* 65/4 (July 1968), 693-701.

Wright, Joseph (ed.). *The English Dialect Dictionary. Being the Complete Vocabulary of All Dialect Words Still in Use, or Known to Have Been in Use During the Last Two Hundred Years*, 6 vols. (London: Henry Frowde, 1898-1905).

Wright, Robert. *The Moral Animal: Evolutionary Psychology and Everyday Life* (London: Little Brown, 1994).

Young, Julian. *Friedrich Nietzsche: A Philosophical Biography* (Cambridge: Cambridge University Press, 2010).

Index